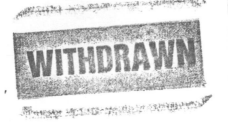
	DATE DUE		

Treading Grapes

Treading Grapes

Walking through the vineyards of Tuscany

ROSEMARY GEORGE

BANTAM PRESS

LONDON · TORONTO · SYDNEY · AUCKLAND · JOHANNESBURG

TRANSWORLD PUBLISHERS
61–63 Uxbridge Road, London W5 5SA
a division of The Random House Group Ltd

RANDOM HOUSE AUSTRALIA (PTY) LTD
20 Alfred Street, Milsons Point, Sydney,
New South Wales 2061, Australia

RANDOM HOUSE NEW ZEALAND LTD
18 Poland Road, Glenfield, Auckland 10, New Zealand

RANDOM HOUSE SOUTH AFRICA (PTY) LTD
Endulini, 5a Jubilee Road, Parktown 2193, South Africa

Published 2004 by Bantam Press
a division of Transworld Publishers

A catalogue record for this book is available from the British Library.
ISBN 0593 053451

Typeset in 11/15pt Minion by
Falcon Oast Graphic Art Ltd

Printed in Great Britain by
Mackays of Chatham plc, Chatham, Kent

1 3 5 7 9 10 8 6 4 2

Papers used by Transworld Publishers are natural, recyclable products
made from wood grown in sustainable forests. The manufacturing
processes conform to the environmental regulations of the country of origin.

For Christopher, who walked every step of the way.

Contents

Acknowledgements

Many people have contributed to this book. Firstly, I would like to thank the powers that be in the City for my husband's timely redundancy, which enabled him to accompany me on all nine research trips. When I first had the idea for this book, I had not fully considered the question of whether I would like to walk alone, to which the answer would have been no, not really. Walking is something that is so much more fun *à deux*, with someone to share the breathtaking views and chance encounters, to help identify an orchid or read the compass when you seem to be off course. Christopher also displayed nerves of steel when confronted with the idiosyncrasies of Italian driving, particularly on the narrow motorways and the frighteningly fast Aurelia that runs the length of the Tuscan coast. And, back home, he has painstakingly read the draft and contributed his observations. Thank you, Christopher.

We are both enormously grateful to the various friends who so generously offered us accommodation in their *agriturismi* or spare bedrooms, namely Maria and Giovanna Manetti at Fontodi, Michele and Lucia Satta at Castagneto Carducci, Laura Bailhache in Montepulciano, Gualtiero and Laura Ghezzi at Camigliano in Montalcino, Edoardo Ventimiglia and Carla Benini at Sassotondo in Pitigliano, Silvana, Ezio and Aleardo Mantelassi in Scansano, Pierpaolo and Rosanna Lorieri at Podere Scuratola in the Colli Apuani, Giampiero and Lucia de Andreis at the Fattoria di Fubbiano in the Colline Lucchesi, Enrico Lippi and his family at Frascole in Rufina, Ugo and Lisa Contini Bonacossi at Tenuta di Capezzana, Enrico Pierazzuoli at Cantagallo in Chianti Montalbano, Ursula Mock at Soiana in the Colline Pisane, and Elisabetta Fagiuoli at Montenidoli in San Gimignano. The warmth of their hospitality, which extended to numerous convivial meals, has enabled us to understand and enjoy yet more of the Tuscan wine world.

Other friends helped enormously in their various ways: Paolo Valdastri of the Consorzio Strada del Vino Costa degli Etruschi, Sammie Daniels, Aileen Hall, Carla Capalbo, Maddalena Mazzeschi, Ursula Thurner, Filippo Magnani, Marriuccia Robbins, Colleen McKettrick and Vassili Siontas, and Dimitri and Nelly Galletti at Montefabbrello on the island of Elba. The three main *consorzi* of Tuscany also played their part in arranging visits, so thanks are due to Silvia Fiorentini from the Consorzio del Chianti Classico, Stefano Campatelli at the Consorzio del Brunello di Montalcino and Paolo Solini from the Consorzio del Vino Nobile di Montepulciano.

However, wine books are above all about people, the men and women who encapsulate the flavours of their particular patch of Tuscany, who feature in these pages. They took time to show us their vineyards and cellars, to explain their *terroir* and its distinctive features, to open bottles and to answer questions. Italian hospitality is warm and welcoming, and never more so than in the wine world, when every producer wants to show you the best that their area has to offer. Without their participation, there would be no book.

Nor would there have been a book if my agent, Maggie Noach, had not sold the idea to Transworld. So thank you, Maggie, and also to my editor, Francesca Liversidge, and publisher, Patrick Janson-Smith, for giving Christopher and me the opportunity to spend so much time in our favourite part of Italy, and last but not least, to Madeleine David for effectively lightening my words with her visual impressions of Tuscany.

Setting the Scene

I HAVE NEVER FORGOTTEN MY first glimpse of the Tuscan countryside. It was over thirty years ago and I was on a train travelling from Florence to Perugia to attend Italian classes at the *Università per Stranieri*. A new course was beginning and the train was filled with students and their luggage. I was squeezed between another body and a rucksack in the corridor. It was hot and airless and, to say the least, uncomfortable. Then suddenly the Tuscan landscape unfolded before my eyes and I was instantly enthralled. This was the scenery of Renaissance paintings, the backdrop to countless Madonnas. There were cypress and olive trees, vineyards and woods, a timeless patchwork on hillsides that seemed not to have changed for centuries. It was breathtakingly beautiful and I quickly forgot the discomfort of the train.

That memory has remained with me, and with it a love of all things Tuscan – the wine, the food, the infinite variety of the countryside, the enchanting hilltop towns and villages and the historical centres of larger cities – all reinforced by friendships stemming from that month in Perugia, and developed over the ensuing years by numerous visits to the vineyards for research for my earlier book on Chianti. This second book has provided a wonderful opportunity to explore the byways of Tuscany in greater depth, and on foot, which is quite the best way to savour a landscape, allowing time to stand and stare, to observe the variations from one area to another, from one season to another. The book is the fruits of nine research and walking trips, between Easter 2002 and June 2003, with my husband as companion, encountering Tuscany in a variety of seasons (but avoiding the height of summer) and during the course of two quite contrasting vintages. Summer 2002 will be remembered as one of the wettest ever, while 2003 hit record temperatures with a succession of days over 40°C; neither are conditions that vines and grapes relish, with each posing a different set of problems for the winemaker. We, however, enjoyed some wonderful spring weather, autumn sunshine and crisp clear days in November and February, and in the course of just over 300 miles walked only once in the rain. Altogether we visited some two hundred wine growers, most of whom feature in these pages, with an apology to those who were omitted, for reasons of space rather than as a reflection on the quality of their wine. I attempted to see everybody who is anybody in each area, but the choice of estates was also determined by our walking routes, which in some instances led us off the beaten track to smaller, less well-known estates.

It all began in Florence on Easter Sunday 2002, with the annual celebration of the *Scoppio del Carro*, which translates literally as the explosion of the carriage. An eighteenth-century gilded cart is dragged into the cathedral square by sturdy white oxen. In most years this entails a lengthy and splendid procession through the centre of the city. Sadly, in 2002 the American Secretary of State had issued warnings against terrorist attacks in major Italian cities, in particular Florence and Venice, and a decision had been taken to cancel the procession. The *carabinieri* were out in force, meticulously checking everyone entering the square. Nonetheless the mood was festive, and the Piazza del Duomo never fails to inspire: the pattern and colour of the marble walls of the cathedral itself, crowned with Brunelleschi's breathtaking dome, and the Baptistery's fabulous gilded bronze doors. The square was packed with people, but thanks to the local knowledge of our Florentine friends we managed to find a spot where we had a view of the cart. To my mind, it looked more like a miniature pagoda, in ornate dark blue and red, festooned with fireworks. We waited and chatted, enjoying the gentle animation and anticipation. Shortly after the appointed hour a mechanical dove flew out of the cathedral door and ignited the fireworks. There were catherine wheels spinning amidst a multitude of brilliant sparks, creating an effect of coloured rain defying gravity. Clouds of gunpowder billowed around the carriage with explosions galore. The noise was deafening and I could not help thinking that if terrorists had chosen to strike, their activities might have initially passed unnoticed amidst the ear-piercing bangs. The display lasted for about a quarter of hour and was deemed a great success by our friends. 'Much better than last year,' said Renato, maybe as a gesture of defiance to the terrorist threats. But, more importantly, Tuscans believe that a particularly successful display foretells a fine harvest, for although the ceremony is ostensibly a celebration of the resurrection, it also has its roots in pagan fertility rites. Unfortunately, the prophecy of a good harvest was not borne out, as Tuscany was to have its worst vintage for ten years, with a wet August and unseasonable rain at the harvest. But at Easter everyone was optimistic.

We waited while the dead fireworks were removed from the cart, an intricate process involving one man inside the cart and two more perched precariously on a mini-crane above it. Then the massive oxen, garlanded with colourful spring flowers and with red ribbons decorating their tails, purposefully pulled the cart away until next year. We adjourned for coffee in a nearby café, pausing to admire the windows of tempting Easter confectionery. And then it was time for lunch, an Easter pie, or *torta pasqualina*, with spinach, ricotta and eggs. It was delicious.

That first trip centred on Chianti and in particular Chianti Classico. Chianti is the name that everyone knows. On first encounter, it is a friendly and unassuming wine, but on better acquaintance you begin to realize that it has hidden depths and many facets to its character. It is produced over a large part of central Tuscany, with various sub-zones surrounding Chianti Classico, the historic heart of the area, in the hills between Florence and Siena. The region has benefited from the enormous transformation over the last ten or twenty years and now produces an ever-growing number of wines with depth and complexity. The tarnished reputation of the 1970s and early 1980s is now a thing of the past, as new landowners with innovative ideas arrived in the wake of the dismantling of the *mezzadria* system and made an impact with their subsequent widespread improvements in vineyard and cellar. Sassicaia from Bolgheri, which was then a little-known area of Tuscany, provided the initial example, quickly followed by Antinori's Tignanello, a wine with Tuscan flavours but designed for the international market, as it combined the Sangiovese of Tuscany with Cabernet Sauvignon, the grape variety of Bordeaux, which has spread to most of the New World as well as to many other vineyards in the Old World. The success of Tignanello surprised even Antinori, and so many others have followed the example that in many corners of Tuscany

Cabernet Sauvignon now features alongside the traditional grape variety of the region, namely Sangiovese.

As well as Chianti and Chianti Classico, there are the other Denominazioni di Origine Controllata e Garantita, or DOCGs, such as the historical wines of Brunello di Montalcino and Vino Nobile di Montepulciano. We spent a happy week or more in each hilltop town, visiting wine cellars and exploring the vineyards. Carmignano is a more recently recognized DOCG, but with a long tradition of including Cabernet Sauvignon in its wine. Pomino, too, has a historical association with French grape varieties, while Vernaccia di San Gimignano remains an island of white wine in a sea of Chianti.

To the north you find the twin Denominazioni di Origine or DOCs of Colline Lucchesi and Montecarlo, both producing red and white wine, although Montecarlo has a reputation for white, while the Colline Lucchesi are better known for red wine. Further north still, almost into Liguria, are the little known DOCs of Candia dei Colli Apuani and Colli di Luni, with yet more vineyards in the foothills of the Apennines and the Val di Magra.

Travelling back south into the Maremma, the region that covers the province of Grosseto as well as the coastal area south of Cecina, you come first to Bolgheri. Since the initial innovatory steps of Sassicaia, the reputation and prestige of Bolgheri have gathered momentum, with some of the great names of Tuscany making wines that are usually based on Cabernet and Merlot rather than Sangiovese. Its neighbours, Montescudaio and Val di Cornia, are inspired by its example and success.

The two principal DOCs of the province of Grosseto include another incarnation of Sangiovese, Morellino di Scansano, with the adjacent white wine, Bianco di Pitigliano.

There has been a veritable wave of new DOCs in recent years, with Sovana, Montecucco, Monteregio di Massa Marittima, Capalbio, Ansonica Costa dell'Argentario all recent creations. Parrina, almost on the border with Lazio, is the smallest DOC, and the island of Elba has its own original flavours with Aleatico *passito*. Orcia and Cortona, too, are new names in the list of Tuscan DOCs, all reflecting the energy of numerous talented winemakers. Others are unconcerned by the lack of DOC in their area, or simply ignore the restrictions of their DOC to make the best they can as an Indicazione Geografica Tipica or

IGT, often at a price that rivals or even exceeds the best of the DOCs or DOCGs.

The creativity of the Tuscan winemaker is astonishing, offering an enormous variety of flavours. Sangiovese may provide the backbone for many of the wines, but there are also shining examples of Cabernet Sauvignon, Merlot, Cabernet Franc, Syrah, Chardonnay and Sauvignon, as well as lesser-known indigenous grape varieties, such as Vermentino Nero, Massaretta, Pollera, Ciliegiolo, and many others that will excite the taste buds. Finally, no book about Tuscany would be complete without mention of that most individual of Tuscan wines, Vin Santo.

It has been a fascinating eighteen months of discovery, with numerous highlights. When you visit a Tuscan wine estate, you never quite know what else you will see, a room of Annigoni portraits, an Etruscan tomb, a Medici villa or a view that is unchanged since Leonardo painted the *Mona Lisa*. Such is the wealth of Tuscan culture, and the warmth of its hospitality. And the versatility of the wines is such that they can be sipped in those most magical of squares, the Piazza del Campo in Siena and the Piazza del Duomo in Massa Marittima; they accompany the local seafood on the seashore of Elba, a hearty dish of wild boar in a village trattoria or the more refined flavours at La Pineta, the stylish fish restaurant on the coast at Bibbona, or at Il Tufo Allegro in Pitigliano – to name but two of my favourite Tuscan restaurants. There is no doubt that the sour-cherry astringency of Sangiovese is the perfect match for Tuscan olive oil, perpetuating a timeless marriage that is repeated in the vineyards and olive groves of the Tuscan countryside.

The Changing Face of Tuscany

IT IS NO EXAGGERATION TO SAY that the face of Tuscan viticulture and winemaking has changed more in the last twenty years than in the previous two hundred. What is not new? Methods in vineyard and cellar have evolved dramatically, as long-accepted precepts have been abandoned. The mezzadria system which had dominated the agricultural pattern of Tuscany for centuries disintegrated after the Second World War, making way for changes in land ownership, which would bring an influx of newcomers to the region. New ideas have followed, with the introduction of new grape varieties and the evolution of vineyard and cellar practices. We have seen the creation of a plethora of new Denominazioni di Origine Controllata, or DOCs, especially in the Maremma, such as Montecucco, Monteregio di Massa Marittima and others, and even more new wines that have no intention of conforming to local winemaking regulations but instead have every pretension and aspiration to quality. The pace of change has been breathtaking, sometimes too exaggerated, and now perhaps things are calming down. All this makes Tuscany the most exciting and rewarding destination.

It is all based on Sangiovese, the grape variety that dominates the red wines of Chianti, forming the backbone, not only of Chianti in its various guises, but also Vino Nobile di Montepulciano, Brunello di Montalcino, Morellino di Scansano and numerous other wines. Bolgheri is perhaps the one exception. Sangiovese is grown all over central Italy, from Emilia Romagna down to the Abruzzo, and the variations in flavour can be enormous, ranging from the often insipid and feeble Sangiovese di Romagna to firmly structured Brunello di Montalcino. The name Sangiovese derives from *sanguis Jovis*, or the blood of Jove, implying an ability to produce deep red, powerful wines, which is certainly not always the case. There is considerable variation amongst the different clones of Sangiovese, something of which much more is understood, following research projects such as Chianti 2000, and other university studies. It is now recognized that some clones are very much more successful than others. However, in broad terms, it seems that there are two sub-varieties, Sangiovese Grosso and Sangiovese Piccolo; the former is so-called because its berries are larger, but in fact they are not that big. In Montepulciano and Montalcino, it answers to the synonyms respectively of Prugnolo and Brunello; Prugnolo for its small plum-like form, and Brunello for its dusky, almost brown hue. Sangiovese Piccolo, for which the common synonym in Chianti is Sangioveto, is grown extensively throughout the vineyards of Chianti.

Until fairly recently it was difficult to generalize about the characteristics of Sangiovese as it was only in Montalcino that it was produced as a single grape variety, without the addition of any other varieties. However, the growing number of pure Sangiovese produced as *vino da tavola* in Chianti Classico led to a change in the law in 1996, allowing Chianti Classico to be a pure Sangiovese, by insisting on a minimum percentage in the blend, but no maximum. The Tuscan DOCs and DOCGs, with the single exception of Brunello di Montalcino, allow for a blend of grape varieties, and consequently considerable flexibility in the style of wine. One of the key flavour characteristics of Sangiovese is a certain astringency, a vivacity, which one winemaker called *una energia*. There is a liveliness and a freshness, a combination of quite high acidity, with some structured tannins, with a fruit flavour of sour cherries, but indisputably ripe ones. In the past Sangiovese has been considered a grape variety that benefits from blending with others, but as methods in vineyard and cellar have improved, that perception is now changing and there are an increasing number of pure Sangiovese, in Chianti and Montepulciano, and elsewhere.

There are also examples of pure Sangiovese in other parts of the world. With the fashion for things Italian, it has travelled to California, but the wines I have tasted have always lacked that inimitable flavour that is essentially Tuscan. Similarly the occasional example from Australia does not have the grip of Tuscany. Sangiovese is also grown on the island of Corsica as Nielluccio, having been taken there by the Pisans and Genoese in the Middle Ages, and forms the mainstay of the island's principal appellation, Patrimonio.

It is Canaiolo that has been most commonly blended with Sangiovese. Canaiolo Nero – there is a very rare Canaiolo Bianco – gives colour to Sangiovese, compensating for its tendency to oxidize, but otherwise has less tannin, acidity and indeed flavour, so that it can soften some of the edges of the rugged Sangiovese. Certainly it is useful in a Chianti *normale* for making a wine suitable for earlier drinking. Other grape varieties may feature in the regulations, such as Colorino, Mammola and Malvasia Nera, as indigenous Tuscan varieties. Then there are others that are more localized, such as Ciliegiolo in Pitigliano and Vermentino Nero and Massaretta in the Colli Apuani, while others such as Foglia Tonda and Pollera are being rediscovered in various research projects.

Tradition dictated the presence of white grapes in Chianti, and also in some other adjoining DOCs, notably Vino Nobile di Montepulciano. The reasons for this are historical, and also economical. It all goes back to the misinterpretation of the findings of Barone Bettino Ricasoli of the Castello di Brolio. When the Iron Baron conducted his research on his estate during the third quarter of the nineteenth century, he found that Malvasia Bianca helped soften a wine, making it ready for everyday consumption. There was no mention at all of the ubiquitous Trebbiano, which still dominates the white wines of Tuscany today. However, the *contadini* of the *mezzadria* system favoured Trebbiano for its generous yields, for the prevalent mentality was that quantity equalled quality. Consequently, when the DOC of Chianti was created in 1967, the regulations allowed for as much as 30 per cent of white grapes in a wine that was supposed to be red, and that 30 per cent was not the percentage of grapes in the wine itself, but the percentage of vines in the vineyard, and so with a high-yielding grape variety like Trebbiano, the percentage in the wine rose yet higher. It is small wonder that Chianti fell into such disrepute. Fortunately, with the subsequent changes in the production regulations, Trebbiano and Malvasia Bianca have both been eliminated from Chianti. The various white DOCs that were based on these two varieties, such as Bianco di San Torpè, Bianco Vergine Valdichiana and so on, have also happily declined in importance. As vineyards have been replanted, Trebbiano, in particular, has disappeared, so now Trebbiano and Malvasia Bianca remain primarily for that most Tuscan of wines, Vin Santo.

More interesting white grape varieties are to be found in San Gimignano, with Vernaccia, and in Montecarlo and Pomino, which have enjoyed the historical influence of France, with the introduction of varieties such as Chardonnay and Pinot Bianco, as early as the middle of the nineteenth century. Vermentino Bianco, which is grown extensively on the Mediterranean coast, and as Rolle in the south of France, makes for some appealing but understated flavours. It must be remembered that Tuscan whites are usually subtle and never overpowering, unless they have been heavily dressed in oak. Their charms are not immediately apparent, but they complement the flavours of Tuscany as perfectly as Sangiovese balances the rich olive oil of the region. Ansonica, otherwise known as the Inzolia of Sicily, is another grape variety with growing success on the Argentario coast, in wines such as Capalbio Bianco and Ansonica Costa dell'Argentario.

Most of the DOC regulations allow for a complementary 10 or even 20 per cent of other grape varieties. These may include the indigenous Tuscan varieties, or, more often these days, the various French varieties that have infiltrated the vineyards of Tuscany. The most obvious of these is Cabernet Sauvignon, which has a long history in the vineyards of Carmignano, but not in Chianti. Cabernet Sauvignon first made its mark in recent Tuscan viticultural history at Sassicaia in Bolgheri, when the Marchese Mario Incisa della Rocchetta planted it in his vineyards soon after the Second World War. The success of the first commercial vintage of Sassicaia, the legendary 1968, paved the way for the acceptance of Cabernet Sauvignon in the vineyards of Tuscany.

There is no doubt that a blend of Cabernet Sauvignon and Sangiovese can make a very happy marriage, for in some respects there are similarities between the two varieties. In this, the lead was taken by Marchese Piero Antinori and his talented oenologist, Giacomo Tachis, who had worked with the Marchese Incisa della Rocchetta at Sassicaia and gained the vital experience that led to the creation of Tignanello, a blend of Sangiovese and Cabernet Sauvignon. Looking back to the 1980s when Chianti was sadly in the doldrums and in need of radical remedies, Cabernet Sauvignon provided the solution. It enhanced the flavours of Sangiovese, camouflaged the effect of the white grapes, and made for a wine with more structure and body. It quickly established its presence in the vineyards, often as an essential ingredient in many of the innovative wines that appeared in the marketplace as the more creative winemakers sought to remedy the deficiencies of their traditional Chianti.

Back in the 1980s, Cabernet Sauvignon was seen as something of a saviour. However, there were also the voices of tradition who argued against it, that it had no place at all amongst the traditional flavours of Tuscany, and that it would deform the taste of Sangiovese, albeit camouflaging defects that might result from the wrong clones or excessive yields. Cabernet Sauvignon is planted all over the world and it would only add to the uniformity. It would be so much better to concentrate on the intrinsic originality of Sangiovese and learn how to enhance its true flavours. At the time Cabernet Sauvignon was even described as the cuckoo in the nest of Chianti.

Twenty years on there is no doubt that Cabernet Sauvignon is here to stay. It does have a worldwide appeal, and can impart a very international and recognizable flavour to a wine. In more traditional regions, it is grown as an adjunct, an addition to a producer's range, allowing them to make another wine that will stand apart from the traditional DOC(G). Amongst the newer DOCs it is often an important part of the blend. Bolgheri is a notable example of this, but other areas, too, concentrate on Cabernet Sauvignon, amongst other French varieties, or maybe the wine growers simply choose to ignore the traditional grape varieties and maintain their own individuality, creating wines according to their whim which might legally be only humble *vino da tavola* or now, with the change in the regulations, an *Indicazione Geografica Tipica* or IGT. In practice an IGT is often more highly rated than the parallel DOC(G). Therein lies the illogicality of Italian wine law.

It is a cliché that Italians are individualists and in the vineyards of Tuscany the cliché is undoubtedly true. The decline in the reputation of simple DOC(G) Chianti has resulted in an enormous amount of creativity, as producers strive to bring their vineyards back to economic viability. Realizing that there is no money to be made from Chianti, they have turned to other wines and planted other grape varieties, notably Cabernet Sauvignon, but also Merlot, Syrah, Chardonnay, Sauvignon and so on. The next hot grape variety may be Petit Verdot, which was only given official recognition in Tuscany in the spring of 2003. A plethora of new wines has been created. Initially there was an attempt to give them some sort of legal status with an association for the so-called Predicato wines based on four grape varieties: Sangiovese, Cabernet Sauvignon, Chardonnay and Sauvignon. The Predicato wines have since disappeared in name, but still exist in the form of IGTs. Most have elaborate fantasy names, which may recall a vineyard, but equally well a child, wife, or maybe a mistress. Indeed it seems that naming your wine is almost as complicated as naming your child. Many of the earlier creations, notably the pure Sangiovese, now conform to the *disciplinari* of the DOC(G); whether their producer chooses to label them DOC(G) instead of IGT is quite another matter. Sometimes there are marketing considerations: an IGT enables you to produce a wine other than your DOC(G), which you can sell at a higher price than your DOC(G). As will be seen, this is particularly so in the Colline Pisane. However, there is no doubt that this surge of creativity has resulted in a wonderful flowering of Tuscan viticulture.

It could be said that the moment was ripe. With the collapse of the *mezzadria* system after the Second World War, many of the old landowners, with vast estates which had been in their families for centuries, found themselves without the means and labour to run their land. The vineyards were planted in the time-honoured method of *cultura promiscua*, with everything all mixed up together. You would find a row of vines, interspersed with an olive tree or two, with wheat and vegetables planted in small patches in between. As the *contadini* left the land, lured by the promise of prosperity in the industrial north, many of these landowners were forced to sell their land. Where once *un podere in Chianti* had been a symbol of wealth, the farm in Chianti became a millstone around the landowner's neck, and in the 1960s and early 1970s it was possible to buy land in Chianti for a song, but enormous amounts of money were then needed for the renovation of buildings and the replanting of the vineyards.

While some of the old-established families, Antinori and Frescobaldi to name but two, remain and have adapted adeptly, many estates have changed hands, resulting in a considerable influx of newcomers. The charms of Tuscany have always attracted people from outside the region, and indeed from outside Italy. The new landowners have arrived from northern Italy, from the industrial cities of Milan or Turin, or they may come from other parts of

Tuscany, having made their money in the textile industry of Prato, or they may come from the capital. They have successful careers in other fields, as lawyers or high-powered industrialists, and having bought what they initially saw as a holiday or weekend home, they have turned their expertise, energy and money into creating something worthwhile from their estate. Those with no experience in wine have the wit and money to employ the appropriate expertise, a consultant oenologist to create some award-winning wines and an *agronomo* to ensure that the vineyards are planted and maintained to the highest standards. The newcomers are often Italian, but there are foreigners too, some investing on a small scale, creating an estate or buying an existing estate to establish their own niche in Tuscany, while others are larger international wine producers, such as Kendall Jackson, who own Villa Arceno and Beringer, who have recently purchased the Castello di Gabbiano, both properties in Chianti Classico.

These are the people who have often been behind the radical improvements in vineyard and cellar of the past twenty or so years. There is no doubt that the technical expertise in winemaking has improved worldwide in that time. Every wine-producing country has seen the proliferation of stainless-steel vats, computerized systems of temperature control and all the adjuncts of modern winemaking. In Tuscany, perhaps one of the most marked changes is the swing from the traditional *botti*, the large oak casks that could hold one hundred hectolitres or more, to the smaller *barriques* of Bordeaux. That is not to say that *botti* have disappeared completely; they are still very much part of a Tuscan cellar, but their use has become more rational, and often they are much smaller and certainly very much better maintained. Traditionally they were made from Slavonic oak by coopers in northern Italy, nor were chestnut barrels unknown, whereas today you can find *botti* of French oak. In reality the large *botti* are containers for storage; they do not make any impact of oak on the wine, but just allow for a very gentle process of oxidation and maturation.

Barriques have been espoused with enthusiasm by the innovators. There is much discussion about the suitability of *barriques* for ageing Sangiovese; the protagonists favour it, while the detractors argue that excessive oak, and in particular new oak, can deform the flavours of the grape variety. Certainly it needs careful attention; too much oak can produce clumsy, heavy-handed results, while just enough will make a wine that is finely crafted and elegant. Paolo de Marchi at Isole e Olena has suggested that it takes a number of years to learn to use new *barriques* properly and that there is a sharp learning curve. Inevitably the newcomer to *barriques* overdoes them, and he admitted that he did. The argument certainly rages in Montalcino where the DOCG regulations demand a minimum of two years' ageing in oak. Here there are people who fervently favour the small barrel, while others refuse to contemplate them. Then there is a middle road, with the so-called *tonneaux* of 500 litres, which allow for a less intense effect of oak than the *barriques*. Often in Chianti the *normale* will be kept in *botti* or in concrete or stainless-steel vats, while the *riserva*, which requires a couple of years of ageing, will be matured in *barriques*. Any IGT wines of Cabernet Sauvignon, Merlot, Syrah and Chardonnay are almost certain to be aged in oak. There is no doubt that the word *barricata*, describing barrel-ageing, is here to stay in the Italian language.

There have been other improvements too. The process that was called *governo all'uso Toscano* has more or less disappeared. It too goes back to Barone Bettino Ricasoli of the Castello di Brolio, who recognized it as a way of rendering tough tannic wine drinkable earlier, by adding slightly dried grapes to the almost finished wine in order to induce a second fermentation and thereby make the wine taste richer, riper and fruitier. It was taken for granted as part of the *contadino* way of making wine, but now as winemaking practices have become more refined, and there is a demand for longer-lived wines, its use is no longer necessary. There is a better understanding of the processes of extracting colour and flavour, with a much better comprehension of the techniques of pumping over or *rimontaggio*, punching down or *pigiatura*, and *délestage*, a French term that is untranslatable and entails a process whereby the juice is run off the skins and then added back to the vat, on top of the skins, so that they float to the top of the fermenting juice. The grapes are invariably destalked these days, thereby removing one source of green astringent tannins. Sangiovese is a late ripener; so how often could the stalks ripen fully as well? And there are many other nuances of cellar practice that will appear on the pages of this book. So much depends on individual winemakers. However, amongst the owners of estates of any size, very few are winemakers, especially in Chianti Classico. Many of the proprietors of the large estates are partially absentee landowners who employ a cellar manager to carry out the instructions of the consultant oenologist. And there are any number of consultant oenologists who make a successful living offering advice to estates all over Italy and indeed much further afield. They could be criticized for adding an element of uniformity to the wines; how easy is it for them to differentiate one Chianti from another? The responsible and conscientious oenologist will tell you that this is not a problem and that he allows the grapes and the *terroir* to guide him.

Everyone will tell you that good wine comes above all from the vineyard and that it is your work amongst the vines during the year that is the key factor in determining quality. Viticultural practices have progressed considerably in Tuscany. First of all there was the dramatic shift from *cultura promiscua* to what are called specialized vineyards. Initially these were planted with very wide rows to accommodate the tractor, thereby encouraging, as Stefano Rizzi of Le Pupille in Scansano quipped, *la viticultura* Fiat. The spate of land-ownership changes in the 1970s prompted an enormous amount of replanting particularly in the vineyards of Chianti Classico, and not always with the best clones or in the most suitable way for the terrain. With the realization that the need to replant would occur again in twenty-five years' time, the Chianti Classico *consorzio* was determined not to repeat the mistakes of the 1970s and replant the wrong clones at the wrong density. With great foresight they initiated a programme called Chianti 2000, which undoubtedly has repaid dividends. Several producers participated with experimental vineyards on their land, planting different clones and rootstock, at various densities, with varying training methods, all in an effort to see what worked best. It was soon revealed that some clones performed very much better than others, and in certain conditions. It was also recognized that higher density plantings gave much better results as vines thrive with some root competition, with each vine producing a limited amount of grapes with much greater flavour.

One of the main viticultural problems of Sangiovese is that it tends to ripen relatively late, especially compared to Cabernet Sauvignon. The harvest in the hills of Chianti Classico usually takes place during the first couple of weeks of October, with the annual gamble: will the weather hold? When will the autumn rains come? It is very rare that Tuscany does not have a summer fit to ripen the grapes, but often a potentially fine vintage is affected by rain during the harvest. However, with a greater understanding of the behaviour of Sangiovese in the vineyard, with appropriate trellising systems, it is possible to encourage an earlier ripening, with the desired effect on the quality of the harvest. There are all manner of details in the vineyards that enhance the quality of the grapes: leaf-plucking will assist the ripening process; a green harvest, entailing the removal of part of the crop while the grapes are still green, will limit the yields still further. Where once the peasant mentality saw the green harvest as the rejection of a gift from God and a waste of the fruits of Nature, most producers, even the more conservative cooperative members, now recognize the benefit to quality that the limitation of their yields will bring.

The wine trade in Tuscany, with its many facets, comprises a wonderful myriad of different characters, opinions, practices and personalities, all helping to make Tuscany one of the most exciting and creative regions to visit. Some of them you will meet on the ensuing pages.

An Introduction to Chianti

CHIANTI IS TUSCANY, EPITOMIZING both the best and the worst of the region. Twenty years ago Chianti was in the doldrums. Its reputation was floundering in a mire of insipid, characterless wine, with quantity rather than quality the key criterion of production. The market was awash with Chianti that nobody wanted, which was sold on price alone. Quite simply, Chianti had lost its way, and lost its friends. But happily there were perceptive producers who were aware of the urgent need to restore the reputation of the wine that symbolizes Tuscany for so many of us. Slowly things began to change. It started in the heart of Chianti Classico, and now, as will be seen, a growing number of like-minded producers in the surrounding wine areas are eager to improve their wines and attain the very best from their vineyards. At its most serious Chianti is a wine with stature and ageing potential, what the Italians call so eloquently *un vino da meditazione*, while at the other end of the spectrum it offers instantly appealing, accessible fruit, as a perfect accompaniment to a plate of pasta, a wine that the Italians would call *un vino da pasto*, an uncomplicated wine, but certainly none the worse for that.

The historical heart of Chianti lies between the two cities of Florence and Siena in the vineyards of Chianti Classico. These are surrounded by various other Chianti sub-zones, namely Rufina in the hills to the north-east of Florence; the Colli Aretini close to Arezzo; the Colli Fiorentini south of Florence, adjoining Chianti Classico; the Colli Senesi over the hills around Siena and the Colline Pisane to the south-east of Pisa. Chianti Montalbano adjoins the vineyards of Carmignano on the south side of the Monte Albano, and Montespertoli is a recently created sub-zone around the village of the same name to the south-west of Florence, and in addition there are other villages that are entitled simply to the denomination of Chianti.

The very first written record of Chianti in fact describes a white wine. In the papers of the Prato merchant Francesco di Marco Datini, best known as the inventor of the bill of exchange or cheque, there is reference to a debt in December 1398 of three florins, twenty-six soldi and eight denari, the price of six casks of white Chianti wine. In correspondence with the same Datini, Amedeo Gherardini of Vignamaggio wrote on 26 October 1404 that he was sending half a barrel of his personal stock from Vignamaggio, one of the choicest wines of Chianti. So the very first reference describes it as a white wine, and it seems that at this time the red wines of Florence were more often called Vino Vermiglio. A century or two later the red wines of the Chianti area began to acquire a reputation in England, where they were known as Florence. Samuel Pepys recorded in his diary for 9 January 1661 a gift of two bottles of Florence, and W. Salmon, writing in 1693 in the *Compleat English Physician*, noted 'Florence white and red are both good stomach wines, but the red is something binding'.

An important milestone in the development of Chianti and also a couple of other Tuscan wines came with the edict published by the Medici Duke Cosimo III in 1716, which defined the boundaries of Chianti, along with those of Pomino, Carmignano and the Val d'Arno di Sopra, which today is part of the Colli Fiorentini. The area of Chianti was determined as extending from Spedaluzzo to Greve and from there to Panzano, including Radda, Gaiole and Castellina, up to the boundary with Siena. This still constitutes the core of Chianti Classico today.

The work of Barone Bettino Ricasoli at the Castello di Brolio in the middle of the nineteenth century has been mentioned in the previous chapter. He kept an extensive diary from 1851 to 1877, which is full of observations on viticulture and oenology, all based on his experiences at Brolio. Rightly or wrongly he bears some of the responsibility for the high percentage of white wine that blighted Chianti's reputation.

The twentieth century saw further attempts to guarantee the quality of Chianti, with the formation of an association of producers in Siena for the *difesa dei vini del vero Chianti*, with the objective of maintaining the quality of Chianti, with members from Greve, Radda, Castellina, Gaiole and Castelnuovo Berardenga, but there was uncertainty as to the precise limits of the area. In 1924 a law was passed which recognized that *vino tipico* should be produced under specified conditions, but it was totally ineffective in that no consideration at all was given to provenance. However, the same year also saw the creation of the *Consorzio per la difesa del vino tipico del Chianti*, again intended to defend the quality of Chianti, with thirty-three founder members from Castellina, Gaiole, Greve and Radda. The *consorzio* took the black cockerel or *gallo nero* as its trade mark, recalling the part played by the cockerels in the boundary dispute between Florence and Siena. Subsequently the *consorzio* lost a legal battle in the United States, when the powerful wine-producing family Gallo claimed that the American public would be confused by the similarity of name. Then in 1927 a second *consorzio* was created to cover the larger area of Chianti, beyond the vineyards of Chianti Classico, which took the *putto* or chubby baby cherub as its emblem. Today this *consorzio* is pretty well defunct, while the consorzio for Chianti Classico continues to function, its members identified by the black cockerel on their bottles.

In 1932 came the first legal recognition of the various zones where *un vino denominato del Chianti* could be produced, namely Chianti Classico, Montalbano, Rufina, Colli Fiorentini, Colli Senesi, Colli Aretini and Colline Pisane. The area recognized as Chianti Classico was almost identical to that laid down by the Grand Duke in his edict of 1716. There were no precise regulations; that would not come until the creation of the system of Denominazione di Origine Controllata, or DOC, which came into effect with the Italian Wine Law of 1963. The DOC for Chianti and Chianti Classico gave legal recognition to the areas agreed in 1932, and the percentages of permitted grape were agreed as follows. Sangiovese formed the backbone, with 50 to 80 per cent; Canaiolo was the secondary variety, with 10 to 30 per cent; the white grapes Trebbiano Toscano and Malvasia del Chianti contributed anything between 10 and 30 per cent, and that left a 5 per cent of complementary grape varieties, which could cover anything grown in the vineyards of Tuscany, such as Mammola, or Colorino, which was particularly recommended for the *governo* method.

The regulations left plenty of room for improvement, especially as the percentages were those in the vineyard, not in the cellar, and yields for Chianti were set at 125 quintals per hectare, equating to 87 hectolitres per hectare, which is far more than is acceptable for a red wine. Chianti Classico was little better, at 115 quintals, equating to 80 hl/ha. Small wonder that the regulations also allowed a 15 per cent corrective of wine or unfermented grape juice from outside the defined area of Chianti, thereby recognizing the existence of a common practice, but one which ran completely contrary to the concept of authenticity of origin. Quite simply it was realized that a red wine that contained such a high proportion of white grapes would need a boost of something deeper coloured and more alcoholic from the warm south, from Puglia or Sicily. The category of *riserva* was also introduced for wines given three years' ageing in cask or bottle from the January after the harvest. It is no wonder that Chianti lost its reputation, as the promulgators of the DOC had merely pandered to the voices demanding quantity, without any realization of the long-term damage that would be done to the wine's quality.

Things began to improve with the introduction of the supposedly stricter regulations of Denominazione di Origine Controllata e Garantita, or DOCG. These were designed to implement a guarantee of origin, but not a guarantee of quality. The grape variety percentages were amended, allowing 70–90 per cent of Sangiovese, 5–10 per cent of Canaiolo, 10 per cent of complementary grape varieties, and 2–5 per cent of Trebbiano and Malvasia Bianca for Chianti Classico and 5–10 per cent for the other areas. Yields were also reduced, down to 75 quintals or 53 hl/ha for Chianti Classico and also Rufina, and 80 quintals or 56 hl/ha for the other zones. The 15 per cent corrective of wine or must from elsewhere was eliminated for Chianti Classico and Rufina, but not yet from the rest of Chianti. That would come later, though it has to be said that a surprising amount of wine from southern Italy continues to travel north and disappear into wine vats north of Rome. The yield for Chianti Classico and Rufina was limited to 3 kilos per vine, and to 5 kilos per vine elsewhere in Chianti. The DOCG regulations can be criticized for retaining the use of white grapes, but at least the percentage became almost insignificant, so as to be undetectable, thus facilitating things for the growing number of winemakers who chose to break the law and make their Chianti without any white grapes. The immediate consequence of the change in the *disciplinari* was the surfeit of white grapes, which resulted in the creation of a brand called Galestro, named after one of the soil types commonly found in Chianti Classico, which enjoyed some popularity in the late 1980s but has now virtually disappeared, certainly from the international wine market. More immediately many of the white vines were grafted with other more desirable varieties, and then eventually replanted with Sangiovese, or whatever. Today on most Chianti estates, Trebbiano and Malvasia remain for that quintessential Tuscan wine, Vin Santo.

It soon became apparent that the new *disciplinari* of the DOCG were inadequate for the restoration of confidence in the reputation of Chianti. The talented and creative winemakers of the area continued to produce an infinite variety of *vini da tavola*, the so-called super-Tuscans, which initially had minimal legal status but were eventually recognized as IGT in 1992, with a further change in the Italian wine law. Many of these wines were made from a single grape variety, Sangiovese, and with increasing success as the producers of Chianti, and Chianti Classico in particular, strove to extract the best from their grapes, with a greater understanding of viticulture than ever before. Consequently in 1996 a further change in regulations finally legalized what so many producers were already doing, and removed the maximum percentage for Sangiovese and the minimum percentage for Canaiolo, Trebbiano and Malvasia, so that Chianti Classico could be made from Sangiovese alone. The new *disciplinari* also allowed for a complementary 15 per cent, a percentage that was increased to 20 per cent in 2000, which could be any of the indigenous Tuscan varieties, or any of the more international varieties, notably Cabernet Sauvignon, Syrah, Merlot and so on. Chianti Classico was recognized as a separate DOCG in its own right, a position to which the producers of Rufina also aspire, for both have long considered themselves to stand quite apart from the mass of Chianti produced all over the centre of Tuscany. Indeed, one of the criticisms of the DOCG was that it attributed a uniformity to wines of quite varying quality. There is a world of difference between a light fruity wine from Montalbano and a more structured wine from Chianti Classico or Rufina, not only in the difference of grapes and methodology, but also in climate and *terroir*, that untranslatable French word, which the Italians would call *terreno*, although it does not have quite the same all-embracing ring as in French, which covers not just soil but aspect, altitude, microclimate and the myriad of different factors that can affect the environment of the vine.

Chianti Classico comprises a multiplicity of different soils and climates for the region is made up of several large valleys, which in turn are divided by numerous smaller ones. The landscape is an inevitable series of folds of hills fading into the distance. With so many hills, the permutations of microclimate are inevitably considerable, and the geological map is a jigsaw puzzle of tiny pieces. Galestro is generally considered to be the most favourable soil for Sangiovese; it is a poor stony soil, which sometimes may be mixed with sand, limestone, chalk or clay. The variations are infinite.

The mountain range of the Apennines plays a huge role in determining the weather, protecting Chianti and Chianti Classico from the prevailing winds from the east, while vineyards further west experience more maritime influence. The higher the vineyard the cooler the average temperature, and altitudes in Chianti Classico can vary from around 250–300 metres near Greve to as high as 400–500 metres around Lamole. Winters can be cold. I encountered clear, bright, but freezing cold days in February, and even snow. Spring and autumn may bring rain, and the summer is usually dry and warm, with little or no rainfall from the beginning of June until October. 2002, the year in which most of the research for this book took place, was the exception, with unseasonable rain in August, which we avoided, deeming that August would be too hot for walking, and also in September, when we were lucky, in that it never seemed to rain on the day that we had planned a walk. Hail can cause damage in summer, while spring frosts are very rare, but do happen, as on Easter Day 2001. Certainly the weather varies enough for vintages to matter.

The charm of Chianti, and in particular of the more compact Chianti Classico, is immediately apparent, with a series of hills, a patchwork of vines, groves of olive trees and lines of cypresses enhancing the landscape, and interspersed with the woods, which are an important part of the fabric of the land. Chianti Classico comprises a collection of small towns, villages and hamlets, each with its own particular character, which reward exploration. The best way to approach Chianti Classico is to take the old road out of Florence, past the monastery of Galluzzo and follow the Chiantigiana, which bends and turns with every hill and valley. You will soon reach Greve, the largest town of the area, with its attractive arcaded square and a statue of Verrazzano, who discovered the mouth of the Hudson River and gave his name to one of New York's bridges. Greve was his birthplace and a nearby estate is named after him. The square comes to life on market day, with colourful animation and the usual selection of market tat. For the gastronomically minded the food stalls are few. It is better to visit the Antica Macelleria Falorni, distinguished by the stuffed wild boar at the door, with its wide selection of salamis and hams from pig and wild boar.

Further down the Chiantigiana, you reach Panzano, where we stayed, and carry on to Castellina, another cheerful town, with the remains of an old tower and an Etruscan tomb. Further east is Radda, with the vestiges of a fourteenth-century Palazzo del Podestà, and further east still Gaiole, which was the starting point for two of our walks.

Chianti Classico is rich in history. It was the battleground of the Guelphs and the Ghibellines, between the two city states of Florence and Siena. Castles still stand – Brolio, San Polo in Rosso, Meleto, to name but a few – and they were succeeded by elegant villas, such as Vignamaggio, La Massa and Rignana. The hillsides have hardly changed since the Renaissance painters first captured them, though inevitably the demise of *cultura promiscua* has altered the agricultural pattern. The variety of the landscape is infinite, with an appropriate complexity in the wines. As we quickly discovered, walking is the pace at which to appreciate it all, and we also took the time to stand and stare, to sip the wine and savour the atmosphere.

THE GOVERNO METHOD

GOVERNO ALL'USO TOSCANO, to give the practice its full name, goes back to Baron Bettino Ricasoli and came to be seen as a way of rendering the often tannic and astringent Sangiovese grape more drinkable and palatable in its youth. Done properly, it is an expensive and complicated procedure. Fully ripe, healthy grapes are picked and set aside to lightly dehydrate for a few weeks, and then pressed and their juice added to vats of wine that has just finished its fermentation so that the fermentation starts again. The aim is to enhance a wine that is intended for early drinking, making a richer and fruitier Chianti. It was rarely used for Chianti destined for ageing in cask, only for young wine. However, as winemaking techniques have improved, the process has been abandoned by all but a few very traditional estates.

Around Panzano, in the Heart of Chianti Classico

· April ·

From Fontodi to La Massa, Castello dei Rampolla, Villa Cafaggio, Vecchie Terre di Montefili and Vignamaggio

PANZANO IS A SMALL TOWN in the heart of Chianti Classico, lying on the Chiantigiana, the SS222, the old road that slowly winds its way from Florence to Siena. Now that the so-called *superstrada* also links the two cities, Panzano tends to be populated by tourists enjoying the fabulous Tuscan countryside, as well as groups of keen Italian cyclists dressed in lurid lycra sports kit. There is a little square with an *enoteca*, the Enoteca Baldi, which is worth a visit for interesting bottles, while a second wine shop, the Enoteca del Chianti Classico, across the street, is a veritable Aladdin's cave of dusty bottles and well worth a lengthy browse for all kinds of treasures. Then you can walk up the main street, through an arched gateway into the old town and up to the church of Santa Maria at the top of the hill, which is always firmly closed, except on Sunday mornings. There are also the vestiges of a ruined castle, while another *enoteca* next to the church, with a less exciting choice of wines, has a sunny, sometimes windy terrace, with views across the valley to the cypress trees of Vignamaggio. Its menu provided a source of amusement, as *saltati* was translated as 'salties' and *panini corretti* had become 'laced sandwiches', as a splash of *grappa* or Vin Santo has been added to the filling.

There are gastronomic reasons too to visit Panzano. Il Vescovino is one of the Chianti's more elegant restaurants, with a wine list of appropriate depth, and for carnivores there is one of the finest butchers in Tuscany, the Antica Macelleria Cecchini, owned by Dario Cecchini. When you visit, don't be in a hurry. Cecchini is a showman; he entertains his customers and friends as he works, preparing *arista*, the classic roast pork of Tuscany, and on Easter Saturday he was autographing photographs rather than serving customers. Somehow it seemed churlish to be impatient. There are mouth-watering pâtés and salamis, and if you are lucky, maybe even a glass of wine while you queue. But if time is not on your side, the butcher's in the square in the old town is an excellent second-best.

However, the real importance of Panzano is the amphitheatre of vineyards outside the village, known as the Conca d'Oro or golden bowl, which includes some of the best names of Chianti, such as Fontodi, Rampolla, La Massa and Cafaggio. Our friends at Fontodi lent us a cottage right in the middle of the vineyards. It was an idyllic spot, with views across the valley towards Rampolla and up the hill to Panzano. We arrived on a wonderful spring afternoon. The vines were just beginning to bud and the rosemary bushes in the garden were in flower, the most intense blue in the sunlight. Maria greeted us with coffee and little cakes and gave us an olive branch, as it was Palm Sunday, and the next day we visited the winery on the hill just outside the village. Giovanni Manetti, who would feature in anyone's list of the most elegantly dressed men in Chianti, with good looks to match, explained how his father Dino had bought the property back in 1968. His family have been important terracotta producers at Il Ferrone since the beginning of the seventeenth century, and maybe even earlier. Nearby Impruneta is known for its *orci*, the large terracotta amphorae which traditionally house the fresh olive oil.

A new cellar had been built since my last visit and Giovanni was justifiably keen to show it off. Everything works by gravity: the freshly harvested grapes drop into the fermentation vats, and from there the new wine is run off into barrels in the underground cellar below, which would not look out of place in one of the more prestigious châteaux of Bordeaux. Altogether there are some 1500 barriques, from several different coopers, but no more large *botti*. They are now a thing of the past. I encouraged Giovanni to reminisce about the changes in Chianti Classico over the last ten years or so, for they have been quite dramatic. The obvious visible differences are the cellars, with the widespread investment in vinification equipment, such as the mechanical, computerized 'feet' for *pigiatura*, and the computerized temperature control of each individual vat. The *governo* is a thing of the past; instead the malolactic fermentation takes place in barrel, making for a more integrated balance of fruit and oak. There are changes in the vineyards too, the results of the research for Chianti 2000, so that planting densities are much higher, with 6500 vines per hectare as opposed to 3000. Giovanni explained how they restrict their yields to about one kilo of grapes per vine; you are allowed as much as two and a half, but the lower yield gives such a better concentration of flavour. And that was apparent in the wines we tasted.

Fontodi's Chianti Classico *normale* has wonderful ripe cherry fruit, with that characteristic astringency and bite of backbone of good Chianti, which complements the local olive oil so well. For Giovanni this is the wine for everyday drinking. If you want more complexity, you choose the *riserva*, in this case Flaccianello, which is a selection of the best grapes, so that the quantity depends entirely on the vintage. 1992 was the last year that they were unable to make it at all, so bad was the summer, and as for 2002, Giovanni has as yet to make the final decision. The winemaking varies slightly for the two wines, with a longer time on the skins and a longer period of ageing in wood for Flaccianello. Vigna del Sorbo, the vineyard just behind the new cellar, includes some Cabernet Sauvignon, as well as Sangiovese, which was grafted on to white vines back in 1980, when farsighted producers were beginning to look at other grape varieties and work out how to improve the quality of their wines. You can taste the impact of the Cabernet in the Vigna del Sorbo, compared to the pure Sangiovese of Flaccianello. There are notes of cassis, with a different structure and a fuller body. They have Syrah, too, making some sweet peppery fruit in the young wine, and also a little Pinot Noir, which to my taste buds served to illustrate just what a temperamental grape variety it can be.

From Fontodi we walked along to the little Pieve di San Leolino, with its portico of Romanesque arches and a fresco of the baptism of Christ. Its simplicity was very appealing. Giampaolo Motta of La Massa keeps his barrels in the cellars under the church, so it was appropriate that his estate was our next destination. Returning to our little cottage, we set off down the track following the edge of the field. At the bottom a large shed housed a number of chocolate-coloured bulls with wide inscrutable faces. Then the path took us back uphill, past a group of cheerful vineyard workers. They suggested it was too cold for walking – there was indeed a chilling wind, despite the sunshine – and the most vocal of the group told us that they were preparing '*il buon vino*'. These were some of Fontodi's vines and we explained we had tasted the wines that morning and agreed that Flaccianello was delicious. They were busy attaching the young shoots to their supporting wires, so that each worker carried a waistband of strands of long green twine. It is a laborious job and we observed their slow progress across the hillside throughout the week.

The track took us past the outskirts of Panzano, which has been somewhat spoilt with the new development of little box houses that have yet to tone into their surroundings. We walked through an olive grove and to the *strada bianca* that leads to the estate of Vignole. As we passed La Massa a large white dog barked at us in a welcoming manner; we later learnt that he is an eleven-year-old Maremma sheepdog and answers to the name of Marvin. The sky was clear, so that the moon was also visible in the late afternoon. There were hawthorn hedges coming into flower and the cherry blossom in the distance looked like a Claude Lorraine painting. Vine-cuttings burning in a vineyard gave off a gentle aroma of wood smoke. Then a pair of deer sprang out of the undergrowth, each boasting a full head of antlers. The road forms a semicircle so that Fontodi came into view, seeming very close, when in fact it is a few kilometres back up the track.

Back at La Massa Giampaolo gave us a warm welcome and an engaging smile. He is passionately enthusiastic, and opinionated, with a sense of humour. The earliest written reference to La Massa dates back to the fourteenth century, while the existing villa was built in 1602. The main entrance has a rather sombre courtyard with statues. Giampaolo has a rabbit warren of small barrel rooms under the villa, and he is planning a new cellar. We tasted in a drawing room in the villa. The walls are whitewashed, but underneath he and his girlfriend have discovered traces of frescoes and painted friezes, which they eventually hope to uncover. Giampaolo is a relative newcomer to Chianti; he comes from Naples where his family have a leather business, but winemaking had captured his imagination. It became a dream to have his name on a bottle. He first came to Tuscany on holiday, and then worked with John Dunkley at Riecine, and also at Rampolla, as well as at a large estate, which he said had best remain nameless, 'for that is where I learnt what not to do!' And in 1992, after looking at nearly a hundred different properties, he bought the bankrupt estate of La Massa as *una grande scommessa*, a huge gamble, which has paid off, for there is no doubt that he has established his reputation as one of the leading estates of Panzano, and indeed of Chianti Classico.

Giampaolo's enthusiasm is infectious and you feel that he allows nothing to stand still as he questions accepted winemaking practices. He is a keen advocate of ageing red wine on its lees, something that is more usual for white wine, firmly believing that this method gives his wine more colour, by fixing the anthocyanins, and makes for better acid stability, with richer tannins and less astringency. But it is a very demanding procedure, he said, 'a labour that keeps you young'. You have to taste every barrel every week, and decide whether it needs lees stirring, or not. 'We can't stay as we are. Possibly this is a time when Chianti will have many different tastes, as people decide how to make their wine. The producers of Panzano still have to find a *tipicità* for their wine.' He is looking for elegance, a certain *dolcezza*, or richness, but not great structure. And his wines are impressive; La Massa, which includes Cabernet Sauvignon and Merlot as well as Sangiovese, is redolent of ripe cherries, with an appealing freshness, while Giorgio Primo, in memory of his grandfather, with 10 per cent of Merlot as well as Sangiovese, is a more powerful wine, structured, but with elegant fruit and length. 2001 was the last vintage that La Massa was labelled Chianti Classico; with the 2002 vintage it became an IGT, in order to create a greater difference between the two wines. Chianti Classico suffers from an image problem. 'If we believe in Chianti Classico, that should be our most expensive wine' – and now Giorgio Primo is.

The Castello dei Rampolla at Santa Lucia in Fauglia was once a convent and came to the de Napoli family in the early eighteenth century as part of a dowry. The house, which dates back to the fifteenth century, is surrounded by olive trees, cypresses and pines, all in a cluster, with a tiny chapel. Maurizia de Napoli took us for a walk through her vineyards, explaining how her grandfather used to come here, but just for holidays. It was her father, Alceo, who began to look after the farm in a serious way back in 1965. He was one of the first to plant Cabernet Sauvignon in Chianti in the late 1970s and the vineyard named after him, on their best site, a steep south-facing slope, is now planted mainly with Cabernet Sauvignon and also some Petit Verdot. Maurizia explained how they began practising biodynamic viticulture some six years ago. They grow broad beans between alternate rows, to provide nitrogen for the soil. The birds and insects are returning to the vineyards and there is a marked improvement in the condition of the soil. The vines are pruned very low, with as many as 8000 plants per hectare.

Altogether they make four wines at Rampolla: Chianti Classico; Sanmarco, from Cabernet Sauvignon, with a touch of Sangiovese; Vigna d'Alceo, and a late harvest wine, from various white grapes, Chardonnay, Traminer and Sauvignon, which are not usually picked until the middle of December. We tasted Sanmarco, which was one of the pioneering wines that helped recreate the reputation of Tuscany. It was sturdy and structured, after two years' barrel ageing, with rounded cassis fruit.

Villa Cafaggio lies further round the amphitheatre of the Conca d'Oro, with views across to Rampolla and La Massa. A medieval Florentine watchtower still stands. Stefano Farkas explained how his father had bought the estate in 1966. Originally they sold their wine *sfuso*, in bulk, but then prices dropped dramatically at the beginning of the 1970s, falling from 40,000 lire per hectolitre in 1970 to 16,600 lire in 1973. The only way to survive was to bottle, so a cellar was built in 1974, which was also Stefano's first vintage at Villa Cafaggio, after studying classics and philosophy. The origin of the name Cafaggio is Lombard and means a closed, cultivated field; apart from vineyards, they also have woods for wild boar and deer. There were workers in the vineyard, replacing some dead vines, prompting Stefano to observe that when he first came to work at Cafaggio, the wine business was so unremunerative that they could only afford four workers. Nowadays the problem is to find the manpower and they use immigrant labour, mainly Muslims from Kosovo, to tend their 32 hectares of vines.

Today Casa Girelli from Trentino has an equal share in the estate, while Stefano Chioccioli has been the consultant oenologist since 1998. The two Stefanos aim to make wines that are more supple than the traditional Chianti. Stefano Farkas observed that people want structure and fruit in their wine, but they are not prepared to wait for it to develop in bottle. The solution is a little gentle micro-oxygenation, with its softening effect. He still has some large *botti* for his Chianti *normale* and they are useful too for blending. A rich fruity smell, redolent of ripe cherries, emanated from an empty *botte*, from which the wine had been bottled that morning. This is an estate that has moved with the times, with its wines remaining amongst the best from the Conca d'Oro, with a *normale*, a *riserva*, Cortaccio from a vineyard of Cabernet Sauvignon, and San Martino, another *cru*, of structured Sangiovese.

Up the road from Cafaggio is Vecchie Terre di Montefili. This has been one of my favourite estates in Chianti Classico ever since I first visited the property back in 1984. The Acuti family, Roccaldo and Franca, with their daughter Maria, and her husband Tommaso, who has been the winemaker since 1994, always give you a friendly welcome and this time was no exception. First we admired various new refinements in the cellar, some equipment for automatic *rimontaggi*, the bottling line and an insulated warehouse, built from stones from their own vineyards. Roccaldo explained how you may use your own stone for building but you are not allowed to sell it, as technically it belongs to the *comune*. There were *botti* for the Chianti *normale*, with *barriques* for the other wines, which we tasted over a convivial lunch. Vigna Regis, the white wine from 80 per cent Chardonnay, 15 per cent Sauvignon and 5 per cent Traminer, fermented and aged in oak, was lightly spicy and accompanied the classic Tuscan dish of *crostini al fegato*. Franca is generous with her recipes. You take some finely chopped onion, fry it till it is golden, add a little water, then the chicken livers and when they are cooked, add anchovies, capers and butter, and a splash of Vin Santo, mince it all up and spread it on slices of toasted bread. Next came the Chianti *normale*, from Sangiovese and a drop of Colorino, with some lovely ripe cherries, which paved the way for Bruno di Rocca, a blend of 60 per cent Cabernet and 40 per cent Sangiovese, which spend thirteen months in oak. The name is a play on words. Roccaldo wanted to make a great wine, like a Brunello, and Rocca is a short form of his name, and the wine was a combination of cedary elegance and firm tannins. It was still very youthful, but none the less delicious with a *stracotta*. Franca was ready with another recipe. This is easy, she said: you seal the meat, add carrots, onions and celery, oh, and a bottle of Bruno di Rocco, and cook it all very slowly. The beef literally melted in the mouth, but I couldn't help thinking that the addition of a bottle of your husband's best wine enhanced the flavours more than the average cooking wine. Anfiteatro, so called because its vineyard in the valley opposite is indeed in an amphitheatre, is a pure Sangiovese wine, which also spends thirteen months in wood. It was more structured than Bruno di Rocca, but with that classic benchmark of ripe sour cherries. '*È toscanissimo!*' exclaimed Roccaldo. No Tuscan lunch is complete without a glass of Vin Santo, and that is how we finished, with further entertainment provided by Roccaldo's three-month-old Labrador puppy, called Brandy as he is the colour of Cognac.

The Acutis bought Vecchie Terre in 1979 and produced their first wine the following year, with the help of Vittorio Fiore. They were one of his first clients, and he remains their oenologist today. When he encouraged them to carry out a green harvest for the first vintage, Roccaldo remembers hearing one of the workers saying: 'My new boss is picking the grapes while they are still green and throwing them away.' So revolutionary was the technique back in the early 1980s that the *contadini* did not understand the process. Today they have 12 hectares in production.

Across the valley from Panzano is the estate of Vignamaggio, where Leonardo da Vinci painted the *Mona Lisa*. The Renaissance villa was the birthplace of Mona Lisa Gherardini, who married Francesco di Zanobi del Giacondo, hence the other name of the famous portrait: *La Giaconda*. A distinctive row of cypress trees, some of the most atmospheric in Chianti, lines the drive up to the villa with its soft pink facade. The villa stands in a formal Italian garden, with statues and box hedges, and the terrace offers spectacular views over Panzano and Montagliari. As a more recent claim to fame, it provided the setting for Kenneth Branagh's production of *Much Ado About Nothing*, and was also used for the television production of John Mortimer's *Summer Lease*.

Vignamaggio used to belong to the Sanminiatelli family. Bino Sanminiatelli was a man of letters, known for a biography of Michelangelo, for his diaries and for *La Vita in Campagna*, a book about life in the Tuscan countryside. Then in 1987 the estate was sold by his widow to Gianni Nunziante, a Roman lawyer, who has invested a considerable amount of money and energy in the property. The old brick cellars have been cleaned with sand to reveal attractive arches, and now house Slavonic-oak *botti* and French oak *barriques*. There are various old artefacts, now museum pieces, an old corking machine, a destemmer and a basket press, as well as their very oldest bottle, dated 1911. The Pope Clement XI also had associations with Vignamaggio, so a new barrel cellar is named La Cantina del Papa.

Today Vignamaggio comprises 52 hectares, planted mainly with Sangiovese, but also including Merlot, Syrah and Cabernet, both Franc and Sauvignon, as well as 11 hectares of olive trees. The wines, made with the guidance of Franco Bernabei, combine tradition and innovation. Chianti Classico *normale*, aged in large *botti*, is a pure Sangiovese. The *agronomo*, Francesco Naldi, explained how they aim for very ripe grapes, picking later and taking more risks with the weather in an attempt to soften the Sangiovese. The wine was firm and structured, with sturdy ripe cherries. The *riserva*, Castello di Monna Lisa, spends eighteen to twenty months in *barriques*, of which a third are new, and comprises Sangiovese with 10 per cent Merlot and Cabernet Sauvignon. It was sturdy but elegant. Unusual in Chianti is a pure Cabernet Franc, made for the first time in 1990, which was nicely rounded and softer than the *riserva*. Next came Obsession, which originates from Nunziante's business friendship with Calvin Klein; it is a blend of Merlot with some Cabernet Sauvignon and Syrah, making a sturdy mouthful of fruit with a touch of pepper. And we finished with some honeyed Vin Santo. Whereas other Chianti estates are expanding into the Maremma, Nunziante has looked further afield and his first vintage of an IGT Salento, from Puglia, will appear in 2005, and for 2004 he is planning a celebration of 600 years of winemaking at Vignamaggio, recalling the reference to Vignamaggio by the Prato merchant Francesco Datini.

ITALIAN WINE LAW

IN A NUTSHELL, Italian wine law is organized like a pyramid. The broad base at the bottom consists of a great mass of *vino da tavola*, anonymous table wine without any distinguishing regional characteristics. Moving up the pyramid, next comes the more recent category of IGT or *Indicazione Geografica Tipica*, which equates to the French *vins de pays* and encompasses many of the new Super-Tuscans and experimental wines, with international grape varieties. Some of these wines may be quite simple; others may be the producer's very best wine with a price to match.

Denominazione di Origine Controllata, or DOC, which seem to proliferate throughout Italy as every unknown wine region attempts to claim some status and individuality, means literally a wine of controlled origin. It is governed by regulations or *disciplinari*, which control its origin in terms of area of production, grape varieties, ageing requirements and so on.

The pinnacle of the pyramid is provided by the *Denominazione di Origine Controllata e Garantita*, or DOCG wines, of which there are five in Tuscany, with even stricter controls as to their origin. The implication is that they are better than the DOCs, but this is not so. DOCG entails a guarantee of origin, but not of guarantee of quality; that comes only from the individual producer.

Lamole
· *April* ·

To the east of Panzano; the village and the estate

I REMEMBERED LAMOLE, OR TO GIVE its correct name, Pile e Lamole, as one of the old traditional estates of Chianti Classico. It takes its name from the village in the hills to the east of Panzano. We took a winding dirt track and wended our way past a ribbon of houses to the little square in front of the church where we had arranged to meet Ugo Pagliai, the manager and winemaker. Things had changed since my earlier visit. In 1994 Lamole, or Lamole di Lamole as it is sometimes called for emphasis, was bought by the Veneto company of Santa Margherita, along with another Chianti estate, Vistarenni, with its elegant villa overlooking the valley on the way to Radda. There is a brand-new winery, a modern block, painted a brilliant yellow that does not blend into the landscape. Rather more discreet was the old barrel cellar, in what were once the storerooms of the castle of Lamole, for the village had been a Florentine lookout post in the fourteenth century. In sharp contrast to the functional warehouse, this was much more atmospheric, with the narrow bricks illustrating the building's age, and filled with the traditional large *botti* with bright red rims. These casks are so large that they have to be assembled *in situ*; nor are they cheap, costing €155 (300,000 lire) per hectolitre. They have *barriques* as well, but Pagliai explained that they were very anxious to retain the *tipicità* of the wine, fearing that an excess of new wood would change its character. Sangiovese should be elegant, but certainly not powerful. They do not want what he called *un vinone*, an enormous wine that needs chewing, so oaky is it.

At Lamole they make six wines from their 35 hectares around the village, a *normale* and a *riserva*; then there is Campolungo from one specific vineyard just outside the village, and L'Oro di Lamole, which contains 20 per cent of Cabernet Sauvignon as well as Sangiovese. However, Pagliai admitted his reservations over the inclusion of more international grape varieties, as he fears that the tipicity of Chianti will disappear. I liked the *normale* best of all, with lovely ripe, easy fruit and the essential backbone of astringency.

Last of all we saw the *vinsantaia*, tucked away in a hidden corner of the village. The smell of maturing wine was memorable, an aroma of nutty honey and old wood, since the wine is aged in tiny 50-litre *caratelli*, for a minimum of three years, or preferably four or five. The barrels are sealed with wax, which looks more aesthetic than the prosaic blobs of grey cement used in some cellars. Pagliai had his theory as to the origin of the name Vin Santo – that the Greek patriarch asked for Vino Xantho, which means 'blond' in Greek, and is a word that can be used to describe the colour of wine. Another suggestion is that you make the sign of the cross over the barrel and then forget about it for a few years! Vin Santo is an essential part of the Tuscan winemaking tradition, and as Pagliai observed, you don't count the cost of making it, you simply make it for your friends.

There is no doubt that it is complicated to make, and expensive. The quantity of wine produced from the grapes is minuscule, as a result of the process of *appassimento*, and the lengthy ageing period, during which the wine inevitably evaporates to offer the angels their share. You pick ripe grapes, Malvasia and Trebbiano, which are left to dry for several weeks, usually until after Christmas, on straw mats or hanging up, in a well-ventilated room, usually an old barn or draughty attic with open windows. The grapes become dehydrated like tiny raisins. Then you press them and put the juice into the traditional *caratelli*, where it slowly ferments and gently matures into something delicious and essentially Tuscan. Opinions vary as to the use of a *madre*, the lees of the previous wine in the barrel. Some keep it, while others believe it is better that the wine be an orphan than have a bad mother. The amount of air left in the barrel also affects the flavour; generally the more air the drier the taste, but there is a delightful lack of predictability about Vin Santo. Somehow it is a wine that defies oenological conventions. The flavour should always recall the *cantuccini* or *biscotti di Prato*, which are the classic Tuscan biscuit, studded with almonds, and so often dunked in Vin Santo at the end of a meal.

The hills behind Lamole offer wonderful vistas of the Chianti countryside, so off we set, out of the village past the stone walls of tiny gardens, and climbing steadily past some overgrown vineyards, through oak and chestnut woods, until, climbing higher still, we reached the dark pine woods. The shade was so dense that it shut out the spring sunshine, and finally we emerged from the trees onto a ridge offering views that well repaid the energetic climb. To the west we could see a series of folds of the Chianti hills, in a gentle haze, making out the town of Greve in the distance and the distinctive avenue of cypresses of Vignamaggio, and to the east were the higher mountains of the Apennines, the mountain chain that runs the length of central Italy.

The track continued to the Villa San Michele, where we stopped to picnic, looking across at a hillside covered in white hawthorn, which created an effect of gentle fluffy white clouds. The tiny chapel was open and there, quite unexpectedly, as it seems to feature in no guidebooks, was a faded fresco of a Madonna and Child with assorted saints, charming in its simplicity. The chapel, too, was sparse, with three rounded arches on either side of the small nave, built in distinctive black and white stone.

From there the path turned back towards Lamole down a footpath that meandered through the hawthorn bushes, with primroses, violets and hellebores. Butterflies flitted in the spring sunshine, brilliant blues, bright yellow and speckled brown. The birdsong was almost deafening; a tiny field mouse scuttled across our path. There were views across the valley towards Lamole, and we passed a couple of houses undergoing extensive restoration, then stopped to chat to an old man who was busy attaching the growing shoots of his vines to wires before the vegetation completely ran away. Our conversation seemed to revolve around food; he wanted to know what time we had set off and where we had had lunch. Our picnic did not seem to satisfy him; we told him that we preferred dinner instead. But then you don't sleep, he countered, but wine helps. And we wished him a happy Easter and went on our way, past an estate calling itself the Castello di Lamole, and back into the village itself.

It was time for a reviving *té al limone*, so we stopped at the cheerful village restaurant, the Ristoro di Lamole, to enjoy the views from the terrace towards the village of Panzano. At the table behind us two men were talking in English, but it was not their mother tongue. I realized that I was being addressed: 'Excuse me. Are you on holiday?'

'No,' I reply firmly, 'I'm working' – which somewhat beggared belief given that I was very casually dressed in T-shirt and jeans, with walking boots and a rucksack. So I admitted to researching a book, and then as English was our common language, we slipped into pleasantries about the weather.

From Badia a Passignano
· *November* ·

West of Greve-in-Chianti; L. & P. Antinori, Poggio al Sole and Rignana

THE IMPOSING TOWER OF the abbey of Badia a Passignano dominates its surroundings. There is something hauntingly magical about seeing it emerging from the trees as you approach from any direction. The abbey has had a chequered history; a notice outside gives you the bald facts: that San Michele a Passignano was founded in 890 and in 1049 the monks accepted the strict Vallombrosan reforms of San Giovanni Gualberto, who is buried in the church. The facade is thirteenth century, while the cloisters date from 1472 when it was a flourishing community. Then the monastery was suppressed in 1866 and the monks did not return until 1987. A fake medieval tower was added in the middle of the nineteenth century, which happily is overshadowed by the original Romanesque tower and remains fairly unobtrusive. Today the abbey is part of the diocese of Fiesole and is run by a small community of Benedictine monks, who returned there when Antinori bought the property from the Lori family.

We had an appointment with Allegra, the youngest of Piero Antinori's three daughters. She has her father's social ease and fine command of English, with a cheerful sense of humour. She explained how the whole estate of Badia a Passignano totals some 500 hectares including woods and a lake, as well as 40 hectares of Sangiovese. The cellars date back to the seventeenth century, replacing the original medieval cellars, and a new extension was added in 2001. People would have taken shelter here during the turbulent times of the Middle Ages and there are still metal steps leading out of the cellar into the old kitchen above. The cellars here are filled with barrels and vats and are ideal for ageing wine, whereas the winemaking takes place in the more modern facilities at the nearby estate of Santa Cristina.

Allegra explained how her family have three estates in Chianti Classico, all close by, namely Badia a Passignano; Santa Cristina with 140 hectares, including the vineyards for Antinori's best-known and trendsetting wines, Solaia and Tignanello; and Pèppoli, which was previously known as Villa Terciona, with 65 hectares. We tasted in the restaurant at Badia a Passignano, with its elegantly vaulted brick ceiling, dating from the seventeenth century.

Arrangements of pressed herbs provided attractive and appropriate pictures for the walls, and the adjoining shop is the only *vendita diretta* on any of the Antinori estates. Antinori's wines are some of the best known of Tuscany. We began with Santa Cristina, a Toscano Rosso, which is mainly Sangiovese, with 10 per cent of Merlot. They make about a million bottles a year of Santa Cristina, with about 40 per cent of the grapes coming from their own vineyards. It is lighter and more accessible than some Chianti, with the hallmark of sour cherries. Pèppoli, a Chianti Classico, also with a touch of Merlot, is aged in large *botti*, and was fuller-bodied on the palate, while Villa Antinori *riserva* was altogether more structured, with some firm cherry fruit. The blend here is mainly Sangiovese, with a little Canaiolo and just a drop of Cabernet Sauvignon, and from the 2001 vintage it ceased to be a Chianti Classico, but became an IGT, to allow greater flexibility in the choice of grapes. Next came Tenuta di Antinori *riserva*, still firmly a Chianti Classico, from grapes solely grown in their own vineyards, namely Sangiovese with just 5 per cent Cabernet Sauvignon. It was rounded with a firm backbone of tannin, and hints of oak on the nose. Badia a Passignano, a Chianti Classico of pure Sangiovese, is aged in *barriques* and seemed more youthful, with oak and tannin as well as fruit.

Then there was Tignanello, the wine that helped set Antinori's reputation as pacesetters in Tuscany. The first vintage of Tignanello, the 1971, was pure Sangiovese; Cabernet Sauvignon was added in 1975, and Antinori were also the first, after Sassicaia, to use French *barriques*, since when the wine has become established as benchmark of the style, a blend of 80 per cent Sangiovese, with 20 per cent Cabernet Sauvignon, with some attractive cedariness on both nose and palate. It was long and elegant with a firm backbone of tannin, and promised well for future ageing; earlier vintages have established a creditable track record of longevity. The reverse of Tignanello is Solaia, a Cabernet Sauvignon with 20 per cent Sangiovese, and consequently much more international in style. I preferred the essential Tuscan flavours of Tignanello.

The Antinori family's involvement in wine goes back over six hundred years, for the city archives of Florence record that in 1385 Giovanni di Piero Antinori was registered as a novice winemaker in the guild of *vinattieri*, and so in 1985 they released Seicento, which could be described as a super-Solaia, to commemorate the 600th anniversary. Back in the fourteenth century wine was not the sole activity of the family; they were bankers and silk merchants too. As affluent citizens of Florence they built their Renaissance palace in the fifteenth century, the Palazzo Antinori, which remains today the administrative headquarters of the company, and where their wines can be enjoyed in the Cantinetta Antinori. In the seventeenth century Francesco Redi, who is known for his poem *Bacchus in Tuscany*, which is essentially a litany of all the fine wines of the region, sang their praises in glowing terms. The merchant house of L. & P. Antinori was founded by two brothers, Ludovico and Piero, at the end of the nineteenth century. Four generations later, another Piero Antinori is the driving force behind the reputation of the company, while his elder brother, another Ludovico, created his own estate of Ornellaia in Bolgheri.

In many ways the name Antinori is synonymous with Tuscany, representing the best of both its traditions and its innovations. Their previous oenologist, the talented Giacomo Tachis, masterminded the creation of wines such as Tignanello and Solaia, and pioneered the use of French *barriques* in Tuscany. He now works as an independent consultant, mainly in Sardinia and Sicily, and has been replaced by the equally able Renzo Coltarello. Today Antinori are noted for their investment in the newer areas of Tuscany, not just in Bolgheri (see page 255) but also in Sovana (page 309), and near Castiglione della Pescaia, within the DOC of Monteregio di Massa Marittima, as well as on the edge of Montepulciano in vineyards which include the new DOC of Cortona (page 177), and more traditionally in Montalcino, with a total of some 1100 hectares of vineyards, representing an enormous commitment to the Tuscan wine industry. In addition they produce wine in Piedmont, Franciacorta, Umbria and Puglia, but those are firmly outside the scope of this book, as are their activities in Hungary, Washington State and California.

Allegra was keen to show us the villa at Santa Cristina, which dates back to the seventeenth century and had been bought for the family by her great-grandfather. A tiny chapel was being restored and in the villa they were installing a series of magnificent paintings depicting country life in the early nineteenth century: large tableaux of hunting and vineyard scenes, in brilliant colours, which needed a vast expanse of wall to accommodate them. There are houses on the estate for *agriturismo*, including one called Tignanello, all beautifully restored in impeccable Italian style. The olive mill was in full production, with rich green liquid spilling out into a small stainless-steel vat, exuding the intoxicating smell of fresh oil.

From Santa Cristina, we walked back to Badia a Passignano, down through the vineyards with their golden leaves, with the Tignanello house perched on the hill behind us. We turned into thick woods and found a forester's track which cut through the trees. Glimpses of the tower of the abbey reassured that our sense of direction was functioning and suddenly we emerged from the woods into the vineyards of the abbey, and walked down an alleyway of olive trees.

The next day we returned to the abbey and continued our walk, down the hill, past more vineyards and olive trees. There were magnificent views back to the abbey tower, surrounded by cypress trees. The road climbed steeply through the woods and we came to the entrance of Poggio al Sole, with an alley of olive trees. A young lad was up a ladder, harvesting the olives, combing the branches with a large red comb. The ground underneath was covered in orange netting to catch the olives, both green and black, as well as an abundant crop of leaves. We observed that this might be like combing your hair: well, not mine, he said, for he was sporting the shortest of haircuts.

Giovanni Dovaz is a lanky German Swiss, with a dry sense of humour and an imperfect command of Italian. His family have vineyards near Liechtenstein but they went to his older brother, so he bought Poggio al Sole in 1991. Why Tuscany, we asked. He admitted that he had looked in France and in Piedmont, and then by chance came to Tuscany and found this estate. It comprises 42 hectares altogether, and he has extended the vineyards from 5 to 14 hectares, adding Merlot, Cabernet Sauvignon and Syrah, 'to see what will work', at the same time increasing the vine density to 7000 plants per hectare. The views over the vineyards stretch towards Fontodi, Rampolla, La Massa and Cafaggio, the other great names of the Conca d'Oro of Panzano, and towards the village of San Donato in the other direction.

The cellars are simple and functional. Giovanni explained how he found working with oak quite difficult initially, for in Switzerland you bottle your wine the spring after the harvest. He had felt rather lost with Sangiovese, which is tannic and needs ageing, and initially sought the guidance of Franco Bernabei. Nowadays a Swiss oenologist friend supplies what he called the outside nose. I liked his wines. The Chianti Classico *normale*, from Sangiovese with some Merlot, is aged partly in *botti* of Slovenian oak and partly in old *barriques* for fourteen months and had the benchmark sour cherry fruit of Sangiovese with a firm backbone. This is a Chianti to age rather than drink immediately. His 2000 Syrah, labelled according to the grape variety, tasted of the grape variety, with peppery fruit. His first vintage was 1996 and the wine is given twelve months ageing in new barrels and promised well. How would it age? And what a relief to have a label that was immediately understandable, rather than the usual confusing fantasy name. '*Mi manca la fantasia*'; I lack imagination, Giovanni immediately responded.

Seraselva, a Merlot Cabernet Sauvignon blend, first made in 1995 and given about sixteen months ageing in barrel before blending and bottling, had ripe cassis flavours. Most stylish of all was 1999 Cascarilla, the *riserva*, from Sangiovese with just a drop of Cabernet Sauvignon, and aged in *barriques* for eighteen months. The classic sour cherries of Sangiovese were there, with a firm backbone of tannin; it was a wine that would need time to show its full potential in the glass.

From Poggio al Sole, we reached a junction of tracks, marked by a shrine, with fresh flowers, and carried on down the hill, past a restaurant, the Cantinetta Rignana, to Rignana itself. This was a complete surprise – the deeply old-fashioned estate that I remembered from a visit nearly twenty years earlier had been completely transformed. It was a fascinating example of what a generation change can achieve. We had an appointment with Cosimo Gericke and his wife Sveva Rocca. First we sat and chatted in the kitchen at a large table. A welcoming fire blazed in the hearth and polished copper pans hung from the chimney breast. Cosimo explained how his father had bought Rignana back in

1967, and in 1999 Cosimo took over and set about restoring everything, the cellars, the villa and the vineyards. The house dates from the eleventh century; the tower was a lookout post, with the river Pesa at the bottom of the hill forming the boundary between the territories of Florence and Siena. The adjoining villa dates from the eighteenth century. At the beginning of the twentieth century as many as three hundred people lived and worked here; now there are just fifteen. They had their own chapel, and cemetery, but then people began moving to the city. Arminio Gericke had bought from the Contessa Biondi, the last of a typical Florentine family who were very much absentee landowners and merely came here during the summer months to escape the stifling heat of the city. Cosimo has studied political science, rather than oenology, but went on to spend time in South Africa, with such notable wine estates as Boschendal, Madeba and Clos Cabrière. He referred to a conflict of generations and observed how things had changed, remembering the old cellar hands scrubbing the barrels every day. There were large casks of chestnut and mulberry, as well as oak, all built *in situ* in the cellar. The wood from these has now been used for new flooring in the villa, and he has brand-new *barriques* in the cellar.

Cosimo and Sveva were keen to show us around. There were far-reaching views from the vineyards in the autumn sunshine, with Barberina Val d'Elsa across the valley, the silhouetted skyline of Castellina in the other direction, and the vineyards of Poggio al Sole nearby. They have 15 hectares of vineyards, some of which are being replanted. It is difficult to prepare the soil; you have to remove the stones, some of which are enormous, and then prepare drainage channels with pipes and stones. There was evidence of wild boar in the vineyard; they are apparently particularly partial to ripe Merlot grapes, though of course by early November these had long been picked.

The villa at Rignana has been converted into several *agriturismi*, allowing Sveva the opportunity to exercise her talent for interior decoration. There are frescoes in many of the rooms; those in the large drawing room are especially fine, portraying bucolic scenes in the manner of Claude Lorraine, on both walls and ceiling. Even the kitchen, with a splendid old tiled stove, had some frescoes, as did many of the bedrooms and also a bathroom. Numerous little touches demonstrated Sveva's artistic flair. The adjoining chapel contains a heavy baroque altarpiece, prompting Cosimo to explain that Rignana had once been the property of the bishop of Prato and Pistoia, Scipone di Ricci. He upset the ecclesiastical authorities by becoming a Jansenist and was exiled here, and when he died in 1810 he was buried in the chapel. His emblem, the *ricci*, or hedgehog, now features on the label of Rignana, and the feast day of Santa Catarina di Ricci is celebrated on 15 August.

1999 was Cosimo's first vintage at Rignana; we tasted the 2000, which had some lovely ripe cherry fruit and hints of oak. It includes 10 per cent of Canaiolo, as well as Sangiovese, and spends several months in *barriques*, but the oak, although present, was not intrusive. It was quite delicious. In fact we enjoyed what might be termed a Tuscan elevenses: a glass of red wine with a slice of *bruschetta*, doused with fresh olive oil, also from the estate.

Thus fortified we set off down the track, past some of the vineyards signed Vigneto il Cimitero and Vigneto Casanova, which now belong to Tenute A. & A. Folinari, and were once part of Tenimenti Ruffino. (For more about Ruffino see pages 198-9 and La Lodola Nuova in Montepulciano.) We could hear the loud cries of hunters in the woods, with the occasional dog barking, intent on encouraging the wild boar to break cover. The track continued past some farm buildings and through more vineyards and olive groves to reach the banks of the Pesa. A couple of hunters clad in luminous orange jackets with guns and walkie-talkies were waiting. We suspected they were rather bored, for they were happy to chat. There were about twenty of them altogether. Isn't the wild boar usually a nocturnal animal, I asked. Yes, but we use dogs to flush them out. They were hoping that the boar might come this way. And is it all right for us to carry on along the river? Yes, but it's probably best to keep talking. So we did; and I felt grateful that my fleece was bright red, and hopefully highly visible. We followed the riverbank, with the shouts of the hunters in the woods above us. Further along we came to a padlocked gate, with a notice about the area being reserved for hunting on Wednesdays, Saturdays and Sundays. It was Saturday.

The wide track followed the river, past a beautifully restored mill, the Molino d'Abate, and then we came to a tiny chapel with simple whitewashed walls. It was firmly locked. We crossed a bridge over the Pesa and then turned up a stone track through the woods. It took us past a house called Gazzolina, with its swimming pool on the other side of the track; in the height of summer this would have been very tempting. The track then turned into a maze of bicycle paths – we had passed a group of cyclists resting at the bottom of the hill so we were confident that we were unlikely to be run over by speeding wheels. Finally we emerged from the woods to see vineyards and olive groves again, and to join the road that leads back to Badia a Passignano. Several people were up ladders in the olive groves, combing the trees, with olives galore at their feet. As always, the tower of the abbey made for wonderful views, what the Italians would call *molto suggestivo*, which is one of those expressions that is well nigh impossible to translate into English. Somehow 'atmospheric' simply does not do it justice.

From Isole e Olena
· April ·

North-west of Castellina-in-Chianti; to the Castello di Paneretta and Monsanto

PAOLO DE MARCHI HAS BEEN making Chianti at Isole e Olena since 1976. In London 1976 might be remembered as the year of the long hot summer, but in Tuscany it was quite the opposite. At Isole a severe hailstorm destroyed 60 per cent of the potential crop, and all over the region it was one of the wettest summers ever. What a welcome to Chianti. And from that inauspicious beginning Paolo has become one of the keenest pacesetters and most talented winemakers in the whole of Tuscany. While many of the other leading winemakers are consultant oenologists who do not work in their vineyards, and many of the estate owners have a career in another field which has allowed them to invest in an estate in Tuscany, Paolo de Marchi is the rare example of a man who makes wine on his family property.

He studied agricultural science at Turin University and then spent time in California, which was an intensely formative experience. Paolo recalls the open-mindedness of the Californian winemakers and the great feeling of discovery and adventure that pervaded the Napa Valley in the early 1970s. It made him realize the need to preserve the balance between innovation and tradition, and once settled at Isole e Olena he quickly came to appreciate that Sangiovese was the key to quality in Chianti. Right from the start he separated the white grapes from the red, which was rare in Tuscany at that time. And the first challenge was to reduce yields, especially of Sangiovese. It is the yield per vine that counts, not the overall yield per hectare. A vineyard with a low density of vines may produce only 40 hectolitres per hectare, but each vine will be contributing as much as 3 kilos. It is much better to have higher-density vineyards, with as many as 7000 vines per hectare, but with each vine producing only about 1 kilo of grapes.

Over the years a considerable amount of the 45-hectare estate has been replanted with Paolo's own selection of Sangiovese. He reckons he has as many as thirty clones in his vineyards, each with different characteristics, which he has been able to identify through a multitude of microvinifications. Paolo is also very aware of the variations in the soil of Chianti and especially in his own vineyards. Since 1987 he has mapped the soil of his estate, recording the temperature and humidity of different plots at one and two feet below the surface. The physical condition of the soil is paramount, for the amount of air in the soil affects the drainage, and the water content is determined by the percentage of clay. This detailed knowledge means you are better equipped to take well-informed decisions.

Although Paolo has vast technical expertise, he is anxious to avoid excessive intervention. 'Knowledge allows you to know what not to do.' He is not a friend of what he calls 'the new oenology', which is too interfering and manipulative and wants to be too much in control. Wine should not be like the food industry. It is special because it is so strongly linked to its area of production. If, for instance, you add extra tannin to your wine, you mask its origin. Tradition is important, but tradition does not mean that things are fixed. Tradition allows for evolution, based on experience, and the changes must make sense. You must respect what you have, but also be open to new developments, and this is what Paolo has done in his expression of Sangiovese, with his Chianti and his *cru*, Cepparello.

Important though the vineyards are, my last visit to Isole e Olena was an opportunity for Paolo to show off his new cellar – at the time of my previous visit, it had been nothing more than a large hole in the ground. This time he said, 'It's almost finished,' while his wife Marta muttered, 'We've been saying that for a year.' And it was truly impressive. There is some high-tech equipment, such as a new pump, which is the latest in technology and supremely gentle. At € 12,500 (24 million lire) it had cost *la lira di Dio*, or an arm and a leg, and Marta observed that she had not even been allowed to replace the noisy fridge in their kitchen. Paolo has also invested in some wooden fermentation vats, which will be used for some of the Cepparello. Apparently they allow for a better extraction of colour. Most dramatic of all was the new barrel cellar. The walls are the colour of dark grey charcoal, contrasting dramatically with the light wood of the barrels. At the far end the original limestone rock has been left in place. From a distance it looks like a sculpture, balanced by two smaller rocks at the entrance. The effect is perfected by atmospheric lighting and that impeccable sense of Italian style, which achieved the perfect contrast of drama and elegance, but without excess.

Paolo's wines are always a delight to taste, and to drink. His Chianti Classico *normale* provides the absolute benchmark example, with wonderful ripe sour cherries, and a firm backbone of tannin, which will go so well with a pasta dish and a sauce based on Tuscan olive oil. Cepparello, a pure Sangiovese from one particular vineyard, which could be labelled *riserva*, is a much more serious wine. It will age beautifully, as a vertical tasting in London once demonstrated, but the 1999, drunk when it was two years old, was remarkably accessible with soft tannins, rich cedary fruit and a wonderful concentration of flavour. Paolo would not be Paolo if he had not responded to the challenge of the international grape varieties. His Collezione dei Marchi label includes a nutty Chardonnay, a Cabernet Sauvignon with some ripe blackcurrant fruit and a firm peppery Syrah. Nonetheless Cepparello remains the epitome of Isole e Olena.

These were once two hamlets. The cellars and house are at Isole, while Olena is now a tumble-down village. When Paolo's father bought the property in the mid-1950s, when the *mezzadria* system was still in place, seven families, totalling 120 people, lived there. Today one worker remains in the village, who once observed to Paolo: 'When your father bought this, there was no tractor, only a donkey.' Paolo's wife Marta took us for a walk through the vineyards to Olena. We passed a small shrine with the gravestones of former owners of Isole and then a new vineyard of young vines. Land was being prepared for planting, with enormous earth-moving machines extracting large rocks from the soil. Next we came to an experimental vineyard run by the University of Florence, and a vineyard of Cabernet and then one of Syrah, along the track to Olena. It is a pretty little village, with a cluster of houses, in soft stone with russet roofs, in varying states of repair or disrepair around the church. Nowadays they are mainly owned by Florentines who visit at weekends, with just two families living there. There are views across the valley to Cortini, an

ecclesiastical property, and further on towards Barberina Val d'Elsa and Tavarnelle in the distance.

From Olena we took a footpath through the woods, heading towards the nearby estate of Monsanto. The path became more and more overgrown and we teased Marta that she is better at winemaking than map reading. She told us that the profusion of white flowers was *scopa*, broom, and that the country people did indeed use it for sweeping. The distinctive *corbezzolo*, strawberry tree, with its dark green leaves and bright red stems, will in autumn produce white flowers and red berries at the same time on the same plant, thus making the colours of the Italian flag. A ground shrub with sharp pointed leaves is *pungitipo*, which will have red berries for Christmas. We also saw some wild asparagus, but it was not yet ready for picking. Marta warned us about adders, which are not uncommon in Tuscany – apparently they have their babies in trees so that the babies immediately fall to the ground, for they are so poisonous that if they bit their mother the venom would kill her. A natural reflex made us look upwards nervously. Soon we came to a stream with a carpeted bank of primroses, violets and periwinkles, and, realizing that we were lost, we scrambled up the hill through the trees, passing a hunter's ladder to a lookout for wild boar, and then found ourselves back in civilization in an olive grove. The road to Monsanto was close by, for the moment still a *strada bianca*, but tarmac was planned for next year and Marta was worried about the increase in traffic that would bring. Hardly a car passed us and we soon reached the magnificent castle of Paneretta; it was built by the Medici and is now owned by a Genoese, Fabio Albizetti, who is gradually restoring it to its former splendour. We peered through the imposing wrought-iron gates into a grassed courtyard with elegant statues.

A few months later, thanks to a mutual friend, we were invited to lunch. This time the gates opened for us to reveal a beautifully manicured, lush green lawn bordered with flowerbeds of white iceberg roses, still in flower on a grey November morning. Fabio is friendly and enthusiastic, and passionate about Paneretta. He had first visited the estate some ten years before he eventually bought it in 1984; it was a case of love at first sight, but he had to wait for the right moment. He took us into the courtyard, where the gallery has some exquisite sixteenth-century frescoed ceilings of bucolic scenes, painted by Poccetti. The original tower of the castle dates back to the 800s, but was enlarged during the wars between the Florentines and Sienese, so that what you see today dates from the sixteenth century.

Records state that wine was made here in the fifteenth century and the cellars under the castle, which house *barriques* and *botti*, are probably older than the castle itself. They are splendidly atmospheric, with evidence of an escape route from the tower. However, Fabio is planning a new underground cellar under the manicured lawn. The first hurdle is to obtain the necessary permission from three different organizations: the *comune*, the *provincia* and the association of historic buildings. He makes three wines, with the help of his oenologist, Attilio Pagli: a Chianti Classico *normale*, a *riserva* Torre a Destra and an IGT Terrine, which is a blend of Canaiolo and Sangiovese. Fabio is passionate about Sangiovese too: 'Why should I *banalizzare* my wine with Cabernet or Merlot? Sangiovese may not be the world's greatest grape variety, but here we can make the best Sangiovese and that is what we should do. We have a mission to defend the identity of our region.' He is also returning to *botti*, in preference to *barriques*, which are not traditional Tuscan containers. However, Terrine does include some *barrique*-aged wine, making for a dry cherry nose, with some elegant structure on the palate. His *riserva*, Torre a Destra, a pure Sangiovese aged half in *barriques* and half in *botti*, had some firm cedary fruit, with a tight oak structure on the palate, while the Chianti Classico was more accessible with some rounded cherry fruit. Torre a Destra went well with the roast beef we were enjoying in the elegant high-ceiling dining room, with a welcoming log fire, but it would deserve some bottle age.

And lunch finished with a traditional Italian dessert, *pane dei santi*, a bread with walnuts and raisins, which is made for All Saints Day on 1 November, and eaten only in early November.

The Fattoria di Monsanto is a little further along the road. We were given a warm welcome by Laura Bianchi, who explained how her grandfather had originally bought the property as a holiday home back in 1961, and then her father Fabrizio began to develop the wine. The family have a textile business in Milan and her grandfather was born in San Gimignano; on a clear day you can see the distinctive tall towers from the terrace at Monsanto. The previous owners had sold the wine *sfuso* but in 1962 Fabrizio made his vintage of Il Poggio from one hillside vineyard and, forever pioneering, 1968 was his first vintage without any white grapes, a revolutionary step at the time and eighteen years before white grapes were officially omitted from Chianti Classico. Part of the original Il Poggio vineyard is being replanted; we looked across the valley to see where they were restoring the old terraces. Altogether they have 72 hectares of vines, mainly Sangiovese, with a little Chardonnay, Cabernet Sauvignon and Merlot.

The villa at Monsanto dates from 1740, but the cellars are older, probably sixteenth-century. Laura showed us round and we were grateful for a guide, for they are a labyrinth of galleries, some old and some much newer. People had sheltered here during the Allies' advance in 1944. One long gallery is 250 metres, lined with stone from the vineyard and filled with a thousand barrels; the subdued lighting rendered it all the more atmospheric. Some of the rocks had been left bare, with *galestro* and limestone; there were statues, a headless naked woman and a bearded man, a prophet maybe, for one of their wines, a pure Cabernet Sauvignon, is called Nemo, meaning no one, and recalling the expression that no one is a prophet in his own land. On one of the large barrels there is a carving of a chimera, with the head of a lion for strength, the horns of the gazelle to represent speed, the beak of the eagle to illustrate far-sightedness and the tail of a snake to indicate shrewdness, and on the paw is the word 'Tinscvil', meaning a votive offering. It is the name of another wine and recalls the Etruscan associations with the property, for they have found a tomb in the woods. The modern vinification cellar was a startling contrast of stainless-steel conical vats.

We sat round the dining-room table, tasting and talking. Laura's grandmother, a silent little old lady dressed in black, who is almost ninety, appeared to see what was going on. Laura explained that she still enjoyed her wine and every now and again a good bottle disappeared from the cellar. Then her six-year-old son returned from school and did his best to distract his mother, mainly by hiding under the table, as he was rather shy. The room had originally been the larder of the house and they had left the old hooks in the ceiling, from which hams had once hung. We began with a Chardonnay, Fabrizio Bianchi, which was rich and buttery with some rounded fruit and a good backbone of acidity. Half of it had been fermented in new oak, and half in stainless steel. The vines are considered quite old for Tuscan Chardonnay as they were planted back in 1974. The 2000 Chianti *normale* was quite sturdy and cedary, more substantial in structure than the wines around Panzano. Laura felt that this part of Chianti Classico produced riper grapes than the vineyards at higher altitudes as they are more open to the warmer sea air and maritime influence. Il Poggio, from the original 5-hectare vineyard, was riper and more complex, with firmer fruit. Then came Tinscvil, a blend of Sangiovese with 25 per cent Cabernet Sauvignon and 5 per cent Merlot; the Merlot is a recent addition to the blend, first introduced in 1999, while Tinscvil has been made since 1979 as a blend of two varieties. The Bordelais grape varieties immediately give the wine a different structure and profile; it tastes sweeter, maybe from the new oak, and more cedary, with less apparent Sangiovese astringency. Nemo, the pure Cabernet Sauvignon, has been made since 1982, from a vineyard planted as early as 1974, for Fabrizio Bianchi was one of the first to plant Cabernet Sauvignon in Tuscany. Again the young wine was quite different from Chianti, with ripe blackcurrant fruit and very obvious oak influence.

But the best was saved till last, two old and quite contrasting vintages of Il Poggio, first the 1968 and then the 1977. The 1968 was revolutionary at the time: made without any white grapes, from destalked grapes, and without using the *governo* method of adding slightly dried grapes into the fermenting juice. In some ways it was extraordinarily Burgundian in style, with almost sweet fruit, notes of cedar wood and tobacco and a long, sweet, smoky finish. On the other hand the 1977 was more reminiscent of Bordeaux, with quite a leathery nose and very marked cedarwood notes on the palate; it was more substantial and beautifully mature. Laura explained how the two wines were made in exactly the same way; however, in 1968 there was some botrytis on the grapes, which accounts for the sweetness, while the 1977 came from very healthy grapes. That wine was aged in Slavonic oak, whereas for the 1968 they had used chestnut barrels. There are few estates that have reserves of wine of this age and we felt that we had tasted a part of Tuscany's vinous history.

Around Fonterutoli
· April ·

South of Castellina-in-Chianti; Etruscan tombs, the village and the wine estate

THE HAMLET OF FONTERUTOLI nestles in the valley below Castellina, just off the Chiantigiana, and stands on the provincial boundary between the cities of Florence and Siena. The name of the village originates from the two springs, which until thirty years ago were the only water source in the village. It played its part in the long struggle between the Florentines and the Sienese, for this is where the boundary was decided back in 1208. It had been agreed that a horseman would ride out from each city when the cocks crowed, supposedly at dawn, and that the boundary would be drawn where they met on the road. Fonterutoli is much closer to Siena than to Florence, but this is less a reflection on the Sienese rider's lack of ability than on the Florentine character. So the story goes, the canny Florentines, who are often described as cunning, or *furbo* in Italian, starved their cockerels the previous night, so that they woke well before daybreak and crowed from hunger, thus giving the Florentine horseman a head start.

The hamlet and its land have been in the hands of the Mazzei family since 1435 when Lady Smeralda Mazzei married Piero di Aguseo di Fonterutoli. However, he died soon afterwards, leaving her the estate, and then on her death in 1437 the property passed to her brother. The present head of the family, Lapo Mazzei, was president of the Chianti Classico *consorzio* and an influential banker. He speaks impeccably elegant English, with a courtly charm, while his son Francesco, who is equally fluent, has succumbed to the American linguistic influence. Francesco is the twenty-fourth generation at Fonterutoli. He took us for a walk round the village. First he explained the origin of the name Mazzei, which comes from *mazza*, meaning a mace, so that the family coat of arms is three iron maces. In the entrance hall to the estate office there is a pair of enormous wooden maces, which Francesco had found in China.

Siena is just ten miles away as the crow flies and from the terrace you can make out its distinctive Torre del Mangia. Below the terrace is an elegant garden designed by Francesco's great-grandmother in the formal Italian style, with neat box hedges and not a leaf out of place. On the next level there is a series of small rose beds, separated by lemon trees, providing a study in perspective, for the garden looks much longer than it actually is. In fact, it is on a slight slope, and is narrower at the top than at the bottom. The villa was completed in 1570, but is only now being given central heating, so chaos reigned. We peered into the library that was covered in dust sheets; the family archives from the seventeenth century onwards are kept here, with earlier documents in the state archives in Florence. Vestiges of the original fortifications, once part of a line extending from Brolio to Fonterutoli and dating from the twelfth century, are marked by an illegible Latin inscription. Another inscription records the visit one thousand years earlier of Ottone III on 26 June 998 when he established the jurisdiction of the bishops of Arezzo, Fiesole and Siena. The church in Fonterutoli, dedicated to San Miniato, was destroyed during the war when the village was occupied by the Germans, and its rebuilding is commemorated with an inscription by Giorgio la Pira, the highly respected mayor of Florence in the post-war years.

The Roman road that linked Florence to Siena passed through the village. Today it is called Via Ottone III di Sassonia, *gia* via Rossini, indicating an earlier name change. Most of the houses along it date from the seventeenth century, and a discreet brass notice indicates the estate office, Cantina di Fonterutoli. Francesco explained how once there were several craftsmen in the village, such as carpenters and an ironsmith. Many of the houses had stables or wine cellars on the ground floor, so that people lived on the first floor. There was evidence of a new cellar being built outside the village, an enormous hole in the ground some 15 metres deep, at its side a gigantic pile of stones. But for the moment their barrels, and a few *botti*, are lodged in a series of tiny cellars throughout the village, along with *orci* for olive oil and a library of bottles. The oldest remaining bottles date back to the 1950s; anything earlier was drunk by the occupying Germans during the war.

The range of wines at Fonterutoli has evolved over the years. Even though they were one of the first to plant Cabernet Sauvignon in the 1970s, they no longer make the so-called super-Tuscans, Ser Lapo and Concerto. Ser Lapo has become Castello di Fonterutoli, with just 10 per cent Cabernet Sauvignon, which nowadays conforms to the regulations for Chianti Classico, while Concerto, which was a Sangiovese and Cabernet blend, has been discontinued.

We tasted around a large table, overlooked by a picture of a magnificent black rooster, as the symbol of the Chianti Classico *consorzio*, recalling the events of 1208. First there was Badiola, an IGT from Sangiovese grapes, which they purchase, not necessarily in Chianti Classico, and age in American oak for six months. It was very accessible, with the ripe vanilla flavours of American oak, and Francesco explained that American rather than French oak was better for a short ageing period, and also cheaper. The 2000 Chianti Classico *normale* is aged for ten months in *barriques*, so that it was much tighter and more structured in flavour. He considers finesse to be the abiding characteristic of Fonterutoli. 1999 Castello di Fonterutoli had spent eighteen months in wood, half of which was new, again giving structured, firm tannins and underlying elegance. And finally there was their *cru*, Siepi, a Sangiovese Merlot blend, which immediately tasted more *bordelais* in style, particularly as it had been aged for eighteen months in French oak. They consider Merlot a better complement to Sangiovese than Cabernet, for Sangiovese tends to be quite acidic and elegant, while Merlot is more rounded and broader. Like so many other producers, they have bought land in the Maremma to produce Morellino di Scansano; it tastes quite different from Chianti, with the warmer climate producing fuller, fatter, ripe flavours. There was no doubt that the tasting amply illustrated an estate bound in tradition, but which has known how to evolve with the times.

There are Etruscan tombs outside Fonterutoli so we walked down the track past an old abandoned farm to find them on a low hill in a grove of cypress trees, which the Etruscans always planted at their burial sites. The tombs date back to the sixth and seventh century BC; at that time this area was quite heavily populated. The tombs, which once would have been covered over, with a door and a series of chambers, were open to the sky; various stones and columns were still in position, but any funeral artefacts or urns had long since disappeared. Then we stopped in the village shop, succumbing to the temptation of lavender soap, made from the lavender that Francesco's mother grows, but we resisted the enticing smells of homely pasta emanating from the Osteria di Fonterutoli. Instead we went to find the hamlet of Badiola, with its little Romanesque chapel of Santa Maria in Colle, appropriately on a hill outside Castellina. Sadly it was firmly locked and the adjoining farm buildings were devoid of people. However, the views towards Radda and Gaiole were worth the detour and the exterior of the chapel was charming in its simplicity.

Around Volpaia
· April ·

Near Radda-in-Chianti; Montevertine

I ALWAYS LIKE GOING TO VOLPAIA, the tiny village perched on a hillside outside the small town of Radda. The road from Radda twists and turns, climbing steeply, or you can take the back road from Lamole, which is little more than a dirt track. Giovanella Stianti and her husband Carlo Mascheroni always give you a friendly welcome. This time it was Easter Saturday and we found ourselves having lunch with their children and numerous friends so that our Italian was given a real work-out in colloquial expressions. Giovanella gave us Easter eggs, not the clumsy chocolate English ones wrapped in garish tinfoil, but real shells filled with melted chocolate, and the meal would not have been complete without the Easter *colomba*, or dove, a delicious delicate brioche with dried fruit and a veil of sugar. Naturally the meal was accompanied by Volpaia's wines. First there was a stylish *riserva* 1997. Then we progressed to the 1998 Coltasala, which was first made back in 1980 as an almost pure Sangiovese with a drop of Mammola. It spends about eighteen months in wood, and now with the change in regulations qualifies as a Chianti Classico; it was satisfyingly rich and rounded. Next came 1998 Balifico, a wine created in 1985, from two-thirds Sangiovese and one-third Cabernet Sauvignon and Cabernet Franc, and which therefore remains a super-Tuscan. It was more tannic and powerful, illustrating the impact of Cabernet on Sangiovese. The final treat was a glass of Vin Santo, with its intriguing biscuity flavours and dry finish.

After lunch we wandered through the cellars that are hidden discreetly in houses around the village. Giovanella was armed with a large set of keys. One discreet arched doorway, once the entrance to a small church, hid the fermentation cellar with its high stainless-steel vats, which had been lowered into position through the roof to fit snugly between each arch. There was a series of barrel rooms, one under yet another church, housing both *botti* and *barriques*, all of new French oak. Once the population of the village was as many as one thousand people. When Giovanella first came here at the end of the 1960s, when her father bought the estate, there were still about a hundred people living here, and today there are just forty-four. Such has been the rural depopulation of Tuscany after the collapse of the *mezzadria* system.

Volpaia was one of the very first Chianti estates that I ever visited back in the early 1980s; the wines were trendsetting then, masterminded by one of Tuscany's leading oenologists, Maurizio Castelli. He has since gone on to other things and yet another of the great names in Italian oenology is now responsible for the winemaking: Ricardo Coltarello, the brother of Renzo at Antinori, and so Volpaia has kept abreast of the changes in the region. They have 45 hectares of vines in production, of which two-thirds have been replanted in the last ten years with some of the new clones, and following the now widely accepted practice of a much higher density of plants. As for winemaking, they have given up *rimontaggi* and now favour *pigiatura* in open-top vats, believing that it gives a better extraction of flavour and colour.

Olive oil is also an important part of the estate, and there is a modern *frantoio*, or olive mill, with the oil kept in small stainless-steel vats rather than the traditional *orci*. This makes hygiene much easier to control, for if the *orci* lose their glaze, as they do, you can have problems of tainted flavours. There is a tempting village shop, not for just wine, but also the olive oil and a variety of flavoured vinegars.

From the village we took a path through the woods, past carpets of violets and primroses, on to the neatly manicured *agriturismo* village of Castelvecchi, and then down to the little Pieve di Santa Maria Novella. The church was firmly locked, but the guidebook tantalizingly told us that we were missing a Della Robbia altarpiece. The path continued through the woods, with a steep climb back up the hill past several isolated cottages. There were views towards the town of Radda, and you could see the elegant facade of the villa of Vistarenni in the distance, which, floodlit at night, almost looks like a stage set with its elaborate columns and fine proportions. Finally we joined an alley of cypress trees and the road back to Volpaia.

Another estate nearby is Montevertine, without which no survey of Chianti Classico would be complete. It was bought in 1966 as a hobby by a steel industrialist, Sergio Manetti, and has been gradually transformed into a serious, pacesetting estate, with a reputation based on one of the very early pure Sangiovese: Le Pergole Torte, made for the first time in 1977. Sergio Manetti died in 2000 and the estate is now run by his son, Martino, along with his son-in-law, Klaus Reimitz, who arrived at Montevertine in 1981 after studying philosophy and Italian literature.

They currently produce three wines at Montevertine, from 13 hectares, namely Le Pergole Torte from a vineyard first planted in 1967, Montevertine and Pian del Ciampolo. There is a fourth wine, their *cru*, Il Sodaccio, which comes from a hillside vineyard near the cellars, but as the vineyard is being replanted the wine is temporarily out of production. Klaus took us for a wander through the cellars, which are a series of small rooms, allowing space for two vintages in barrel. An inside window onto the rock showed the solid *galestro* stone, with an attractive 1900s wine carafe, with a space for ice, on the sill.

Then we adjourned to the kitchen, with its large welcoming fireplace, to taste. 1999 Pian del Ciampolo is an IGT from Sangiovese with some Canaiolo, which spends eighteen months in *botti*, with elegant cherry fruit on nose and palate, with a touch of spice. Montevertine is Sangiovese, with 10 per cent Canaiolo, given two years in *botti*, with more depth, spice and soft tannins. 1999 Pergole Torte was more than living up to its reputation for elegance and structure, with layers of intriguing fruit and flavour. From Montevertine, it was a short drive to the Castello di Ama.

THE COLLAPSE OF THE
MEZZADRIA SYSTEM

THE *MEZZADRIA* SYSTEM of share-cropping was the backbone of Tuscan agriculture for centuries. The landowner provided the necessary capital expenditure, buying seeds, tools, equipment and so on, and housing the peasant farmers or *contadini* and their families on his land, and in return they contributed their manual labour. All the crops were then divided, usually equally between landowner and *contadini*. As the landowner was often an absentee, the estate was run for him by a *fattore*, or manager.

The industrial revolution came late to Italy, after the Second World War, but it brought the collapse of the *mezzadria* system, as people left the land to work in factories, and consequently the inefficiency of many estates came to light, as the landowners were left without the manpower to run their estates. The mechanization of agriculture, particularly the advent of the tractor, also made an impact. Consequently many landowners, who found themselves without the means to run their estates, sold their properties, which brought a new generation of innovative estate owners to Tuscany, people with experience in other fields and broader horizons than the old aristocratic families.

From Castello di Ama
· *November* ·

South of Radda-in-Chianti; to the village of Vagliagli; Dievole and Aiola

A MA IS A TINY HAMLET in the southern part of Chianti Classico. The origins of the village are Etruscan, while the castle formed part of the Florentine defences against the Sienese, until it was destroyed in the seventeenth century. A villa built in the nineteenth century was in ruins when Lionello Sebasti and his partners bought the property in 1982, and has subsequently been restored. We were given a friendly welcome by his daughter, Lorenza, and her husband, Marco Pallanti, who has been the winemaker at Castello di Ama since 1982.

Marco explained how the vineyards have developed over the last twenty years. The oldest vines date from the mid-1960s. In the 1980s, they carried out lots of different experiments and made as many as five different wines, with various blends of Sangiovese, and also Merlot and Pinot Noir, all in an attempt to see what suited the clay and limestone soil best. They now have 85 hectares, including some of the new clones of Sangiovese, and the wines have become rather more streamlined, as our tasting revealed. But first we wandered through the cellars; the barrel-ageing cellar had that wonderfully evocative smell of new oak laced with young wine. Transported there blindfolded, you could be nowhere else than in a wine cellar. They favour *barriques* – anything larger is too difficult to clean – and Seguin Moreau, Taransaud and François Frères are their favourite coopers. They have also tried Russian oak, but it is nearly as expensive as French oak, and they do not like American oak. They last used *botti* in 1995.

We sat at the dining table of the villa, with a veritable forest of glasses in front of us, for a tasting of recent vintages of Castello di Ama Chianti Classico. Lorenza and Marco fervently believe in Chianti Classico; they want to raise its reputation to that of the most respected of French appellations and they firmly spurn the concept of the IGT wines. You sense that quality is their driving force. 2000 Chianti Classico is a blend of about 85 per cent Sangiovese, with some Merlot and a little Malvasia Nera and Canaiolo, with about twelve months' ageing in *barriques*, of which a small part are new. It was redolent of ripe cherry fruit, with soft tannins. 1999 is an even better vintage, making a more structured wine, with elegant tannins and sour cherry fruit. 1998 was less successful in this part of Chianti, and there is a little more Merlot in the wine, giving a cedary nose, and a sturdy, drier palate. Best of all was the 1997, with some stylish smoky fruit on both nose and palate. Castello di Ama has always produced *crus* or single vineyard wines, which are now concentrated into two, Vigna Bellavista, a blend of Sangiovese and Malvasia Nera, and Casuccia, a blend of Sangiovese and Merlot. Marco made an apt comparison: the *cru* is like *haute couture* in fashion, whereas the *normale* is your *prêt-à-porter*. 1999 Vigna Bellavista had a certain richness on the nose and palate, and Marco explained that Malvasia Nera might not be an elegant variety, but it gave weight and body to a wine, without drowning the Sangiovese. In Casuccia you could sense the presence of the Merlot, as it was quite chunky and sturdy, with body and fruit. We finished with a treat, a couple of older vintages. First there was the 1989 Chianti Classico, which Lorenza described as a very average year. The colour was quite developed with an elegant, vegetal nose that was reminiscent of Pinot Noir, with some cedary fruit on the palate. Marco observed that he thought there was a similarity of flavour between Sangiovese and Pinot Noir, but that you could also find a resemblance with Cabernet Sauvignon. It all depended on whereabouts in Chianti the Sangiovese was grown. Although nine years old, the 1993 Bellavista was still youthful, with cherry fruit, firm tannins and a hint of liquorice. Lorenza and Marco are very optimistic for the future, and confident that there is a greater consistency of quality, not only in their own wines, but also in the whole of Chianti Classico.

We set off from Ama to walk to the village of Vagliagli. The sun was shining, which lifted our spirits, and the *frantoio* was in full swing, exuding the fragrant aroma of fresh oil as we passed the open door. We carried on down the hill, past vineyards and then to another tiny hamlet, with Casa Nuova di Ama, advertising *vendita diretta*. Out of the village we joined a tarmacked road, with a sign to La Mandria, but instead we turned off down the dirt track towards

San Polo in Rosso. The path took us along a ridge with views over vineyards in both directions, towards Radda on our right and back towards Ama on our left. Soon we reached the tiny cluster of houses of Poggio San Polo. Everything looked neatly manicured, with pots of bright red geraniums still in flower. The track continued downhill towards San Polo in Rosso, passing neatly tended vineyards. San Polo in Rosso had a certain reputation for its wines in the mid-1980s, but the Canessa family have since given up bottling and are content to sell their wines *sfuso*. The tall Romanesque tower of the fortified church of San Polo dominates the surrounding countryside. Its origins lie in the eleventh century when it stood on the much disputed boundary between Florence and Siena. Today there is a sign telling you very firmly that this is private property, together with a list of the dozen or so days in the year when mass is said. We had just missed All Saints Day on 1 November and would have to wait for the Immaculate Conception on 8 December, and then Christmas Day.

The path disintegrated into a stony dirt track winding down through the woods. There were acorns underfoot, juniper bushes in the undergrowth and bright red pyracantha berries, as well as the occasional wild flower valiantly resisting the autumnal chill. In the distance we could hear the soothing tinkle of water from the river Arbia at the bottom of the valley below us. We passed a pretty little shrine, a Madonna and Child, with its roof covered in moss, and right in the middle of nowhere; it seemed a curious place for a shrine, so off the beaten track and almost overgrown by vegetation. We crossed the river and climbed quite steeply up the other side of the valley to find a picnic spot by a firmly shuttered farmhouse; in the foreground were vines, on the hill behind, the village of San Sano, and in the distance the dramatic outline of Monte Amiata. The path carried on past the farm buildings of Bottaccio, towards the wine estate of Dievole. A steep slope was being prepared for planting on the other side of the valley, and we noticed a curious formation of vines, planted in a circle with narrowing rows meeting at the cypress tree in the centre, which was reached along a pathway of rosemary, lavender and rose bushes.

Dievole caters for tourists, with a restaurant and bedrooms, as well as a cellar and vineyards. There was evidence of a circuit for those intent on exercise, with hanging bars and other gymnastic paraphernalia. However, our visit at Dievole did not start well; we were told that we were late and that we had been expected fifteen minutes earlier. Needless to say we were somewhat taken aback, as such exacting standards of punctuality are most unusual in the Tuscan wine world. However, it transpired that cellar visits are usually guided tours, and our tardiness had quite upset the programme. We were given a glass of wine, 1999 Divertimento, from a blend of Mammola, Canaiolo and Colorino, which was curiously sweet, and then taken into the chapel with our glasses of wine. A minute later inappropriate canned music suddenly blasted away the silence of the chapel and a waiter appeared, bearing a tray of salami. We begged for silence, as the tiny chapel was a delight, dating from the fifteenth century, with a picture depicting two vintners paying rent, which comprised three loaves, two capons and six silver coins, to the Emperor Henry III in 1080. The coins apparently came from Lucca, which had its own mint at the time, and there was an imitation coin to show us. According to Mario, our guide, Dievole can boast nine hundred years of history with written references in the archives of Siena. We continued our way through the cellars. There were outsize black and white pictures of various farm workers on the walls of the barrel cellar, and an intriguing display of sixteen different soil types, an example from each vineyard, with contrasting colours and texture, illustrating the infinite diversity of soil in Chianti Classico.

Dievole is now the property of Mario Felice Schwenn, who is apparently very much the instigator of the extraordinary atmosphere. It was quite unlike any other wine estate that I have ever visited and somehow I had the impression that I had walked on to a film set. We tasted in the restaurant, well after lunch had finished. There were old photographs on the walls of previous owners and an enormous chess set in the garden outside. Paolo Vaggagini is the consultant oenologist, who masterminds the range of nine wines. They have numerous different grape varieties on their 96 hectares of vineyards, including several clones of Sangiovese, as well as other traditional Tuscan varieties, some well known like Malvasia Nera and Mammola, and others much rarer such as Saragiolo and Pugnitello, as well as international varieties like Syrah, Merlot and Cabernet Franc, but no Cabernet Sauvignon. Rinascimento is a blend of Malvasia Nera and Canaiolo, with some rich cherry fruit; Broccato was more international in flavour, with the influence of sweet oak, and the same could also be said for Novecento *riserva*. Plenum is the fruit of a joint venture, with a different partner each year. We tried the 1997, for which a Côtes de Provence estate had provided the Syrah and Dievole the Sangiovese; in 1998 Sangiovese was partnered with Barbera and next will come a Tempranillo blend. It was an intriguing idea, but perhaps a bit of a gimmick, which could well describe the place itself.

The main drive to Dievole is lined with cypress trees; some old and some newly planted, with views between the trees across to Aiola on the other side of the valley. The entrance to the estate is marked by a flamboyant sign. We emerged onto the road just before the village of Vagliagli. The mountain range of the Apennines was visible in the distance with a pale line of snow on the summits, the first of the year, which had fallen the previous night. But Vagliagli was sunny and we sat outside the village café in the square, with its *alimentari* and church, cheerfully waiting for Donatella who was coming to give us a lift back to our car at Ama.

A day or two later we went back to Vagliagli to visit Aiola. A castle was built here in the thirteenth century and played its part in the war between the Florentines and Sienese, and in particular, as a defensive position against the nearby castle of Brolio. It was subsequently destroyed in the fifteenth century, then substantially rebuilt, with the thick walls of an impregnable fortress. The remains of the moat are still visible, with evidence of the old drawbridge and tunnels that once provided escape routes. Inside, a large vaulted room is sometimes used as a theatre, but the shuttered rooms were very sombre. The estate was bought in 1936 by Giovanni Malagodi, who was a prominent figure in Italian politics. In the 1980s the enterprise became a limited company, with his daughter continuing to represent the family interests. They are well organized for visitors, welcoming the casual caller who would like a tasting, but for a cellar visit you need to make an appointment. The cellar dates from the 1960s and I suspect not much has changed since then. There are lots of *botti*, which are used for Chianti, including some of French wood, which is an innovation, as well as some *barriques* for their IGT, Rosso del Senatore, in memory of Giovanni Malagodi. A tiny *vinsantaia* was full of old *caratelli* of traditional chestnut, where the wine stays for five years.

Aiola is one of the few estates that continue to make the DOC Bianco Val d'Arbia, which covers the southern part of Chianti Classico as well as land towards Montalcino. It is a mixture of Malvasia and Trebbiano, and with its firm almondy acidity amply illustrates the reasons for the decline of this marginal DOC. They also carried on adding white grapes to their Chianti right up until the change to the *disciplinari* in 1996. Aiola is also unusual in continuing to bottle Chianti in the traditional straw-covered *fiaschi*, for private customers and restaurants; it is very laborious as each bottle needs to be filled by hand. You really sense that things are slow to change here. The Chianti Classico *normale* had some sturdy cherry fruit, the Rosso del Senatore a certain austerity of pure Sangiovese, while Logaiolo, from 70 per cent Cabernet Sauvignon with Sangiovese, was more accessible with some cassis fruit from the Cabernet. Next came an intriguing comparison of two vintages of Vin Santo: the 1992 was rich and nutty while the 1996 was pale in colour, with delicate honey, but there was no obvious explanation for the difference. Vin Santo has a mind of its own, and that was how it was. Perhaps best of all was the *grappa*, made by a local distillery, Bonolla, which had a delicate inviting aroma, even at 10 o'clock in the morning!

From Gaiole-in-Chianti
· April ·

Badia a Coltibuono, Riecine, Colombaio di Cencio and Capannelle

IT WAS A SUNNY SPRING morning as we strode eagerly out of Gaiole. The first old man we met asked if we were going up into the hills; we answered in the affirmative. The second suggested that we might slow down a little: *piano, piano*, he muttered under his breath. And the path began to climb, so that we were soon level with the tiny village of Barbischio on the other side of the valley. The track continued its gentle climb, past a profusion of spring flowers, hellebores, violets and a lone orchid, maybe an early purple. There was cherry blossom, hawthorn and white broom, and as we climbed we reached the dark shade of the pine woods. The air felt cool, in contrast to the spring sunshine, but soon we emerged onto a *strada bianca* and made our way to the village of Montegrossi. A ruined castle dominates the village, yet another reminder that the boundary between the city states of Florence and Siena was much disputed in the Middle Ages. Sheep with jingling bells around their necks grazed contentedly between the crumbling walls of the terraces below the castle.

Soon we reached Badia a Coltibuono, today a wine estate, but once an important house of the Vallombrosan order, which was founded in the early eleventh century as a splinter group from the Benedictines. The name comes from the Latin, *cultus bonus*, referring either to a religious cult or to land suited for cultivation; whichever, it was good. The abbey dates from the eleventh century and there are written records of the monks planting vineyards here in 1080, including the earliest references to Sangiovese. When Napoleon secularized the monastery at the beginning of the nineteenth century, just five monks remained, and in 1846 the property was bought by the Stucchi family, to whom it still belongs. Our appointment was with Roberto Stucchi, who would not look out of place in a monastery himself; he has a full head of hair, with a substantial ponytail, and with his finely chiselled features and greying beard and moustache has a somewhat biblical appearance. More significantly, he is the first member of his family to train as a winemaker, at U.C. Davis in California. First he showed us round. The attractive courtyard was built in the eleventh century. Today there are the traditional amphorae, *orci*, with small olive trees; the distinctive bell tower, which you can see from afar, was built at the same time. The cloisters have been enclosed and the monks' refectory is now a sitting room, with restored frescoes from the fifteenth century. They depict the life of San Lorenzo, to whom the abbey is dedicated. He met a grisly end: he was toasted alive by the Romans, and his symbol is a grill pan. Adjoining the refectory is an elegant stuccoed pale-green dining room, for guests, who ate separately from the monks. The garden is a pattern of box hedges, with barely a leaf out of place, and roses trained over archways. In a few weeks it would be a profusion of flowers and scent.

The cellars are in the original crypt of the church, dating from the fifteenth century. Where once they had the traditional enormous chestnut *botti*, they now have French oak *botti*, of more modest proportions, 15–25 hectolitres. There is a library of old bottles, the oldest dating back to 1937, although the first commercial bottlings at Badia a Coltibuono did not take place until the early 1950s. Previously the wine had been sold *sfuso* and in *fiaschi* to Antinori and Ricasoli. It is really Roberto, and his father Piero, who are responsible for the current commercial success of Badia a Coltibuono. Such a cellar is totally impractical for modern-day winemaking, and so they have built a new winery, first used for the 1997 vintage, on the outskirts of the village of Monti, closer to their main vineyards. From the outside the design could be described as space age, but it blends unobtrusively into the hillside and inside it is definitely state of the art. Everything operates by gravity; there are squat stainless-steel tanks, fed by a sorting table and a conveyor belt, allowing for *pigiatura* and finely tuned temperature control, and under the roof there is a large space for drying Vin Santo grapes. Although the fermentation cellar will accommodate several small batches of grapes, from separate vineyards, Roberto is adamant that there will always be an estate blend, rather than several individual *crus*. Vineyards are not always consistent and for him the growing trend towards single-vineyard wines, *crus*, does not make sense.

He expounded his ideas as we tasted, discussing the changes since my previous visit a few years earlier. These start in the vineyard. Since 2000 they have practised organic viticulture. No herbicides or insecticides have been used since the mid-1980s, and since the late 1990s they have only used organic fertilizer, practising much better soil management, including cover crops. They are following the trend towards a higher density in the vineyards, with about 5550 vines per hectare. This limits vigour, but nonetheless Sangiovese is a challenge. Rain or drought at the wrong moment encourage mildew; they remove leaves to improve the aeration, and cluster thinning helps to regulate the balance of the vine, making it more resistant to disease. Roberto is convinced that healthier soil leads to better flavours in the wine, and that organic viticulture helps in the cellar. The fermentations are easier, more spontaneous, and he has had fewer problems with stuck fermentations, with no likelihood of chemicals upsetting the yeast.

More than half their production comes from outside their estate. The white Trappolino is made from Chardonnay and Pinot Bianco grown near the coast. There is a cheerful Chianti Cetamure, as well as wines under Roberto's own personal label. In addition they make three wines from their vineyards near the village of Monti, a *normale*, a *riserva*, and in the best years, Sangioveto, a pure varietal. 'However, you must be careful; the *riserva* will suffer if you remove your best Sangiovese; it all depends on the overall quality of the vintage.' For instance, no Sangioveto was made in 1998, as the quality would have been no different from the *riserva*. All the estate Chianti is aged in wood, for it helps to stabilize the colour and soften the tannins, but while the *riserva* spends time in *botti*, Sangioveto is aged only in small French *barriques*, which are replaced in a four-year cycle. The first vintage of Sangioveto was 1980, making it one of the pioneering pure Sangiovese. Roberto has mixed feelings about the influx of Cabernet Sauvignon and, more recently, Merlot. For him, what makes Chianti is Sangiovese, as his 1998 *riserva* illustrated, with its ripe flavours of sour cherries and firm structured fruit.

From the abbey we wandered back down the lane, with the taste of Sangioveto lingering in our mouths, ignoring the temptation to stop at the abbey restaurant. It is now run by Roberto's brother, Paolo, with some serious input from his mother, Lorenza, who is a talented chef and cookery writer and also runs cookery courses at Badia a Coltibuono. Paolo apparently used to be a violinmaker, with, as Roberto put it, five clients a year; now he has a hundred a day. But we did succumb to honey in the estate shop with its tempting local produce.

From Badia a Coltibuono it is a short walk downhill to Riecine, with some wonderful views over the valley. A cellar hand was puffing on a cigarette at the cellar door, with a remote control in the other hand for a piece of machinery inside the cellar. 'I'm not allowed to smoke in the cellar,' he grumbled; and quite right too. There was a large tub of young vines in water, awaiting planting.

I have long had a soft spot for Riecine. The former owner, John Dunkley, could always be relied upon to give you the unexpurgated version of whatever was going on in Chianti, sprinkled with some provocative opinion and a healthy disrespect for Italian bureaucracy, in particular that generated by the wine industry. I remember the first time we met, back in 1984, as DOCG was being discussed for Chianti. John dismissed it with a snort: 'Yes, guaranteed, like the postal service and the railway timetable,' both of which are notoriously unreliable in Italy. Then he taught me that well-known Italian proverb, *fatto la legge, l'inganno trovato*, which means that no sooner is the law made, than the loophole is found. It is vividly illustrated by the many Tuscan winemakers who gave up using white grapes in their wine long before it was allowed by law.

John bought Riecine back in 1971 with his Italian wife, Palmina Abbagnano, when he tired of life as a successful advertising executive in London. Their first vintage, in 1972, was not a good one, neither for Riecine nor for Chianti. As John remembered, they made a small amount of rather bad wine and learnt an enormous amount in the process; he recalled Maurizio Castelli giving him the sound advice to buy a thermometer, in order to check his fermentation temperatures. Sadly John died in 1999, a few years after his wife, but had sold a larger share of the estate to an American wine enthusiast, Gary Baumann, and given shares in the estate to his winemaker, the engaging Sean O'Callaghan, so that the future of Riecine is assured. Sean continues John's tradition of warm hospitality, with a relaxed but conscientious approach to his winemaking, and a perceptive view of things in Chianti. He is tall and

lanky, and barely squeezes into his tiny Fiat 500, with his head brushing the roof.

A new neat little wine cellar has been built, to accommodate the crop of 9 hectares of vines. There is a small barrel cellar, with 225-litre *barriques*, as well as some 500-litre *tonneaux* and a couple of larger *botti*. Blending is all-important, with each batch of wine spending time in both new and old wood of different sizes, with the one exception, the *cru*, La Gioia, which matures only in new wood. We wandered through the cellar, glass in hand, tasting barrel samples from the 2001 vintage, which at six months old was showing ripe cherry fruit, with good structure and backbone. Then we sat in spring sunshine on the terrace, looking over the very first vineyard that John planted back in 1971, while Sean explained how they had practised organic viticulture for the last three or four years, and are gradually moving towards biodynamic viticulture, as advocated by Rudolf Steiner. It all depends upon the phases of the moon. A calendar determines when is the best moment for various treatments; this may sound far-fetched, but in the past winemakers would, for example, filter their wine when the moon was waning, for the simple reason that the wine was less turbulent and therefore easier to filter. More far-fetched is the practice of burying a cow's horn filled with manure for a year, so that the manure composts and the horn begins to crumble. The mixture is then sprayed onto the vineyard, but, in fact, is that so very different from adding bonemeal to your roses?

John always had mixed feelings about following the popular trend of making a *vino da tavola* that would be more expensive than your Chianti. He felt strongly that it reduced Chianti to the status of a second wine and detracted from its quality, for you used your best grapes and drew attention to only a very small part of your production. He called it public suicide, but then succumbed to the trend and began making La Gioia, a pure Sangiovese aged in new *barriques*. Currently it comes from vineyards in Chianti, but Sean envisages that the future source will be their new vineyards in the Maremma, at Montecucco, once these are in production. Meanwhile La Gioia di Riecine remains one of the most elegant and stylish of wines and a fitting tribute to John's achievements.

From Riecine we wandered down the dirt-track road back towards Gaiole, passing Gittori, who rent out their vineyards, down to Colombaio di Cencio, which we identified by the ostentatious W on each gate post. Modesty is evidently not the strong suit of the owner, Werner Wilhelm. Here outside Gaiole there are just two hectares of vines, with the main cellars near Brolio, so with a later appointment there we met the manager, Jacopo Morgante. Jacopo explained how the land had been bought from Cacchiano and the vines planted in 1996, with a state-of-the-art cellar constructed in 1998. He used to renovate houses and obviously has an eye for the aesthetics, even in a cellar, and evidently he was allowed to spare no expense. The black marble floor emitted a sparkle; it looked like diamonds, or stardust. Jacopo said he had taken the idea from a museum in North America. But the cellars were also very functional. The stainless-steel vats are divided into two, which simplifies the process of *rimontaggio*, and everything is computerized, with meticulous temperature control. There is a large barrel cellar, with a variety of French coopers, but no American oak. At the moment they make three wines, but are giving up producing a *riserva*, for commercial reasons, preferring to concentrate on Chianti *normale* and an IGT, Il Futuro, from equal parts of Sangiovese and Cabernet Sauvignon and 20 per cent Merlot. The problem is that the price of Chianti can never be as high as that of an IGT, even if the quality of a *riserva* would be comparable. It is all a question of market demand and acceptance. The Chianti *normale* includes 10 per cent Merlot with the Sangiovese, and is given fourteen months of oak ageing. The Merlot fills out the Sangiovese to give it some ripe fruit and a long finish. It was good, but it did not taste of Tuscany. Il Futuro 1999 was smoky, cedary and concentrated, but again lacked tipicity, although the quality was indisputable.

Continuing our path down the *strada bianca*, we could see Capannelle across the valley. When I first visited Capannelle in the mid-1980s, its cellar seemed as innovative as that of Colombaio di Cencio does today. Things have moved on since then. Raffaele Rossetti, who began planting vines at Capannelle in 1975, sold his estate in 1997 to James Sherwood, who runs Sea Containers, which owns the Orient Express. The cellars have been enlarged; there is a new barrel cellar of which one wall is bare exposed rock, which looks stark and dramatic. The bottles are stored in glass cages with black frames, which enhances the dramatic impact still further. They have added wooden fermentation vats and everything remains super-hygienic and streamlined, with stainless steel galore down to the last hammer, just as I had remembered.

The wines have gently evolved. The 2000 Chardonnay was given twelve months in new oak, with plenty of lees stirring, making a rich buttery wine with well-integrated oak and layers of flavour. Capannelle, which could be a Chianti as a pure Sangiovese but remains a *vino da tavola* for historical reasons, spends two years in wood. The 1994, which was not a fine vintage, was nonetheless finely structured with some dry leathery fruit. 1997 Solare, a Sangiovese with 20 per cent Malvasia Nera, spends two years in *barriques*, and was the star, elegant and harmonious, the Malvasia Nera adding some *rotondità* to soften the Sangiovese. Capannelle also run a joint project with Avignonesi from Montepulciano; they provide the Sangiovese and Avignonesi the Merlot, and the two winemakers decide the precise blend, with each estate taking it in turns to age the wine. Just 10,000 bottles are made, which are sold for *la lira di Dio*, an exorbitant price. Outside they were picking olives, combing the trees with giant combs, and in a corner of the cellar large plastic bags held *vinacce*, the skins left from the fermentation, waiting to be sent to the distillery in Greve.

Back in Gaiole in the middle of the afternoon, the town seemed rather sombre and unwelcoming, with shuttered shop windows. The only sign of life was an old lady sitting outside her front door, knitting. It would be evening before the streets became animated again.

South of Gaiole-in-Chianti
· *November* ·

*To the Agricoltori del Chianti Classico, the Castello di Meleto, Valtellina,
Rietine, Rocca di Castagnoli and Montiverdi*

IT WAS A WONDERFULLY SUNNY MORNING, despite the heavy rain that had fallen
during the night. We set off down the main street of Gaiole and soon turned
up a track into woods past a small farmhouse to reach the little square of
Spaltenna, with its tenth-century church. We were lucky; the door was open
and we were able to admire the grey stone arches with their simple lines. There
is an intriguing *trompe-l'oeil* altarpiece, which looks as though it is made of
richly ornate marble but is nothing more than painted wood. It was amazingly
deceptive, and the atmosphere in the church was both uplifting and
welcoming. The church adjoins what is now an expensive hotel, with rooms
round an elegant courtyard. We walked on past vineyards, with leaves turning
golden in the autumn sunshine, and turning back there were rewarding views
over to Spaltenna, with the tall church tower dominating the skyline. A grassy
track took us through the woods to emerge by a deserted farm, San Pierone,
which was really more of a tiny hamlet, with the eleventh-century church of
San Pietro in Avevano firmly closed. There were the remains of an outdoor
bread oven, as well as the old well, with some substantial buildings, which now
looked sadly neglected. We continued down the hill past a villa with bright red
Virginia creeper growing up its walls, softening its contours. Across the valley
we could see the cellars of the Agricoltori del Chianti Geografico, with some
unsightly large tanks outside, inadequately camouflaged by a row of cypress
trees.

This is one of the two large cooperatives, *cantina sociale*, in Chianti
Classico; the other, Castelli del Grevepesa, is in the northern part of the area,
outside Greve. Altogether the Agricoltori del Chianti Geografico comprise 200
members covering 570 hectares, producing some 700,000 bottles per year,
mainly from the southern half of Chianti Classico. However, they also work

with a member with vineyards in Montalcino, at Castello Altesi, and have another cellar in San Gimignano. There had been numerous improvements since my last visit to their cellars in Chianti, as the director, Carlo Salvadori, explained. An extensive replanting programme is underway, some 40 hectares per year, with the members following very precise guidelines. It all represents a considerable investment, and the members are paid per hectare instead of per quintal of grapes, which enables them to encourage more demanding quality criteria, and also allows for a greater selection of the grapes. In some ways this has become possible as attitudes have changed, with the members taking greater care of their vines and listening to advice from the cooperative viticulturalist. At vintage time there are four different quality selections for the grapes each day. Their attitude to wood has changed too, with a shift towards smaller wood, less time in oak, and a preference for bottle ageing. The greater selection of the grapes enables them to maintain the separate identity of some vineyards, such as Pulleraia in the Maremma near Grosseto, which is an IGT Merlot. Ferraiolo is their other super-Tuscan, a blend of Sangiovese and Cabernet Sauvignon from a vineyard between Vagliagli and Siena. Their best-known wine, Contessa di Radda, is an honest, reliable Chianti Classico with some rounded cherry fruit, while the *riserva* Montegiachi is more substantial, and the basic Chianti *normale* a cheerful quaffing wine for drinking with pasta.

Across the valley is the medieval castle of Meleto; first we passed its modern cellars, and then allowed ourselves to be sidetracked into a centre for local crafts. The building had originally been a kiln supplying plaster for the castle walls, and the remains of the old kiln were still visible. We resisted the temptation of bowls of olive wood and Tuscan pottery and carried on up the cypress-lined drive to the castle. There were views of Vertine and Spaltenna back across the valley. The Castello di Meleto meets everyone's idea of a medieval castle; it was part of the fortification line, including Brolio, Rocca di Montegrossi and Cacchiano, between the Florentines and Sienese in the Middle Ages.

We had arranged to meet Gianfranco Campioni, who has long worked in Chianti Classico; he was eager to explain the changed and chequered fortunes of Meleto. It was originally part of the considerable Ricasoli lands, at a time when the family owned as much as a third of Chianti Classico, but had been sold during the problematic period of the 1960s, when the family was rich in land but had insufficient money to run all its estates. There was no doubt that Meleto, although it had a reputation as one of the traditional estates of Chianti, had been seriously neglected by its subsequent owners, a real-estate group with some six hundred shareholders who were actually not interested in making wine, so that the wine was sold *sfuso* and the Meleto label and any reputation disappeared with the neglect of the vineyards. But happily things have changed and the controlling shareholders are now the Swiss Schuler family, who have been wine merchants since the end of the seventeenth century. They once had the Brolio agency in Switzerland but wanted their own vineyards in Chianti Classico, and are now intent on restoring Meleto to its former glory. The vineyards are being replanted, with the help of Stefano Chioccioli, one of Tuscany's leading viticulturalists, while Vittorio Fiore is the consultant oenologist.

Gianfranco was happy to show us round the castle. The towers at each corner date from the eleventh century, while considerable improvements were made in the eighteenth century. We walked through a series of rooms with some wonderful *trompe l'oeil* of wood painted as marble. A mural of the original map of Chianti Classico included Gaiole, Radda and Castellina, but not Greve, Panzano or Lamole, and depicted a line of castles, Castagnoli, Meleto, Spaltenna, Vertine and San Polo in Rosso. There was a fresco of the Madonna and Child with a host of saints from the Perugino school and a portrait of Geremia Ricasoli who renovated Meleto in the eighteenth century. He was a landscape designer and is shown holding a compass. An eighteenth-century chest depicts the castle on the front panel, but if you look at it closely you realize that the artist has exercised a certain licence and that the towers are in the wrong position by 180°. There is a coat of arms, with the Ricasoli lion and the motto *riens sans paine* (sic). Best of all and quite charming is a tiny theatre, built by Geremia Ricasoli in the middle of the eighteenth century. It would hold no more than thirty people with a tiny gallery for the family, and is painted in soft pastel colours with a painted beamed ceiling. Various pieces of scenery remain on the stage, while some of the original costumes are on display at the Theatre Museum in London's Covent Garden. They are sumptuously rich with the embroidered brocade of the period. The theatre is still occasionally used for concerts, and somehow, for a castle, Meleto felt surprisingly cosy.

Then we went down into the old cellars, with rows of 350-litre casks, which have a less intrusive impact of new wood than the smaller 225-litre *barriques*. We sat and tasted in what had once been a dungeon, but was now transformed into a tasting room. The wines were impressive. A 1999 Chianti Classico *normale*, a pure Sangiovese, with ten months in *botti*, was quite rich and spicy on the nose, with some firm tannins and the acidity typical of the cooler climate of this part of Chianti. The 2000 had some attractive ripe fruit, while the 1999 *riserva* was more concentrated and firmer in stature, after ten months in 350-litre barrels and a longer period in *botti*. Fiore, from 85 per cent Sangiovese, a selection of the best in the vineyards, and 15 per cent Merlot, was first made in 1996, the year of the renaissance of Meleto, as a homage to Vittorio Fiore. It spends fifteen or sixteen months in small wood; as always the Merlot made the wine seem fuller and fleshier, changing the style and, as Gianfranco observed, responding to a marketing demand. Rainero, named after the first Ricasoli, who built Meleto in the twelfth century, is a blend of Cabernet Sauvignon, Merlot and Sangiovese, which are aged in *barriques* for about fifteen months. As the Merlot ripens some three weeks before the Cabernet Sauvignon, it is easier to blend the wine before bottling, rather than before ageing. The colour was deep, with some firm sturdy flavours that owed more to Bordeaux than to Tuscany. We finished with that most Tuscan of wines, Vin Santo; it was quite amber in colour, with a certain sweetness and a mature nuttiness with long hints of honey on the finish.

As we left, we walked through the formal gardens, with flowerbeds lined with neatly trimmed box hedges, with lavender and thyme, and past the *enoteca*, with its tempting bottles. The track took us past some vineyards and back into the woods. There was a tiny shrine where someone had left some fresh flowers for All Saints Day, and then we reached the turning for Valtellina. I had first visited this tiny estate when it was the property of Giorgio Regni, but since then it has been sold to a German family, Fuchs, and in their absence is run by their likeable Swiss winemaker, Andreas Stössel. There are just eight hectares of vines, in a natural amphitheatre, which protects them from the north-east winds. The cellar is neat and compact, with *barriques* and *botti*, as it was in Giorgio Regni's day. We tasted and Andreas explained that his aim was to make wines that would age. The Chianti *normale* is mainly Sangiovese, as well as grapes from a very old mixed vineyard of Colorino, Ciliegiolo, Malvasia and Canaiolo, with some appealing fresh fruit and firm tannins. The 1997 Chianti *riserva* spent two years in wood, mainly *botti*, and exuded rich cedary fruit, while the 1999 *riserva* was more structured and concentrated. Next came Convivio, a blend of 25 per cent Cabernet Sauvignon with Sangiovese that is aged in *barriques* for two years, with a smoky nose and dry cassis fruit on the palate; the Cabernet gives the wine more body and weight. The first vintage of the pure Merlot, Il Duca di Montechioccioli, named after the previous proprietor of this particular vineyard, was 1995. We tasted the 1998, which was rich and oaky, with dense fruit and concentration. Andreas admitted ruefully that the first vintage had been 'Parkerized' with a rave review from the American wine critic Robert Parker, and the wine simply took off. The Fuchs family has also bought land in the Maremma, in the DOC of Capalbio, where they have planted Cabernet, both Franc and Sauvignon, as well as Merlot, Sangiovese, Alicante, which is the local name for Grenache Noir, and Petit Verdot. The conditions are much warmer than in the heart of Chianti, but as yet the nine hectares are not in production.

The road took us back into the woods and past a farmhouse that was undergoing extensive restoration. Another solid farmhouse with imposing walls looked firmly closed and uninhabited, and then the path took us into the little village of Rietine, where we tracked down Galina Lazarides. Despite her name, she is British, and is married to a Swiss, Mario Caffuri. She explained how they bought a house in Radda when they first married back in 1970, together with some olive trees and half a hectare of vines. Then in the mid-1980s they began looking for a winery, and in 1989 found Rietine. The previous owners had simply sold the wine *sfuso*; they did their first bottling in 1992, and now have 12 hectares of vines, of which they have replanted nine, as so many vines were missing. Their Chianti *normale* is a blend of Sangiovese, with 20 per cent Merlot. Sangiovese does not always ripen properly, so the Merlot adds structure, filling out the palate. In contrast the *riserva* is a pure Sangiovese, with a proportion aged in *barriques* to give a tightly structured wine with some firm fruit. And most original was Tiziano, a blend of Merlot and Lambrusco, the grape more commonly found in Emilia Romagna for sparkling red wine. Lambrusco was already in the vineyards so they decided to keep it. The 1997 Tiziano had an intriguing tarry character, with some smoky fruit and rugged tannins, while the 1999 was more chocolatey in character, and quite unusual.

A short walk on the tarmac road from Rietine led to Rocca di Castagnoli, a cluster of houses dominated by a church. The director, Marco Crini, and his winemaker, Maurizio Alongi, showed us round the cellar. They explained how Rocca di Castagnoli is made up of four different farms; the main vineyards are here, and there is land at nearby San Sano below Lecchi, and in Castellina, as well as some vineyards at Rapolana between Siena and Arezzo where they make an IGT, rather than Chianti Colli Senesi. Altogether they have 230 hectares of vines, including 170 of Chianti Classico, which makes them one of the largest estates of the area, and there are also five or six thousand olive trees. These days the estate is the property of a Milanese lawyer, but like Meleto it was once part of the vast landholdings of the Ricasoli family. There is a large functional cellar behind a discreet wall at the entrance to the village. Much more atmospheric is the barrel cellar in La Rocca, the old castle, with its simple brick arches in the traditional Tuscan style. However, there was an ultra-modern system for turning the barrels, a black frame allowing stacks three barrels high, and permitting an automatic lees stirring. It is expensive to install but saves on labour, both in terms of time and expense. There are *botti* for the Chianti, as well as *tonneaux* and *barriques* for other wines. A document dated 1050 refers to La Rocca when it was linked to Badia a Coltibuono, while the villa dates from 1700, with a cluster of houses around it, in varying states of repair or disrepair. Some are being renovated for *agriturismo*. Altogether some fifty people live in the village.

We tasted in a light airy room with the most breathtaking views over the surrounding countryside, looking over the never-ending folds of hills of Chianti in the weak autumnal sunshine. There is no doubt that they make an impressive range of wines at Rocca di Castagnoli, seven in all. First there was Molino delle Balze, from a vineyard of Chardonnay that was planted at the end of the 1980s, at an altitude of 800 metres. Only a third of it is fermented in oak and consequently it was refreshingly elegant, compared to some Tuscan Chardonnay. Their Chianti Classico, which is a blend originating from all three estates, is mainly Sangiovese, with a drop of Canaiolo and also of Merlot, which has a welcome softening effect, as the wines round this part of Chianti can be quite tough and acidic. Maurizio explained that the Merlot had not softened the intrinsic taste of the Chianti; it had simply filled out the fruit, so that the wine still retained the benchmark notes of ripe cherry fruit, after a year's ageing in 30-hectolitre *botti*.

Poggio ai Frati, from a single nearby vineyard, planted with Sangiovese and a little Canaiolo, is the traditional *riserva* of the estate. It has been aged in 500-litre *tonneaux* and was elegant and sturdy, with firmer tannins than the *normale*, and attractive cherry fruit. Capraia, from the vineyards near Castellina, includes some Cabernet Sauvignon as well as Colorino with 85 per cent Sangiovese. It spends eighteen months in *barrique* and the Cabernet Sauvignon made it more international in style, as did the more obvious oak. However, they consider that there is a return to the traditional taste of Tuscany, with a concentration on Sangiovese. Le Stielle from the vineyard by the cellars, which we had passed on our way into the village, is an IGT, a blend of Sangiovese and Cabernet Sauvignon, with eighteen months' ageing in *barrique*. It was elegant and stylish, an appealing and successful marriage of two grape varieties. A couple more IGT followed, Merlot Le Pratole, from a vineyard in Gaiole, which was ripe and rounded with some body and weight, and Buriano, a Cabernet Sauvignon with some firm blackcurrant fruit and a backbone of tannin. There is no doubt that the wines of Rocca di Castagnoli have the hallmark of elegance.

Just outside the village we took a track down through the olive groves and found a picnic spot looking across the valley where land was being prepared for new vineyards. A large yellow digger was at work, excavating large rocks. We carried on down the hill, over a stream and then climbed up the other side of the valley, past a couple of firmly shuttered houses and into woods of sweet chestnut. We spotted the occasional mushroom, but no identifiable *porcini*, and the path slowly climbed and joined a wider track that led into the tiny village of Barbischio. Just outside is a tiny cemetery; there were fresh flowers at every gravestone, while the village is dominated by a tenth-century tower that looked recently restored and inhabited. A group of American walkers were taking photographs of each other; we ignored them and continued on through the village, to find that the road petered out by a house with its facade covered in old farming artefacts. A track carried on down the hill through the woods and at the bottom we followed the stream to emerge onto the road by an old farmhouse that had once been the village mill. We turned towards Gaiole and came to the wrought-iron gate at the entrance to Montiverdi.

The driveway takes you up into the hills above Gaiole, offering wide sweeping views over the town on one side and toward Meleto and the cellars of the Agricoltori del Chianti Geografico on the other side. We had a meeting with Graziella Ferrari, a charming Milanese, who runs the estate for the absentee owners. She explained how the owner, Nicolò Longo, originated from Puglia and made his money in heating engineering. He bought this land from nearby Badia a Coltibuono in 1972 and gradually planted vines where there had once been none, but just a chicken farm. There are now 20 hectares of vines, as well as woods and olive trees, on the other 30 hectares. This has remained a very traditional estate, with the classic *bottaia* of enormous *botti* holding the wine of several vintages. The biggest is a breathtaking 120 hectolitres. And there was that convincing vinous smell; your nose alone told you that you could be nowhere but in a wine cellar. There were *barriques* for the *crus*, and cement vats for fermentation, making what Graziella called *la vera cantina toscana*, the true Tuscan wine cellar.

As for the wines, Graziella suggested that their main characteristic was elegance, and that they needed time. This was certainly true, for the 1998 vintage had only been bottled in 2002; it was quite light in colour, with firm cherries on the palate, elegant, with an indefinable old-fashioned feel about it, but none the worse for that. The 1998 *riserva*, a selection of their best vineyards, was more substantial and tannic, again with some firm fruit. Next came Il Cipressone, a blend of equal parts of Sangiovese and Cabernet Sauvignon, with some cedary fruit. Ventesimo, created to mark the twentieth anniversary of the purchase of the estate, is a blend of Sangiovese with small parts of Cabernet and Merlot, which give the wine more body and weight. 1993 Vigneto Carpinaia, a pure Sangiovese, was long and elegant, with mature vegetal notes, while 1997 Le Borranine, a pure Cabernet Sauvignon, had some sturdy young blackcurrant fruit. I had visited Montiverdi without any preconceptions; somehow the mainstream of Chianti Classico seems to have passed them by, but the wines provided a pleasant backwater of tradition. And from there the road took us back to Gaiole.

VIN SANTO

VIN SANTO IS THE traditional dessert wine of Tuscany, and most estates make a little to offer to friends and family, even if they do not sell it. It relies upon the process of *appassimento*, of drying healthy, ripe grapes, usually Trebbiano and Malvasia Bianca, in a well-ventilated place, so they shrivel and become raisin-like. After pressing, which is easier said than done, the viscous juice is put into small barrels, traditionally called *caratelli*, where it very slowly ferments, and remains for a minimum of three years, but often longer, with the bung sealed with cement or wax. Permutations in the process entail the amount of air left in the barrel; more will make for a drier wine, but one of the charms of Vin Santo is its unpredictability. Some producers favour the use of a *madre*, the lees of the previous wine in the barrel, believing that it enhances the flavour. Others disagree, arguing that it is better for the wine to be an orphan than have a bad mother. Theories as to the origin of the name abound, of which more in the pages of this book. And the wine is inevitably expensive, as so little is produced, after the *appassimento* and the ageing in barrel, during which time a considerable amount of wine evaporates. Traditionally Vin Santo is drunk with *cantuccini* biscuits, as a delicious finale to a meal.

A word of warning – avoid Vin Santo with the mention *liquoroso* on the label, for this implies that the wine has been fortified, by the addition of alcohol, which is contrary to the concept of true Vin Santo.

From the Castello di Brolio
· *November, with some cellar visits in February* ·

South of Gaiole-in-Chianti; San Felice and the frantoio at Villa Sesta,
Castello di Cacchiano, Rocca di Montegrossi, Castello di Bossi and San
Giusto a Rentennano

THE CASTELLO DI BROLIO is one of the historic estates of Chianti, for this is where the Barone Bettino Ricasoli, the great-great-grandfather of the present baron, conducted his experiments with the *governo* method and with the blends of different grape varieties to create the forerunner of the modern Chianti. Since then Chianti Classico has moved on, with the advent of modern vinification methods that no longer necessitate the softening effects of the *governo*, nor the need to add white grapes to the blend. Initially Brolio was the property of the Vallombrosan monks, until the Ricasoli family arrived here in 1141, following an exchange of land. However, they are known to have been settled in Tuscany since 770, which makes them one of the oldest recorded families of the region. They were powerful warriors, supporting the Florentines against the Sienese, and the castle of Brolio was destroyed on numerous occasions. It was rebuilt for the last time in 1486 by the city of Florence in gratitude for services rendered during the wars. At one time the Ricasoli family owned other large estates in Chianti, Meleto, Castagnoli and Montefiridolfi, while the Castello di Cacchiano belongs to their cousins. Brolio was one of the very first estates to bottle its wines back in the eighteenth century.

The estate had a chequered history during the latter half of the twentieth century; not only were there family vineyards, but also a merchant business, which was sold to the large international company, Seagrams, in the mid-1960s by the present baron, who had inherited a difficult financial situation and needed capital. Subsequently the company was bought by United Wine Producers, which in turn sold a controlling share to the Australian company BRL Hardy. This meant that although the Ricasoli family still retained their vineyards, all their grapes were destined for the merchant house. It was not a happy situation and Francesco Ricasoli, the son of the present baron, realized that something needed to be done: that either he and his father had to invest in their vineyards, or sell the estate. He chose the first option and managed to acquire the company back from Hardy's; he admitted that it was a gamble, that everyone thought he was mad, and that it would never have been possible if the company had been financially viable. He can look back over the last ten years with pride and measure his achievement by the recognition of the *Gambero Rosso*, one of Italy's most influential wine guides. In 1993 there was no mention at all of Brolio in the *Gambero Rosso*; in 2002 the Castello di Brolio was named the winery of the year.

Francesco explained how they were making as many as thirty-five different wines when he took over. He set about streamlining the range, insisting on the importance of quality in quantity, providing a critical global mass at a reasonable price. It has been what he called '*una sfida affascinante*': a fascinating challenge. The range of wines is now reduced to just two wines from the family vineyards, Brolio, and Castello di Brolio. The difference between the two is one of selection; Francesco dislikes the term *riserva* for he considers that it does not tell the consumer much, as a *riserva* can vary so much in style and quality. Also, some of the most successful wines of Tuscany are IGT, whereas Brolio has to be successful as a Chianti Classico, and similarly the Castello di Brolio, not because it is a *riserva*, but because its quality is indisputable. Since my visit, Francesco, along with five other leading Chianti Classico producers, namely Castello di Ama, Fonterutoli, La Massa, Le Corti and Podere il Palazzino, have joined together to work for what they are calling a Super Chianti Classico, in preference to making either a *riserva* or an IGT, thereby emphasizing their Chianti Classico as their very best wine, and the truest expression of their *terroir* and its tipicity.

The 2000 Brolio, with its elegant label taken from a painting of the castle from the 1930s, has sturdy ripe cherry fruit, with freshness and vivacity, while the Castello di Brolio, made for the first time in 1997, has more stature, but with an underlying elegance. It spends eighteen months in *barriques*, whereas the Brolio is kept in cement or concrete vats, as well as large barrels. Four or five other wines are made from bought grapes, sometimes blended with their own, namely Casalferro, a Sangiovese and Merlot blend; Torricella a

Chardonnay; Formule, a pure Sangiovese; Rocca Guicciarda, a Chianti Classico *riserva,* and then there is Vin Santo. Essentially they concentrate on Brolio.

The cellars have undergone an impressive renovation since my last visit back in the Seagrams days. Many of the old concrete vats have been destroyed – easier said than done as they were built to last and are well nigh indestructible – and they now have several magnificent barrel halls housing some 6000 *barriques* altogether. There is also a welcoming *enoteca* where passing wine enthusiasts may taste and buy.

Francesco himself is something of a surprise. He was a very successful photographer with his own studio, concentrating on fashion accessories, and once he had taken the decision to resurrect the fortunes of his family vineyards he closed down his studio and moved into wine in the matter of a couple of weeks. For someone with an artistic bent, he has an astonishing amount of business acumen. We chatted over dinner in his local restaurant in the hamlet of Villa Sesta, the Bottega del Trento, with its original flavours and eccentric owner. Francesco is a perceptive observer of Chianti; he talked about the new players in Tuscany, observing how the new generation is more motivated and more focused than their parents. There is also a greater awareness of business demands. Many estates will not survive; they will either be sold or will close down. We also talked about food, for cooking is a great enthusiasm, and he expressed a passion for cowrie shells, producing one from his jacket pocket.

The next day we walked up the cypress-lined driveway to the castle of Brolio, past what was described as *un bosco inglese*, an English wood, which was planted by the first Barone Bettino Ricasoli in the 1840s. It includes fine examples of sequoia, cedars of Lebanon and other trees, some of which still have splinters of shrapnel, a reminder of the fighting that took place here during the Second World War. Further up the hill there is an old icehouse built of red brick. The castle is open on occasions to the public. You have to pull a heavy bell cord, which hangs down from the castle wall, and a bell clangs loudly in the courtyard. A notice informs that you may have a ten- or fifteen-minute wait, and after a while the imposing door opens electronically to allow you access and a custodian appears to proffer an entry ticket. The castle is an architectural hotchpotch in sombre grey stone with a red-brick addition with arched gothic windows from the nineteenth century, reminiscent of the Scottish baronial style. You can visit the chapel with its painted walls, and underneath there is the crypt of the Ricasoli family, with the tombs of Bettino and his wife Anna, amongst others, all with fresh flowers for All Souls' Day. We walked round the walls, looking down on a formal garden with neat box hedges, and views over the vineyards towards San Felice and Cacchiano. A plaque informs you that the Grand Duke of Austria, Leopold, stayed here in July 1773.

We walked down the hill past a vineyard. Two bulldozers were at work, excavating enormous piles of stone. These days it is no longer necessary to leave the land fallow as the diggers can extricate all the old vine roots. They work in pairs, one to dig and the other to sieve the earth, removing stones and roots; then, depending on the amount of clay in the soil, drainage pipes are usually necessary. We went past a little shrine, and then a small chapel in a grove of cypress trees, and past a vineyard of tiny young vines. Posts were lying on the ground waiting to be installed with wire trellising. The path continued towards San Felice and we fell into conversation with a friendly American couple, who were staying in the hotel at San Felice and hurrying back for a cellar tour. They came from Oregon, but my reference to Pinot Noir did not excite a response; instead, we discussed Italian driving habits!

San Felice is a pretty little hamlet, essentially comprising a wine estate and a smart hotel in the main villa. The population of San Felice totals just fifteen people these days and the hamlet belongs to the German insurance company Allianz. However, you feel that the wine estate is left very successfully to its own devices, with Leonardo Bellaccini, who has been the winemaker here since 1984. San Felice has a total of 190 hectares of vines, including 120 for Chianti Classico as well as vineyards for IGT. They were very much involved in the Chianti Classico 2000 project, conducting experiments with microvinifications of different clones, rootstock and pruning systems. They have also worked on old varieties, names I had never heard of, like Pugnitello, Abrostine and Volpolo. The Pugnitello has proved particularly satisfactory and they have finally obtained permission to plant more. San Felice has always had a reputation for experimentation; the former manager, Enzo Morgante, was the first winemaker to produce a pure Sangiovese, Vigorello, back in 1968, and from 1979 he took the then revolutionary step of including a small percentage of Cabernet Sauvignon in it. The wine has evolved over the years so that the blend is now 45 per cent Sangiovese, 40 per cent Cabernet and 15 per cent Merlot, and given as much as 22 months' barrel ageing. We later drank the 1999 Vigorello with a barbecued *bistecca alla fiorentina*; the oak was still very obvious, but the wine was rich and rounded, promising a long life.

Their *cru* Poggio Rosso has also evolved over the years; first it was kept in *botti;* then in *barriques* and then in 500-litre *tonneaux.* Now they are returning to *barriques.* Leonardo explained that it is easy to overdo the oak; tannins need oxygen, so with the 500-litre *tonneaux* you obtain a good balance on the nose but not enough suppleness in the mouth, whereas with the 225-litre barrels, the opposite is true. Now they are going to try the malolactic fermentation in wood, which should also have a softening effect. The 1999 Poggio Rosso, from the vineyard just by the hamlet, is Sangiovese with 10 per cent Colorino; it was quite sturdy and oaky, but with some rich fruit. Leonardo observed that you must control the yields of the Colorino; otherwise you just get colour and water. Il Grigio is a pure Sangiovese and a blend of several different vineyards; it is kept in large *botti,* as well as old *barriques,* and is more classically Chianti in style.

The chapel at San Felice is worth a visit. There are murals by Enzo Cini, a follower of Chagall, portraying the evolution of humanity, from monkeys to the Etruscans and then to the present day; and behind the altar another mural depicts people from different religions. Most moving of all was a sculpture of the Crucifixion carved from an olive branch from a tree that had died in the great frost of 1985, which destroyed many of the olive trees that had survived the earlier hard winter of 1956. The altar too is made from olive wood.

Then they took us to see the *frantoio* at nearby Villa Sesta. An intoxicating smell of fresh oil assailed our nostrils. Leonardo explained how the olives, both black and green, are hand washed; the leaves removed and the olives crushed in the olive mill, producing a brown paste that looks not unlike a *tapenade.* The oil then coagulates, so that the solids are separated from the liquid, which in turn is centrifuged to separate the oil from the water. One hundred kilos of olives will produce just 15.5 litres of oil. We watched the fresh oil drip out slowly into a stainless-steel container. A notice warned: '*È severamente vietato di assaggiare l'olio.'* It is strictly forbidden to taste the oil. It was very tempting, but we were lucky, we were invited to lunch, and for a meal that was designed to show fresh oil at its very best. There was *cecino*, a crisp bread made with oil and flavoured with rosemary; *bruschetta* was sprinkled with a little salt and an optional rub of garlic and doused rather than drizzled with oil. That classic Tuscan vegetable soup, *ribolita*, provided a vehicle for yet more oil, as did the barbecued steak. Leonardo explained how his mother cured olives: you dry them in an oven in order to remove any bitter flavours, and then you add garlic, orange skins and parsley and leave for a few days. It sounded delicious.

From San Felice we took the path through what they called the Vitiarium, a vine-covered pathway, with views back towards Brolio and the hamlet of San Felice at the other end. From there the track continued into woods and down to a babbling stream, which was deeper than usual following the recent heavy rain. We managed to ford it without getting too wet and continued up through the woods, past bushes of pyracantha with bright red berries, and juniper with black berries, to join a track by some vineyards. We continued past what had once been the church of Nebbiano, which is now converted into a private house, and then we turned down a track through Brolio's Torricello vineyard, a vast expanse of vines changing colour, with splashes of oranges, yellow and a surprisingly deep red. Red is indicative of Colorino, and also Merlot, while Sangiovese tends to yellow; in contrast, Cabernet Sauvignon keeps its leaves for much longer, and was only just beginning to turn colour. The track followed the valley floor, above a large drainage system; every 15 metres you could see a wide pipe, with an overflow, under a grate, which Francesco Ricasoli had explained was essential as there is so much·clay in the soil. The house of Torricello seemed to be undergoing serious renovation, for it had recently been sold. The track continued past yet more Brolio vineyards, affording views across the valley towards the Castello di Cacchiano, Rocca di Montegrossi and the village of Monti. An old man had stopped to pick some grapes that had been left hanging in the vineyard. Are they any good? I asked. No, they are much too sour, he said and spat them out.

We followed the road back towards Brolio. A couple of estate workers were out, one cutting down the weeds among the cypress trees while the other was much more interested in looking for *porcini*, and indeed there was quite a haul in the back of his van. However, we remembered what the restaurant had said the previous evening, that it is too late in the season for *porcini* and that they are now full of worms. Certainly the only fungi we had spotted in the woods were of the non-edible variety. We continued on our way back past the castle, enjoying imposing views of the grey walls and the somewhat incongruous brick addition, and back down the alleyway of cypress trees to our car at the bottom of the hill.

Our next appointment, the following day, was at the Castello di Cacchiano, which has belonged to the Ricasoli-Firidolfi family since the middle of the twelfth century. The castle was destroyed by the Aragonese in 1478, but rebuilt by the Florentine republic in recognition of the family's loyalty. Today the property is run by Giovanni Ricasoli-Firidolfi, while his brother Marco has created his own estate at Rocca di Montegrossi, after a division of the vineyards of Cacchiano in 1998. Their mother, Elisabetta, continues to play an active part in the estate whose reputation she helped to create, for originally the wines of Cacchiano were sold *sfuso* to Brolio. The first bottling was only in 1974, sadly a year after Elisabetta's husband died. It was Elisabetta who showed us round the cellars; she is *une femme formidable* in the nicest possible way, exuding confidence and ability, with an aristocratic friendliness. But first there was a comic scene: Elisabetta had left her keys to the castle in Florence, so we witnessed her banging loudly and energetically on the solid oak door, with an equally solid metal knocker. There is no electric doorbell here. Her knocks became louder, with growing impatience, and eventually an elderly housekeeper appeared, shuffling in her slippers, complaining under her breath that she had been in the kitchen and hadn't heard the knock.

You sense that this is an estate that is keeping apace of new developments. The oldest vines were planted by Giovanni's father in the early 1970s, and the newest in 1999, with a density of 9200 vines per hectare, while some extensive planting in 1985 included two experimental vineyards for the Chianti 2000 project. There are 30 hectares altogether in the valley towards Monti, with more behind the castle, adjoining San Felice and Brolio, with extensive views over the hills towards Meleto and Vertine. The cellars combine the modern and the traditional. There are concrete vats alongside new oak conical vats. The wood entails more work and you cannot control the temperature as easily, but it does give better results, fixing the colour and the tannins, making a wine that will age. *Barriques* were first used for the 1984 vintage, housed in a series of small cellars, one of which had previously been used for storing potatoes. And the wines are finely crafted. They no longer have any Trebbiano so the *bianco* is a pure Malvasia, with fresh herbal notes. A Toscano Rosso is mainly Sangiovese with 'a little of everything else', making for some ripe cherry fruit after a few months in *botti*. The 1999 Chianti Classico *normale*, from Sangiovese with just a drop of Merlot, had some soft cherry fruit – 1999 is above all characterized by fruit – and it was elegant and beautifully balanced. And only in the very best years do they make Millennio, their *riserva*. A *riserva* really must be outstanding, and not merely represent commercial expediency. We compared 1995 and 1997; the 1995 was stylishly elegant with some cedary fruit, while the 1997 was richer and more structured, but with an underlying similarity of balance and elegance.

We timed our arrival at Rocca di Montegrossi to see the preparation of the grapes destined for Vin Santo. Bunches of Malvasia that had been hanging from plastic nets on movable frames for several months were being carefully sorted before going to the press. The mobility of the frames enables you to meticulously check the grapes for any grey rot during the drying process. By early February they looked like little dry currants and I wondered if there was any juice in them at all. At Rocca di Montegrossi they rely on ventilators to dry the grapes, rather than the uncertain process of an open window, entailing a discussion of what Elisabetta called *la politica della finestra*. The first three weeks of drying are the most critical; the more water the grapes lose, the less risk there is of grey rot. The next day we had an opportunity to taste the juice. It looked very murky, a sludgy brown colour and to my nose it was not particularly appealing, but rather stalky. However, on the palate it was viscous and sweet. Marco Ricasoli explained how his Vin Santo is aged in three different woods, mulberry, cherry and oak, with seven years in *caratelli*, to become what he called 'a small jewel'.

The very first vintage of Rocca di Montegrossi was 1994 and since 1998 Marco has been working with one of Tuscany's leading oenologists, Attilio Pagli. Marco laid down some ground rules right at the beginning: that he did not want his wines to be too oaky, and he also insisted that the basic Chianti Classico *normale* should be his best wine, while the *riserva*, San Marcellino, named after a tiny church on the estate, represents the icing on the cake. Then there is Geremia, after Geremia Ricasoli from the Castello di Meleto, which has been changed from a pure Sangiovese to a super-Tuscan Merlot and Cabernet Sauvignon blend. The wines have an elegance combined with structure and the *energia* of Sangiovese, with the promise of fine ageing potential, while the cellar includes the best of modern winemaking philosophies. The wooden vats have metal plates for temperature control and are organized for automatic *pigiatura*; both the humidity and temperature can be regulated in the *barricaia* and there is no cultured yeast, no concentration machine and no filter, with the winemaking representing an accumulation of many little details.

Just down the road from San Felice is the Castello di Bossi. Marco Bucci is genial and relaxed, with an underlying energy and professionalism in his approach. He explained that his family's main business is in the clothing industry in Prato and that they had bought the Castello di Bossi in 1980. Altogether there are 124 hectares of vines on the 650-hectare estate, with many of the vineyards planted in the 1970s, so that they are now replanting extensively. However, they have found some old Cabernet and Merlot vines, which would have been amongst the first planted in Chianti.

There was once a defence garrison here, with a tower dating from 1170. The more substantial castle was built in the fourteenth century around a courtyard. There are views in every direction, across the valley to Cacchiano and to the estate of Castell'in Villa. A fireplace in the large reception room is dated 1500, with a carving of bread and fish, which is also depicted on their labels. The wines represent an intriguing range: the Chianti *normale* has firm cherry fruit, after eight months ageing in old *botti*. The *riserva* Berardo is quite a contrast and Marco explained that, for this wine, their aim is a Chianti with a long life, for a *riserva* should be quite different from a *normale*; it comes from just one vineyard of Sangiovese and a little Merlot and is aged in *barriques* after a three-week maceration. The flavour was rich and sturdy, and with oodles of potential, but the purist in me asked: is this really Chianti? Somehow the combination of Merlot and *barriques* seems to give it a certain international ring that was not truly Tuscan. Corbaia is another *cru*, a blend of 70 per cent Sangiovese, from an old vineyard, with Cabernet Sauvignon, which spend between eighteen and twenty-four months in *barriques*. Again, the Cabernet immediately makes for a more international flavour, with rich cassis fruit, a firm backbone of tannin and a long powerful finish. Finally there was Girolamo, a pure Merlot from thirty-year-old vines, with a rich, intense nose and the ripe fleshiness of the Merlot. It was much more accessible than Corbaia, and for Marco the most representative of Castello di Bossi. He talked of other projects: they have planted vineyards in the Maremma, near Tallone, with Sangiovese, Cabernet and Merlot and also some Vermentino, a clone from Corsica. Also they have bought land in Montalcino, which they are currently replanting. You sense that nothing will stand still here.

Even further down the road is San Giusto a Rentennano. An eleventh-century castle was destroyed and the villa dates from the sixteenth century, standing next to a cluster of houses. A hound called Moses was surveying the various comings and goings. The estate is run by two brothers, Francesco and Luca Martini di Cigala. Once this land had belonged to the Ricasoli family, for the brothers' paternal grandmother was a Ricasoli. Francesco took us to see the old attic where they dry their Vin Santo grapes; in sharp contrast to Rocca di Montegrossi here they put the grapes on straw mats and the large windows are left wide open. Down in the cellar we could see the lees left from the first pressing; they were still very liquid and sludgy, and really not inviting, but definitely worth a second pressing. We wandered through a labyrinth of cellars, with Francesco's brother Luca, who explained that they have 28 hectares of vines altogether, in three different spots, close by, at Monti and by the Arbia river. We tasted in a snug room with a blazing fire. The wines were as good as I had remembered them on an earlier visit. Luca is very pleased with the Chianti 2000 and rightly so, for it exuded the fresh fruit of dry cherries, and was 'very Chianti' but not a wine for ageing. The 1999 *riserva*, kept in barrel and *botti* for twenty months, was structured and elegant, and Percarlo, a pure Sangiovese, and a selection of the best grapes, which usually come from an old vineyard planted in the 1970s, was finely crafted, with cedary smoky fruit and an elegant finish. 1983 was the first vintage of this wine, while the first bottling of the estate's Chianti was 1978. Next was La Rocorma, a pure Merlot, which was first made in 1996 from vines planted in 1993. It was much richer, but less elegant than Percarlo, and Luca admitted that they still had a lot to learn about Merlot. 'If you pick it too late, it goes flabby.' We finished with 1995 Vin Santo, with Luca explaining that this would be the last vintage to be called Vin Santo. Instead the wine will be called Vin San Giusto. The reason is one of alcohol content in the face of bureaucracy. The DOC for Chianti Classico Vin Santo was created in 1995 and demands a minimum alcoholic degree of 13°, whereas their wine is usually only 12°. Luca felt that there was an error in the regulations, in that they should insist on a minimum sugar, not a minimum alcohol, level. The wine was deep brown with a yellow-green rim and rich raisiny nose. On the palate it was intense and unctuous, rich and raisiny with a dry finish. It seemed incredible that such liquid gold could come from the brown sludge that we had seen earlier in the cellar.

Around Felsina Berardenga
· November ·

North of Castelnuovo Berardenga

WE ARRIVED EARLY FOR our appointment with Giuseppe Mazzocolin so that we could walk through his vineyards first. It was one of those sunny, almost warm days of autumn that are too good to be true, and Giuseppe was distracted by the sunshine; it was much too nice a day to be confined to an office and he succumbed to the temptation of joining us for a walk, which was to our definite advantage, for we now had a guide, and a knowledgeable one at that. Giuseppe is a fountain of information about Tuscan culture. However, he was not born into wine. In a previous existence he had taught Italian literature, specializing in Dante, and came to wine through marriage, for Felsina is the property of his father-in-law. Gloria's father had bought the estate in 1966, when it was an *azienda di caccia*, a hunting estate, with just two and half hectares of vines, as well as eleven farmhouses and lots of olive trees. Giuseppe first began working here in 1975 and since 1981 has devoted his energy and enthusiasm to making some of the best wines of Chianti Classico, with the help of his consultant oenologist, Franco Bernabei.

Felsina is on the southernmost edge of Chianti Classico, just north of the town of Castelnuovo Berardenga. You approach it along an alleyway of cypress trees to come into an attractive courtyard. A large family of grey cats with countless fluffy kittens were snoozing in the sunshine. Giuseppe explained how each century had left something. The earliest written mention of Felsina dates back to the twelfth century, while the original house was built in the seventeenth century, when it was a guest house, not far from the pilgrims' route of the Via Francigena. The small chapel with its soft pastel-coloured walls was built at the end of the eighteenth century. You enter the cellar through a solid wooden door, locked with quite one of the largest keys I have ever seen, but first we explored the vineyards. Giuseppe led the way down a dirt track towards another tiny chapel, surrounded by cypress trees, and explained that the track, on the edge of the valley of the Ombrone, provided the boundary between Chianti Classico and the Colli Senesi, with Sangiovese planted on the left and Cabernet Sauvignon on the right. And there is a difference in the landscape. If you look south towards the Creti Senesi, the countryside changes, from vineyards to open hills of wheat and grazing land. 'It's another world,' Giuseppe said, '*un paese stregato*, a bewitched landscape.' There are no vines or olive trees, just sheep and wheat.

Then we passed an old vineyard that Giuseppe has just bought for its indigenous clones of Sangiovese; for every row of olive trees, there are two rows of vines. Giuseppe enthused about his olive oil, how this year he is picking every variety separately, and according to the maturity of each plant. In past years all the olives have been mixed up together, but there are quite discernible differences between the varieties. Thanks to the earlier rain and sunshine, weeds were rampant in the vineyards, almost smothering some young vines. Giuseppe talked about his replanting programme; he bought the nearby estate of Pagliarese in 1995, which has enabled him to maintain the same number of hectares in production while renewing some of his older vineyards.

Our path took us up to the old farmhouse of Rancia, which gives its name to Giuseppe's Chianti Classico *cru*. There is a written reference to Rancia dated 1165, to the *strata* (sic) *di Rancia*, which was a Roman road. The name Rancia originates in *granaia*, meaning a grange or barn where grain is stored, and the house was inhabited until the hard frost of 1956 which destroyed so many of the olive trees, for the farmers here made their living from oil rather than wine. It is a beautiful spot, with views towards the Creti Senesi, even the towers of Siena itself in the haze. We suggested to Giuseppe that he should restore the house so that we could rent it as an *agriturismo* one summer; he protested that he had other more pressing investments to consider. But there was no doubt that Rancia would provide an enchanting base for a Tuscan holiday, with elegant porticos and views over the vineyards. We walked through the woods, which are a hunting reserve for pheasants, and emerged into a clearing where there were enormous chunks of rocks, dug from land that was to be replanted with vines. The white *albarese* rock, which almost glistened in the sunlight, formed a stark contrast against the rich brown soil and clear blue sky. It was a dramatic sight.

*

Back at Felsina we went down into the cellars. The design is cunning. You go through the old stables, with their tall arches and high oval *botti* fitting into each original stall and an old basket press displayed at the end, and then you follow a gentle slope into the large barrel cellar, filled with countless *barriques*. It looks as though it is a natural continuation of the stables but was built 250 years later, deceptively, from old materials, so that the divide between the old and the new is imperceptible.

Then we had to admire the new *frantoio*. Giuseppe is very proud of the new system, which avoids any oxidation of the oil. Any leaves are removed, the olives are washed and the stones removed. Then the olives are very slowly mashed into a paste, under a blanket of nitrogen, which prevents the paste from turning brown. Without the olive stones, it is a much more gentle process. The oil and water are separated and the oil is run into small stainless-steel vats, still protected by nitrogen. To my inexpert eye, it all seemed very high-tech and beautifully streamlined. Giuseppe is excited: *Adesso comincia la storia per capire.* Now we are going to start understanding about oil. There are some five hundred different varieties of olive tree in Italy, as they grow all over the country, except in the Val d'Aosta. He explained how the removal of stones is the *metodo* Veronelli, after the eminent Italian wine writer, and Olioro is an association of the producers who follow this method. 'Vines are the present and olives the future,' he exclaimed. We tasted three oils from last year, out of tiny glasses. Pendolino is the pollinator, with a rich peppery nose and a hint of apples. Next came Leccino, which was distinctly peppery though softer on the finish, while Raggiolo was quite soft and rounded, with a touch of pepper on the finish. We concluded with some Leccino that had been pressed the previous day. It was a vivid fresh green, the result of the protection from oxygen, and deliciously fresh and ripe.

Wine-tasting with Giuseppe is always a pleasure, for he is thoughtful and discursive about his wines. This time we began with a 2000 Sauvignon from his other estate in the Colli Senesi, Castello di Farnetella, which had some fresh varietal character. The Sauvignon was grafted onto old Trebbiano vines back in 1984 and he first bottled the 1990 vintage. Next came I Sistri, his Chardonnay, which is made very much in the Burgundian way, fermented in oak and given regular lees stirring. It was rich and buttery, with some satisfying flavours, balanced with acidity. Chianti Colli Senesi, with a dash of Merlot, from a vineyard just 15 kilometres away from Felsina, was fresh and youthful with a refreshing astringency. Next came Lucilla, a blend of Sangiovese with 15 per cent Merlot and Cabernet Sauvignon, which was fuller and riper than the Chianti. Giuseppe explained how he keeps the estate at Farnatella for these international varieties the market demands. For him Chianti Classico is Sangiovese, and it must not be diluted with the likes of Cabernet or Merlot. He likes Sangiovese as a *monovitigno* – 'if I add Canaiolo, I impoverish the Sangiovese' – and Sangiovese will age beautifully, as older vintages of Giuseppe's wines always illustrate. 'The problem is that people need to be educated about Sangiovese.' His Chianti *normale* 2000 was structured with some cherry fruit and a certain smokiness; the 1999 Rancia Chianti Classico, which had spent sixteen months in *barriques*, was wonderfully elegant. Now he is punching down, rather than pumping over, during the fermentation, which gives more finesse as well as density. Finally we enjoyed another pure Sangiovese, Fontalloro, which is an IGT, for the legal reason that part of the vineyard is in Chianti Classico and part in the Colli Senesi. It was richer and more full-bodied than Rancia, more tannic and mouth-filling, with a long promising finish, and a good note on which to leave the vineyards of Chianti Classico.

SANGIOVESE

THE SANGIOVESE GRAPE is the backbone of most of the red wines of Tuscany and of central Italy. It comes in many guises, depending on where it is grown. In Chianti it is called *Sangioveto*, in Montalcino *brunello*, in Montepulciano *prugnolo* and in Scansano *morellino*. The name is said to derive from *sanguis Jovis*, or the blood of Jove, implying an ability to produce deep red wines, which in fact is not always the case, for there is considerable variation amongst the different clones of Sangiovese. Following the research of the Chianti 2000 project, it is now understood that some clones are very much better than others, and respond in different ways to different treatment. It is also recognized that there are two sub-varieties, Sangiovese Grosso and Sangiovese Piccolo; in fact, both produce pretty small berries.

Until fairly recently it was difficult to generalize about the characteristics of Sangiovese as Brunello di Montalcino was the only permitted varietal wine. That has now changed with the amendment to the *disciplinari* for Chianti Classico and the growing number of pure Sangiovese from the hills between Florence and Siena. Taste-wise, the distinguishing characteristic of Sangiovese is sour cherries, but they must be ripe cherries, so that there is fruit combined with a certain astringency of acidity, with some structured tannins. There should always be an underlying vivacity or *energia*. Often, but not always, it benefits from some subtle ageing in oak, possibly in larger rather than smaller barrels.

Chianti Rufina and Pomino

· April ·

East of Florence, including Frascole, the Castello di Nipozzano with the Frescobaldis, Selvapiana, Villa di Vetrice, Colognole and Pomino

FROM PONTASIEVE, EAST OF Florence, we took the narrow road that runs along the valley of the Sieve, through the little town of Rufina, which gives its name to this part of Chianti, and on to Dicomano. There we turned sharply uphill, following a steep winding route up to the little hamlet of Frascole, which is the northernmost estate of Rufina. Enrico Lippi explained how he had bought Frascole as a collection of ruined houses, without any proper cellar, back in 1992 and now runs the estate with his wife Elisa, and his sister Paola, who is married to Elisa's brother, Carlo. The previous owner had made *vino sfuso* and *vino da tavola*, but Enrico had quite different ambitions. He has carried out some extensive replanting of the vineyards and now has 15 hectares of vines, and 9 of olive trees. Here you are in the foothills of the Apennines and there is indeed an almost alpine atmosphere, a complete contrast from the hills of Chianti Classico, or the more gentle valley of the Arno. The vineyards lie at between 320 and 480 metres, and when the grapes are ripening in September there is always cold air blowing off the Apennines at night, so that the harvest is always at least a week later than further west down the valley, giving the wines of Rufina a structure and an acidity that you do not find in Chianti Classico.

Enrico now has a neat little cellar, with several vats and just two small rows of barrels. He said he buys so few he almost knows each barrel by name! A little *vinsantaia* has the traditional old chestnut barrels, sealed with large slabs of cement. They are left untouched for eight years, and the 1993 Vin Santo, which we drank later at dinner, was rich and unctuous, with a firm dry finish. As for Enrico's red wines, they were finely crafted, with an underlying elegance and firm backbone of tannin. His *riserva* benefits from just 10 per cent of Merlot, which softens some of the potential austerity of Rufina.

The next morning we awoke to birdsong and watched a falcon hovering over its prey in the vineyard below our feet. It was a sunny morning and one for a walk, with our destination the Etruscan remains up the hill. We set off past Enrico's newly planted vineyards, pinstriped with alternate rows of grass between the vines. Further up the hill there was a view back towards Frascole, an attractive cluster of houses, with cypress trees and parasol pines, and later the views opened up over the valley, with verdant pastureland enhancing the alpine atmosphere, alongside contrasting groves of olive trees. We passed a tiny walled cemetery with a small chapel, and then an old-fashioned vineyard, with the tall vines planted in wide rows, using trees as their supports. Next we came to a ruined villa, first passing two large pillars which constituted the original entrance to the estate, to reach the sadly neglected building, with an elegant double staircase up to the main entrance. It looked forlorn, its former glory long forgotten. According to Enrico, it had belonged to a noble Florentine family, and they had sold it, and now it has been sold again to some Venetians who are planning its restoration and possible conversion into a hotel. The Etruscan remains were at the top of the hill, with two tombs, excavated in 1988, surrounded by a ring of newly planted olive trees. It was a peaceful spot for a picnic, with no noise apart from the birdsong.

Frascole is an example of one of the several new estates in Rufina; in sharp contrast to Chianti Classico, the vineyards here are very much owned by local people, with little of the outside investment you find in more fashionable parts of Tuscany. Rufina is something of a rural backwater, but nonetheless boasts some serious estates. The Frescobaldis are one of the old Florentine families, who can trace their winemaking activities back to the fourteenth century, while their ownership of the Castello di Nipozzano dates from the end of the nineteenth century, when Leonia degli Albizzi married Angelo Frescobaldi in April 1863. The castle of Nipozzano was built in the tenth century by the Guidi family and occupied a strategic position on the road to Florence as an important garrison. Then in the 1300s it became the property of another powerful Florentine family, the Albizzi, who were enemies of the rulers of Florence, the Medici dukes, and consequently spent much of the ensuing three hundred years in exile. Vittorio, the brother of Leonia degli Albizzi, was born in France near Auxerre, and when his father summoned him back to

Florence in 1855, he brought cuttings of French vines, which explains why Pomino, the adjoining wine area to Rufina, includes some French grape varieties. There are records of wine production at Nipozzano since the 1500s. Today 220 hectares of the 580-hectare estate are devoted to vineyards, with olive trees, woods and arable land as well. Members of the public are greeted in a welcoming tasting room, which is decorated with old photographs and houses some defunct bottling equipment. You may also see the cellars, with the enormous *barricaia*. Tiziana Frescobaldi explained that they have a total of 9000 barrels, 1300 of which are housed at Nipozzano, and they buy around 1500 new barrels a year. The old *botti* that I remembered from an earlier visit have all gone.

Tiziana's uncle, Leonardo, has the quintessential elegance of an Italian aristocrat. His tweed three-piece suit would not have looked out of place in parts of Gloucestershire and his brilliantly polished shoes could well have come from Jermyn Street. We sat in an elegantly proportioned drawing room, with rather sombre furniture, and Leonardo talked about the family business, emphasizing that it is very much a family business, with a diversity of different estates throughout Tuscany, which are run as individual family properties. In addition to Nipozzano and Pomino, they have Castelgiocondo in Montalcino, where they produce not only Brunello di Montalcino, but also Luce, in partnership with Robert Mondavi from California; Castiglione in the Colli Fiorentini, and like so many others they are also investing in the Maremma, at Santa Maria, for Morellino di Scansano. In addition they have a 50 per cent share in Ornellaia, the Bolgheri estate that was created by Ludovico Antinori. Over lunch in the old kitchen with a large hearth, where you could have turned a spit, we savoured the wines of Nipozzano, beginning with the 1999 *riserva*. It is based on Sangiovese, with some Malvasia Nera, Merlot and just a drop of Cabernet Sauvignon, which had spent 24 months in barrel, and was wonderfully ripe with a firm backbone. The *cru*, Montesodi, a pure Sangiovese from the 21-hectare vineyard, given about eight months in barrel, had some appealing cedary fruit, while Mormoreto, another *cru* from a particular 20-hectare vineyard planted with Cabernet Sauvignon and Cabernet Franc, with some Merlot, again aged in barrel for two years, was riper with some intense cassis fruit and the influence of new oak. Leonardo explained that Cabernet and Merlot could sustain a longer ageing in oak than Sangiovese.

From Nipozzano it is a short downhill walk to Selvapiana, the other estate of international note in Rufina. We turned down a track through the vineyards of Nipozzano, all neatly pruned, with not a shoot out of place, nor a weed to be seen, heading towards a ruined house with, curiously, a neatly tended vegetable plot. Then we crossed a stream and followed the path into the woods, past carpets of primroses, violets and hellebores, to emerge a short while later into the vineyards of Selvapiana. There was a newly planted vineyard, the tiny vines barely discernible amongst the weeds, which had grown profusely following some spring rain. Someone had erected a flag, *PACE*, a demand for peace and a protest against the Iraq war, and the track passed the vineyard of Bucerchiale, the *cru* of Selvapiana.

I always enjoy visits to Selvapiana. The elderly owner, Dott. Francesco Giuntini, is one of the eccentrics of the Italian wine world. The previous time we had met, I found myself discussing English nursery rhymes, about which he knew a lot more than I did; he can also recite Edward Lear, which I cannot, and speaks impeccable, elegant English. In 1826 his ancestor Michele Giuntini, a successful banker, used his wealth to buy estates all over Tuscany, not just Selvapiana, but also La Parrina and Badia a Coltibuono. Today there are still family ties between these estates, and Dott. Giuntini is related through his mother to the Antinori family. His adopted son, the genial enthusiast Federico Massetti, whose father was the previous *fattore*, was born at Selvapiana, and now runs it, living there with his young family, so that you sense that it is very much a home for three generations.

Federico gave us a friendly welcome, apologizing for the chaos caused by the renovation and extension of the cellars. Vats were sitting outside by a cluster of cherry trees with deep-pink blossom, a line of washing adding to the rustic scene. A mobile bottling line was in full swing, the clatter of machinery rendering conversation well nigh impossible, so we adjourned to the cellars for a walk through the picturesque part, with rows of *botti* for their Chianti Rufina, and *barriques* for their *crus*, Bucerchiale and Fornace. Federico explained how they have stopped making *riserva* as they want to improve the quality of their basic Chianti Rufina; if you also make a *riserva*, your *normale* is inevitably going to suffer. They have stopped making white wine too, with 1998 the last vintage of Borro Lastricato, and they are working hard on their Vin Santo, which for my taste buds is one of the best in Tuscany, giving the grapes a longer period of drying, until March, and using small new *caratelli*. We talked about the influence of the *madre* or mother and how it can affect the level of sweetness; for Federico his wine seems sweeter without a mother. There are large earthenware *orci* of olive oil; Selvapiana used to have its own *frantoio*, and they are hoping to have one again.

We drank the wines over dinner with Dott. Giuntini; they have the elegant structured hallmark of Chianti Rufina. The Chianti 2000 had rounded cherry fruit; 1999 Fornace, which is mainly a Cabernet Sauvignon and Merlot blend, with just 20 per cent Sangiovese, was firm and structured but with a richness that contrasted with the pure Sangiovese, the 1999 Bucerchiale, which is more structured and tighter in flavour, with elegant complexity and the Vin Santo provided a delicious finale.

The next morning we went to see the Grati family. They have been making wine in Rufina since about 1900, although the parish church in Rufina has records of the name Grati from the fifteenth century. They own two estates, Villa di Vetrice and further up in the hills, Galiga, which is also a hunting reserve. Altogether they have about 100 hectares of vines and produce a considerable range of different wines and styles. We were treated to a large tasting. Although it was a sunny April day, there was a chilling wind coming down from the Apennines, and a roaring fire had been thoughtfully lit in the tasting room.

Three generations were there. The grandfather, Grato Grati, serenely and silently observed the proceedings while his granddaughter, Cristina, bubbled enthusiastically; her father, Gianfranco, is more measured in his manner. There is an old-fashioned feel about their wines, with the hallmark of dry, cedary fruit and an underlying elegance; they still use the traditional old *botti* for their *riserva* wines but are also trying out some new *barriques* and even buy the occasional new *botte*. Some Merlot has been planted too, in the mid-1990s, for Campo al Sorbo. Best of all is Grato Grati; we were treated to the 1988 vintage, which had not been bottled until 1996, spending the first eight years of its life in large *botti*, in the cellars below the sixteenth-century villa. It comes from fifty-year-old Sangiovese vines, with the traditional blend of Canaiolo, Colorino, and even some Trebbiano. The taste was long and lingering, with elegant fruit. In between tastes of wine we enjoyed slices of *bruschetta*, liberally drizzled with the Grati's olive oil, which had recently won a prize in the *frutta intensiva* category.

Reluctantly we declined a pressing invitation to stay for lunch and instead set off to walk up into the hills behind Rufina. We took a way-marked tarmac road, looking down on some allotments on the riverbank. As well as vegetables and a row of neatly pruned vines, there were chickens and rabbits roaming freely in one allotment, and next door, a cacophony of hunting dogs, who barked ferociously as we walked past, but were obviously quite oblivious to the potential meal behind the adjoining fence. We turned off the road to follow a path that rambled along the riverbank through woods that were full of violets and primroses galore, bringing back memories of childhood walks. Every now and then there was a roar of water from a small waterfall, and then the path began to climb up through the woods to reach a farmhouse, Le Pialle, on a dirt-track road, which ran along the crest of the hill, giving us views over the valley. We picnicked in an olive grove, and then continued along the track past various farmhouses and signs indicating that the woods were the hunting reserve of La Galiga. The track brought us to an old windmill, which has been restored to its full glory with resplendent sails, and here our path turned downhill past the neatly tended vines of Villa di Vetrice. As well as vineyards there were olive groves, one with small daffodils still in flower. It was a beautiful spring afternoon, with birdsong interrupted by the occasional cockerel. A man was making a bonfire of olive pruning and a group of riders came slowly up the vineyards.

Later on we went to Colognole to see the Marchesa Gabriella Spaletti. Spaletti was the name of a popular Chianti brand in the 1960s, now marketed by Ruffino. The marchesa explained how her family came originally from Emilia Romagna and had bought three estates in Tuscany, including Colognole, in the 1890s. For many years it was a traditional estate selling wine *sfuso*, but in 1990 they began to pay more attention to their wine and to bottle it. It was drizzling gently, not the weather for a walk, but the marchesa volunteered a drive through her vineyards; the property totals some 650 hectares, of which just 30 are vineyards, and they have olive trees too. The marchesa explained that the slopes of Monte Giove, which dominates the valley of Rufina, are particularly suited to olive trees as the wind maintains good ventilation and keeps the olive flies away. Rufina was once important for its peach trees, but production costs eventually proved too high. A small lake, which once provided for water for irrigation for the trees, now provides a habitat for wild ducks, to the benefit of the hunters. The vineyards of Colognole were very scattered. Some are still in the old style with high trellising, while they replanted a considerable amount in the mid-1990s with higher densities, shifting from 3000 to 5000 plants per hectare; any tighter and they would need new machinery. We passed a number of small houses, and a fallow field, destined for replanting next year. The woods were dense with oak trees, and the track lined with white broom. There was a newly planted vineyard of Syrah. First they had had to break up the thick slabs of *galestro* rock, and the marchesa remembered how her father had tried to plant this same hillside, but without modern machinery it had proved impossible to break the rocks. Even now it looked quite barren and volcanic, with dark grey stones. We had hoped to see the wine museum in the old palace of Poggio Reale, which had once belonged to the Spaletti family, but museums in Italy are firmly closed on Mondays, so instead the marchesa offered to drive us up to the top of Monte Giove; there were wonderful views over the valley, even on a rather grey day, and a memorial to partisans who had fought here during the Second World War. On summer days a restaurant is open and a small lake provides fishing opportunities.

The cellars are under the villa of Colognole, an imposing building painted in bright yellow ochre, which dates from the 1500s and is built around a central courtyard. There was the usual mixture of tanks and barrels of various sizes, including some tiny *barrilotti* that were used for carrying wine. An old-fashioned filter, called *calze,* looked like a large pair of baggy linen trousers; it was once used for filtering thick, viscous Vin Santo. For the moment they make just three wines at Colognole, as yet no super-Tuscan or *cru,* but a simple Chardonnay, a Chianti *normale* and best of all, the Riserva del Don, with some attractive cedary fruit and a picture of the marchesa's grandfather on the label. For the moment it remains a traditional estate that is gently trying to renovate itself.

Pomino is now a quite separate DOC, recognized as such in 1983. Hitherto it had been considered part of Chianti Rufina, and indeed the tiny hamlet of Pomino is a *frazione* of the town of Rufina. Nevertheless Pomino had enough individuality in the seventeenth century to merit mention by Francesco Redi, and in 1716 the Grand Duke Cosimo III laid down boundaries for it, which are those of the present-day DOC. In 1897 Pomino Chablis won a gold medal at the Paris exhibition.

It was Vittorio degli Albizzi who was responsible for laying the foundations of Pomino as we know it today, for the originality of Pomino is the presence of Pinot Noir in the red wine, and Chardonnay, Pinot Bianco and Pinot Grigio in the white wine, grape varieties he brought back from France in the middle of the nineteenth century, long before they became fashionable in the vogue for so-called super-Tuscans. The atmosphere is quite different from the vineyards of Rufina. The vineyards are at a much higher altitude – between 400 and 730 metres – making them some of the highest in Tuscany. There is often snow in winter, and a sign at the bottom of the hill remains there even in summer, warning motorists not to take this road without snow chains on their tyres. Frescobaldi is the principal producer of Pomino. Tiziana Frescobaldi describes it as *una zona di frontiera*; they are keen to retain the individuality of its traditions, taking up the challenge to produce great white wine in Tuscany.

The villa, just outside the village of Pomino, where Frescobaldi has its cellars, was built at the end of the sixteenth century by the Florentine architect Gherardo Silvani. There is an attractive arched portico and behind this elegant facade some streamlined facilities, with new wooden fermentation vats and a neat *barricaia* with two old basket presses. The *vinsantaia* is under the eaves, with *barriques* rather than the tiny *caratelli*. Altogether Frescobaldi have 95 hectares, accounting for 99 per cent of the DOC, with Selvapiana renting 3 hectares from Petrognano, and it is almost impossible to increase the area of Pomino as the vineyards are strictly limited to the valley confines. Two-thirds of the production is white and it is the white wine that is the more original in flavour. It is based on Chardonnay, with complementary varieties, Pinot

Bianco and Pinot Grigio, while they are working on other aromatic varieties such as Rhine Riesling, Gewürztraminer, Sauvignon and Kerner, just to see if the blend would benefit. I thought the 2002 Pomino Bianco was delicious as it was, and that it did not need the input of any other variety, with its fresh grassy notes and acidity on the finish. In contrast, Pomino Il Benefizio, from the highest vineyard of the estate, is a pure Chardonnay, fermented and aged in oak for twelve months. It was one of the very first Tuscan whites to be fermented in *barriques*. The wine was rich and rounded with a dry nutty backbone and layers of flavour, which you felt would allow it to develop in bottle.

As for the red wine, 2000 Castello di Pomino, it was good, but less original. Sangiovese remains the mainstay, with 30 per cent Pinot Noir and 10 per cent Merlot. They used to have Cabernet Sauvignon, too, but recognized that it simply would not ripen and did nothing but impart herbaceous notes to the wine. Without Cabernet the wine tastes more rounded; the Pinot Noir softens the Sangiovese and the Merlot adds body and soft tannins, so that it is long and understated. Tiziana quoted Luigi Veronelli, one of the leading Italian wine authorities, who likened the wines of Pomino to people who have something worthwhile to say, but say it quietly, *sotto voce*, so that you really have to pay attention to them.

Chianti Colli Fiorentini

· *November visits and an April walk* ·

South-west of Florence; Castello di Poppiano, Castelvecchio, Corzano e Paterno for cheese as well as wine; Le Corti Corsini in Chianti Classico

THE VINEYARDS OF Chianti Colli Fiorentini sprawl around Florence, adjoining both Chianti Rufina and Chianti Classico. Quite simply, they are defined by the provincial boundaries. They meet Rufina at Pontasieve and then extend south, almost into the suburbs of Florence and to the north edge of Chianti Classico at Strada-in-Chianti, to continue around the western edge of Chianti Classico to Tavernelle Val di Pesa and Barberina Val d'Elsa, to reach the recently created sub-zone of Montespertoli. Altogether the Colli Fiorentini cover some seventeen *communi* and include producers who make both Chianti Classico and Chianti Colli Fiorentini, if their land crosses the provincial boundary. There is no doubt that the Colli Fiorentini suffer from lying in the shadow of the much better known and now much more prestigious Chianti Classico. This is a problem they are trying to address.

We went first to the imposing Castello di Poppiano, which is owned by the Count Ferdinando Guicciardini, who is a cousin of the Strozzi Guicciardini family at Fattoria di Cusona in San Gimignano, and there are other cousins across the valley at Lucignano. I asked the count how long his family had been at Poppiano. 'Well,' he replied, in his impeccable English, 'the first written record relates to an inheritance of land divided between two brothers back in 1192.' He showed us round; there are new stainless-steel fermentation tanks outside, while the old *botti* are in the cellars of the castle, as well as some American and French oak *barriques*. Two large stone vats dating from the 1700s remain as a reminder of the past. Until 1938 there was no electricity here and it took two oxen to turn the stone wheel of the olive press. But best of all was the *vinsantaia*, housed in the Torre Grande, as opposed to the second, smaller tower. There are rows of hundred-year-old *caratelli*, housed on four floors; we climbed the tower, inhaling the wonderfully intoxicating bouquet of

Vin Santo, a nutty honeyed aroma that pervaded the whole tower, and then emerged into fresh air at the top. This was not a lookout tower for nothing, with far-ranging views towards the four compass points, of Florence, Siena, San Gimignano and Pisa, as well as the nearby Castello di Montegufoni, the former home of Osbert Sitwell. Then we sat in the kitchen and tasted; there was a battery of splendid copper saucepans, with dried flowers and some incongruous bunches of plastic oranges hanging off the wall.

The count's family may have been at Poppiano for some eight centuries, but he has a very perceptive appreciation of the current problems besetting Chianti from the Colli Fiorentini. He feels strongly that it was a mistake to lump all the various sub-zones of Chianti together in the all-embracing *consorzio* of Chianti Putto, as was done in the past, for not only are they very different in climate and *terroir*, but also it simply meant that you were a second-class citizen, as you were not a member of the Gallo Nero, the *consorzio* for Chianti Classico. Chianti Putto no longer exists as an organization, and now the various sub-zones are working to create their own individual identities.

Although the Colli Fiorentini is a very diverse area, covering the hills south of Florence, it does have a strong regional identity, with its links to the city of Florence. A *consorzio* has been formed, initially consisting of just fifteen members, who are wine producers, not merchants. The producers particularly want to link the image of the wine with its territory, and they consider themselves fortunate to have such a strong link with the city of Florence. Consequently their labels bear the emblem of the rampant lion, which is also the symbol of Florence. The count insisted on the differences between Chianti Colli Fiorentini and Chianti Classico. Here the soil is mainly *albarese*, well-drained stony clay, rather than the *galestro* of Chianti Classico. The hills are lower, with the vineyards between 150 and 350 metres, and consequently the climate is milder and the vintage is usually slightly earlier than in Chianti Classico. He talked about the market, commenting on how much Chianti owes to media coverage, but that it is in danger of becoming its prisoner, with producers not just trying to make good wine, but also wine that conforms to an international taste. If they are both made using new oak, with Cabernet Sauvignon and Merlot blended with Sangiovese, 'Bordeaux and Chianti will start to taste the same and they will all get 90 to 100 in the *Wine Spectator*.' Attention must be paid to *tipicità*, while improving quality. It is a constant struggle between tradition and progress, a challenge with a finely balanced path.

The count had seen at first hand the dismantling of the *mezzadria* system, the time-honoured system of share-cropping which had been the backbone of Tuscan agriculture for centuries, whereby the landowner provided the necessary capital expenditure, bought seed, tools and so on, and also housed the peasant farmers or *contadini* and their families, and in return they contributed their manual labour. All the crops, olives, wheat and wine were divided, usually equally, between the landowner and his farmers, who could then sell any that were surplus to their needs. A Tuscan estate at the beginning of the last century was an example of self-sufficient subsistence agriculture and frequently was run in the landowner's absence by his *fattore* or manager, a position that often passed from father to son.

The Italian government was partly responsible for the disintegration of the system. It encouraged the breaking up of large estates and in some cases helped the *contadini* to buy land. At the same time many people succumbed to the lure of the city. Life on the land was hard and the attraction of the towns, offering, they thought, easy wages, created a rural exodus. The inefficiency of many estates was brought to light, as the landowners were often left without the manpower to farm their estates and labour costs became all too significant.

A further element in promoting change was the mechanization of agriculture. Tractors did not arrive in any number in the vineyards of Chianti until the 1960s, and then suddenly there was not the same demand for manual labour, which further hastened the depopulation. In the space of ten or twenty years a system that had remained unchanged for centuries disintegrated. Often the same *contadino* family had held the same farm on the same estate for centuries, for it was the only way of earning a living. Then in the 1960s the so-called Italian miracle of the industrialization of the masses took place and there was a dramatic population shift to the cities. The count explained how the 270-hectare estate of Poppiano had been farmed by thirty-three *mezzadria* families in the early 1960s, which meant some 150 to 200 people working in the fields and vineyards. Today the same land provides employment for just twenty-five people; such is the effect of mechanization. He remembers families coming to return the keys to houses in which they had lived for generations, almost on a weekly basis at one time. Inevitably it was the most energetic and ambitious who left, those with initiative, in the same way that it was the more adventurous Sicilians who left their island to find a new life in America. So the only way for these very labour-intensive estates to survive was by mechanization.

A series of four aerial photographs in his office amply demonstrates the change. In 1962 Poppiano was a patchwork quilt of tiny fields, in sharp contrast to the vast expanses of huge fields in 1998. The most marked difference came between 1962 and 1972, with the greatest consolidation of land. Today there are 120 hectares of vines, all in production, apart from the annual replanting of 10 hectares.

Castelvecchio, outside the village of San Pancrazio, has also undergone a transformation, but more recently and on a different scale. Today it is run by the immediately likeable and enthusiastic brother and sister team, Stefania and Filippo Rocci. They explained how their grandfather had bought the estate back in 1960 and until 1991 the wine was sold *sfuso*. Then their father began to initiate a move towards quality, which the younger generation has enthusiastically followed, with Filippo taking over from his father in 1998.

The name Castelvecchio denotes an old castle and indeed there are the remains of a castle that was destroyed after the battle of Monteaperti in 1260. The villa dates from the fifteenth century and there is a charming little chapel, La Chiesetta, dating from the twelfth century and dedicated to San Lorenzo, where both Stefania and Filippo were married.

The estate totals some 73 hectares, of which 22 are olive trees, and 36 vineyards, planted mainly with Sangiovese, and also Canaiolo, Colorino, Malvasia and Trebbiano, and, since 1997, a little Cabernet Sauvignon and Merlot. We looked out on some tiny Merlot vines which had been planted the previous day, with 6000 vines to the hectare. They have some *barriques*, housed in a small cellar with three-metre-thick walls, and also some small *botti*, but are insistent that they do not like too much wood. It should be a garnish, but never dominate the fruit, and certainly their wines had a lively fruitiness, with a fresh

Chianti Colli Fiorentini, a more structured *riserva*, and Il Brecciolino, their IGT with some Cabernet as well as Sangiovese, which was ripe and sturdy. They deserve to do well.

Corzano e Paterno lies just 200 metres outside Chianti Classico within the zone of the Colli Fiorentini. The difference is one of administrative geography rather than geological distinction, as it is within the *comune* of San Pancrazio rather than neighbouring San Casciano. We took a dirt track and travelled hopefully past olive trees and vineyards to reach a cluster of houses around a courtyard. Aljoscha Goldschmidt is a striking example of the internationalism of Chianti, to the extent that he is not quite sure what his mother tongue is. He is of German origin but was born in Holland, and came to Italy in 1972 when an uncle bought the estate. He has since married an English wife, Toni, who is friendly and vivacious. Aljoscha, too, is welcoming, with an unruly mop of dark hair and a winning smile.

First we wandered through the neat little cellar, with an olive press amidst the barrels and an old-fashioned basket press, and then we adjourned to the kitchen for a tasting. First came a white wine: Il Corzanello, a blend of Trebbiano, Malvasia and Chardonnay, with some delicate fruit, and a lift of flavour originating from the Chardonnay. It was immensely drinkable, as we discovered later that evening. A barrel-aged Chardonnay Aglaia was altogether more serious, with some structured fruit, but Aljoscha admitted that it entailed a lot of work and hassle for just 3000 bottles. His 2000 Chianti, Terre di Corzano, is a blend of Sangiovese with Canaiolo and Colorino and this year he added a drop of Merlot for the first time. He described 2000 as a strange vintage; the grapes were ripe, and produced high alcohol and low acidity, but somehow they were just not good enough for a *riserva*. Nonetheless it had some attractive perfumed notes of fresh cherries. Nor does he place any credibility in the Colli Fiorentini as a name for his wine, preferring to call it simply Chianti. I Tre Borri, after the three streams in the valley, is a *riserva* that is given twelve months in *barriques*, making for some sturdy fruit, with firm tannins. It was ripe and harmonious with good ageing potential.

Aljoscha observed how 1997, 1998 and 1999 were all very good vintages, whereas in contrast 2000, 2001 and 2002 have all been difficult for one reason or another. Next came a Rosso Toscano, Il Corzano 1997, from Sangiovese, with Cabernet Sauvignon and Merlot, aged in *barriques* for several months. This was altogether more international in flavour, with some new oak on the nose, and ripe blackcurrant fruit. We finished with Vin Santo, from Trebbiano and Malvasia, which are left hanging up drying until mid-February. Then the wine spends five years in *caratelli* with a *madre*. They have the same problem as San Giusto a Rentennano in Chianti Classico, that legally the wine is not Vin Santo, as at 9.5° it does not have enough alcohol – the requirement of the *disciplinari* is 13° – so Aljoscha calls it Il Passito di Corzano. It was richly honeyed with a firm bite, with notes of apricots and marmalade, making a smooth, rich mouthful, with balancing acidity on the finish.

Then Toni took us to see their dairy and the flock of sheep, for the reputation of the estate also rests on her talent as a cheesemaker. A large flock of creamy Sardinian sheep ran past us, herded by two dogs, and what she described as the modern shepherd, for he was riding a Vespa. She explained that she makes an enormous range of different cheeses, but it was the wrong time of year to see anything much; there was some *pecorino* ageing in the dairy and she gave us some Blu di Chianti, saying that it would be delicious with Vin Santo. And it was.

An invitation to visit the dairy when it was in full operation in the spring was readily accepted, so six months later we were back at Corzano, with Aljoscha giving us directions to walk through the valley. We followed the track, the Via San Vito di Sopra, to the next house and then took a path downhill through the vineyards. An elderly man was collecting wild asparagus; he looked to have a good harvest, but when I asked if he was finding much, the reply was distinctly non-committal: *Boh!*, which is one of those Italian words that means all or nothing, or, in this case, not as much as he would have liked. The path took us through the woods, past a pond, over a couple of streams and then up a hill to join the Via Paterno by a farm. We turned along it, to meet a couple of horses, a tethered mare with her young foal, and then a couple of friendly dogs of indeterminate breed, with their tails wagging eagerly, no doubt in expectation of a walk, and we were at the dairy.

We left our muddy walking boots outside and donned voluminous pristine white wellies. Toni and a colleague were busy kneading curds and putting them into containers; they would eventually become Chianti Blu. She was happy to chat as she worked, explaining that the curds needed to be well aerated, to allow the mould to grow, and every few days the cheese is injected with needles to encourage the mould still further. There was a large stainless-steel cauldron, with whey being heated to make *ricotta*. A fig stick was floating on top; apparently the sap of the fig tree is acidic and this helps the *ricotta*, and almost adds a hint of vanilla. Every now and then steam was released from the bottom of the cauldron, making a dramatic roar.

Toni explained how she began by selling milk from her flock to a Sicilian shepherd who made the traditional *pecorino* of Tuscany, but it simply was not remunerative, so she decided to learn cheese-making, working with the Sicilian for a year and also with a Tuscan who had cows and made butter and ice cream. She wanted to diversify away from traditional *pecorino*, partly to avoid creating any ill-feeling with her mentors. Now she makes about eleven different cheeses, and has a technical consultant to give her advice. Some of the cheeses were created by accident, such as Buccia di Rospo, which translates literally as toad's skin, and that is indeed rather what it looks like. The taste, however, is delicious; it was originally intended to be a *pecorino*, but something went wrong. The cheese still tasted good, so her consultant helped her work out just what they had done, and now it is an important part of the repertoire. It turned out that the curds were too wet, taking twelve hours rather than 45 minutes to harden. We also tried Rocca, a creamy cheese, named after their fifth child, and another experiment with Vin Santo grape pips coating the outside, and came away with a delicious semi-*stagionato pecorino*.

Our route carried on along the Via Paterno, with views of an imposing yellow ochre villa in the valley, the Fattoria di Sorbigliano, surrounded by cypress trees, to meet a tarmac road by the *agriturismo* of Il Corno. Il Corno is another important wine-producing estate in the Colli Fiorentini, but repeated phone calls to make an appointment failed to elicit a response until it was too late and we were in San Gimignano. We carried on past the hamlet of Santa Cristina a Salavolpi; we were lucky that the little church with its attractive three-arched portico was open. In fact, it was being energetically spring-cleaned, so we peered in through the open door, admiring its simple lines. We turned back down the Via San Vito di Sopra, past vineyards, some new, some old and high, with bundles of vine cuttings neatly tied up. Not all were neatly manicured; there was an untidy field of vines that had been pulled up, looking rather forlorn, next to some sawn-off olive trunks. We passed an occasional house; then the track took us through some woods, and past a pretty pink house with a tower, and we enjoyed views across the valley, as we reached our car at Corzano.

Across the valley you can see the villa of the Chianti Classico estate, Le Corti Corsini, which is now run by Duccio Corsini, or to give him his correct title, the Duke of Casigliano. He speaks impeccable English, which he said he had learnt in Scotland, and maintains the cultured elegance of the Italian aristocracy. Duccio Corsini is now intent on restoring the fortunes of the family vineyards. Until the early 1990s most of the wine was sold *sfuso*, usually to Antinori, and the vines were treated like any other agricultural crop. Duccio was instrumental in the first proper bottling in 1993 and the wines have improved apace with Carlo Ferrini as their oenologist; and together they are intent on turning Le Corti into a serious wine estate. Le Corti has belonged to the Corsinis since 1427, and until the Second World War totalled 500 hectares, with 35 farms, scattered over Tuscany. Very much larger was another family estate near Manciano in the Maremma. Initially 8000 hectares were rented from the Grand Duke of Tuscany in 1759; then the Corsini family purchased the land in 1886, and in 1952 it was reduced to 2650 hectares, as part of a programme of agrarian reform. Duccio showed us round the Renaissance villa where he now lives; it had been unoccupied for fifty years. Originally there was a fortification tower here, and then the villa was built in the middle of the seventeenth century. There were elegantly painted and very deceptive *trompe l'oeil* panelled doors. The family tree is on a wall in the drawing room. Pope Clement XII was a member of the family; he was elected at the age of 80 in 1730, and much to everyone's surprise lived for another ten years, and is known for the building of the Trevi fountain, the Quirinale and the facade of San Giovanni in Laterano.

We tasted in Duccio's office. Le Corti Chianti Classico *normale* had some ripe cherry fruit. Duccio described the *tipicità* of this northern part of Chianti Classico, suggesting that the wines have more elegance than power. The harvest here tends to be relatively early as the climate is warmer than in some of the higher vineyards around Radda. 2000 Don Tommaso, from Sangiovese, with 15 per cent Merlot, is a blend taken from the best vineyards, and given fifteen months' ageing in barrel. Tommaso is a family name, recalling amongst others his grandfather, who helped write the constitution of Italy. Merlot helps soften the Sangiovese in Chianti and is much less intrusive than Cabernet Sauvignon. The 2000 was ripe and rounded, with some body from the Merlot, while the 1999 was cedary and more elegant, with soft tannins and a long finish. Our tasting finished with the first vintage from their vineyards in the Maremma. They are in the DOC Capalbio but are not planted with the appropriate grape varieties to conform to the *disciplinari*, so they produce a Maremma Toscana from Cabernet Sauvignon, Merlot and tiny drops of Petit Verdot, Tannat, Syrah, Mourvèdre and Grenache Noir, or Alicante. They have just five hundred plants of each, allowing a microvinification for experimental purposes, what Duccio called *un fritto misto*. The wine is aged for sixteen months after blending and the 2000 promised well, with some rounded oaky fruit on nose and palate, with quite firm tannins. Somehow it tasted more international than the Chianti Classico.

There is no doubt that Duccio is intent on putting Le Corti on the map. He organizes an annual wine festival, inviting some seventy-five of the best Tuscan producers to show their wines, each with a stand in the elegant courtyard of the villa, observed by Roman busts. His aim is to increase the contact between producers and consumers. His aunt is a renowned landscape gardener, and thanks to her inspiration there is also an annual garden show; the tenth was held in 2003. So Le Corti represents an intriguing example of an estate undergoing a transformation, motivated by the energy of the new generation.

AGEING IN BARREL

TRADITIONALLY TUSCANY HAS USED the large *botti*, which could be as large as 100 hectolitres or more. They were intended more for storage than for influencing the taste of a wine, and hygiene was often an issue as they needed to be meticulously maintained in order to avoid any off-flavours. As Tuscany has espoused more modern winemaking methods, the French *barrique* of 225 litres has become much more widespread. Opinions vary as to the suitability of Sangiovese for maturation in small oak; maybe larger barrels, such as the 500-litre *tonneaux*, might be better, or even small *botti* of 10 or 20 hectolitres. It all depends on the ratio of wine to oak, and also on the amount of new oak. A new oak barrel will have an immediate effect on the taste of the wine, imparting a sweet vanilla flavour in a matter of weeks, whereas an older barrel will be more gentle in its impact and allow for a subtle process of oxygenation, which will help the wine to evolve. While there is no doubt about the suitability of Cabernet Sauvignon and Merlot for ageing in *barriques*, with Sangiovese it is still very much open to discussion.

Chianti Colli Aretini
· March ·

North-west of Arezzo; Sette Ponti, Fattoria Petrolo, Manucci Droandi and Villa Cilnia

A S A CHIANTI, THE Colli Aretini have little identity. They form the most easterly vineyards of Chianti, covering the hills of the Arno valley and around the city of Arezzo, and are limited by the provincial boundaries of Florence and Siena. Arezzo is known as the birthplace of Petrarch, and for its enchanting frescoes by Piero della Francesca, while the Aretini, as the inhabitants of Arezzo are called, are known among other Tuscans as the worst drivers of the region.

The best part of the area adjoins the hills of Chianti Classico. Over the past few years there have been interesting developments, with the renovation of old estates and investment by outsiders. There are fashionable names amongst the newcomers: the British singer Sting has bought a property near Figline Val d'Arno, and Ferruccio Ferragamo has restored the old estate of Il Borro near Loro Ciuffenna.

Antonio Moretti at Sette Ponti is intent on creating a reputation for his family property. His father, Alberto, who was an architect, bought the estate in the 1950s from the royal house of Savoia, mainly for its hunting opportunities. Back then the vineyards were very much a secondary consideration and the estate was run by a *fattore*, as was the custom for absentee landlords. Meanwhile, Antonio Moretti, after graduating from Siena University with a degree in economics and banking, developed a successful business in the fashion industry. It is only latterly that he has turned his attention to the family vineyards. He would be the first to admit that his practical knowledge of the wine business was extremely limited, but he knew how to find the expertise that he needed and had the means to pay for it, and, more importantly, he knew how to learn from that expertise, employing Carlo Ferrini as his consultant oenologist and Sean O'Callaghan, who is based at Riecine, as his winemaker.

While Sean is no longer involved, there is no doubt that he laid solid foundations for the wines of Sette Ponti. And why Sette Ponti? The name refers to the number of bridges crossing the Arno on the road from Arezzo to Florence. The first, which is close by at Ponte Buriano, took nearly forty years to build in the middle of the thirteenth century, and if you look carefully at the backdrop to Leonardo's *Mona Lisa*, this is the bridge you will see, with six elegant arches spanning the river.

The 300-hectare estate includes some 64 hectares of vineyards, which have undergone extensive replanting. However, the original vineyard, La Vigna del Impero, a two-and-a-half hectare vineyard planted back in 1935, still remains, with the vines, Sangiovese, Canaiolo and Colorino, all mixed up in the traditional manner. They are much taller vines than is usual today, forming wonderfully gnarled twisted shapes, and, in deference to their age, they are attached to the supporting wires with osier, the supple reed of a willow, which before the advent of plastic was always used as the traditional material. It is infinitely more fiddly, demanding greater manual dexterity.

It was a sunny spring morning, with views stretching towards the hills of the Pratomagno, which were almost purple in colour. After admiring the venerable vines, we continued through the vineyards of Sette Ponti. The blackthorn was just coming into flower, with a gentle haze of white blossom. We passed a small shrine to the Madonna, with a posy of flowers, and an old terraced wall with steps built into it. In places the earth was very sandy, and deep red in colour with its high iron content, and in other parts very rocky; consequently all the new plantings require extensive drainage channels. An elderly man was tying down shoots in a vineyard, while a bulldozer nearby was preparing land for another vineyard, breaking up some gigantic boulders. We walked down an alleyway of young cypress trees, with wire netting around them, not only to persuade them to grow straight, but also to protect them from the ravages of the deer. The *barricaia* is in a house built in the eighteenth century, and our guide, Susanna, explained how they were considering a new cellar, but for the moment it had not progressed beyond the architect's plans. Sette Ponti is also known for its Chiana cattle, the distinguished breed that provides *bistecca alla fiorentina*, an intrinsic part of Tuscan cuisine. They also have some *cinta senesi* pigs, which they sell for breeding rather than for their contribution to Tuscany's cuisine. A group of nervous piglets ran off squealing as we approached, while their rather solid mothers, black with a distinctive white saddle, stared at us inscrutably.

For the moment they make three wines at Sette Ponti, and none of them is Chianti. Vigna di Pallino is a pure Sangiovese, with the classic Tuscan flavours, the ripe fruit of sour cherries, and unadulterated by oak. It could be Chianti, but like most serious estates in the Colli Aretini, Antonio Moretti rejects the name Chianti. Crognolo is a blend of Sangiovese with 10 per cent Merlot, which spends about seventeen months in *barriques*. The young wine had the inevitable vanilla sweetness of new oak on the nose, but the palate was rounded and harmonious, showing plenty of ageing potential. Then there is Oreno, a blend of 50 per cent Sangiovese, with some Cabernet Sauvignon as well as Merlot, which has a more international flavour, with the higher percentage of French grape varieties and more marked oak. Some white grape varieties, Viognier, Chardonnay, Sauvignon and Roussanne, have been grafted, just 500 plants of each, to see how they perform, but the first harvest was not until 2003. The Colli Aretini have a reputation for light wines, but those of Sette Ponti show this to be anything but true. Antonio Moretti has come a long way since his first vintage in 1998, and recently he has bought more land in the Maremma at Magliano-in-Toscana, and also in Sicily, near Noto. He is not a man to stand still.

Fattoria Petrolo is another of the rising stars of the Colli Aretini, near Mercatale Val d'Arno. Luca Sanjust explained how the property is of Etruscan origin; the Romans had a *castrum* here and in the Middle Ages it was on a pilgrims' route to Rome. The villa dates from the 1700s, and there are the remains of a lookout tower on the hill, dating from AD 1000, a vestige of the wars between Siena, Florence and Arezzo. His grandfather bought the property just after the war in 1947; at that time it produced simple Chianti, obtaining some 3000 hectolitres from just 30 hectares of grapes, with just 1600 vines per hectare. Things are rather different today. The newly planted vineyards have a density of something between 4500 and 6500 vines, giving a yield of 500–600 hectolitres, but still from 30 hectares. Essentially you reckon a kilo of grapes per vine.

Luca is particularly enthusiastic about Merlot; he likens his *terroir* to that of Chianti Classico, which is only a few kilometres away. There is *galestro* here, which suits Sangiovese, while other parts of his vineyards are wetter with clay soil, which suits Merlot. The climate in the Colli Aretini also tends to be more humid than in the Chianti Classico, again suiting Merlot. The first plantings of Merlot were in 1990, originally with the intention of blending it with Sangiovese, but it proves much more successful on its own. Luca talked of the need to find a third path, between the two great wines of Tuscany, Brunello di Montalcino and Chianti Classico; maybe it is not the right answer to concentrate on Sangiovese when Merlot offers such interesting possibilities. However, blending is important too; each vineyard is vinified separately, so there are at least ten different batches of Sangiovese, and also of Merlot. Each vineyard ripens at a slightly different time.

They make just two wines at Petrolo, and again neither of them is called Chianti. Galatrona is a pure Merlot and Torrione mainly Sangiovese. For Luca, Torrione represents what he called the *anima toscana*. There is a little Merlot to soften the Sangiovese, making a beautifully rounded wine with ripe fruit and supple tannins so that it is less astringent than some Chianti. In contrast, Galatrona is pure Merlot, representing the *anima bordelese*, and the taste was immediately so much more international, with ripe fruit, a tannic backbone and more vanilla on the nose.

The next day we came back to walk up to the lookout tower, but first we had arranged to see the Pieve di San Giovanni Battista a Galatrona, the little church on the property for which the first documentary evidence is as early as AD 963. This had necessitated a phone call to Don Alessandro, and while we waited for his colleague to arrive with the key, we talked to the elderly lady who lived in the adjoining house. She tends the small garden outside the church, an attractive rock garden, with lilac in bud and rosemary bushes in bloom. She used to have the key to the church, but it got too much, cleaning up the dead flies. And when a chubby priest, Don Stefano, arrived, she teased him: *Quanti morti?* How many dead bodies are there in there? I mean flies, of course. It was a simple church with thick whitewashed arches, and worth the detour for its beautiful font with intricate carvings in marble by Giovanni della Robbia. There was also a fine statue of St John dated 1518, also by della Robbia, and hints of frescoes under the whitewashed wall.

As we set off up the hill, the geese opposite the church honked loudly at us. It was a gentle climb, following a track through the woods, past a couple of vineyards which were fenced to keep out the wild boar, who are particularly partial to ripe grapes. There were fine views back over the valley, and down to the villa and the *pieve*. Hellebores, violets and crocus were in flower and the butterflies flitted in the spring sunshine. A small shrub with bright red berries is *pungitopo*, Italy's answer to holly, and just as prickly. The tall stone watchtower was curious in that there was no obvious door, but there were some serious cracks in its façade, and an abandoned farmhouse nearby. We slowly retraced our footsteps back down the hill.

Our next visit was to Manucci Droandi, outside the nearby village of Camposelvi, to see Roberto Giulio Droandi. Again, as at Petrolo, the vineyards are almost on the edge of the Chianti Classico, and Signor Droandi has a second estate within the *comune* of Gaiole, just 10 kilometres away. He has managed to overcome Italian bureaucracy and obtain permission to vinify his Chianti Classico outside the zone of production, as he does not have a cellar in Gaiole. Signor Droandi is a cheerful bearded individual who explained with great enthusiasm how all the wine until 1998 was sold *sfuso*, but how he had decided that the time had come to make something of his wines. He still sells a lot *sfuso* to various merchants, but now makes a Chianti Colli Aretini, as well as a Chianti Classico and an IGT Campolucci. We were treated to an extensive tasting of the early vintages. Signor Droandi explained the differences, as he saw them, between Chianti Classico and Chianti Colli Aretini. The soil is different; the Colli Aretini are lighter and sandier; average temperatures are different, it is milder in winter and a little warmer in summer in the Colli Aretini, and usually there is a bit more rain. Certainly in the glass the Chianti Classico was sturdier, but it had spent time in new barrels, while Campolucci, which is currently Sangiovese with some Cabernet and Merlot, and may include other old Tuscan varieties as they come into production, such as Foglia Tonda and Barsaglina, was quite sturdy and leathery. Our conversation was interrupted by the chimes of the nearby church bell, still rung by hand by the sacristan, and we adjourned to the nearby Osteria di Rendola for a nourishing plate of pasta.

*

We got lost finding Villa Cilnia at Pieve di Bagnoro, in the confusing suburbs of Arezzo. You approach it along a drive lined with cherry trees, about to burst into blossom in late March. It was worth persisting, for Villa Cilnia has been one of the pioneering estates of the Colli Aretini since Giovanni Bianchi arrived here in 1974. He developed what was then an innovative range of wines, blending Tuscan varieties with more international grape varieties. Then in 1991 he sold the estate, and after brief ownership by a German company it was sold again and is now managed by Luigi Segala and Orietta Gustand, who arrived here from Milan in November 1998. The move was very much a career change for them. They have simplified Giovanni Bianchi's extensive range to a more manageable four wines, from 10 hectares of vines. There is a Chianti Colli Aretini, with a drop of Cabernet and Merlot, which fills out the palate, as well as a *riserva* – they admit that they are one of the very few to put Colli Aretini on a label, but not for much longer. It is difficult to sell at a sensible price, and they are planning to extend the range of fantasy names instead. Vocato, a Sangiovese with 20 per cent Cabernet Sauvignon, given twelve months in oak, has attractive cedary notes with a firm finish, while Cignoro, made for the first time in 1998 from Sangiovese with 25 per cent each of Merlot and Cabernet, has some nicely rounded flavours.

Luca Sanjust was right when he said that the problem with the Colli Aretini is that there is no *azienda pilota*, or pacesetter, in the area, nor any recognition of the region. Each producer is intent on creating his own individual reputation, and that for the moment is how they will survive.

Chianti Colline Pisane and Nearby Estates

· April ·

South-east of Pisa; Soiana with Ursula Mock, Badia a Morrona, Tenuta di Ghizzano, I Giusti e Zanza, Villa Vestri, Tenuta di Fibbiano, Varramista, Montellori a Fucecchio

AMONGST THE VARIOUS zones of Chianti, after Chianti Classico and Rufina, the Colline Pisane is the one with the most coherent individual identity. While the others are mostly limited by the boundaries of the respective provinces, such as Arezzo or Siena, the Colline Pisane comprises a group of hills to the south-east of the city of Pisa. They are not to be confused with the Monte Pisano, which is to the north-east of the city of the leaning tower and the magical Piazza dei Miracoli.

None of these gentle hills rises much above 200 metres, in sharp contrast to the higher altitudes of Chianti Classico. This is softer, more peaceful countryside, with scattered villages and hamlets. It is very much a backwater, on the way to nowhere, with few passing tourists. The centre of the area is the village of Terricciola. Casciana Terme, as the name implies, is a spa town, noted for its cures for rheumatism, while Fauglia, Lari and Crespina are other important wine villages, as is Soiana, a hilltop village with the vestiges of a castle destroyed in the wars between the Florentines and the Pisans in the late Middle Ages. In fact, the vineyards of the Colline Pisane are much closer to those of Montescudaio than Chianti Classico. However, for better or for worse, history and tradition have thrown them into the millpond of Chianti, from which they are now trying to escape, with the creation of a new DOC, Terre di Pisa, which will encompass the more international grape varieties being planted in the area. Today there is a hardly a producer who puts the words 'Colline Pisane' on their label; they virtually all make simple Chianti, as well as a more expensive IGT, which ultimately will become Terre di Pisa, as and when officialdom has accepted the putative DOC. The white wine of the region, Bianco di San Torpè, which depended on Trebbiano and Malvasia, has virtually disappeared.

There have been changes in the region since my earlier visits. Bruno Moos, an enterprising Swiss, who was one of the pioneers of the area, has crossed the Atlantic to make wine in Ontario and sold his estate in 1999 to Ursula and Pieter Mock. Ursula studied history of art and ran an art gallery in Bremen, where her husband still works, coming to Soiana most weekends. Ursula admits that she is learning from experience; she did the 1999 vintage with Bruno's help, and has since employed Attilio Pagli as her consultant oenologist. His guiding hand is apparent in the wines. From just two and a half hectares she makes a stylish Soiano Bianco, from Vermentino and Malvasia, which is fermented and aged in oak for eight months. Vermentino provides a note of originality from the Tuscan norm of Trebbiano and Malvasia; you also find it in the wines of the Ligurian coast below Genoa, and further round the coast in the south of France, where it is commonly called Rolle. In the Colline Pisane they say it likes the salt that blows in on the sea breezes. Soianello is a cheerful fruity Sangiovese, with a touch of Malvasia Nera, Ciliegiolo and Canaiolo, with no oak ageing, and wonderfully drinkable with a plate of pasta, while Fontestina, which is matured in barrel for twelve months, is more structured and sturdy, with ageing potential. In appreciation of what Bruno had achieved for the region, Ursula has retained his name for the estate and also keeps the names of his wines. Note that there is no mention of Chianti.

Ursula lives in an imposing town house in the main street of Soiana, while her atmospheric cellars are in a tunnel just opposite that was once part of the castle of Soiana, of which not a vestige remains above ground. A knock at Ursula's front door brings an immediate response, with loud barks from her two beagles, Otto and Auguste, with smart brown-and-white patchwork coats. They were eager for a walk and Ursula offered to be our guide, even though it was raining, but more an English drizzle than a heavy Tuscan rain with an attitude. We set off out of the village, with Otto and Auguste pulling eagerly at their leads, through the hamlet of Stibbiolo and then down a dirt track, with a sign offering *vendita diretta* at Panta Rei. 'Let's see if they're in,' suggested Ursula, and we were welcomed by Alberto and Cristina. Otto and Auguste were firmly attached to a small basket press in the garden and immediately took up guard-dog positions, while we adjourned to the kitchen and Alberto opened a bottle of their very first vintage 2001 Chianti le Costie. He is a chubby-faced bespectacled man from Lombardy, and she is a *petite* Norwegian blond. They explained how they found their vineyard on the internet; they wanted to come to Tuscany and this area was still affordable, unlike more fashionable areas. However, since then, there has been investment from a couple of larger producers, Ferrari and La Spineta from northern Italy, and prices look set to rise. It is noticeable that there are very few locals amongst the producers in the Colline Pisane. Alberto explained that his vineyards are thirty years old and really need replanting; there is Colorino, Ciliegiolo and Malvasia Nera as well as Sangiovese, and his wine was wonderfully refreshing, a lively fruity Sangiovese, with a good acidity and tannin balance. I was impressed that he could achieve this as a complete novice. We refused offers of a second glass, released Otto and Auguste from the basket press and carried on down the track, our feet sinking into the soft muddy clay.

Badia a Morrona's vineyards came into view. Ursula cast a critical eye over them; there were some old vines that were pruned much too high, by modern standards. They were just starting to come into leaf, a delicate fresh green, but there were too many buds; some will have to be removed, she declared. We continued up the track to the road and on to the Badia. Two noisy Alsatians barked ferociously at Otto and Auguste as we went past; they showed enormous restraint and decorum in completely ignoring the threatening growls.

Badia a Morrona belongs to the count Alberto Gaslini, but is now managed by Arrigo Depaoli, a ginger-haired serious young man, who had just arrived at the estate when we met him. There are 600 hectares in total, including 60 of vineyards, of which 25 have been replanted since 1996. They also have olive trees, wheat and extensive woods that are a hunting reserve for pheasants and wild boar. *Agriturismo* is another activity. The records of the abbey go back to the twelfth century, for it was founded in 1152 by an offshoot of the Benedictines, the Camaldolese, and subsequently expropriated by the bishop of Volterra in 1482. The estate was bought by the Gaslini family at the end of the seventeenth century. A little church remains, Santa Maria a Morrona, with rounded arches and frescoes of saints. The villa is built around a simple courtyard, with walls painted an elegant pale yellow, offset by green creepers and lemon trees in pots. There was a magnificent Banksia rose growing up through a tall pine tree, its bright yellow flowers contrasting vividly with the dark green leaves of the evergreen.

They make five different wines: a basic Trebbiano; an oak-fermented Chardonnay, La Suvera, a name that originates from *sughera*, or cork oak, and recalls the fact that there were once cork oaks on the estate; I Sodi del Paretaio, their Chianti; N'Antia, meaning *andare nella via antica* – and indeed an old road runs nearby – a blend of Sangiovese, Cabernet Sauvignon and Merlot; and Vigna Alata, the highest vineyard of the estate at 220 metres with 35-year-old Sangiovese vines, ripe and oaky after eighteen months in wood. It will be interesting to observe the changes under the new management.

From the Badia we took a different route back to Soiana, past a sculptor's house with terracotta heads in the garden, and then past some newly planted vines. They are sitting too deep in the soil, observed Ursula's critical eye. Next we saw some vines pruned in a low espalier method. 'That looks nice,' said Ursula, 'but there are far too many buds; that's old-style viticulture.' Some adjoining vines were left unpruned, waiting to be pulled up. There were olive groves, breaking up the vineyards, some with statuesque artichoke plants in between the trees, others with rows of broad beans already in flower in early April. Then we slithered down the side of a muddy field and past some peach trees in blossom, the deep pink flowers providing a cheerful contrast with the grey sky. Our path continued through some woods, with violets and white anemones. 'Let's go and see someone else,' suggested Ursula. 'Azienda Vallorsi is just along the road.' Ursula doesn't know Signor Vallorsi very well, but even so, she was somewhat taken aback by the response to her friendly approach. 'I've brought a couple of wine-writing friends to see you.' '*Non c'è più vino*'; we don't have any wine left, despite the *vendita diretta* sign at the gate. We decided not to take this cool welcome, which quite contradicted the usual warmth of Italian hospitality, too personally; well, we were looking a bit damp, and maybe Otto or Auguste had let out a growl. Instead, further down the road, they found some guinea fowl to chase, but not catch, and then we took a steep track back up to the village of Soiana, past the API petrol station that is run by Gigi. This is the social focal point of the village; a group of elderly men keep him company most afternoons when he is at the pump, and nothing happens without Gigi knowing. The old Roman road into the village has now become a track, passing some vegetable patches and turning into the main street. Soiana has a population of about 500 people; after living here for four years, Ursula knows most of them by sight, and exchanged several *buona sera, che brutto tempo*, good evening, what horrid weather, as we walked down the street.

Other producers in the Colline Pisane were not within walking distance of Soiana. The Tenuta di Ghizzano is now run by Ginevra Pesciolini; her family has been in the village of Ghizzano since 1370 and it is her father, the count Pierfrancesco Veneroso Pesciolini, who takes the credit for realizing the need to do something with his vineyards, rather than just selling the wine *sfuso* to the merchants. The choice was either to invest or to pull up the vineyards. He decided to invest and their first wine, Veneroso, was born, in 1988. The blend has changed over the years and now consists of 50 per cent Sangiovese, 45 per cent Cabernet Sauvignon and 5 per cent Merlot. Right from the beginning it has been aged in Allier *barriques*. The estate used to produce Chianti too, but gave up doing so with the 2000 vintage. Ginevra explained the reasons for her decision: it simply was not financially viable. She only has 14 hectares of vineyards, from which she wants to obtain the very best wine possible. The cost of producing Veneroso and Chianti are very similar, but she can sell her Veneroso for €23 (45,000 lire) a bottle, whereas her Chianti was the most expensive on the market at €7 (14,000 lire) a bottle. Instead she is developing a second wine, Nambrot, named after the founder of her family at the time of Charlemagne, from 70 per cent Merlot and some Cabernet Sauvignon and Petit Verdot, which was planted before it was officially allowed in Tuscany in the spring of 2003. Ginevra admitted that she felt guilty about withdrawing from the DOCG of Chianti, but feels that the Colline Pisane has an insurmountable image problem; so few people make it now, that you cannot influence the market with only a few bottles. She, like all the other producers we saw, is pinning her hopes on the new DOC of Terre di Pisa.

 She showed us round her cellars; there were conical stainless-steel vats for *pigiatura*, and *barriques*, with the Sangiovese put into older wood, and all the

Nambrot into new wood. Then we climbed the tower of the house, and enjoyed hazy views towards Volterra. There is a large gallery, and off it a small room containing numerous pictures by Annigoni, who was a friend of her grandfather and often stayed on the estate. He painted not only her grandparents but also workers on the estate, and there were also sketches of the Tuscan scenery. Then we tasted in an elegant dining room, with a collection of silver spoons hung on the wall, and the wines illustrated the potential of an overlooked area and the changes that can be achieved by some committed investment.

Paolo Giusti and Fabio Zanza bought the old property of Scopicci in 1995, and having renamed it I Giusti e Zanza are now intent on making the best that their vineyards will offer, without any preconceptions based on tradition or history. On the contrary, they like Cabernet Sauvignon and Syrah, and believe Sangiovese to be a handicap, not a marketing tool. They want an international profile for their wines, and their wines do indeed have a certain international flavour, and are none the worse for that. They make two: Dulcamara, a Bordeaux blend of Cabernet Sauvignon and Merlot, and Belcore, from Sangiovese and Merlot, as well as Syrah, which came into production in 2001, as did Petit Verdot. They have invested in a new streamlined functional cellar, and are gradually replanting the old vineyards with high density, as much as 10,000 vines per hectare, which is very unusual for Tuscany. The vigour of the vines needs to be contained, and for that you need weak rootstock. And with such narrow rows, you also need a tractor *enjambeur*, which straddles the wines. The early vintages promise well and they too are looking forward to the creation of Terre di Pisa.

Isabelle and Christoph Fahrni are a friendly brother-and-sister team who described themselves as refugees from Switzerland. She had been a teacher and he was an anthropologist. They planted their first vineyard in 1991 and now make three wines from just two and a half hectares at Villa Vestri outside Lari. L'Ora Blu, referring to the blue hour at the end of the afternoon just before dusk, is a blend of Trebbiano and Vermentino. The red wines were more impressive; Sotto il Vento, a pure Sangiovese, without any wood ageing, exuded sour cherry fruit. It used to be labelled Chianti but sells so much better as an

IGT. Isabelle admitted that it was absurd, *ma è così*, but that's how it is. You can buy a Chianti Classico in Switzerland for €1.5 (3000 lire), so you certainly would not be able to sell a Colline Pisane for €4.5 (9000 lire). It all comes down to marketing. Their second red wine, Notte, which they described as *un vino da meditazione*, is a blend of Syrah and Merlot, with some peppery fruit and subtle tannins, and had been aged for a few months in small *botti*. Christoph admitted that they have an oenologist who gives them technical advice, which they do not always follow, such as his suggestion to put the Notte in *barriques* rather than *botti*. They have no Cabernet for the simple reason they don't like it: 'It makes everything taste the same and can dominate the flavour, as can too much wood ageing.'

San Gervasio is a vivid example of an estate that is moving with the times. Luca Tommasini explained how his father had bought the property in 1960. The original estate, owned by five Florentine noblemen, had been reduced from 1600 to 400 hectares and had produced cereal and fruit, cherries and peaches, with wine very much a secondary activity. Until ten years ago the wine had been sold *sfuso*, but Luca had realized that they needed to change. There was simply no point in carrying on as they were. The only way to create a reputation and a good market is by putting your wine in bottles. He does not believe in the Colline Pisane, and has stopped making Chianti. 'You can't even sell it in Florence; people are so parochial.' So for him, too, the solution is Terre di Pisa, which will extend from Fauglia as far as Volterra and San Miniato and up to the FIPILI, the *superstrada* that links Florence to Livorno, and thus unite a group of like-minded producers. He hopes things will be decided for the 2006 vintage. The regulations will be much stricter than for Chianti, with a maximum yield of 1.5 kilos per vine and a minimum density in the vineyard of 5000 plants. The wine will be based on Sangiovese, with a minimum of 85 per cent, making it truly Tuscan, but also allowing for some Merlot, Syrah or Cabernet Sauvignon, depending on the producer's preference. And there will be a mandatory ageing period of twelve months in wood, followed by six months in bottle, making a much more serious wine than a Chianti from the Colline Pisane.

Altogether Luca has 22 hectares of vines, concentrating on Sangiovese with 13 hectares, as well as some Merlot and Cabernet, planted in 1994. He favours very high densities, 6000 to 10,000 and maybe even as many as 12,000 plants, and there is also some Trebbiano, Vermentino, Chardonnay and Sauvignon. We had a quick look round the cellars – it was raining too heavily to appreciate the vineyards in any comfort. The barrel cellar, originally the fermentation cellar in the 1950s, was built in the eighteenth century, with elegant arches and the original stone floor, while the bottling line was in the former laundry, which retained the old heater for boiling water, and large stone sinks. As for his wines, Luca makes three reds: Le Stoppie is a pure Sangiovese, with ripe cherry fruit, and would be a Chianti, while A Sirio, after his grandfather, is much more serious, from Sangiovese and 5 per cent Cabernet Sauvignon, which spends sixteen to eighteen months in wood. Originally it was called Rosso dei Colli dell'Etruria Centrale, a DOC created in 1989, which has failed to acquire any marketing cachet or recognition. Now it is an IGT, and, hopefully, in 2006 will become Terre di Pisa. The 1999 was quite solidly oaked and needed to develop. I Renai is a pure Merlot, aged in new oak for sixteen to eighteen months, with good structure and firm fruit, and even firmer oak. Luca was adamant that this was no international Merlot, for it has what he called the *acidità di questo terreno*, with its *sapidità* and *vivacità*. The maritime influence is apparent in both soil and climate; with sandy soil with fossils of shells, and sea breezes tempering the climate.

Two brothers, Giuseppe and Matteo Cantoni, at Tenuta di Fibbiano, are still very much finding their way. They come from Milan, where Matteo had been a sommelier and bought the estate in May 1998. It was all rather chaotic, for the cellars were a building site, except for the *barricaia*, housed in an Etruscan tomb. It was dug out of the tufa and the temperature remains constant throughout the year, never fluctuating beyond 12–15°C. In the nineteenth century, the tomb had been used as a larder. The two brothers are full of ideas and projects. Matteo talked about the different vines that existed in Tuscany a hundred years ago; as outsiders they are very much in favour of the indigenous grape varieties, and referred to a research project by the University of Florence focusing on some long-forgotten vines, such as Foglia Tonda. 'They do Merlot and Cabernet so much better in France, so it is much better to concentrate on Sangiovese.' They have 8 hectares in production, with Sangiovese, Canaiolo, a little Malvasia Nera, as well as Malvasia Bianca and an old variety Colombena, from which they make four red wines and one white: Le Pianette, Chianti, l'Aspetto and Ceppatello for red, and Fonte delle Donne for white. I liked the Ceppatello best, which benefits from some oak ageing, but I left with a feeling that this was an estate still trying to find its way – not unlike the whole region of the Colline Pisane.

We had first tasted Varramista's Syrah at the Antiprima tasting in Lucca. This is now an annual tasting that provides a preview of the previous year's vintage for the wines of the Tuscan coast from Bolgheri down to La Parrina. I had never before been to a tasting in quite such magnificent surroundings, in a fine *palazzo* with painted ceilings and frescoes, set in a large garden in the middle of a bustling town. It was quite awe-inspiring. And the quality of Varramista sang out, as one of the best Syrah of Tuscany, alongside Isole e Olena and Manzano.

Varramista is situated in the Arno valley, close to one of the main roads linking it with Florence, and although theoretically it comes within the Colline Pisane, the wines have absolutely nothing to do with Chianti. The estate originally belonged to the Capponi family, who are also the owners of Calcinaia in Chianti Classico. They acquired the land sometime towards the end of the fifteenth century, and built the imposing villa around 1490. A few centuries later the estate became the property of the Agnelli family; Umberto Agnelli ran the company Piaggio, which developed the Vespa scooter that is so popular all over Italy. Today Varramista is a private company.

There is a total of 480 hectares, including a game reserve of woods and a plantation of poplar trees, as well as an estate at Capalbio in the Maremma, but for olive oil rather than for wine. The original vineyards comprised the usual Tuscan mixture of grape varieties, in the traditional planting of *cultura promiscua*. Then in 1990 a decision was taken to create a small but high-quality vineyard, and so they began a programme of grafting and replanting, initially concentrating on just two varieties, Cabernet Sauvignon and Syrah. Subsequently they have added Merlot, for its early ripening and *rotondità*, and also Sangiovese. The director of the estate, Andrea Barbuti, explained that they make just two wines: Frasca, from 60 per cent Sangiovese with 20 per cent each of Merlot and Syrah, aged in oak for twelve to fourteen months; and Varramista, the pure Syrah on which the reputation of the estate is founded. The wine spends fifteen months in oak barrels, of which two-thirds are new. The intrinsic peppery character of Syrah was undoubtedly there in the young wine, with some weight and structure, while older vintages had developed a certain meaty character. Why Syrah? I asked. It had quite simply been 'a flight of fantasy'. There had been no preliminary studies, but it had undoubtedly paid off. Federico Staderini, the first winemaker at Ornellaia, has been involved since the beginning; he is keen and intense, and has created a highly successful, brand-new wine, an example of the wonderful creativity that abounds in Tuscany.

Montellori does not really fit into the pattern of Chianti; nor does it provide any walking opportunities, situated as it is on the bypass of Fucecchio. However, its wines more than merit the detour. The new cellars and an elegant eighteenth-century villa with its formal gardens are in the suburbs of Fucecchio, an unprepossessing town in the Arno valley, while the vineyards are in the hills, towards Monte Albano at Ceretto Guidi. Alessandro Nieri explained how they were hoping for the creation of a Chianti sub-zone, Ceretto Guidi. When I expressed doubts as to the marketability of the name, he told me firmly that the project was *allo studio*, and that the wines would require a minimum of 90 per cent Sangiovese and a period of ageing in wood. As for white wine, there is a DOC, Bianco dell'Empolesi, created in 1990. Unfortunately, the regulations made the complete mistake of insisting on 80 per cent Trebbiano, despite the lack of support for this by any potential producers, and consequently the DOC may exist on paper, but rarely in practice. Alessandro Nieri does make two white wines; neither is Bianco dell'Empolesi, nor do they contain any Trebbiano. His IGT Manderlo is an original blend of Roussanne, Marsanne, Clairette, Chardonnay and Viognier, with intriguing herbal notes and a full, slightly almondy finish, not unlike a Montecarlo, while Sant'Amato is a pure Sauvignon. The vineyards for it are on the slopes of Monte Albano at 450 metres, with 7500 plants per hectare, and the wine had the attractive herbaceous character of Sauvignon, with Alessandro explaining how there are two harvests, ten days apart, achieving a very successful blend, balancing ripeness and acidity.

Montellori is the only private estate in this part of Tuscany; any other nearby vineyards are part of the local cooperative, the Cantina Leonardo, outside Vinci, which produces a very palatable Chianti. Montellori was bought by Alessandro's great-grandfather in 1895 and they first put their wine in bottle in the 1950s. Today half of the 100-hectare estate is devoted to vineyards; the rest is arable land. A second estate, Fattoria le Caselle, was bought at nearby San Miniato in 1998, which produces Chianti and an IGT Bramasole, a blend of 70 per cent Sangiovese with Syrah, with some peppery fruit and firm tannins.

When I first visited Montellori back in 1989, Castelrapiti was their flagship wine, both red and white. But things have evolved; the white is no longer made as the rewards of trying to make a great white wine – that is to say, with oak – are uncertain in Tuscany for there is too much competition from elsewhere. As for the red, from the 2001 vintage, it will be called Dedicato, in memory of Alessandro's father, who died in 2002. Castelrapiti, which was first made in 1985, has been a valuable learning process and now they want to implement that experience by creating a new wine, a pure Sangiovese, rather than the previous Sangiovese and Cabernet Sauvignon blend. There is no doubt that the use of oak has become more subtle and refined over the year, for the 2001 Dedicato had youthful fruit and tannins, with a fine structure and good ageing potential.

Moro, with a mulberry on the label, is a blend of 80 per cent Sangiovese and 10 per cent each of Cabernet and Malvasia Nera, aged for a year in *barrique*, and is seen as providing a bridge to the more expensive super-Tuscans, Dedicato, and Salamartana, which is a blend of Cabernet and Merlot, given fourteen months' ageing, half in new *barriques*, and was first made in 1992.

Over lunch with Alessandro's mother we tasted old vintages, an elegantly cedary 1995 Castelrapiti and a more vegetal, smoky 1997 Salamartana. Maria Carla had cooked a delicious pasta, a simple *farfalle*, the butterfly-shaped pasta, with finely chopped onions, young peas and olive oil from the estate. The fresh flavours amply illustrated the appeal of simple ingredients. Not so simple was the devastatingly rich chocolate cake that was our dessert. The walls of the villa are hung with numerous paintings, vivid splashes of bright colours, by the artist Salvo, who has also designed some of Montellori's wine labels. They, too, were worth the detour before we returned to the more traditional areas of Tuscany.

YIELDS

YIELD IS A KEY FACTOR in wine quality. If a vine produces too many grapes, the wine will be thin and dilute, but if the yield is too low, the wine will be unbalanced and excessively concentrated. Balance is crucial. Traditionally in Tuscany vine density has been low, with about 3000 plants per hectare, each producing a fairly generous amount of grapes, to give what sounds like a reasonable yield per hectare. However, these days research has proved that it is preferable to have more plants per hectare, as many as 7000 or even more, with each producing a much smaller quantity of grapes. The yield for Chianti Classico is fixed at 3 kilos per vine, and 5 kilos in the rest of Chianti, but any conscientious producer will tell you that they produce much less than that. Vines thrive on a bit of competition, so that narrower rows are also beneficial to wine quality.

Initially yields are determined by the severity of pruning in the spring, but the growers also have to hedge their bets, as their crop may be affected by spring frosts or hail; consequently the practice of green harvesting has also developed, allowing for excess grapes to be removed in mid-summer.

Brunello di Montalcino, Sant'Antimo and Orcia

· June walks, with some cellar visits in February ·

Round the walls of Montalcino. From Camigliano to Banfi at Poggio alle Mura. Col d'Orcia, Argiano. From Buonconvento to Montalcino, via Emilia Nardi at Casale del Bosco, Badia Ardenga, Donatella Cinelli at Il Casato, Colombaio di Montosoli and Il Paradiso di Manfredi. Altesino, Caparzo. From Montalcino to Sant'Antimo. Fanti, Costanti, Sirò Pacenti, Poggio Antico, Fattoria dei Barbi

MONTALCINO IS SYNONYMOUS with one of Tuscany's finest red wines, Brunello di Montalcino. It was the Biondi Santi family who did much to establish the early reputation of the wines and it really all began with Ferruccio Biondi Santi in the 1870s. However, before that the naturalist Giorgio Santi had written in the eighteenth century of his estates and their 'exquisite fruits, much and above all, rich wine'. The next generation Clemente Santi won a prize at a local fair for his 'vino rosso scelto (brunello)' in 1865. He favoured a particular variety of Sangiovese, called Sangiovese Grosso, as opposed to the Sangiovese Piccolo, or Sangioveto, that is more common in Chianti. When Sangiovese Grosso ripens, the grapes take on a dark dusky colour, described as *brunello*, hence the name given to this particular sub-variety of Sangiovese, which Clemente Santi had planted on his estate at Il Greppo.

Ferruccio Biondi Santi was a courageous young man who fought with Garibaldi's troops at the battle of Bezzecca in 1866, and his interest in winemaking developed when he took over his grandfather Clemente's cellar. It was a difficult time as two diseases, oidium and peronospera, had affected the vineyards of Montalcino. The white Moscadello vines suffered particularly, while Sangiovese seemed to fare better, so Ferruccio set to work to isolate this particularly variety of Sangiovese and replant his vineyards with it. He took cuttings from the best vines; in effect, some of the earliest work on clonal selection. His work was particularly innovatory because, at that time, not only was most of the wine of Montalcino still predominantly white, but any red wine was made in the style of a young Chianti, including white grapes and with the use of the *governo* method, to produce a fruity wine for early drinking. By making a wine from Sangiovese alone, limiting the yields and keeping the juice in contact with the skins for a long period of fermentation, followed by a period of ageing in large oak barrels, Ferruccio Biondi Santi was anticipating the trend for pure Sangiovese of the late twentieth century. The 1888 and 1891 vintages were particularly praised.

Ferruccio's son Tancredi continued his father's work and began to establish the international reputation of the family and its wine, and things have continued in much the same way under the succeeding generations, Franco and then his son Jacopo, who has gone on to produce wine on his mother-in-law's estate of Poggio Salvi and also in Scansano at the Castello di Montepò (see pages 299-300). It was appropriate that Franco Biondi Santi was able to host a celebration to mark a hundred years of Brunello di Montalcino. In some ways the date was rather arbitrary, for it just happened that 1888 was the vintage of the oldest surviving bottles. For those of us privileged to attend, it was a splendid occasion.

Phylloxera decimated the vineyards of Montalcino during the 1930s and production declined still further during the Second World War and its aftermath. It was not until 1980 that the vineyard area of Montalcino returned to that of 1929. However, already in the 1950s several other estates had begun to sell their Brunello too, notably the Colombini at Fattoria dei Barbi, and also the Lisini, Franceschi, Costanti Lovatelli, Mastropaolo, Camigliano, Casale del Bosco, Castiglion del Bosco, to name but a few, some of whom will appear on these pages. The reputation of Brunello di Montalcino, combined with the energy of these producers, led to the creation of a DOC in 1966, which laid down the guidelines for production, defining the area, limiting the yield, and confirming a four-year ageing period in cask, and the classification of *riserva* for five years' ageing. With the end of the *mezzadria* system, the new DOC gave an impetus to the development of several smaller estates and encouraged investment from outside the region, a trend that continues to this day.

The next stage was the creation of the DOCG, in 1980. It was an opportunity for a modification in the regulations, reducing the yield to 80 quintals, making 56 hl/ha, and the ageing period to three and a half years from 1 April following the vintage. The possibility of a corrective of wine from elsewhere was firmly squashed. Subsequently the ageing period has been reduced still further to a minimum of two years in cask, and a minimum of four months in bottle. However, the wine must stay in the cellar until five years after the harvest, allowing for a certain flexibility and choice between vat, cask and bottle.

Not all the grapes will produce wine suitable for such a long ageing period, so that the creation of the DOC Rosso di Montalcino recognized the existence of a younger style of wine, with a shorter period of ageing, and not necessarily in wood. The wine may be sold from 1 September following the harvest. Rosso di Montalcino at its best conveys the flavour of Brunello, but without its weight or structure. The third wine of Montalcino, Moscadello di Montalcino, recalls the medieval tradition for sweet white wine in the region, the Moscadelletto, which was lavishly praised by Francesco Redi in 1685. In practice very few people make it, but those who do, passionately maintain the tradition.

The last decade has seen some notable developments in Montalcino, with an enormous growth in the number of producers, as the international reputation of the wine has soared. Every February Montalcino hosts a tasting, Benvenuto Brunello, to welcome the new wines; in 2003, the 1998 Brunello, the 1997 *riserva* and the 2001 Rosso di Montalcino. It is a tremendous occasion, some 120 producers participating in the tasting and showing off their wines. It's the only time I have been to a tasting attended by the local *carabinieri* in dress uniform, with swords, gold braid and tassles galore.

The *comune* of Montalcino covers a number of little villages and hamlets, and is limited by three rivers, the Orcia, the Ombrone and the Asso. We were lent an *agriturismo*, a snug little flat in the tiny hamlet of Camigliano, which provided a comfortable base for a week's stay. The view on one side overlooked a building site; we were reliably informed that the open-air village discotheque was being refurbished. On the other side we looked across the valley over vineyards and woods towards Argiano, and Poggio alle Mura, which is now part of the Banfi empire. Maddalena had enthused about Carmigliano. 'I just love this place; it is so peaceful. You never hear a thing.' Those proved to be famous last words. It did indeed seem peaceful and yet at 6 o'clock the next morning the tranquillity was shattered by a sound remarkably similar to that of a Boeing 747 slowing down its engines after landing. I looked out of the window somewhat bleary-eyed to see an eager red tractor in the vineyard across the valley, already at work in the early-morning sunshine, spraying the vines. Somehow the valley walls seemed to amplify the impact of the noise. But fortunately the spraying was completed in one morning. And I was equally relieved that the disco was still a building site.

Camigliano belongs to Gualtiero and Laura Ghezzi. His father bought the property in 1958 and now Gualtiero, who is a construction engineer in Milan, is turning his attention to renovating the estate and improving the quality of his wine. First we explored the village, a cluster of houses, with a riot of flowers in pots around a tiny square. An elderly woman was washing her lettuce under the village pump. The villa where the Ghezzi live had a breathtakingly vivid bougainvillaea growing up the wall. We went into the simple church, which dates back to the fourteenth century, with the vestiges of carvings over a lintel. The key was carefully hidden between stones by the door. A door discreetly advertising *vendita diretta* quite belies the large cellar behind it. Originally there might have been as many as 350 people living here, but now that number has dropped to about forty, all of whom work on the estate.

Gualtiero took us for a drive through the vineyards, which are all around the village. He now has 50 hectares, mainly of Brunello, but also a little Cabernet Sauvignon, Merlot and Syrah for the new DOC of Sant'Antimo. Originally the estate totalled 1000 hectares and although they have sold land to Antinori, at Pian delle Vigne, they still retain 60 hectares of olive trees, as well as vast expanses of woodland. Back in the cellar there was a feeling that things were about to change, with plans for extensive modernization and the arrival of a new oenologist, Lorenzo Landi, and also an *agronomo* to help in the vineyards. For the moment the wines seemed a touch rustic, but certainly the potential is there.

Montalcino is one of my favourite hilltop towns. There is a long street that runs through the middle of the town from the Piazza del Popolo with the town hall to the Piazza Cavour. It is lined with tempting shops, bakers that sell *panforte*

and the traditional *biscotti, ossi di morti*. Inevitably there are wine shops, and a delightful café, the Fiaschetteria, with sumptuous red banquettes and its original *art nouveau* decor. Much of the city walls are still intact, so it is possible to walk round them. We started our circuit near the Santuario della Madonna del Soccorso and went through the Porta Suvelli and past the hospitals, both old and new. Then the path at the foot of the walls led past numerous little vegetable gardens, tiny pocket handkerchiefs of land, crammed with every imaginable vegetable in early June. There were peas, French beans, artichokes, tomatoes, a cherry tree, where someone had temptingly propped a ladder, some olive trees and even a few vines, as well as some noisy chickens. Then we came to the Fonti Castellana, an old fountain and *lavatoio*, or washing place, that was being restored, before the path took us back into the town though the Porta Castellana and up to the *fortezza*. This is fourteenth-century in origin and you can walk round most of the walls and climb the towers for views over the town, a patchwork of russet-coloured roofs, punctuated by the inevitable television aerials, with the Tuscan hills stretching into the background. The fortress also houses an *enoteca*, with wines from just about every estate worth its salt in Montalcino. They offer tastings and light lunches, but the canned music drove us away.

Later we took the path out of Camigliano, down a steep track, to cross an almost dried-up stream, save for a pond with some noisy frogs. A steep climb took us up the other side of the valley and along to a tiny walled cemetery. It looked somewhat neglected, with faded plastic flowers, and a little further along the road was the Pieve di Poggio alle Mura, dedicated to San Sigismondo. It is Romanesque, dating back to 1462. We were lucky: the door was open, and we found a plain nave, with rounded arches and some simple carvings. The restaurant next door, the Osteria del Vecchio Castello, was once the priest's house. At dinner later that evening we found that it boasted one of the best wine lists of Tuscany, in three volumes: Montalcino, the rest of Italy, and the rest of the world. We contented ourselves with the local one, which had an array of tempting older vintages of all the best names, and the menu offered food to match, with a series of elegant courses of traditional Tuscan flavours.

We carried on along the track to Poggio alle Mura, passing their vineyards. The Banfi bus, which provides transport for the vineyard workers, was parked by the side of the road and people were busy leaf-plucking and tucking the shoots into the wires. Where this had not yet been done, the vineyards look quite unruly, as though each vine was sprouting an overgrown shaggy hairstyle and was badly in need of a short back and sides. Some electric fences were in place to protect the vineyards from the ravages of wild boar, and we also passed some irrigation pumps, with black tubes discreetly running through the vineyards, for drip irrigation. A tiny chapel marked the beginning of the driveway to the castle and we turned up the avenue of cypresses. An earthmover was at work, first flattening the soil and then ploughing it deeply; the strength of this yellow monster was mesmerizing, shifting soil and enormous rocks, and at the side there were piles of some huge stones that had been removed from the old vineyards. Further along we came to the old icehouse, a brick building with a domed roof, in the shade of a grove of cypresses. It would have been filled with snow from nearby Monte Amiata.

The large American company of Banfi Vintners was created by the Mariani brothers, John and Harry, and their subsequent investment in Montalcino, following their success with Lambrusco from the large cooperative of Reunite, caused more than a little unease and suspicion amongst the more conservative members of the winemaking fraternity. But twenty years on, it seems that they are well integrated into the community, producing a serious range of wines, both Rosso and Brunello di Montalcino as well as the recently created DOC of Sant'Antimo and various other IGT. They have a considerable amount of technical expertise at their disposal as well as the financial means to invest in cellars and vineyards. The entire estate totals some 2830 hectares, of which under a third, 850 hectares, is planted with vines, concentrating on Sangiovese, Cabernet Sauvignon, Merlot and Syrah for reds, and Chardonnay, Sauvignon, Pinot Grigio and Moscadello for whites. Much work has been done on clonal selection for Sangiovese, with the choice narrowed down to about twelve significant ones, of which Banfi are working on three or four, linking a clone with the most appropriate soil. Sangiovese clones can be very diverse, with varying fruit and tannins, so that a mixture in the vineyard makes for a more balanced wine. Research has indicated at least thirty different soil types, with an on-going project of soil definition, but with so much land they have the luxury of being able to select the very best sites for their vineyards. Elsewhere they have plum orchards and grow sunflowers and wheat.

Poggio alle Mura provides the historic contrast to the modern public face of Banfi, an eleventh-century castle which has been carefully restored and now houses a glass museum, which can only be described as fabulous. It covers the history of glass from Roman times to modern-day Riedel, with some exquisite Venetian glasses, and some wonderfully ornate bottles, some decorative, some comic, and all beautifully displayed. There is a visitor centre, where you can taste and buy, and also a restaurant, offering typical Tuscan dishes. Next door there is what they call the *balsameria*, where they make balsamic vinegar. Legally balsamic vinegar comes only from Modena, so although this is made in exactly the same way, it is sold as *salsa etrusca*. Trebbiano and Moscato must, which has been concentrated with some gentle simmering, and with the addition of a yeast culture, is aged in a *solera* system, with barrels from five different woods, beginning with 60-litre oak barrels, then chestnut, next cherry, followed by ash, and finishing with just 25-litre mulberry barrels. The barrels do not have a bung, so that the contents are left open to the air, protected simply with a cloth and a chain to keep the cloth in place. Every so often, a third of the contents of the mulberry barrel is run off for bottling and the *solera* is refreshed. The minimum ageing period for balsamic vinegar is twelve years, and may be as long as twenty-five. It is far more valuable than Brunello di Montalcino.

Every time that I visit Banfi, it seems that the cellars have grown, and there is yet more modern equipment. Ezio Rivella, who masterminded the whole development, has now retired to his own estate near Massa Marittima and the head winemaker is Rudi Buratti. They have new bladder presses, squat fermentation tanks, with an internal paddle that removes the bitter pips from the skins, and a new barrel cellar, with refined humidity and temperature control. They are now ageing and seasoning their own staves, in association with the Italian cooper Gamba, so there were piles of wood stacked in the yard outside the cellar. They use both *barriques* and *botti* for ageing their Brunello, with a total of 7000 *barriques*, of which a third are renewed every year. This is everything that a modern cellar should be, producing wines that are consistently representative of Montalcino. The cellars are also open to the public for a daily tour.

From Banfi it is a short distance to Col d'Orcia on the outskirts of Sant'Angelo in Scalo. This used to be part of the Cinzano empire, but since the family sold the brand is now owned by Francesco Marone Cinzano. Pablo Harri, a friendly Swiss, who used to make wine for Banfi, is now the winemaker at Col d'Orcia and describes their style as classic and traditional, and indeed it is. However, the wines have moved with the times. They have invested in their vineyards, planting international varieties, as well as replanting Sangiovese. Altogether they have 150 hectares (which ranks them third after Banfi and Frescobaldi at Castelgiocondo), of which 110 are Sangiovese. They favour *botti* rather than *barriques* for their Brunello. However, Cru Banditella is a barrique-aged Rosso di Montalcino from a single vineyard, making it a more serious and structured wine than some. Their Brunello di Montalcino is rounded with soft tannins, while best of all is their *cru* Poggio al Vento, a 7-hectare vineyard, which is only made in the very best years. It is given a total of seven years' ageing, before sale, first in 50-hectolitre barrels, and is bottled after four and a half years. The wine was sturdy and dense with a great concentration of fruit and flavour. Later we walked to the vineyard, which is close to the hilltop village of Sant'Angelo in Colle, to admire a magnificent 200-year-old oak tree, which features in a list of the 100 most beautiful oak trees of Tuscany. It spans some 80 feet in diameter, a breathtakingly majestic tree, surrounded by neatly tended vineyards. Nearby there was a dilapidated farmhouse, which we fantasized about restoring as a holiday house. Instead we took the cistus-lined track back to the road and up to the little village of Sant'Angelo in Colle. It was rather sombre in the spitting rain. A group of elderly ladies chatting on the steps of the church were scattered by the diatribes of a drunken carpet salesman; they retreated muttering to their various houses and we took refuge in the café.

Argiano, which is close to Banfi, also belongs to a member of the Cinzano family, Noemi Maroni Cinzano, the sister of Francesco, and is not to be confused with the nearby Castello di Argiano. This was built in the thirteenth century, and fell into ruin in the sixteenth century, so that only the tower remains, surrounded by a cluster of houses. In contrast, the wine estate of Argiano is centred on an elegant villa, which was built in 1570, with an avenue of cypress trees and a double-arched courtyard, with flowering jasmine. There are some fine old cellars, with vaulted ceilings and arches in soft red brick, with the remains of an old water cistern, under the villa, which was filled with rainwater; a precautionary measure in case of siege during the troubled period of the Middle Ages. Once this was an enormous estate of some 7000 hectares, but is now a shadow of its former self, with a manageable 48 hectares of vineyards. A sleepy Alsatian, Ringo, stirred himself to greet us. Pepe Graciani gave us a tasting, which illustrated the elegance that is the hallmark of the wines of Argiano. Rosso di Montalcino spends nine months in *botti*, and was quite tannic and sturdy compared to some. The Brunello was everything that a Brunello should be, while their IGT Solengo, a blend of equal parts of Cabernet Sauvignon, Merlot and Syrah, was rich and concentrated, with a more international flavour.

There is an extraordinary diversity in the terrain and *terroir* of Montalcino, which you only really appreciate as you cross the *comune* on foot. The map of Montalcino comprises a 30-kilometre-square outline of hilly terrain, with Tuscany's highest mountain, Monte Amiata, off to the south-east. In general terms, the vineyards to the north-west tend to be cooler, whereas those to the south are more influenced by the warm winds of the Tyrrhenian Sea blowing across the Maremma. Monte Amiata helps protect Montalcino from extremes of climate. Altitude plays a part, too, with most vines planted between 300 and 500 metres, and certainly no higher than 600 metres. As for geology, *galestro* is the main soil type, usually mixed with some clay.

We caught the local bus down the hill to the town of Buonconvento. The driver firmly ignored the notice *Non parlare all'autista* and chatted to his passengers; he was quite clearly a vital cog in the efficiency of the local grapevine. Buonconvento is a pretty town, in soft red brick. Its old walls and gates still stand and the main street contains some medieval houses, and on Saturdays there is a lively market outside the walls. We crossed the river Ombrone, which was a tiny trickle in early summer, and took a dirt track towards a farm and continued up into the woods. The outline of a castle tower appeared through the trees, not medieval but a modern one in red brick, and further up the hill there was a castellated lodge, again in red brick and firmly shuttered. It seemed rather incongruous. We learned later that this was the Castello di Rosi, which had been built in 1800, though it looked even more recent. The path continued between fields of wheat and broad beans, past a grove of olive trees to an alleyway of cypresses that led to what we thought at first was yet another fake medieval castle. In fact, it was the Castello di Bibbiano, with origins in the tenth century. Then we reached the village of Segalari. On the outskirts there was a traditional vineyard with the wide rows of high vines, and a little shrine, surrounded by cypress trees. We chose not to refresh ourselves at the *bieraria*, as the village café described itself, but walked on past a newly restored *agriturismo*, Podere Casalone, with some new vineyards. They are too low in altitude for Brunello and outside the denomination.

We crossed the railway track at Stazione Torre-Bibbiano and immediately afterwards warning lights began to flash, and, after a very long pause, a two-carriage train eventually chundered past, on its way to Grosseto. Then we crossed the Ombrone again, this time a rather fuller river, and passed a distinctly uninviting *agriturismo*, and a dilapidated farmhouse. Our path started to climb, and we stopped for a picnic, looking at a field of ripening golden corn. A cockerel in a nearby farmhouse kept crowing loudly, and when we set off we soon passed a sign telling us that we were within the denomination of Brunello di Montalcino; then we saw our first vineyards, belonging to Castiglion del Bosco, and a signpost to Nardi.

Castiglion del Bosco has recently changed hands, to be bought by Massimo Ferragamo, a member of the well-known fashion house, representing perhaps an example of the appeal of a wine estate to the lavishly rich, who see it as an accoutrement to their mainstream business. Our destination instead was Casale del Bosco, which is one of the two estates belonging to the Nardi family.

Emilia Nardi gave us a friendly welcome, telling us that her father had bought the property back in 1950 and had extended the family holdings, buying more land, in 1962, including Manechiara, which is close to Fattoria dei Barbi, with more favourable vineyard land. The family business is agricultural machinery and based in Umbria; she is one of eight children. After Emilia had tried the family business for a couple of years, her father gave her the opportunity to run these two estates, and she jumped at it. And that is what she has been doing since 1993. She manages some 80 hectares of vines in all, which are currently undergoing an extensive replanting programme. The oldest part of the cellars dates back to the seventeenth century, with lovely stone arches, where the *barriques* for their *cru*, Manechiara, from the very oldest vineyard planted in the 1950s, are housed, and the entrance to the cellars at their upper level is down a spiral staircase, cunningly fitted into the old well. Nardi are one of the protagonists for the use of *barriques* in Montalcino, following the advice of Professor Yves Glories from Bordeaux. Emilia talked admiringly of his work, of how he has revolutionized their wines. Previously everything had been very traditional, but Glories made them look at every detail, assessing the identity and character of each vineyard, considering the maturity of the grapes and the *terreno*. In some years they might do a pre-fermentation maceration, but not in 2002, as that was a very difficult vintage. They do *rimontaggi* and *délestages*, all depending on the quality of the grapes. The wines are a blend from several different vineyards, with the aim of elegance, in preference to concentration. Certainly those that we tasted from the fine 1998 vintage had achieved an elegant balance of fruit, tannin and finesse.

Continuing our walk, the skyline of Montalcino came into view and we realized just how steep a climb we had ahead of us, and in the other direction the mock castle dominated the landscape, with Buonconvento in the distance. The attractive bell tower of Badia Ardenga announced our arrival there, with a welcoming sign saying *cantine aperte*, left from the open day for cellars earlier in the week. The *cantine aperte* is an initiative designed to encourage members of the public to visit wine cellars in their regions, with the various member cellars offering a visit and a tasting. There is a nationwide opening once a year in early June. The Badia, a Vallombrosan monastery of the eleventh century, founded by the count of Ardenga and subsequently suppressed by Pope Pius II, was firmly closed. A door left ajar next to the church revealed the old cellar, with a couple of disintegrating barrels and a dilapidated concrete vat. It transpired that the functioning cellars are down the road at Torrenieri, and that is where we went on a later visit to Montalcino, the following February. Mario Ciacci was keen to tell us something of the history. The building was on the Via Francigena. An archbishop of Canterbury, Sigerico, had stayed there in 990, when the Pope had summoned all the archbishops to Rome, as an act of submission. It was a 118-day journey, with seventy-nine stops, either in a sanctuary or a fortified place, such as Torrenieri. The name derives from 'a tower built of dark stone'. Under the Sienese it was incorporated into a castle to defend and control a strategic point on the Via Francigena, and was destroyed by the Lucchesi in 1315. The Sienese had wanted to rebuild it, but they were always short of the necessary cash. However, the house was rebuilt as an important staging point on the pilgrim route and was to remain a strategic crossroads on the road between Siena and Rome until the middle of the nineteenth century. Torrenieri was appreciated for its fresh water and the healthy air, as well as the ample space for accommodating carriages. Apparently Eleanor, Princess of Portugal, stayed here on her way to Rome to marry the emperor, Federico III, in 1452. A local observer noted that she was 'as beautiful as Nature could make her', and also that she travelled with forty doubles, who wore the identical clothes and hairstyle, in order to protect the princess.

Abbadia Ardenga consists of 10 hectares of vines around the old abbey, but the wine is made in cellars at Torrenieri. It was a freezing cold February day, and the cellars seemed even colder than outside, as we wandered through a series of rooms full of barrels and vats. Signor Ciacci pointed out the date over the arch, 1449, and there was a well dating from 1450, while the vestiges of the old tower were discernible as particularly thick parts of the walls. There were various old artefacts, a hand pump, a destemmer and a plough that would have been drawn by a pair of oxen. A library of bottles included Badia Ardenga from the 1950s and a collection of bottles of Brunello representing everyone who bottled their wine in the 1970s. The wines were cold, too; tasted again later they had a certain rusticity, with dry cedary notes on the Brunello and more immediate fruit on the Rosso di Montalcino.

After Badia Ardenga the path began to climb gently, past an old drinking trough and numerous beehives, for Montalcino is also known for its honey. The flowers in June were spectacular with hedges of wild dog roses, and beautiful brilliant purple and pink vetches, as well as pyramid orchids and wild fennel. We saw some wild boar tracks, but never an animal, and then reached Il Casato, Donatella Cinelli's neat-looking winery, in a beautifully restored farmhouse, next to a building site, with the inevitable tall crane.

Donatella Cinelli has always been very much in favour of wine tourism, and her cellar is beautifully designed to welcome the visitor, with a fascinating introduction to the history of Montalcino. Her friendly colleague, Antonella Marconi, took us on a guided tour. First there were three tiles that explained the origins of Montalcino, the *mons* or hill, while ilex is an oak tree, which gives you Mons Ilicini, which became Montalcino. The tannin from the oak trees was used to tan leather from AD 1000, and the charcoal from the trees fired the kilns for pottery. A local artist, Giovanni Salto, has illustrated various key moments in the town's history. By 1260, Montalcino was a wealthy city state and an important republic in its own right. However, both Florence and Siena had designs upon it. The two city states met in battle at Monteaperti, and the Montalcinesi were asked to participate, but could not decide which side to support. In fact, they arrived too late, just as the Sienese had won the field, and consequently Montalcino became part of the republic of Siena. Giovanni Salto's mural depicts the Montalcinesi burying the dead; the battle was so bloody that the waters of the Arbia are said to have run red with blood, and to this day the Montalcinesi retain the nickname *becca morti* or grave-diggers, and for this reason the local biscuits are called *ossi di morti*.

Montalcino spent the ensuing 300 years defending itself against the might of Florence, and then, in 1553, Florence besieged the town with Spanish help. The mural depicts the Spanish general confronted by a vision of the Madonna, protecting the town. This was taken as a sign from God and the siege was called off. Thus the Madonna became the patron saint of Montalcino, with celebrations on her feast day, 8 May, centred on the church La Madonna del Soccorso. However, by 1559 Florence had seized Montalcino so that it became part of the Grand Duchy under the Medici and there was no longer any need for the town to defend itself. Instead, it needed to recover its former prosperity. The shoes and terracotta that contributed to its earlier wealth were no longer significant and so it turned to agriculture, and also to wine. Agriculture alone was not enough as there was always the risk of famine, as the picture for the year 1840 depicts. By 1920 wine was becoming important alongside other crops, and by 1970 Brunello di Montalcino had begun to acquire a wider reputation. It was the history of the town imaginatively told in a nutshell. Next came Donatella's family tree. Il Casato came to Donatella from her grandmother, but has been in the family since 1592, often used as a hunting lodge and also as a honeymoon house, and always passed through the female line. It could be said that on first acquaintance Donatella looks an unlikely feminist for she has an elegant Renaissance face that would not be out of place in a portrait in the Uffizi gallery, and yet she feels passionately that women deserve a more important role in agriculture and the world of wine. For this reason her best wine is called Le Prime Donne. After admiring the renovated cellars, we settled down to a tasting confronted by a forest of glasses.

Not only does Donatella produce Brunello, but she is also involved in the new DOC of Orcia, at another family property at Fattoria il Colle at Trequanda. The DOC of Orcia, created in 2000, demands a minimum of 60 per cent Sangiovese, but otherwise anything else goes, except that pure Sangiovese is not allowed, in order to differentiate it from Brunello di Montalcino. Prior to 2000 the wines were plain Rosso Toscano, from an area that stretches from Torrenieri to Pienza and on to Cetona. There are now some thirty producers, mostly with a strong dominance of international grape varieties. Donatella makes two Orcia. Leone Rosso, as her father's family crest is the red lion, is from Sangiovese with 30 per cent Merlot. It was young and fresh and eminently drinkable. More serious was Cenerentola; in English, Cinderella. Donatella explained the reason for the name: the wine is sandwiched between two stepsisters, Brunello di Montalcino and Vino Nobile di Montepulciano, which are older, richer and more famous. Cenerentola is an intriguing blend of Sangiovese and a little-known grape variety that Donatella is trying to revive called Foglia Tonda. It was apparently the main grape variety of the Orcia valley, and provides colour and structure to a wine, complementing the perfume and elegance of the Sangiovese. Although most of the other producers of Orcia favour the inclusion of some international varieties, Donatella adamantly insists on Tuscan grapes. She compared Foglia Tonda with Sagrantino, a grape variety from Montefalco in Umbria, which had similarly nearly disappeared.

1998 was Donatella's first vintage, but she had to wait until 2002 to use the renovated cellar at Il Casato. The new cellar allows her to give her wines a year in *barriques* and a year in *botti* and then they will have a couple of years of bottle ageing before they are released for sale. The 1998 Brunello, without any *barriques*, just small *botti*, was ripe and rounded, with some supple fruit. More serious were the three Prime Donne, which came next. The 1998, which had been in *barriques*, was sturdy and firm, with a structured palate. 2001, straight from a *barrique*, had some perfumed oak, with silky tannins and promised well, while the 2000 was less elegant, with a richer concentration of vanilla and tannin and a firm, fruity finish.

After Il Casato, the road took us past La Magia and then Le Gode di Ilano Ripaccioli, where a silent dog sniffed us, and the gradient increased. Soon we reached Colombaio di Montosoli, where there was a riot of colourful flowerpots in the courtyard, with an old well and a pomegranate tree in flower. Nello Barricci, a sprightly 80-year-old with a twinkle in his eye, explained how he had bought his land in 1956, as the *mezzadria* system was being dismantled, observing that it was much better to work for yourself than for a *padrone*, or boss. His first fermentation vats were wood, then cement, and now they are stainless steel, and the neat little cellar was built in stages, mainly under their house. 1971 was the first wine they bottled, which they could not sell until 1975. He has 13 hectares of land, including 5 of vineyards, as well as olives and wood, for the land had been very much used for mixed farming in the traditional manner. Signor Barrici has a traditional view about barrels, which is shared by his son Graziano; their wine spends at least three years, if not three and a half, in *botti*, when it need only be two. We tasted the 2001 from barrel, which will not be bottled until 2005; it was nicely understated with closed, firm fruit; the nose had begun to develop on the 2000, making for richer cedary notes, while the 1999, which was to be bottled before the summer of 2003, was elegantly stylish. 'That's already a Bruncllo,' observed Nello. And we finished with 1998, with its elegant cedary fruit and rounded bottle, amply illustrating the quality of this estate, which was one of the pioneers of the Brunello *consorzio*.

Next we passed signs to Capanna, Pertimali and Il Paradiso, and the road continued to climb relentlessly, past a fine old stone wall with an arched drinking fountain set in it. Then we reached a sadly neglected stone chapel; we peered in through a window to see the remains of frescoes on the wall. The date on the outside wall was 1577. Eventually we caught our first glimpse of the Porta Burelli, the way into Montalcino, at which moment our step lightened noticeably.

I have a soft spot for the wines of Il Paradiso di Manfredi. It was a chance bottle in what is now one of my favourite restaurants in Siena, Le Logge, that first led me there. Le Logge is owned by Gianni Brunelli, who is now a Bruncllo producer in his own right, but back in the mid-1980s he was an enthusiastic advocate of his cousin's wine from Il Paradiso. Florio Guerrini is a school bursar by profession, but looks after his mother-in-law's vineyard of one and a half hectares on the steep hillside outside Montalcino. 1982 was his first vintage, of which he made just 300 bottles, one of which we drank at Le Logge. On this last visit the whole family gave us a warm welcome: Florio, his wife Rosella, his mother-in-law Fortunata, and their daughter Silvia, who is learning about wine with a view to taking over from her father eventually. Their large black dog, Annibale, charged round the garden, enjoying his favourite game of chasing the cats. The olive trees were in flower and the view from the terrace showed us how steeply we had climbed, with the vineyards of Montosoli, Altesino, Caparzo and Capanna, and the cellars of Val di Suga. On a clearer day we would have been able to see Pienza and even Montepulciano. You are at 830 metres here.

Florio has a neat little cellar under the house; essentially he makes one *botte* per vintage. The 2001 wine was doing its malolactic fermentation, and every now and then the cask emitted a loud gurgle, not unlike a giant stomach rumbling. 2000 was an excellent vintage for Florio; he talked about the importance of microclimate, explaining how it does not get too hot here, on the north-east side of Montalcino, as there is very good ventilation and consequently no fog. The wine had some wonderfully elegant fruit, with supple tannins. Everything is very simple, and done with meticulous attention to detail; there is no fining or filtering and bottling is by gravity. Then Florio opened a bottle of 1997, the latest vintage to be bottled, and we sat round a dining table laden with *salami, prosciutto* and *pecorino.* The wine was everything that fine Brunello should be, with an appealingly smoky nose, and cedary fruit on the palate, with a long lingering finish. Florio talked about the smell of wine left in the empty glass, detecting not only honey but also red fruits, cherries, raspberries, blackberries and plums.

Altesino is just outside Buonconvento, on the southern edge of the *comune* of Montalcino. The name means 'small Altesi', and next door is the Castello Altesi, with vineyards run by the Agricoltori del Chianti Geografico. Both estates had once been a single property belonging to the Altesi family over many centuries; then Giulio Consonno, the creator of Prénatal, had bought Altesino in 1970, when there was just a ruined house and no vines. Since 2001 it has belonged to Elisabetta Angelini Gnudi, who has also acquired the adjoining estate of Caparzo, as well as nearby Val di Suga, and Borgo Scopeto in Chianti Classico. New investments are planned, with an underground cellar and a modern vinification cellar, as little has been done since the 1970s. There is a fifteenth-century villa, once one of the palaces of the Altesi family, which was used as a school in the 1940s and 1950s. It now houses the enormous oak *botti,* some as large as 120 hectolitres, on the ground floor. Altesino was also one of the first, if not the first estate in Montalcino, to use *barriques,* both for Brunello and for a range of IGT.

The range of wines has since been streamlined and we sat outside in surprisingly warm winter sunshine, for the month of February, and tasted, enjoying wonderful views from the terrace, over the vineyard of Montosoli, their *cru*, a small and particularly sunny hill crowned with a cluster of trees, totalling 5 hectares of 30-year-old vines. The distinctive outline of Monte Amiata formed the backdrop. The Rosso di Montalcino was quite firm with intriguing notes of liquorice, after seven months in oak; 1999 Alte d'Altesi, a blend of 70 per cent Sangiovese with some Cabernet Sauvignon, is given twelve months' ageing in barrel, making for a firm smoky palate, and a distinctive Italian flavour. From 2001 the blend will also include Merlot. Palazzo Altesi is a pure Sangiovese, which also spends twelve months in barrel, and includes a proportion of wine fermented by carbonic maceration. It was quite oaky and tannic, with a certain Burgundian sweetness. A small percentage of the Brunello spends three to six months in French *barriques*, which soften the aftertaste, and there was no doubt that the 1998 Brunello had a certain spiciness that may well have come from the French oak. It had spent three years in oak altogether, followed by a minimum of four months' bottle ageing, so that it was smoky, with dry cherries on the nose, and closed on the palate, with a tight tannic structure, promising plenty of potential. Montosoli also spends three years in wood, compared with four for the *riserva*, followed by six months' bottle ageing. And we finished with the traditional Tuscan taste of Vin Santo, a rich honeyed wine, with layers of flavour.

Caparzo is just down the road. This was one of the innovative estates of the 1970s, for it all began when four friends from Milan decided to buy a house in Tuscany. What started as a quest for a holiday home turned into a serious company with twelve shareholders, which was then sold to Signora Gnudi in 2000. Vittorio Fiore has been the consultant oenologist since the beginning, with the very first bottling in 1970 from just one hectare of vines, and Massimo Braccalante is the current winemaker. Altogether there are 74 hectares of vines in Montalcino, 25 here at Caparzo, with other plots scattered over the *comune* at La Casa, Il Cassero and San Piero Caselle. The entrance of Caparzo is quite deceptively small, but behind is a large new cellar and a considerable capacity of storage in vat and barrel.

An extensive tasting illustrated the range of their wines. Le Grance, which now conforms to the DOC of Sant'Antimo, as a blend of Chardonnay, with 5 per cent Traminer and 20 per cent Sauvignon, was beautifully layered with fruit and length, after eleven months in barrel. The nose was intriguingly perfumed, and a contrast to the dryness of the palate. The Rosso di Montalcino spends twelve months in Slavonic oak *botti* and had some lovely dry cherry fruit with a firm backbone. We then deviated into Chianti Classico to taste Borgo Scopeto, a pure Sangiovese, which spent eight months in barrel and *botti*. It provided an intriguing contrast with the Rosso di Montalcino; the Chianti Classico was richer with more body, while the Rosso di Montalcino had more structure. Brunello di Montalcino spends three years in both French and Slavonic oak *botti*. Massimo talked about the differences between the two. The French wood is more delicate while the Slavonic is more rustic, but the price is not so very different. On the palate you were certainly aware of the oak, with firm structure and dry cherries. The *riserva*, which is a selection of the best barrels, usually from La Caduta vineyard, had a deep colour and a richer palate, with ripe fruit and more layers of flavour. It certainly deserved the extra accolade of *riserva*. Ca del Pazzo is another Sant'Antimo, from equal parts of Cabernet Sauvignon and Sangiovese, which are blended and then aged for twenty months in barrel. This wine was particularly innovative at the time of its first vintage in 1982. The Cabernet fills out the Sangiovese, making for a rounded fleshy tannic wine with a certain richness of cassis fruit and an elegant finish. We finished with Moscadello di Montalcino, of which they are one of only about ten producers to maintain the tradition. The Muscat or Moscadello grapes, which are lightly *passito* with a little noble rot, are fermented in barrel and the wine stays in wood for twelve months, to give an intensely rich flavour of dry apricots and honey, with a refreshing edge of acidity.

The path to Sant'Antimo, the awe-inspiring Benedictine abbey by the village of Castelnuovo dell'Abate, begins in Montalcino. We went down the Via Poggiolo, which soon turned into a dirt track, affording fine views back towards the town. The path continued past a stone farmhouse with an olive grove and some wonderful views over the valley and then past an elegantly renovated farmhouse, Il Poggiolo. We encountered an American couple who, like us, were trying to walk to Sant'Antimo, where they had left their car, and had hitched a lift into Montalcino. 'We daren't tell the kids we hitch-hiked,' they said. The

path went on towards Villa a Tolli, a neat little village with a tiny chapel, and some well-appointed houses, and others more run-down, surrounded by a vast expanse of vines. We met a young man and an elderly lady; the vines belong to Villa Tolli, he said; we make *rosso*, Brunello, *grappa* and *olio*, and indeed there is a winey smell exuding from one of the buildings. Sadly a subsequent request to visit met with a negative response; there was building work in the cellars and it was quite impossible.

The terrain on the southern side of Montalcino is softer and more gently undulating, with the vineyards at a lower altitude. Some vineyards in the distance across the valley looked like green pinstripes, neatly manicured with grass between every other row. Next we came to Casinano Colombaia, with one sign advertising *vendita diretta*, and several others saying *privata*, which looked distinctly unwelcoming. We passed a pair of cyclists. 'It's going to rain,' they said, and indeed it looked as though it would, with a dramatic grey sky and threatening clouds behind us. Ahead, however, the sky was brighter and the light made a dramatic play of shadows on the hills opposite, with Sant'Angelo in Colle in the distance. So we optimistically carried on towards Sant'Antimo. There were pink cistus and dog roses in the hedges, with yellow broom, making a dramatic splash of colour, with its heady scent in the warm air. At Ventolaio we were greeted by noisy barking dogs – we were undoubtedly the most exciting thing to have happened all day – and continued into the woods of Poggio d'Arno, before the track began its sharp descent towards Sant'Antimo. The abbey suddenly came into view, and we slithered, rather than walked, down the steep gravelly path, past olive groves and ilex trees. The bells were chiming as we descended and the view was perfect, with the village of Castelnuovo d'Abate perched on the hillside behind.

Sant'Antimo is one of the architectural gems of Tuscany, a Romanesque church dating from the early twelfth century. It is wonderfully simple, with awe-inspiring arches and little details, such as carvings over a doorway, portraying eagles, gryphons and monsters. The capitals in the nave also have some fine carvings. Quite the best way to appreciate it, as we did, one evening, is at Vespers, a sung service, conducted by a priest in a green and gold cope, with the monks in austere white robes. The air was thick with incense and the open doors allowed the evening sunshine to flood into the nave, so that birdsong competed with the monks' mesmerizing chanting, in a ceremony that has remained unchanged for hundreds of years. There is a simple timelessness about the abbey.

Baldasarre Filippo Fanti has his cellars in Castelnuovo d'Abate, underneath his house in the middle of the village. They are a contrast of ancient and modern. Modern was an electronic gate that denied us access; ancient was the old basket press outside and an array of *botti* squeezed alongside stainless-steel vats into a minute space; the back wall of the cellar was provided by the rock on which the village is built. We arrived seconds before the start of a tremendous gale, causing everything to rattle noisily, but curiously there was hardly a drop of rain. Signor Fanti's daughter explained how her grandfather had bought the property, a 300-hectare estate with 30 hectares of vines, with olive trees and grain as well, and that her father had began bottling his wine in

1983. He is now planning a new cellar, and when I asked the elderly cellar hand, Fernando, how old this cellar was, he replied *da sempre*; in other words, how long is a piece of string. Afterwards we sought out the village café; it was empty apart from a group of women playing cards, observed by a small boy, and a little old lady with a chubby face, capped by a thick woolly hat, even though it was the month of June, who kept repeating to us, almost like a mantra, 'I'm 90, you know.'

Back in Montalcino we went to see Andrea Costanti at Colle al Matrichese on the outskirts of the town. The Costanti are one of the old Montalcino families, arriving here in 1555, at the end of the wars between Florence and Siena, and they were one of the first to regularly bottle their wine in the 1950s. Plaques in the cellars commemorate two pioneering members of the family, Tito Costanti, *avvocato e viticoltore* (lawyer and wine grower), 1827–1895. There is a record that he bottled some of the 1865 vintage for an exhibition in 1867, but sadly no bottles remain. Emilio Costanti, *medico e viticoltore* (doctor and wine grower), 1906–1983, was Andrea's grandfather's cousin, who turned winemaker when he retired from being a doctor. Andrea explained how his own father had combined running the estate with a career as a chemist, but that he had taken the decision to make the estate his profession; it could no longer be a hobby. The Costanti property consists of 10 hectares of Brunello and 4 for their IGT, Ardingo, a blend of Cabernet Sauvignon and Merlot. Andrea explained how he found these newcomers to Montalcino more constant than Sangiovese, with a suggestion that Sangiovese resembles Pinot Noir, in that it is very tied to both climate and *terroir* and reacts to every annual variation. The cellar is full of barrels of different sizes, *barriques*, *tonneaux* and *botti*, but Andrea feels that it is a mistake to keep the wine in wood for too long. It only oxidizes and ages too much; he prefers less time in wood, but better wood, and longer in bottle.

In the twelfth century there was a Romanesque church here; various additions were made in the sixteenth and seventeenth centuries. He led us into a pretty courtyard with a profusion of geraniums and petunias in pots, up the steps to the first floor, past a very vocal cat with a litter of tiny kittens. We tasted at a long table, in a rather sombre reception room, dominated by a chest dated

MDCLIII. Vermiglio is a blend of Sangiovese, with 20 per cent Merlot and 10 per cent Cabernet Sauvignon, which is given eight months in barrels, *barriques* for Merlot and Cabernet, and *botti* for Sangiovese, with a rich international flavour which contrasted with a sturdy Rosso di Montalcino and an elegantly cedary Brunello di Montalcino. Ardingo, from 65 per cent Merlot and 35 per cent Cabernet Sauvignon, given eighteen months in *barriques*, was first made in 1997; the 1999 vintage was rich and cedary with firm tannins and more obvious oak. Andrea is currently president of the *consorzio* of Brunello di Montalcino and he is generally optimistic about the development of the wine and the town, asserting firmly that the wine is linked to a very precise territory.

Giancarlo Pacenti at the estate of Sirò Pacenti has broken with tradition in that he is the only producer to age his Brunello in small *barriques* alone. His father Sirò bought the estate in 1970 and until 1988 it remained the classic Tuscan estate, with cereal and animals as well as olive trees and vines. How things have changed. He gives his Rosso twelve to fourteen months' ageing and his Brunello twenty-four months, replacing about a third of his barrels each year, buying about 120 to 150, so that most of the Brunello goes into new wood. He uses five or six different coopers, some of the big names amongst the French, Seguin Moreau, Demptos, Taransaud and so on. He first tried out *barriques* for the 1988 vintage and since 1995 has used nothing but *barriques* for his wines, saying that he wanted to do something individual, *con una forta dosa di personalità*, or in other words stamp his personality on his wines. Neither Merlot nor Cabernet Sauvignon tempt him. He considers that he would be in competition with the great wines from other regions, notably Bordeaux, which he certainly does not try to copy, but instead enjoys drinking. Ageing in small wood gives the wines better colour stability, with more elegant tannins, while the light oxygenation of the tannins, which you do not get with large *botti*, makes them more stable. You can certainly taste the oak in the 1997, with firm tannins and some vanilla flavours, making for a more international taste. The question is: how will the wines age?

Giancarlo's cellars and some of his vineyards are on the north side of Montalcino, with views towards the town, as well as an old basilica, the

Osservanza, in the woods, while another 13 hectares are between Sant'Angelo and Castelnuovo d'Abate. He chooses the best grapes from each area for his Brunello; there are differences between the two, but they complement each other. The grapes from the southern vineyards make for more structured and alcoholic wine, while the north is more elegant, with more fruit. There is a difference in altitude; here we are at 300 metres, where it is cooler, whereas at 150 metres in the south there is more wind with a greater maritime influence and the climate is generally drier and hotter. Generally he reckons that a vineyard needs to be at least fifteen years old to produce good Brunello, rather than Rosso.

Paola Gloder explained how her father had bought Poggio Antico in 1984 from a friend, who had bought it ten years earlier, when it was in a sorry state of disrepair. There were no vines or cellars, just an abandoned farm, with a few chickens and crumbling buildings, so he had to start from scratch, and developed 20 hectares over the ensuing ten years. Then it was the moment to sell, and when Paola graduated in 1985, her father, an investment banker in Milan, offered her the job of managing the estate. It was an enormous challenge for someone with no particular experience of rural life, but she discovered that she likes working on the land and she and the estate have grown together. She now has 33 hectares in production from which she makes, with the guidance of Carlo Ferrini, four different wines: a *riserva* in the very best vintages, with five years' ageing, including three and a half in large wood; a Brunello di Montalcino, with four years' ageing, including three in wood; a Rosso di Montalcino, which includes the fruit from young vines, and Altero, which was originally an IGT, but with the change in regulations reducing the ageing period in wood for Brunello to two years, now qualifies as a Brunello. The classic Brunello is kept in old wood, while Altero is aged in smaller *tonneaux*. The cellars are well conceived and functional, with that appealing aroma, the combination of wood and wine. The wines speak for themselves and are best enjoyed at the restaurant at Poggio Antico, which is run by the talented and imaginative chef, Roberto Minnetti, whose dishes include such delights as a *porcini risotto* and a *fegato grasso* or hot *foie gras* that simply melted in the mouth, while a piece of succulent beef showed off Paola's Brunello to perfection.

Fattoria dei Barbi is one of the old traditional estates of Montalcino. It first belonged to the Tamante and Padelletti families, who came to Montalcino some 400 years ago, and now it is the property of the Colombini, who arrived in Montalcino with the Medici troops in the 1550s. Some time around 1850 two Colombini brothers married the Padelletti and Tamante daughters. Today the estate is run by Signora Francesca Colombini and her son Stefano, while her daughter Donatella Cinelli has established her own estate at Il Casato, as we have seen earlier in the chapter.

Not only do they make wine at Fattoria dei Barbi, but they also have olive trees, pasture for sheep, providing milk for *pecorino* cheese, fields of wheat and vast expanses of woodland, and they rear pigs for *salami* and ham. On one visit I saw hams being smoked, the preparation of *salami*, and *pecorino* cheeses in various stages of maturity. All this home produce can be sampled at the cheerful restaurant attached to the farm, or bought from the farm shop, along with bottles of Brunello and their other wines, which makes the estate a popular tourist attraction, with regular cellar tours. Their cellars are a veritable rabbit warren of small rooms, stuffed with barrels and vats, finishing with a tasting area, filled by a long lopsided table, made from a piece of wood that had come out of an old stable. On the walls and on every other surface there was a mixture of knick-knacks and old photographs, swords, pieces of china in a cupboard, old wicker-covered bottles and even a large Russian babushka.

Stefano Colombini is a fountain of information. We sat in his office, admiring the view of Monte Amiata which dominates the skyline, and Stefano talked about the past prosperity of Montalcino, explaining that at the beginning of the twentieth century it was a rich community at an important crossroads, linking the Maremma, Rome and Arezzo, and very open to outside influences. In 1920 there were 2000 hectares of vines, and as many as 12,000 inhabitants before the Second World War, with a group of innovative families, such as Colombini, Biondi Santi and Costanti. Stefano's grandfather began selling wine by mail order in 1934, and some of the original letters still exist. Then with the Second World War came the crisis; in the ensuing battles the cellars were drunk and then in the 1960s the motorway was built so that the road to Rome no longer passed through Montalcino and the town lost the reason for its prosperity. People left to find work elsewhere and the population dropped to about 5000 inhabitants. Now with the development of the vineyards, prosperity is coming back to the town again, but Stefano criticizes some of the new arrivals in the wine-growing community for ignoring the past.

Stefano is equally impassioned when he talks about changes in the vineyard and in the cellar. They have steadily replanted their vineyards, but will keep two pre-war vineyards as museum pieces, as a reminder of traditional Tuscan agriculture. They are experimenting with pruning systems, including *cordone speronata libera*, vines without wires, which allows for double the amount of leaves exposed to sunshine, with better ventilation. Stefano is convinced that the climate is changing; the weather is hotter, with strong rains in short bursts, incurring the risk of drought and also erosion. Also the climate change has affected the chemistry of the grapes. Originally the harvest took place towards the end of October, with the grapes benefiting from the cool October nights, so that they would be cold when they arrived in the cellar in the morning. Now the vintage is in late September, when there is less difference between the night and day-time temperatures, so that the grapes often arrive at 30°C or more. To counter this, they are experimenting with pre-fermentation maceration, but maybe the wines have less ageing potential today.

The wines at Barbi are chiefly Sangiovese, with a Rosso, a Brunello, a *riserva* which spends three and a half years in wood, and one from their best vineyard, Vigna dei Fiori, which spends a total of 30 months in wood, both *tonneaux* and *botti*. Brusco dei Barbi enjoys a particular fermentation technique that makes for softer, more accessible wine than standard Brunello. Barbi have 100 hectares of vineyards in Montalcino, and have also bought land in Scansano, from which they make Birbone, a new wine, with the first vintage in 1999. In the Tuscan dialect the name describes a mischievous young child, and the wine is an intriguing blend of grapes, not only from Montalcino but also the Maremma, namely Sangiovese, Canaiolo, Alicante, the local synonym for Grenache, and not to be confused with Alicante Bouschet that can be found in the south of France, as well as a little Merlot which apparently was introduced to the Maremma by the French some 200 years ago. With Stefano running Fattoria dei Barbi, the estate maintains a happy combination of the progressive and the traditional, combining the best of Montalcino.

Vino Nobile di Montepulciano and Cortona

· June ·

A walk round Montepulciano, with Avignonesi, Contucci, Talosa and the Cantina del Redi. Walk from San Biagio to Montefollonico and on to Gracciano, via Canneto, Poliziano and Innocente. From Pienza to Montepulciano, with a visit to Triacca. Walk around vineyards in Gracciano and a visit to Fassati. Cantina Dei, Le Casalte, La Braccesca, Fattoria del Cerro, Salchetto, La Lodola Nuova. Fattoria di Manzano in Cortona. Trinoro in the Val d'Orcia in the snow

WHEN I FIRST VISITED Montepulciano, I thought it a rather sombre place, but my impressions have been revised over several visits since. Quite simply it is one of the wonderful hilltop towns of Tuscany and a delight to explore, with splendid *palazzi* and some atmospheric wine cellars. Not for nothing was it called the pearl of the sixteenth century. An English friend, Laura Bailhache, has a vineyard at Gracciano just outside the town, and has lived there for many years, so she proved an excellent guide and a fine source of local knowledge.

It is a gentle climb up through the main gate, the Porta al Prato, up to the Piazza Grande, with the cathedral and the Palazzo Contucci. You pass the imposing lion on a column, the Colonna del Marzocco, erected in 1511, which as the symbol of Florence demonstrated Montepulciano's allegiance to that city, after years under Sienese rule. It is just by the Palazzo Avignonesi, so we went in to admire their old cellars, with Elena Falvo.

The Palazzo Avignonesi was built around 1550, but the cellars underneath date from the fifteenth century, and there are even the remnants of an Etruscan tomb, as well as the customary *botti* and *barriques*. One of the *botti* has the Avignonesi coat of arms, the sun, the half moon and two clubs, which Elena said were an indication of the family character! She explained that her mother was an Avignonesi, from one of the old families of Montepulciano, who traditionally have been doctors and pharmacists. It was her father, Ettore Falvo, who had the land. Originally the wine was sold *sfuso* and it was only in the mid-70s that they began making wine seriously, with their first vintage of Vino Nobile made in this atmospheric but totally impractical cellar, in 1978.

To show us the modern face of the company, Elena took us to Le Capezzine, one of the four estates they now own, on the edge of the vineyard area of Montepulciano, adjoining the new DOC of Cortona, which encompasses the vineyards around another atmospheric hilltop town. 2000 was the first vintage of the new DOC, which allows for wines from single grape varieties, with 15 per cent of a complementary variety, such as Chardonnay, Sauvignon, Merlot, Cabernet Sauvignon, Syrah, Pinot Noir, and curiously Gamay, which apparently was grown in the region in the eighteenth century, as well as the traditional Sangiovese. Accordingly wines like Avignonesi's Il Marzocco, a pure Chardonnay, will now become DOC Cortona. Le Capezzine comprises a cluster of cellars around a simple courtyard, with an elegant chapel where the Falvo children have been married and baptised. The former owner of the estate, Angiolo Vegni, was buried there too, with his wife Giuseppina. Below ground there are barrels galore, large *botti*, old *barriques*, and also new 500-litre *tonneaux*. These are a new introduction, and so far the oak effect seems far less aggressive than with the smaller 225-litre *barriques*. Most of the wood is French, but they also have some American oak, though find that it tends to make the wine mature too quickly.

The *vinsantaia* has the wonderful intoxicating aroma of heady wine. The barrels for this are tiny, just 50 litres, which are filled with 43 litres of juice, 2 litres of *madre*, with 5 litres left empty. A piece of linen is put round the bung and then it is sealed with wax and left for as many as eight years. Over the years Avignonesi have established a justifiable reputation for their Vin Santo; both from white grapes, and most unusually red, making what they call *occhio di pernice*. These are the most unctuous and deliciously concentrated of wines; only a tiny amount is made each year, and a bottle costs *la lira di Dio*. To dunk your *biscotti* in it, as Tuscans usually do, would be sacrilege.

In the vineyards at Le Capezzine there are several experiments with different planting systems, with the vines in the form of a hexagon, and the *alberello* system of training, with a supporting pole and no wires, and each plant 1.27 metres apart, which gives you 7158 plants per hectare. In this way, no vine shades another. Another vineyard is circular, with narrowing rows, so that you obtain varying densities, from three and a half to one metre, going from 2500 plants to 8500 plants per hectare. It is all Sangiovese but planted on six different rootstocks, and they make 30 litres of wine from the vines of each density, aiming to produce a kilo of grapes per vine.

There were many more grape varieties at the beginning of the nineteenth century, maybe as many as three hundred, but so many of them disappeared with phylloxera that when people replanted it was with quantity rather than quality in mind. So a third vineyard contains some ninety-five different grape varieties, as well as clones and variations of Sangiovese, each planted in a separate row. This is run in conjunction with the University of Florence, but as yet there are no conclusive results.

While the Avignonesi range has undergone some modification over the years, Vino Nobile di Montepulciano remains very much the backbone of the estate, accounting for half of their production. It is a sturdy, oaky wine, a blend of Prugnolo Gentile, the local name for Sangiovese, with Canaiolo and Mammola, aged in both *barriques* and *botti*. The *riserva*, which spends thirty months in *barriques*, contains some Cabernet Sauvignon, but there is none in the *normale*. The *disciplinari* for Vino Nobile dictate two years' ageing for the *normale*, of which eighteen months must be in oak, with a three-year ageing period for the *riserva*, of which a minimum of six months must be in bottle. Their Bianco di Toscana is a blend of equal parts of unoaked Chardonnay and Sauvignon, while Rosso di Toscana, which includes Merlot and Cabernet Sauvignon, as well as Sangiovese, was lighter and fruitier than the Vino Nobile. They first planted Cabernet Sauvignon in 1981 and Merlot in 1988. Desiderio, which replaces I Grifi, as the new DOC of Cortona, comes from Merlot with 15 per cent Cabernet Sauvignon, amply illustrating the quality of these varieties, with some rich oaky concentrated fruit on the palate.

Later we returned to the town and continued our way along the *corso*. There are more imposing facades, while others are more elegant. The Palazzo Bucelli has the carvings from Etruscan and Roman funeral urns incorporated into its facade and the Torre di Pulcinella sports a wooden statue of Pulcinella, which chimes the hour. We made our way past wine shops, the cheese shop where Cagusi, one of the leading producers of *pecorino*, offers a range of cheeses in varying stages of maturation, and the inviting Café Poliziano. Tiny churches are tucked in between the palaces and finally we reached the old fortress at the highest point of the town. More recently it had housed the local school and, according to Laura's children, is riddled with underground passages, where they used to hide when playing truant; before that, it had been a silk factory. Nowadays it is used for exhibitions. Then we emerged into the imposing Piazza Grande, with the Palazzo Communale, with its tranquil arched courtyard and the cathedral with its unfinished facade. There is a well, framed by two Doric columns, with two griffons, the emblem of Montepulciano, and two lions of Florence, with the crest of the Medici in between, attributed to Antonio da Sangallo the Elder. The wine shop run by the *consorzio* was firmly closed, so we headed into the Palazzo Contucci to see Count Alamanno Contucci and to visit his cellars. He is a cheerful, chubby-faced man with a bushy moustache and a friendly smile, who has been president of the growers' *consorzio* for several years.

Cellars in the town cellar are far from practical, but the count observed that his family have been here for nearly one thousand years, so they do not really feel inclined to move. They are the only ones to vinify their wine in the town; others have ageing cellars. The earliest part of the cellars dates from the thirteenth century, and includes part of the inner walls of the town, built during the conflict between Florence and Siena. There is a veritable rabbit warren of barrel rooms, which are open for tourists to visit, providing a picturesque showpiece, confirming the romantic image of winemaking. There is not a *barrique* to be seen, just *botti*, some stained almost black, with deep-red iron bands; some are quite new, while the very oldest are made of chestnut. At the height of the season they have as many as 250 visitors a day, providing a ready market for their wines. The palace, which dates from 1520, is another work by Antonio da Sangallo the Elder. It has belonged to the Contucci family since the end of the seventeenth century and earlier it was the property of Pope Julius III.

The count took us up on to the terrace, with its views over the rooftops of Montepulciano, a maze of russet-coloured tiles and the inevitable forest of

television aerials, interrupted by church towers. The heart of the town was built during the sixteenth and seventeenth centuries, when it was a bishopric and an important administrative centre. The Medici were a strong influence on the cultural life of the town, which supplied two popes during the fifteenth century, and the count boasted that there were more works of art per square metre in Montepulciano than anywhere else in Tuscany. In the distance you could see the lakes of Chiusi and Montepulciano, and further away Trasimeno and then the blurred outline of the Apennines.

The Contucci have 21 hectares of wines, but like every traditional Tuscan estate also produce wheat and olives. As well as Rosso di Montepulciano and Vino Nobile they make a Bianco della Contessa, a very traditional Tuscan white wine from Trebbiano and Malvasia, which has spent six months in oak. Pietra Rosso comes from a 4-hectare vineyard, planted with Canaiolo and Mammola as well as Prugnolo, and spends at least two years, if not more, in barrel, to give a wine that is quite tight-knit with some concentration. They also make Sansovino, named after Andrea Contucci, a sculptor and architect, who lived at the end of the fifteenth century. Unlike many other more go-ahead producers in Montepulciano, they firmly eschew Cabernet Sauvignon, Merlot or Chardonnay. Alamanno Contucci is adamant that he does not want to give his wines an international flavour: 'Sometimes we are criticized, but we have broad shoulders, or in Italian, *resistenti* shoulders.' You sense that he is content with his traditional path.

Just round the corner from the Palazzo Contucci are the ageing cellars of Talosa, which the cellar master, Roberto Cangini, proudly described as the finest cellar in the whole of Montepulciano. They in fact form the foundations of two *palazzi*, dating from the fifteenth century, with a mixture of brick arches and bare rock face for walls. It is all wonderfully atmospheric, representing the traditional face of Tuscan winemaking, with large *botti*, which will apparently be replaced in favour of new *tonneaux*. The winemaker, Ottorino de Angelis, explained that Talosa represents a name change with new ownership from the former Fattoria di Fugnano. Like Siena, Montepulciano is divided into *contrade*, of which Talosa is one; the name is a deformation of Toulouse, and was chosen as the offices are within the *contrada* of Talosa, while their labels portray the symbol of the *contrada*, the rose. Montepulciano is divided into eight *contrade* and on the last Sunday of August they race in the Bravio delle Botti. Barrels are pushed up to the Piazza Grande from the main gate. The 1.2-kilometre route is far from being uphill all the way; there are two places where it goes sharply downhill, and much of the skill lies in keeping control of the barrel on the declines rather than in manifesting brute strength on the inclines. Each team comprises two men per barrel, with lots drawn for positions at the starting line, with four at the back and four in front. Like the Palio of Siena, the Bravio used to be a horse race, but was changed to empty barrels in the mid-1970s.

Returning to the wine of Talosa, Signor de Angelis explained that their style is very traditional, especially in comparison with Canneto, the other estate he manages. They are more attached to their *terroir*, *più legato alla terra*, and aim for longevity in their wines. Consequently they make Chianti Colli Senesi,

Rosso di Montepulciano and Vino Nobile di Montepulciano, but no super-Tuscans, from some 30 hectares of vines. The Chianti is fresh and fruity, an easy drink, while the Rosso di Montepulciano has more structure, even though neither has spent time in wood. As for the Vino Nobile it was a mixture of ripe cherries with a firm backbone; the use of oak was understated, with stylish fruit, while the *riserva* was even more elegant, with fine ripe cherry flavours. De Angelis laughingly said that he was aiming to make Montepulciano's best wines, and then he would retire. We talked about the problems of a cellar in the centre of the town. It is quite impossible for dispatching large quantities of wine; everything has to be taken down the hill on the back of an Api, one of those little three-wheel trucks you see causing traffic jams all over Tuscany.

The cooperative, *cantina sociale*, of Montepulciano also has some atmospheric cellars in the heart of the town, the Cantina del Redi. As you go in, there is a notice telling you to behave properly and not to yell or touch the barrels; you make your way slowly down a wide spiral staircase past barrels and *botti*, to a high-arched cool room where there are yet more *botti*. Here an echo picked up our voices and there was indeed an almost overwhelming temptation to shout very loudly. We peered through an iron grille at the Etruscan origins of the cellar, where bottles were quietly maturing, and came past a tasting counter to emerge into the street, a hundred feet or so below the entrance, blinking in the bright sunlight.

The main cellars of the cooperative are situated outside the town. It had been a while since my last visit here, and the winemaker, Valerio Coltellini, was keen to explain the various developments. Above all, he was extremely proud of their brand-new barrel cellar, which will be fully functional in 2004. It was certainly breathtaking: long galleries, with elegant arches and atmospheric lighting, were waiting to be filled with barrels. And the cost was a mere twelve *miliardi* lire.

Altogether the cooperative is responsible for 1500 hectares of vines, with 396 active members, from which they produce some forty different wines and labels, not just Vino Nobile, but Chianti, Valdichiana Rosso and Bianco and five different IGT. Coltellini talked about some of the improvements they are trying to instigate; only three members have a mechanical harvester, and they want more control over the harvesting, and are planning to check the temperature of the grapes to see how long they have been sitting in the sun before being delivered to the cooperative. 'That won't go down too well,' muttered Laura under her breath. There lies the key problem of most cooperatives: how to raise the quality level above lowest common denominator and motivate your members, when there are so many. There are four selections at the harvest, with payment according to the quality of the grapes. The cooperative works well for its members and for the wines of Montepulciano. Its Rosso di Montepulciano is a ripe fruity wine; the basic Vino Nobile has an elegant balance of fruit and tannin, while a *cru* Briareo has more depth and structure. I have even enjoyed on various occasions copious quantities of the *sfuso* wine that the cooperative members buy at advantageous rates. Putting the world to rights, or relaxing after a hard day of winery visits, around Laura's dining table, it has slipped down a treat.

The Tempio di San Biagio, outside Montepulciano at the foot of the hill, is described in the guidebooks as one of the most significant monuments of the Italian Renaissance. For me it is a perfect example of elegant proportions, with its domed roof and simple lines. Inside the church takes the form of a Greek cross in perfect symmetry, with some simple carvings, and the dome is simply awe-inspiring. It is another work by Antonio da Sangallo the Elder.

From San Biagio we set off down the road, enjoying views up to the town, with its evocative skyline, and towards our destination, the village of Montefollonico on the skyline. Our path passed through vineyards belonging to Talosa and then Canneto. The cellars of Canneto are at the foot of Montepulciano, with a terrace offering views over our route. This is a 60-hectare estate, with a block of 30 hectares of vines, all in one piece. Originally it had belonged to various wealthy families from Montepulciano, and then to a Roman who merely sent his grapes to the cooperative, and finally in 1987 it was bought by Ottorino de Angelis with a group of Swiss partners. He is a friendly, straightforward man, whom we had also met at Talosa. He explained that Canneto is more innovative. They are planting Petit Verdot and planning a super-Tuscan, which may include a little Sangiovese but will concentrate on *bordelais* grape varieties. The trouble with Sangiovese is that it is so difficult to get it fully ripe; if the pips are still green, you have to get rid of them, or else you will end up with some very unwelcome astringency. As for the wines of Canneto, Signor de Angelis suggested that you can sense the influence of their oenologist, Carlo Ferrini, and that was so. The wines are finely crafted, with elegant fruit, and appealing smoky oak notes.

We finished on an unusual note, a late harvest wine made of Malvasia, and a little Trebbiano and Grechetto; they are also planting Sauvignon and Sémillon. The first vintage was 1995; it was *una cosa strepitosa*, something quite tremendous; they had beginner's luck, and then waited until 1998 to see how the wine would develop. We tasted the 1999, which was unctuously rich, redolent of honey, apricots and toffee, but with refreshing balancing acidity. They spray water over the ripe grapes to encourage the development of noble rot and it works. The grapes are usually harvested in December, when it is easier to find willing pickers, and they go through the vineyards twice, selecting and rejecting the berries, and obtain about 5000 bottles from a hectare and a half of vines. The wine is fermented in vat, with the fermentation stopping naturally at 15° leaving about 30gm/litre of residual sugar, then it spends twelve months in wood. It made a refreshing change from Vin Santo.

We continued on our way. A man was driving a tractor, which Laura called a dirt-eater, *una mangiasporca*, slowly mowing between the rows. We passed the old farmhouse of Podere Colombelle, which has been converted into *agriturismo* flats. Then we came upon Claudio, sitting on a tractor, filling in an irrigation channel for a new vineyard planted by Signor Chiasserini – you will never see that name on a label as he only produces *sfuso* wine. Next we came to some of the vineyards of Poliziano.

Along with the Falvo family, Federico Carletti has been one of the pioneers of Vino Nobile di Montepulciano, creating one of the leading estates of the denomination. The first vines were planted in 1962 and the first cellars built in 1970, but it was not until 1980 that they began selling wine in bottle. Federico took over the management of the estate the following year and over the last twenty years has overseen an amazing growth. Poliziano is named after Montepulciano's most famous son, the classical scholar and poet Angelo Ambrogini, who lived in the second half of the fifteenth century, and was known as Il Poliziano, so that nowadays *poliziano* describes an inhabitant of Montepulciano. The estate now consists of a total of 140 hectares of vines,

120 here, of which 45 hectares are Vino Nobile, 25 hectares Rosso di Montepulciano and the rest for Chianti, and 20 hectares in the Maremma, in the DOC of Morellino di Scansano. Over the last ten years there has been an intensive replanting programme, shifting towards denser plantings, of 6500 vines per hectare. Some Canaiolo and Mammolo remain in the old vineyards, and Merlot has been planted in preference to Cabernet Sauvignon for blending with Sangiovese.

The cellars have been modernized over the years, culminating in a new cellar which was built in 1999, 'eradicating the mistakes that were made twenty years ago'. Everything works by gravity, to avoid unnecessary pumping, and they prefer *pigiatura* as that softens the tannins, making for earlier drinking. They have stainless-steel conical vats, equipped with a metal plate for automatic *pigiatura*; they had also tried wooden vats, but these need renewing every three or four years. It is all very streamlined, with meticulous controls following the evolution of each vat. A new *barricaia* is being built, to house *botti* of French oak as well as some 2000 *barriques* and *tonneaux*. There is a little American oak, but certainly none of the traditional Slavonic oak of Tuscany.

I have always liked Federico's wines. The Rosso di Montepulciano, including 20 per cent Merlot and ageing in American oak, has some firm cherries, with a fruity finish. The Vino Nobile, from 80 per cent Sangiovese with some Canaiolo, Colorino and Mammola and a little Merlot, enjoys just fourteen months in wood, mostly in *barriques* and also in *botti*, as Federico and his consultant oenologist, Carlo Ferrini, feel that the customary two years in wood is too long. Certainly the wine has soft tannins and hints of vanilla on nose and palate. They do not make a *riserva*, but instead prefer to make a *cru*, Asinone, from the vineyard that we passed between Montepulciano and Montefollonico. It is the same composition as the Vino Nobile, but enjoys a different maturation, spending between fourteen and sixteen months in *barriques*, of which 70 per cent are new. As a young wine, it has dense firm fruit, and should develop well.

From the Asinone vineyard, we crossed a stream, the Fosso dei Grilloni, and climbed a hill which afforded views over the valley, where the wind rippled through fields of wheat, creating waves. New vineyards provided evidence of the intense development currently taking place in Montepulciano. The countryside is more open and undulating, compared to the tighter valleys of Chianti Classico, and you never quite lose sight of the distinctive skyline of the town. We passed a row of mulberry trees; apparently before the Second World War everyone grew mulberry trees for the silk worms, but this industry has long since disappeared from the region. The dilapidated chapel of Santa Anna was firmly closed; and there were some untidy vines in the churchyard.

Then we reached the Podere Abbadia, a newly renovated farmhouse. More interesting were the ruins behind it, of the Monastero di Santa Maria. It seems to have had a chequered history, according to a noticeboard erected for the benefit of passing tourists. The first records date from 1170 and it featured in disputes between the bishops of Arezzo and Siena. First there was a Benedictine order, then Camaldolese monks arrived in about 1127, until it was taken over by Augustinians in 1306, and finally it was demolished in the eighteenth century. A pile of rubble remained, with three arches still standing, by a field of sunflower plants. We looked around and found a host of lizard orchids, with their long dangling purple and white tails.

Our path continued through the woods, climbing steeply towards Montefollonico, and then suddenly we came out on to a tarmac road, but were rewarded with some wonderful wild flowers on the verge, more lizard orchids, bee orchids, a Bertoloni orphys, a man orchid and violet limodore and a birds nest orchid, as well as colourful cistus in abundance. The birdsong was loud and a hoopoe was whooping in the distance. We walked through the narrow streets of Montefollonico, past the simple church of San Leonardo, and the cheerful, inviting restaurant of Tredici Gobbi, or thirteen hunchbacks. Apparently both are considered lucky in Italy; seventeen is the number that the superstitious fear.

Our destination was the cellar of Vittorio Innocente in the heart of the village. Officially Montefollonico lies outside the *comune* of Montepulciano and so Vittorio had to obtain special dispensation to make his wine here, rather than in Montepulciano. His cellar, under his house, was built in the fourteenth century, on rock, so that it follows the contours of the hillside, and is as atmospheric as any of the old cellars in Montepulciano. In contrast to Montefollonico, Montepulciano is built on tufa, which is much softer and easier for digging out a cellar. Vittorio's cellar is a series of small barrel rooms, stuffed with *botti* and barrels, with a little *vinsantaia* exuding the most delicious aroma. It all created an impression of organized chaos, leading Vittorio to observe '*non sono una persona ordinatissima*', which could rate as one of the understatements of the year. 'Modern cellars these days are so hygienic,' he said, 'it's more like going into a chemist's.' At the end of the series of barrel rooms, we emerged onto a pretty flowering terrace, with views over the Val di Chiana.

It was time for a tasting and so we went back to a small tasting room just off the main street. There were some genuine old *fiaschi* covered in straw on a shelf. Vittorio explained how his father had initially made Vin Santo and how his first vintage of Vino Nobile was 1981. Now he has 15 hectares of vineyards and has recently planted a little Cabernet Sauvignon and Merlot. He finds Merlot, with its more neutral taste, more suitable for masking any deficiencies in the Sangiovese. You are allowed to put 10 per cent of each in your Vino Nobile, but not 20 per cent of either. We began with Rosso di Montepulciano, with some ripe fruit and firm tannins. It had spent eight months in vat, followed by six months or so in chestnut *botti*, recalling an earlier tradition of Tuscany. Vittorio explained that chestnut can give the wine very bitter tannins, so you have to clean the barrels with salt and water to get rid of the wood tannins. The wine was sturdy, but certainly not bitter. A pretty grey cat called Minou sat on the doorstep and loudly demanded access. Then an American couple arrived, with the introductory words: 'Franco sent us,' Franco being the owner of Montefollonico's smartest and most expensive hotel and restaurant, La Chiusa. They stayed to taste, too, until their dinner reservation called. Vittorio's Vino Nobile spends two years in *botti*, with nicely rounded fruit, while a *riserva*, with three years in wood, has the vanilla hints of American oak. Vittorio finds that American oak softens the wine more than French oak, making the palate quite rounded, but I wondered if the strong aroma of vanilla would have led me to mistake the wine for a Rioja in a blind tasting. Then another American couple arrived. 'Franco sent us,' they said. Vittorio smiled a welcome and gave them a glass. Next came Acetone, a pure Sangiovese that spends twelve months in French *tonneaux*; it had fine fruit and a firm backbone. We finished with Vin Santo, which smelt just like the *vinsantaia*, richly sweet and unctuous.

Vittorio was summoned for dinner and we set off down the hill back to Gracciano, taking a track out of the village, an old stone path, lined with flowers – elderflowers, poppies and yellow broom – past the late-fifteenth-century church, the Chiesa del Triano. It was firmly closed. We detoured past one of Vittorio's neatly tended vineyards, and past some Contucci vines, where every other row was neatly grassed, while some neighbouring vines were very much less tidy. There were wonderful expanses of rolling fields, planted with wheat or broad beans, a patchwork, interspersed with vines and olive trees and the occasional house, sometimes ruined, and sometimes undergoing extensive restoration, and Montepulciano never seemed far away.

Pienza is a delightful little Renaissance town, created by Aeneas Silvius Piccolomini, on his election to the papacy as Pius II in 1458. He transformed the original fortified village of Corsignano, which was his birthplace, and renamed it Pienza, by papal bull in 1462. The centre of the town is dominated by an elegant square, appropriately the Piazza Pio II, with a cathedral and palaces. Pienza is also known for its tasty *pecorino*, a hard sheep's cheese which improves with ageing, but it has no vines. Nonetheless the path from Pienza to Montepulciano provided a wonderful walk, with vistas of open rolling countryside, with wheat fields, shimmering in the sunlight, interspersed with groves of olive trees. At every turn there were views back towards Pienza, on the hilltop, and towards the village of Montechiello in the distance, and at one moment we could even see the distinctive silhouette of the skyline of Montalcino in the far distance. Our route took us along a *strada bianca*, past clusters of houses, with occasional welcome shade from cypress trees. At one point we passed a newly planted avenue of diminutive cypresses, in memory of Lorenzo Martelli. '3.9.2000', so a discreet brass plaque told us. The yellow broom was in flower and its scent was heady in the warm sunshine. There was a riot of wild roses, pale pink fading into white, as well as statuesque purple thistles, and orchids in profusion. We arrived at the outskirts of Montechiello feeling hot and thirsty, but ignored a sign offering *degustazione* and *vendita diretta* of *vini tipici locali* and *olio extra vergine di frantoio* at the Oleificio Chianti. Instead we found a café for a much-needed, long cool drink. Montechiello is known for its *teatro povero*, theatrical spectacles written and performed by the local population each summer in the village square, in front of the church that is dedicated to Santi Cristoforo and Leonardo, coincidentally the Italian names of my husband and my father. There are the vestiges of a ruined fortress, with a shady path taking you round the remaining walls.

The path took us on towards Montepulciano, passing little vegetable plots on the outskirts of the village. Some were large enough to accommodate olive trees and vines, and there was even a haystack in another. A flock of sheep were grazing peacefully in an olive grove. We found a comfortable wall for a picnic, looking over another olive grove, its trees festooned with tiny flowers, and in the distance we watched a man on a tractor mowing a large field in slowly decreasing circles, his movement weaving a mesmerizing pattern on the hillside.

From there the path went sharply downhill before beginning a long ascent. Finally Montepulciano appeared on the skyline and, with it, the first vineyards, which became denser as we neared the town. A rather smart new cellar, that of Triacca, was under construction, dominated by the usual crane, and eventually we emerged onto the main road, close to San Biagio. An avenue of cypress trees runs down to the church, each planted to commemorate a soldier who fell in the First World War, with a plaque and a date for each tree, and, in some instances, vulgar plastic flowers.

We had an appointment a day or two later with Luca Triacca, and an opportunity to admire another state-of-the-art cellar that was just nearing completion. Luca explained that his family originally came from Switzerland but have been making wine in Valtellina in northern Italy since the end of the nineteenth century. It was his father who began the expansion process, first buying La Madonnina near Greve, in Chianti Classico, in 1969, and then Santavenere in Montepulciano in 1990. That estate has been renamed Triacca and the previous owner, Massimo Romeo, has gone on to create a new estate, Romeo. The new cellars are built in thick red brick, a nine-sided building, in keeping with nearby San Biagio, suggested Luca. Inside it is an impressive circular cellar, with fifteen large stainless-steel vats lining the walls, each divided into two, so that the top part is for fermentation and the bottom half for storage, allowing the cellar to operate by gravity. The vats are equipped with pistons for automatic *pigiatura*. In the middle there is a large open space, almost like a theatre auditorium, so that everything seems airy and spacious. The barrel cellar is underneath, containing both *barriques* and *botti*. We tasted the 2000 Vino Nobile from barrel; it is almost pure Sangiovese, with just a drop of Merlot, and was still closed and tannic, with a firm structure, while the 1999, which had recently been bottled, was a touch more supple, but nonetheless needed some bottle age.

Laura took us for a walk through her vineyards in the early evening sunshine, and she talked about the trials and tribulations of growing grapes, and also the rewards. She arrived in Montepulciano in 1983, with her Italian husband, and now has 5.8 hectares of vines around her house at Gracciano. She is a member of the *cantina sociale*, but sometimes wonders whether she should try her hand at winemaking. Her vines are of various ages, the oldest over thirty years old and planted in much wider rows than her newer plantings. It was early June and everything was growing apace, vines and weeds together in profusion. Laura was worried about getting the shoots tucked in between the wires in time, and then they would need trimming before the vegetation became too dense. Her old vineyard still has a mixture of grape varieties, with the traditional varieties of Montepulciano, Grechetto, Malvasia, Trebbiano and Canaiolo as well as Sangiovese, whereas her newer vineyards are pure Sangiovese. She also has just one experimental row of Merlot, with the vines coming from a big nursery near Udine. The cooperative now insists that each variety is harvested separately and will no longer accept an unspecified mixture of grapes, which is laudable from the quality perspective, but poses problems for those with more mature vineyards, planted in the traditional Tuscan way. Laura observed how fashions in pruning had changed; when she first arrived everything was trained in a spur cordon, then *guyot* became popular and now there is a trend back towards *cordone speronata*. Laura likes to mow between the rows, retaining some vegetation; she commented on some of the vineyards where there is not a weed to be seen, that they look like the Sahara desert, with all vegetation sprayed out of existence. She dubbed the absolute opposite of this, a completely overgrown vineyard, a 'virgin forest', while hers, I thought, resembled a summer meadow, with some pretty vetch, pink columbine, wild mint and love-in-the-mist. We startled a hare, which ran at speed into the nearby undergrowth. In early June the vines were just beginning to flower, with the tiniest little white flowers, and a delicate scent that intensified in the evening air. In the next field sheep were grazing, with bells tinkling around their necks in a soothing sound. Laura's experienced eye can tell one vine variety from another; the leaves of Canaiolo are furry underneath with a more rounded shape, while Malvasia has red stems, and Grechetto particularly profuse vegetation. We carried on up the hill, past Caggiole al Mezzo, and the new plantings of Fassati, whose new cellars are just down the road from Laura's house.

My very first visit to Fassati, back in 1979, was to some wonderfully old-fashioned vaulted cellars, stuffed with old *botti*, in nearby Sinalunga, but in 1986 they moved to these smart streamlined premises. We met Barbara Giannotti, with the oenologist, Roberto da Frassini, and first of all went to look at the vineyards just outside the cellar. Barbara explained how the Marchese Fassati had founded the business in 1913 at Gaiole-in-Chianti. Then in 1969, her grandfather, who already owned the Verdicchio company, Fazi-Battaglia, decided to invest in Tuscany, with the purchase of Fassati, and in 1974 bought the first vineyards in Montepulciano. They now have 70 hectares of vines, 40 of Vino Nobile and 30 for Rosso di Montepulciano and Chianti, which may be labelled Colli Senesi. The vineyards are planted mainly with Sangiovese, with a couple of hectares of Merlot and Cabernet Sauvignon, and also some experimental Cabernet Franc, Syrah and Pinot Noir. They are not convinced by Syrah or Cabernet Franc; Merlot works well, while Cabernet Sauvignon is more of a challenge to get the yield in balance. With 5000–6000 vines per hectare, they need to irrigate the young vines. Really they favour the indigenous Tuscan varieties, including Mammola and Colorino, preferring Colorino to Canaiolo as it gives more colour and flavour, whereas Canaiolo is more susceptible to disease. They have vineyards in three different places: here, around the cellar, called La Vigna Nuova, as these were the first to be replanted; at Graccianello where the soil has a much higher clay content; and at Le Caggiole, the vineyards we had passed the previous evening, where the soil is sandier. Various microvinifications allow them to see the differences in the style of Sangiovese from each vineyard.

As for the wines, there was Selciaia, a Rosso di Montepulciano, with some rounded fruit; a Vino Nobile Pasiteo with ripe plummy flavours – Roberto observed that they have renewed many of their barrels recently and invested in 500-litre *tonneaux*, which have had a marked impact on the quality of their wines. Vino Nobile Gersemi includes some Cabernet Sauvignon and Merlot, as well as Sangiovese from all three vineyards. The wine from Graccianello is more powerful and longer lasting, while Le Caggiole is more elegant, and La Vigna Nuova provides body. Each is vinified and aged separately, and then blended together just before bottling. Salarco, little stream nearby, gives its name to the Vino Nobile *riserva*, which consists of Sangiovese, with fifteen per cent Canaiolo and Mammola, and spends three years in wood, two in *botti* and one in *barriques*. With its elegant smoky fruit, it was a good note on which to finish our tasting.

There are several other estates, which are well worth the detour, but by car rather than on foot. Cantina Dei is not far from the walls of Montepulciano, down a long winding track. Today it is run by the extrovert and welcoming Catarina Dei. She explained how her grandfather had bought the property as a holiday home; there were some vines, but they simply sold off the grapes, until the first vintage of 1985, and then her father, who is in the marble business, persuaded her to join the estate. Her world was the performing arts; she had studied theatre and loves music and was initially reluctant to consider her father's suggestion, until she did her first vintage. It was 1992, a lousy year, so they only made 100 hectolitres of Vino Nobile, but it was love at first sight, and, as she puts it, she has grown with the estate. They now have 36 hectares of vines, with a further 12 being planted. It is now impossible to find land to buy. As well as the classic grape varieties of Montepulciano they have planted Syrah, Cabernet Sauvignon and Petit Verdot, all as an experiment in 1991, and since 1996 have made Santa Catarina, with a blend of 30 per cent each of Prugnolo, Cabernet Sauvignon and Syrah, with 10 per cent of Petit Verdot, taking care that the Cabernet Sauvignon does not dominate the blend. We tasted the 1998 vintage of Santa Catarina, which had spent a year in *barriques*, 50 per cent of which were new. The new wood was obvious on the nose, with hints of vanilla, ripe cassis fruit and firm tannins. The structure and flavour is quite different from Vino Nobile, which for Caterina is the true expression of the *terroir*, with a blend of Prugnolo, some Canaiolo and some Mammola, with elegant structure and firm cherry fruit. Her wines, which are made with the guidance of Nicolò d'Afflitto, are the epitome of elegance.

Chiara Barioffi at Le Casalte is someone else who has grown with the family estate, which was bought by her father in 1975. The farmhouse had not been lived in for thirty years and the land had been farmed very much on the old system, producing grain, with a row of vines and olive trees at every 20 metres. Everything has since been replanted and Chiara took us to see the vineyards. She has nearly 13 hectares altogether, including almost 8 in one large plot on the Collina Querciatonda, which once had a lookout tower and one large oak tree. The tower is now reduced to rubble and they have planted several oak trees. Part of the vineyard is trained on wires, with 4500 vines per hectare, and there are also one and a half hectares of *albarello*, with single supporting poles, and 9000 plants per hectare, reviving a traditional planting pattern. Chiara has five different clones of Sangiovese, and also some experimental Merlot, which only came into production in 2002. In the distance there are views of Montepulciano, and in the opposite direction the hilltop town of Chianciano *medievale*, which is worth a detour for its narrow alleyways, flowering balconies and views over the valley, but you are best advised to avoid the thermal spa, in the modern town below, with its garish shops and now half empty hotels.

Chiara's barrel cellar is best described as a *piccola grotta*, a series of little rooms with as many barrels and *barriques* as possible squeezed into a tiny space. A larger cellar is being planned. The barrels are meticulously labelled; you cannot call your wine Vino Nobile until it has passed all the prerequisite tests at the end of its ageing period. Therefore the future Vino Nobile in barrel needs to be classified not as Vino Nobile, but as *vino atto a divenire* Nobile di Montepulciano; such is the power of Italian bureaucracy. The old farmhouse has been beautifully restored and in early June was surrounded by roses in flower, while the vineyards nearest the house have artichoke plants, rather than roses, as a more practical warning against oidium. Adjoining the house is a tiny sixteenth-century chapel that is delightful in its simplicity; Chiara's cat, who had given birth fifteen days earlier to some enchanting grey kittens, basked in the sun with her litter.

We sat and tasted and Chiara talked articulately about her wines. She is adamant that Rosso di Montepulciano is not a lesser Vino Nobile, but a different and simpler wine, that is fruity and easy to drink, and immediately appealing. And it was just that. Her Vino Nobile is an elegant combination of sour cherries and oak; here she wants a wine that is helped by the wood, but is not overwhelmed by it, and with that in mind, she uses a mixture of woods, for the large *botti* will retain the perfume and structure of the wine. Super-Tuscans simply do not interest her; she has planted Merlot to see if it helps the Vino Nobile, but does not want to make an international wine. The Merlot would only ever account for 5 per cent of the blend, certainly not as much as 10, as that would change the character of the wine. She is adamant that your DOCG should be your best wine. She has stopped making a *riserva*, as that detracts from the quality of the basic Vino Nobile, but she might consider a *cru* from Querciatonda, as the newer plantings come into production. It all promises well for the future, as an estate with a strong proprietor presence and a sense of purpose and commitment.

Antinori may have been producing wine in Tuscany for some six hundred years, but they are relative newcomers to Montepulciano, buying their first vineyards here in 1990. The estate of La Braccesca is on the edge of the *comune*, close to the village of Petrignano, which is in Umbria. Nearby is the nature reserve of the *lago di* Montepulciano and you can see the town of Cortona on the hilltop opposite, so that the vineyards across the valley are part of the new DOC of Cortona, and not part of Montepulciano. It is administrative geography that makes the difference here, rather than precise variations in *terroir*, and that is emphasized still further by the choice of grape varieties, not only Sangiovese, but also Merlot and Syrah. After further purchases in the mid-1990s, they now have some 240 hectares, and are planning an increase to 310, within the next few years, which will make La Braccesca Antinori's largest estate. The cellar was still under construction, with a large hole in the ground where the *barricaia* will eventually be, and a streamlined fermentation cellar, with the usual battery of stainless-steel vats, all programmed for temperature control and *rimontaggi*.

Fortunately for us the tasting room was operational, a room with landscape windows on three sides, affording views of the vineyards and across the valley to Cortona. The vineyards were planted with mechanization in mind, and particularly machine harvesting. These machines are so sophisticated now that you can regulate their vibration according to the particular grape variety you are harvesting. The new vineyards benefit from drip irrigation, with water coming from an artificial lake nearby. The regulations regarding irrigation are becoming more flexible, so that you may irrigate young vines, and also more mature vines in a drought situation, in order to prevent excessive stress in the vineyard.

For the moment Antinori produce three wines under the La Braccesca label, with no mention of the name Antinori. Sabazio, their Rosso di Montepulciano, named after a monk who produced wine here in the Middle Ages, is a blend, mainly of Prugnolo with 5 per cent Merlot and 15 per cent Canaiolo. The aim is to maintain the primary fruit flavours, so the wine spends four months in large *botti*. The Merlot provides a certain roundness of flavour, what the Italians call *rotondità*, balancing the tannins of the Sangiovese. There is some Merlot too in the Vino Nobile, which enjoys fourteen months in wood, in both small *botti* and *barriques*, but not new ones. Again the impression was of ripe sweet fruit. Finally there was a Merlot, which with fourteen months in new wood was quite international in style. They were planning a DOC Cortona from Merlot, with 15 per cent Syrah, which would appear in 2003. Currently there are about 200 hectares of Cortona in production, with Antinori, Avignonesi, Manzano and Ruffino the main producers, but the DOC is unlikely to ever total more than 900 hectares.

No visit to Montepulciano would be complete without a mention of Fattoria del Cerro, which is now owned by Italy's largest insurance company, Fondaria Sai. It was Saiagricola that bought del Cerro back in 1978 and the estate now totals some 167 hectares of vines altogether. The cellars are what you would expect, streamlined, functional and efficient, with a forest of stainless-steel vats and a large barrel room, with both *botti* and *barriques*. We tasted in the fourteenth-century villa, which had once been the bishop's summer palace. There was a variety of wines, with numerous highlights, accompanied by some Piemontese biscuits that resembled the crisp Sardinian bread *carta di musica*, but wickedly they are called *lingue di suocera*, or mother-in-law's tongues. The Rosso di Montepulciano was redolent of fresh cherry fruit, while the Vino Nobile, from 90 per cent Prugnolo with some Colorino, Canaiolo and Merlot, was quite sturdy and tannic. Half of the *riserva* spends eighteen months in *barriques*, making for more intense oaky flavours, while Vigneto Antica Chiusina, their *cru* from the best vineyards, from 90 per cent Sangiovese and 10 per cent Colorino, exuded layers of flavour with tannin and firm fruit, demanding bottle ageing. It promised well. Tiziana Mazzetti, the competent and likeable public relations officer, explained that Colorino has nothing to do with colour, despite its name, but that it adds structure, harmony and complexity to the Sangiovese. There was also a pure Sangiovese, Manero, and a pure Merlot, Poggio Golo. They have tried Cabernet Sauvignon too, but it was not as successful. They also make a late-harvest wine, with noble rot, Corte d'Oro. We tasted the first, 2001 vintage, from equal parts of Sauvignon and Sémillon, which were planted in 1996. There was no obvious botrytis on the nose, more a bouquet of ripe honey, with some unctuous sweetness and good acidity on the palate. The wine is fermented in oak, and the fermentation stops naturally; in 2001 they made just 2000 half bottles. We were lucky to share one.

A visit to Salchetto is a must for the stunning views of Montepulciano from the courtyard. Cecilia Naldoni explained how her husband Fabrizio was in the navy, while she worked in a photographic laboratory, and then in 1983 they bought 26 hectares of land, mainly arable and grazing land. There were just 3 hectares of vines and initially they sold the wine *sfuso*. It was not until 1990 that they bottled their first wine, and gradually they have developed the estate. You could buy planting rights ten years ago, but nowadays it is impossible for small people to buy land here. Now they have 15 hectares in Montepulciano and 8 of Chianti, Colli Senesi, near Chianciano. There is a neat compact cellar, with a head of Bacchus at the cellar door and some wonderful flowering jasmine creeping up the wall. Unusually, they do not add any other grape varieties to their Vino Nobile, preferring to make it from pure Prugnolo, which since 1999 conforms to the *disciplinari*. The wine was elegantly structured. Salco, which is a selection of grapes from the best part of their vineyard, and the equivalent of the *riserva*, which they no longer make, spends eighteen months in new wood, making some concentrated fruit, with well-integrated oak. 1999 was their first vintage, which we enjoyed later over lunch at one of Montepulciano's more elegant restaurants, La Grotta, just by San Biagio.

The name Ruffino, not to be confused with Rufina, is one of the big players in the Tuscan viticultural scene. The business began in 1913, dealing in grapes, and the first land purchases were made in 1942. We met Luigi Folinari at La Lodola Nuova, one of their two estates in Montepulciano, and he explained how the family had divided up their land holdings in June 2000, so that the large Chianti estate of Nozzole now belongs to his cousin, while his side of the family retain the Tenimenti Ruffino with nine estates: Montemasso, Santadame and Greppoli in Chianti Classico; Poggio Casciano in the Colli Fiorentini; Solatia near Monteriggioni, where they grow Chardonnay; an estate in Montalcino; Il Greppone Mazzi; Il Murlo in the Colli Senesi; Pietraia in nearby Cortona, and Il Greppo, as well as La Lodola Nuova in Montepulciano, and a head office and warehouse in Pontasieve. Altogether this represents some 1500 hectares of land, including 600 of vines. Over the past few years they have been carrying out an extensive replanting programme, adopting the newer practices of Tuscan viticulture. As for La Lodola Nuova, they bought it in 1988 and were one of the first outside investors in Montepulciano. There was hardly anything here at all. Now they have 35 hectares of vines and are building a brand-new cellar, yet another building site scarring the Tuscan landscape. Their vineyard in Cortona will be part of the new DOC and is planted mainly with Syrah as well as Sangiovese and Merlot. I quizzed Luigi about the Maremma, as the obvious choice for any future investment. He admitted that it could be interesting, but for the moment they prefer to concentrate on what they have, and for them central Tuscany will always be better; in contrast the Maremma is less elegant and more homogeneous. In Montepulciano he considered that they held the middle road, between traditional and innovative. Their Vino Nobile from 90 per cent Sangiovese and 10 per cent Merlot spends twenty-four months in *botti*. Here they are traditional in that they tend to be anti-*barriques*; however, that does not stop them from putting part of their *riserva* into *barriques*. The wine had an attractive nose, with a ripe rounded palate and good tannin structure. The *riserva* in contrast had a tight-knit nose, with a fuller, richer palate. We ended with a quite individual wine from Santedame, Romitorio di Santedame, made from 65 per cent Colorino with 35 per cent

Merlot, which had spent at least eighteen months in new barrels. It was chocolatey and intense, with tannin and ripe fruit, and quite unusual.

There is an overlap of producers between Cortona and Montepulciano, with most of the producers of the new DOC of Cortona, created in 1999, producing Vino Nobile. One exception is the innovative estate of Fattoria di Manzano. It had changed out of all recognition since my earlier visit back in 1989; then the reason for my visit was for the now virtually defunct DOC of Bianco Vergine della Valdichiana. This time it was the reputation of their pure Syrah, Il Bosco, which is generally considered to be one of the best in Tuscany, and rightly so. We met Francesco d'Alessandro, who explained how his father had bought the property back in 1967, and how, with his brother Massimo, they began experimenting in the mid-1980s, pulling up the old traditional vines, and planting varieties like Syrah and Viognier. Syrah is firmly part of the DOC of Cortona, but for the moment, Viognier is not even on what he described as the national *alba* or list of permitted grape varieties, but that omission should soon be rectified. As it is, the DOC allows the producers to decide which varieties suit their land, with a choice of a minimum of 85 per cent of one variety in a wine. The only thing that is forbidden, happily, is Trebbiano.

Alessandro took us for a drive through the vineyards, with views towards Cortona, which never fail to delight. He showed us where they are recreating the old terraced vineyards, which is a true labour of love for these are steep slopes and often the walls have completely collapsed. The newest plantings reach a density of 8500 vines per hectare. Then we returned to the pretty eighteenth-century villa with its attractive yellow facade, and tasted in an elegant dining room, with an elaborate frieze around the walls. A certificate showed that the estate had won a medal for Vin Santo in Palermo at the end of the nineteenth century. First we tried the white wine, Fontarca, which is a blend of 60 per cent Chardonnay, fermented in wood, and 40 per cent Viognier, vinified in stainless steel. The new oak dominated the flavour to give a long sweet finish.

They used to make Vesco from Gamay, which was brought here by Napoleon's troops. Instead today they produce Vescovo II from Syrah, which had an attractive peppery fruit, with a certain structure and freshness. Only part of it is kept in wood. Alessandro talked about the differences between Italian Syrah, and French or Australian. He felt that the fruit in the Italian Syrah was more obvious, what he called *frutta di bosco*. His oldest vineyards of Syrah are fifteen years old, and the best grapes are used for Il Bosco, which spends about fifteen months in *barriques*. The very first vintage of Il Bosco was 1992; we were treated to the 1995, which was evolving nicely, with some peppery fruit. With its subtle elegance, I found it quite French in style. The oak influence was still very apparent on the 2000, with some dense tannic fruit, while the 2001 was youthful and concentrated with dense leathery fruit and firm tannins. It could only improve with age. Last of all was the Vin Santo, and yet another explanation of the name, that the grapes are left to dry until Holy Week. The wine was ripe and unctuous, but with a certain freshness that comes from the lack of *madre*. It was a good note on which to finish.

Our visit to Trinoro was magical. It was early February and it had unexpectedly snowed overnight. We could see a sprinkling of light snow across the valley on the slopes below Montefollonico, but as we took a narrow road out of Sarteano the snow became thicker, and as the road turned downhill into the Orcia valley towards Trinoro, the valley floor was covered with a thick white carpet. It was a world of white basking in gentle sunshine, and would soon melt, the unexpected reminder of winter vanishing almost as suddenly as it had come.

In the absence of our host, Alessandro Franchetti, his *fattore*, Stefano, took us for a drive around the estate, which totals 200 hectares altogether, but only 25 of vineyards, with woods, lakes and arable land. Everything is gated and fenced, what the Italians call *fondo chiuso*, in order to keep the hunters off the land. Obtaining permission for this from the *comune* is not easy and requires tenacity in the face of obstinate bureaucracy.

There were wonderful views over the valley, with 300-year-old olive trees covered in snow, which looked like a scene from a fairy tale. It was the first time I had ever seen snow in Tuscany, although at higher altitudes it is not so unusual. Here we were at just over 400 metres – not so high. We passed four endearing orphaned wild boarlets in a pen, together with some *cinta senese* pigs. Although Franchetti bought the estate in the early 1980s, he did not come and live here until 1990, and so the first vineyards were planted in 1991, Cabernet Sauvignon and Cabernet Franc, Merlot and Petit Verdot, with 10,000 plants per hectare in the traditional *bordelais* manner. There is also an unusual variety that originates from Lazio, Cesanese di Affile. In theory Trinoro lies within the new DOC of Orcia, which runs from Sarteanno to San Quirico, including Pienza and Torrita di Siena, but in practice the lack of Sangiovese at Trinoro makes the wines IGT rather than DOC. However, given the reputation and resultant price that Trinoro has established in a short space of time, whether it is IGT or DOC is quite irrelevant.

We returned to the cellars and our host appeared, looking somewhat dishevelled, with unkempt hair and three-day-old stubble, with that confident self-assurance of someone who has no doubts about their place in the world, lacking neither money nor social position. He spoke English with ease, explaining that with an American mother, he was born in New York, but brought up in Rome. As for his interest in wine, he had a distribution company in New York in the mid-1980s, and has been much influenced by friends in Bordeaux in his choice of grape varieties to plant. 1995 was the first vintage of Trinoro, with 1997 the first commercial vintage; Franchetti said he simply followed his nose; he does not employ a consultant, but may ask friends for advice. There is no doubt that the results are very fine, with two wines: Tenuta di Trinoro, of which just 600 cases are made each vintage, and the second wine of the estate, Le Cupole, named after the various dome buildings scattered around the property, which includes some Cesanese di Affile, but no Petit Verdot. It is more accessible than Tenuta di Trinoro in both price and flavour.

We compared the 2001 vintage of each. Tenuta di Trinoro was tight-knit and finely structured with ripe fruit and elegant tannins, while Le Cupole was softer and smokier, with more rugged tannins, ripe fruit and a long finish. Franchetti enthused about Cabernet Franc, which accounts for 60 per cent of his vineyards. He likes the concentration that comes from low yields, and wants no more than 18 hl/ha, with a rigorous green harvest and careful picking, seeking out the very ripest, indeed almost overripe, grapes. Manual *pigiatura* and some *rimontaggi* extract fruit and flavour; the wines are kept in barrel for ten months and then spend the second winter in concrete vats, before bottling in their second spring. Franchetti suggested that Tuscany is not really truly

Mediterranean, whereas Lazio, just over the next hill, is. Here there is no sea influence and the grapes are picked much later than on the coast. They may stop ripening, during the stress of summer heat, and then set off again as the cooler weather returns. As for the wines, they promised well, but with such a short history, their true potential for the moment remains untested.

But Franchetti is not resting on his laurels at Trinoro. He talked with enthusiasm about a new project on the slopes of Mount Etna, where he hopes to produce a truly great wine from Sauvignon Gris, Chardonnay and Viognier, from high-altitude vineyards, at 1000 metres, on the north face of the volcano. Some terraces on the 18-hectare estate were lost to lava in the 1970s, so by the law of averages, the vines should be safe from eruptions for a few years yet. And as we left, the snow was melting fast in the February sunshine.

Carmignano and Chianti Montalbano

April

West of Florence; Villa di Capezzana, Pratesi, Piaggia, Ambra and the Fattoria di Cantagallo in Chianti Montalbano

THE VILLAGE OF CARMIGNANO, to the west of Florence on a hillside overlooking the Arno valley and the plain of Pistoia, gives its name to one of the few Tuscan wines with a historical association with Cabernet Sauvignon. However, the village's origins are Etruscan, with remains at Artimino and tombs at Fattoria della Calavria. One of the earliest references to the wine of Carmignano comes from the Prato merchant Francesco Datini, who bought some, paying a Florentine *sugello* per *soma*, apparently some four times the price charged for the most prestigious wines of the period.

The Medici dukes of Florence contributed to the fame of Carmignano. The proximity of the city of Florence meant that this was perfect land for hunting, so they built villas and hunting lodges here, which still stand. The substantial villa at Artimino, called La Ferdinanda, with its hundreds of chimneys, was designed by the architect Buontalenti for Ferdinand I at the end of the sixteenth century. His father, Cosimo I, was responsible for the construction of the long stone wall to enclose the *barco reale*, or royal property, as a hunting reserve for the Medici dukes.

Duke Cosimo III issued the famous *bando* of 1716, which stands as one of the very first attempts to limit a vineyard area and guarantee the authenticity of a wine. Four areas were mentioned, Chianti, Pomino, the Val d'Arno di Sopra and Carmignano, and wine not produced within those specific areas could not be sold by that name. Today the DOCG of Carmignano covers much the same area as defined in 1716, namely the *comune* of Carmignano and part of adjoining Poggio a Caiano. Cosimo III also despatched people to France to collect cuttings of different vines and it was at that time that

Cabernet Sauvignon was first planted in Carmignano. A few plants have always remained, referred to as *uva francesca*, or French grapes. At one time there were over a hundred different grape varieties grown in the region, nearly all of which have now sadly disappeared.

When the vineyard area of Chianti was delimited in 1932, Carmignano was absorbed into it and no attempt was made to distinguish it from adjoining Chianti Montalbano until the mid-1960s, when there was a move, instigated by Ugo Contini Bonacossi of Tenuta di Capezzana, to plant more Cabernet Sauvignon in an attempt to reinforce the separate identity of the region, for it is the long-established use of Cabernet Sauvignon that really differentiates Carmignano from Chianti. With the change in the regulations for Chianti allowing for the inclusion of Cabernet Sauvignon and the plethora of new Tuscan DOCs, which permit its use, the differences are now of course less defined, but in 1975 Carmignano was recognized as a separate DOC, with an obligatory percentage of Cabernet Sauvignon, at a time there was very little Cabernet Sauvignon planted elsewhere in Tuscany. Then in 1990 it was elevated to DOCG.

The Monte Albano dominates the skyline of Carmignano and gives its name to the adjoining sub-zone of Chianti. Many Carmignano producers also have vineyards in Chianti. Those of Carmignano are on the eastern, cooler slopes of the hill, whereas the vineyards of Montalbano and the village of Vinci, where Leonardo was born, are on the other warmer slope. There is also a difference in the soil, with Montalbano having more sandstone, while Carmignano is heavier, with limestone, schist and *galestro*, in other words, not so different from the soil of Chianti Classico, and the climate here is a little milder and damper, with more rainfall.

I have always had a soft spot for the wines of Capezzana. Ugo Contini Bonacossi was one of the very first Tuscan wine growers I visited back in the early 1980s. He and his wife Lisa are amongst the most welcoming people in Tuscany. Ugo was brought up by an English nanny and speaks impeccable English with an old-world aristocratic charm. He is now a sprightly 80-plus years old and quite belies his age. You drive up an alleyway of cypress trees to the tiny hamlet of Capezzana and ring the doorbell at 108 Via Capezzana. A discreet brass plaque tells you that you are indeed at the Fattoria di Capezzana, but behind this discreet facade there is a magnificent villa, built by the Medicis in the fourteenth and fifteenth centuries, with further additions in the seventeenth century. After various changes of ownership, the estate was bought by Ugo's grandfather in 1920. However, the first written reference to Capezzana goes back to 804 with the granting of the leasehold of part of a property in a place called Capezzana, inhabited by the farmer Petruccio, with the house, its buildings and land, the courtyards, gardens, vineyards, wood and olive trees. Already at the beginning of the ninth century, Capezzana was producing wine and olive oil, as it does today. Now the vineyards total some 100 hectares of the 650-hectare estate, along with 150 hectares of olive trees and 330 hectares of wood, as well as some arable land.

Capezzana is very much a family concern, with three of Ugo and Lisa's children following in their parents' footsteps. The youngest, Filippo, is responsible for the vineyards and he took us for a drive, pointing out the large expanses of new plantings, some 22 hectares over the last three years. Syrah is a fairly recent introduction, originally sent by the nursery in mistake for some Sangiovese back in 1992, and since 1998 it has been included in their IGT Ghiaie della Furba. However, the average age of the vines is around twenty years, with some as old as forty. The Syrah vineyard is planted in what Filippo called the *sistema francese*, with 9600 vines per hectare.

We looked at the site of a new vineyard; from just 1.8 hectares of land they had removed a breathtaking 3000 square metres of rocks, so that there were gigantic boulders lying at the side of the vineyard. It was *un lavoro di Cyclops*. Drainage channels have to be installed. Filippo explained how the planting systems have changed over the years. At one time rows were much wider, and then in the early 1980s, in an attempt to increase the density, Ugo added a second vine, so that you had two vines side by side sharing a single supporting post, almost looking as though they were a single vine.

There was a vineyard of Trebbiano, planted in narrow rows by Ugo's father in 1948, before the advent of the tractor demanded wide rows to accommodate machinery. A group of Moroccan workers were busy tying the vines to their supporting posts, and in another vineyard, supporting wires were being installed, with the spacing accurately measured. We crossed the little stream, the Furba, which gives its name to one of their wines. It rises on the Monte

Albano and remains unpolluted, so that there are freshwater shrimps for the taking. Merlot is planted nearby on lower land and on the nearby hill the church of Tizzano provides a prominent landmark. Sadly, the area has become a dormitory for the growing cities of Prato and Pistoia, making the land more valuable for construction than for vineyards. Consequently, Carmignano remains a small area of about 200 hectares, with eleven producers who bottle their wines.

Ugo showed us round his cellars, a labyrinth that runs not only under the villa, but also under the large courtyard and the *limonaia*, where the lemon trees spend the winter. There had been some changes since my last visit, with more *barriques* and the introduction of *botti* of Allier oak, in preference to the traditional Slavonic oak. This prompted Ugo to make an observation about the old school and new school of Carmignano – the Cabernet Sauvignon now stands at 20 per cent, with Sangiovese as the backbone. You are also allowed 10 per cent of complementary grape varieties, which could be Merlot or Syrah, or Canaiolo. At Capezzana they keep to Sangiovese and Cabernet Sauvignon. However, the introduction of malolactic fermentation in *barriques* enhances the fruit, counterbalancing a tendency of Sangiovese to lose its colour and dry out with too much oxygenation. The oldest bottles in the cellar are 1925 and are overlooked by an inscription carved in granite:

Della tua bontà
Abbiamo ricevuto questo vino
Frutta della vita
E del lavoro dell'uomo

Words which sum up Ugo's personal philosophy that wine is the fruit of a gift from God and the result of man's hard work.

We tasted his wines over dinner in an elegant dining room, with a host of family photographs, a family group at Ugo and Lisa's fiftieth wedding anniversary, and Lisa's mother as a little girl, with her older sisters; she was born in 1899 and died in 2001 at the age of 101. An imposing portrait of Ugo's grandfather looked down on us. As for the wines, the 2002 Chardonnay was lightly buttery and refreshingly unoaked; 2000 Carmignano amply illustrated the influence of Cabernet with ripe fruit; 1999 Trefiano, their second estate, a slightly different blend with 15 per cent Cabernet Sauvignon and 10 per cent Canaiolo, had a similar elegance, with subtle nuances of flavour, and 2000 Ghiaie della Furba, for which the blend has evolved into 30 per cent Merlot, 10 per cent Syrah and 60 per cent Cabernet Sauvignon, had some rich cedary fruit with a peppery note. These were accompanied by Lisa's memorable cooking, including *caramelli*, which is the Italian not only for a toffee but also for a pasta shape that looks just like a wrapped-up boiled sweet, stuffed with ricotta and spinach. Strawberries were the basis of the fruit salad, but with the original addition of pine nuts and raisins.

The next morning we explored on foot, first taking the road up the hill through the hamlet past the elegant thirteenth-century Oratorio di San Jacopo, which has the addition of a twentieth-century bell tower, by Ugo's grandfather. The architectural distinction is so subtle that the difference in age is barely perceptible. A road took us round to another hamlet, Coli, with views across the valley. Sadly, you never seem to escape from the urban encroachment, and then we joined a track through the vineyards, passing a house hidden in some trees on the edge of the vines. A young Alsatian, called Kira, we subsequently found out, barked furiously at our walking sticks and, ignoring her owner's exhortations to stay, followed us on a gentle stroll through olive groves and vineyards of various ages. We returned her home before our appointment further down the hill at Pratesi, but not without some difficulty as she seemed determined to effect a second escape.

Fabrizio Pratesi, who is also the local Mercedes dealer, was away, but his wife Cristina and their toddler Niccolò were expecting us. Pratesi is one of the new estates in Carmignano, or rather, one of the more recent ones to start bottling its wine, in 1998. The land has been in the family for several generations. They have 7 hectares, just below Capezzana, planted with Sangiovese, Merlot and Cabernet Sauvignon, some even with 10,000 plants per hectare. This necessitates a double *enjambeur* tractor, which can straddle two rows at a time. There is a neat cellar, with fat stainless-steel vats for fermentation, which gives better skin contact than the more customary tall thin vats, as well as lots of *barriques*, from Seguin Moreau and Taransaud, and not a *botte* in sight.

They make three wines, a Carmignano from 70 per cent Sangiovese, 20 per cent Cabernet Sauvignon and 10 per cent Merlot, which are blended after sixteen months maturation in *barriques*. There was a rich concentration of oaky fruit on the nose and palate and it was definitely a wine to age. Locorosso, an IGT, with 90 per cent Sangiovese and 10 per cent Merlot, without a drop of Cabernet, is given twenty-four months' ageing in oak, and illustrates how much Merlot adds flesh and body to the Sangiovese, much more than Cabernet Sauvignon, it would seem. Finally, Carmione 2002, a 60 per cent Cabernet Sauvignon and 40 per cent Merlot blend, with twenty months' ageing, was full of intense youthful fruit. The potential seemed enormous, but with the underlying reservation that these are new wines with no established track record, as yet. The style of Pratesi, with its more international flavours, contrasts with more traditional Carmignano. Cristina described their enormous investment as *una scommessa*, a gamble, but one that is paying off.

Mauro Vannucci at Piaggia also favours a more international style of Carmignano. With Ugo's help we traced him down on the edge of Poggio Caiano, in his neat functional cellar, without a sign to indicate the presence of a winery. There are all sorts of local rumours as to how Mauro Vannucci made his money; he admits to a previous career in knitwear, with nearby Prato the centre of the Tuscan textile industry. Now he is passionately involved in his wine, admirably self-taught, and able to pay for good advice. He is a short stocky man, exuding formidable energy and passionate enthusiasm. *Mi sono appassionato*, he said at every other breath as he took us to see his vineyards. He began by buying just 3 hectares from Ugo, and now when everything comes into production, he will have a total of 15 hectares, 12 in a splendid position in a veritable suntrap just below the hamlet of Poggetto. It entailed two years of lengthy negotiations with six different owners to achieve the single plot of land. There had been olive trees there, but mostly they have been replaced by Sangiovese, Cabernet Sauvignon and Merlot. You could certainly appreciate the microclimate and the intense heat generated by the sheltered position, and if there had not been a gentle mist in the distance, we would have been able to see the cathedral dome of Florence.

Mauro Vannucci makes two wines, Carmignano *riserva* and a *cru*, an IGT called Il Sasso, after a nearby hamlet. The blend is the same for the

Carmignano, but with marketing astuteness he realized the value of producing a more expensive wine. The Carmignano, from 70 per cent Sangiovese, 20 per cent Cabernet Sauvignon and 10 per cent Merlot, spends two years in Allier barriques. The influence of the new oak is very apparent, while the body of the Merlot and Cabernet mask any astringency in the Sangiovese. The wine was ripe and dense, from almost overripe grapes, with structure and tannin, but somehow it was not very Tuscan. Il Sasso, which only spends twelve to fifteen months in *barriques*, was slightly less sturdy and structured. Vanucci said that he was looking for power and elegance; he claimed to be the first to make Carmignano in this way, contrasting his wine with the other extreme permitted by the regulations, namely 50 per cent Sangiovese, 20 per cent Canaiolo, 10 per cent Cabernet Sauvignon and 10 per cent complementary varieties, which may include Merlot or, equally well, Trebbiano and Malvasia. Again, it will be interesting to see how these wines develop with age and experience. However, we were left in no doubt of Mauro Vannucci's passionate commitment to Piaggia.

Giuseppe Rigoli at Ambra, with cellars just down the road on the outskirts of Poggio Caiano not far from the Medici palace, is quite a different character, both in wine and personality. He is a tall lanky man, in his mid-40s, with a friendly smile. His *fattore*, Leonardo, is a cheerful *contadino* who has worked at Ambra for over forty years. Giuseppe described him as *la coscienza storica* of the estate. As Giuseppe is a trained oenologist, he is rare in Tuscany in not employing a consultant; all the decisions are his alone. *Il vino è veramente il suo*, said Leonardo. Giuseppe explained how he cultivates 18 hectares, some from his parents' estate and some rented, with four vineyards, each making quite different styles of Carmignano, as our tasting subsequently illustrated. In addition he produces a Trebbiano, a pink Vin Ruspo and a young red wine, Barco Reale.

The vinification differences for the Carmignano are subtle. They are fermented in stainless steel and then aged in *tonneaux, botti* or *barriques*. Giuseppe talked of the permutations in the blend for Carmignano. The regulations are fine as they are, with the flexibility allowed by the complementary varieties, but he would also like the possibility of a pure Sangiovese, and maybe more international varieties. 'Everything is possible' –

especially considering that there were once as many as two or three hundred different grape varieties grown here in the 1700s, which the experimental vineyard at Artimino is trying to salvage. I was not sure that I agreed about a pure Sangiovese, for it is the obligatory percentage of Cabernet Sauvignon that singles out Carmignano from the other wines of Tuscany.

Giuseppe's wines are really very classic. Rosato di Carmignano, otherwise known as Vin Ruspo, from Sangiovese, Canaiolo and a little Cabernet, run off after a day of skin contact, was light red in colour, with ripe strawberry fruit and fresh acidity. There is an anecdote attached to the name, which literally translates as 'stolen wine', and recalls the days of the *mezzadria* system when the *contadini* did not deliver the last picking of the day until the following morning. Inevitably the grapes were lightly crushed by their own weight overnight, and some light red wine was the result, which the *contadini* always kept for themselves.

Barco Reale is the young version of Carmignano, a DOC in its own right and named after the wall protecting the royal hunting forests of the Medici. Giuseppe's is Sangiovese, with 10 per cent Cabernet and 5 per cent Merlot. White grapes are still allowed, in the *disciplinari*, but no one uses them any more. Dry cherries with some rounded tannins was the dominant flavour. Carmignano, Vigna di Montefortine, with 10 per cent Cabernet and 10 per cent Canaiolo blended with Sangiovese, grown on tufa and kept in small *tonneaux* of 350–500 litres and also some 25-hectolitre *botti* for a year, was elegant and perfumed with cedary overtones and a dry finish. The DOCG regulations demand eight months' ageing for Carmignano *normale*, and twelve months for a *riserva* with a further twelve months in bottle before sale.

Santa Cristina in Pillo, a vineyard near Artimino, is *albarese* with clay and a blend of 75 per cent Sangiovese, 10 per cent Canaiolo, 10 per cent Cabernet and 5 per cent Merlot and Colorino. Giuseppe explained that *albarese* makes for richer wines with more structure, and this was certainly the case, compared to Vigna di Montefortine. Montalbiolo, a Carmignano *riserva*, from tufa and *galestro*, with a slight variation on the blend, with no Colorino, spends twelve months in *barriques* and *tonneaux*, including a percentage of new oak for the malolactic fermentation. The nose was richer, with more obvious oak, and on the palate the wine was both elegant and structured with cedary overtones.

Giuseppe began working with *barriques* in 1990 and has used them consistently since about 1998.

2000 Elzana *riserva*, predominantly Sangiovese with 5 per cent Cabernet Sauvignon, grown on *galestro* and clay and first made in 1995, had some lovely smoky fruit. It was richer with more vigorous tannins. Giuseppe explained that Sangiovese is not always very suitable for ageing in *barriques*. Sometimes a 5- or 10-hectolitre barrel may better enhance the fruit and not overwhelm it with oak.

Over lunch in the friendly restaurant at Artimino, Da Delfina, we were treated to various more mature vintages, such as 1996, which Giuseppe described as *la vecchia scuola*, the old school, for the dominance of Sangiovese. 1992 Montalbiolo was rich and elegant, with 1989 Vigna Cristina delicate and vegetal and almost Burgundian in character, and the final 1983 Carmignano, made in the traditional manner in old *botti*, had intriguing herbal notes with a dry backbone, amply illustrating the ageing potential of Carmignano in a wine that was almost twenty years old.

Da Delfina merits the detour. Delfina is an elderly lady who sits at the entrance to the restaurant quietly observing the comings and goings, while our enthusiastic host, Carlo Croni, encouraged us to sample yet another speciality. 'I insist that you try the *tagliatelle* with freshly picked wild asparagus; it is just the season for it.' How could we refuse? Next came succulent young rabbit with olives and pine nuts. This is the signature dish of the restaurant, and you are given a colourful plate depicting the dish as a souvenir, but sadly not the recipe.

After a quick look at the outside of the Medici villa at Artimino with its host of chimneys, it was time to head over the Monte Albano, taking a winding road past another estate, Baccheretto, and then on to Vinci, past the birthplace of Leonardo, which is now a museum with reconstructions of his various machines, and then on to the banks of the Arno and town of Limite e Capraie. Our destination was the Chianti Montalbano estate of Cantagallo, which is the property of the Pierazzuoli family, who also own the Carmignano estate of Le Farnete. Enrico Pierazzuoli is the keen young president of the *consorzio* of Carmignano. His grandfather had bought Cantagallo in the early 1970s and the family acquired Le Farnete as an abandoned estate in 1992 and there is now a third estate, Matronero, in Chianti Classico. Enrico's grandfather had produced wine in the traditional manner and sold it *sfuso*; his father works in textiles in Prato and so it was up to Enrico and his three brothers and one sister to do something with the family land.

Enrico described himself as *un uomo della vigna*; it is the vineyards that are central to everything. Sangiovese needs so much more work in the vineyard; it is like a thoroughbred horse that needs taming, whereas Merlot is much easier and provides more fruit and colour. He talked of the green harvest: how the elderly *contadini* said, 'These people have got money to throw away.'

Tasting with Enrico illustrated the differences between Chianti Montalbano and Carmignano and just why Carmignano deserves its separate DOCG. 2000 Montalbano Cantagallo was a pure Sangiovese with five months in *tonneaux*. It had the attractive cherry fruit of Sangiovese, but nothing more. 2000 Carmignano, from 80 per cent Sangiovese and 20 per cent Cabernet, had a smoky elegance on the nose and palate, with much more depth, with the cedary notes of the Cabernet balancing the energy of the Sangiovese. Enrico may grow Merlot for an IGT, but for him it has no place in Carmignano. The 1999 *riserva*, an identical blend, with two years in *barriques*, was long and complex with smoky fruit and herbal undertones.

Enrico spoke of Ugo Bonacossi with great admiration and professional respect. 'He allowed us to escape from Chianti' – for it was all Ugo's efforts in the 1970s that really achieved the DOC of Carmignano. 'Now we must take care not to enter into the *mirasma del mondo*' – in other words, not become too international. How true.

San Gimignano – Vernaccia and Rosso

· April ·

Montenidoli, Signano, Panizzi, Fugnano, San Donato, Castello di Montauto, Casale, Vagnoni, Cesani, San Quirico, Il Paradiso, Fattoria di Cusona

THE TALL MEDIEVAL towers of San Gimignano loom out of the haze, making a dramatic skyline, which someone once described as a Tuscan Manhattan. The distinctive silhouette of this hilltop town is visible from far away; often it is nearer as the crow flies than the twisting winding roads would have you believe. The towers were built by local families as a measure of defence during the struggles between the Guelphs and the Ghibellines; the higher the tower, the more important the family. Today just thirteen of the original seventy-six remain. The Piazza della Cisterna lies at the centre of the town, an attractive triangular 'square', lined with buildings from the thirteenth and fourteenth centuries, and with a *cisterna*, a well, that was also built in the thirteenth century. You can sit at a café and watch the world go by; the world in this instance being the two million or so tourists who flock to San Gimignano every year. The narrow streets are lined with wine and other souvenir shops, with almost impassable crowds on a spring Sunday afternoon. It is so much more atmospheric later in the evening when the coaches have disappeared and the streets are almost empty.

The origins of San Gimignano are Etruscan and in the Middle Ages it owed its importance to its position on the Via Francigena, the pilgrim route that ran through northern Italy to Rome. Grain, wine and saffron were the principal crops, and the wine, Vernaccia di San Gimignano, is said to have been enjoyed by several popes. Martin IV was placed by Dante in the sixth circle of Purgatory where he 'purged through fasting the eels of Bolsena and the Vernaccia wine'. In medieval London Vernaccia was known as *vernage*. There are poetic references to Vernaccia. Michelangelo Buonarroti the Younger wrote in 1643 that Vernaccia 'kisses, licks, bites, slaps and stings'. Vernaccia di San Gimignano, in common with any Tuscan wine of any merit, features in Francesco Redi's poem of 1685, 'Bacchus in Tuscany'. He condemns all those who do not appreciate it, particularly the Vernaccia of Pietrafitta, which is still a reputable estate today, to drink inferior wines, and to be crowned with beetroot and whipped by a satyr.

No one can explain why it is that Vernaccia is grown in the vineyards of San Gimignano while the ubiquitous Trebbiano is the principal grape variety for virtually all the other white DOCs of Tuscany, except Montecarlo and Pomino. There are two other quite different Vernaccias in Italy: Vernaccia di Serrapetrona, from the Marche near Pescara, which is a red wine, while Vernaccia di Oristano, from Sardinia, could be described as Italy's answer to sherry. There is a suggestion that the word derives from the same root as 'vernacular' and therefore it may simply have been a way of describing a native or local wine, which would also explain the diversity of the three different Vernaccia. The first written reference to Vernaccia in San Gimignano dates back to 1276, when the Ordinamenti di Gabelle or tax list of the town established that the tax for a *soma*, a medieval measure of about 76 litres, was two *soldi* for Vernaccia.

Vernaccia di San Gimignano was the very first wine to be recognized as a DOC in May 1966, and then in 1993 it was elevated to DOCG status. The *disciplinari* recognize Vernaccia as the dominant variety, but as always, there is the flexibility of a tenth percentage of complementary varieties, which could be Trebbiano or Malvasia, but more probably Chardonnay. More often than not

Vernaccia stands alone. The vineyards also lie within the Chianti zone of the Colli Senesi, but there have been moves, which are coming to fruition, to create a more precise DOC of San Gimignano Rosso, which will come in several forms, pandering to the increasing internationalization of the vineyards of Tuscany. The basic San Gimignano Rosso demands a minimum of 70 per cent Sangiovese, with various other possible complementary varieties, Cabernet Sauvignon, Merlot, Syrah and Pinot Noir, and in addition it is possible to make a red wine based on any of those varieties, with a minimum of 85 per cent in the blend, with the grape variety featured on the label.

The soil composition of the vineyards of San Gimignano favours white wine, with tufa or yellow sandstone, which is sometimes mixed with clay. At its most basic, Vernaccia di San Gimignano is a simple white wine, made in the simplest of manners, by pressing the grapes, chilling the juice and fermenting it at a cool temperature. However, all kinds of nuances are possible, and there is no doubt that the quality of the wine has benefited from the considerable technological advances in Tuscan cellars over recent years. The diversity of style is amply illustrated by the wines of Montenidoli. Elisabetta Fagiuoli bubbles with enthusiasm, passionately expounding her ideas. The *tradizionale*, which includes some pressed as well as free-run juice, has a grassy nose, with hints of minerality, with herbal and almond flavours on the palate. The Vino Fiore, only from free-run juice, is more subtle and mouth-filling, with some intriguing herbal flavours, while Carato has been fermented in barrel, some new, and is nicely rounded with well-integrated oak, making a harmonious whole. There is also Templare Bianco di Toscana, from Vernaccia, blended with Trebbiano and Malvasia. The first vintage of this was 1999; we tried the 2000, which presented a mouthful of different flavours, with nuances of herbs. Elisabetta also makes red wine, a light, fresh Rosso di Toscana, Il Garrulo – she explained that this is how Chianti used to be, while there is also a Chianti Colli Senesi, with some dry cherry fruit, and a more substantial Sono Montenidoli, a Rosso di Toscana, which benefits from some oak ageing.

The first time I went to visit Elisabetta at Montenidoli, a number of years ago now, she explained how she had bought the vineyard with a legacy from her grandmother. There were family vineyards in the Veneto and both her grandmother and great-grandmother had made wine; her mother was a wonderful cook, as indeed she is, but she came from an intellectual family, of teachers, and arrived in San Gimignano as 'an illiterate' as far as wine was concerned, to make her first vintage in 1971. Then she quoted Veronese, 'the last love of a woman is the earth'. You know instinctively that she is more widely read than a many a winemaker, and an element of the aesthetic is provided in her functional cellar by a statue of Achilles.

We chose a sunny Sunday morning in spring for our walk through the vineyards of San Gimignano, setting off down a *strada bianca* close to the town. You very quickly leave the madding crowd behind you and the valley opens out into wide vistas, with views of many towers behind you. The road is lined with olive groves and well-tended vegetable gardens, and the occasional house. The first estate we reached was Signano, the property of Manrico Biagini, who is also a butcher by trade, raising *cinta senese* pigs, for salami and hams. He is a cheerful man with a mop of grey hair and a bushy moustache, who evidently enjoys what he does. His father bought the estate in 1961 and the vineyards have gradually been increased to a total of thirteen, with another dozen rented. The cellars, which were rather chaotic, with an air of Heath Robinson about them, were built in 1965, and the first bottling at Signano was in the mid-1970s. There was a row of concrete vats, one receiving the full force of a gas heater in an attempt to persuade a recalcitrant vat of Merlot and Sangiovese to get on with its malolactic fermentation. We tasted first a Vernaccia *normale*, which was crisp and fresh; next was the *cru* Poggiarello, from a vineyard we had passed on the road; the grapes are picked a little later, so that the wine has more body and substance. Then came the Vernaccia *riserva*, which is fermented and aged in wood for twelve months; it was nicely oaky with a note of ginger, but as Signor Biagini observed, the problem with *barriques* is that they standardize the flavour, so that you lose the *tipicità* of the grape variety, making an oaked wine that may be good but could come from anywhere. The range was completed with a Chianti Poggiarello, with some attractive cherry fruit. He plans to plant more vineyards for San Gimignano Rosso, but wisely intends to concentrate on Sangiovese rather than the international varieties.

Further up the hill we reached Panizzi. There was a neatly tended vineyard, pruned in the lyre system, with the vines forming a V shape. We were told later that it requires a lot of work, much more than the more traditional training systems, but it gives much better exposure and riper grapes. Giovanni Panizzi, who comes originally from Milan, bought the farm in the mid-1970s, when it consisted of one hectare with a farmhouse. Then in the mid-1980s he began to take wine more seriously, extending the vineyards. He has a neat efficient cellar, with stainless-steel vats and *barriques*, mainly French, as well as a few American, as an experiment. Currently he makes more white than red wine, but is developing more vineyards with San Gimignano Rosso in mind, planting Cabernet Sauvignon, Merlot and Sangiovese. There are two different Vernaccia, a *normale*, which is fresh and leafy, and an oak-aged *riserva* that is more substantial, but for my taste buds loses the intrinsic delicate fruit of the Vernaccia. Bianco di Gianni, made for the first time in 1996, is a blend of Vernaccia and Chardonnay; the Chardonnay spends a year in barrel and fills out the palate. A Chianti Colli Senesi Vertunno is a pure Sangiovese, with a touch of oak, named after Vertunnus, the god who presided over the change of the seasons. The San Gimignano Rosso, called Folgòre after a fourteenth-century poet who wrote sonnets about the months of the year and described the grape harvest, is a blend of Sangiovese with 15 per cent Merlot and 10 per cent Cabernet Sauvignon, all picked together when the late ripening Sangiovese is ready and the others overripe. It spends fourteen months in *barriques*, and was quite *bordelais* in character, with some rich fruit.

After Panizzi's cellars the path began to climb quite steeply towards Montenidoli. It was Sunday and Elisabetta's gate was firmly locked – an understandable protection against curious tourists. There is no sign to her estate, for, as she rightly points out, 2 million people a year come to San Gimignano and 'my wine is known all over the world', so she does not want endless unexpected and unannounced visitors. The other problem is the hunters. Property may be marked as private in Italy but many of the hunters consider that they have a right to roam, irrespective of whose land they are on – they are not supposed to come too near to houses, but often they do – and so to keep them out of her vineyards, Elisabetta has gone to great trouble and expense to fence her land. We followed the perimeter fence, taking a detour to avoid two ferocious-sounding geese that were intent on acting as guard dogs, and then the dogs in the nearby farm heard us and set off a cacophony of barking. Soon we were out of earshot, following a dried-up riverbed up into the woods to find a pleasant track with spring flowers, violets, primroses and hellebores, wild cyclamen, through a soft bed of oak leaves. We picnicked with a view, looking through the trees at the towers of San Gimignano. There were signs allocating the hunters their spot – *appostimento fisso per la caccia no. 1053*.

Tracks through woods can be confusing and have a habit of petering out; this one did, so we got lost and were forced to retrace our footsteps and take a path that led sharply downhill to emerge from the trees into an olive grove, and from there we managed to find a track that took us to Fugnano, and on to a path that led back into San Gimignano. This approach to the town gave us a glimpse of the other face of San Gimignano, the one the tourists do not usually see: an unattractive modern sprawl of houses and flats, built in distinctively uninspiring urban Italian architecture, with washing hanging from every balcony.

Fugnano proved to be a charming discovery and well worth the detour through the woods. The next day Laura Pensabene gave us a warm welcome as we sat in the sitting room and chatted. Her family comes from Sicily and it was her grandfather who had bought this property some forty years ago; he was an industrialist, but also enjoyed the finer things of life, and had come to know many of the Florentine painters of the time. There were some wonderful pictures on the walls, mostly by Guido Borgianni, who was part of the Macchiaioli movement. Laura explained how her grandfather had fallen in love with Tuscany, and with San Gimignano in particular, and had initially planted vines as a hobby. She had studied jurisprudence at Palermo, and when her grandfather died in 1997, she took over the running of the estate.

Originally the grapes had been sold to various larger producers, such as Teruzzi & Puthod and Baroncini, as well as some *sfuso* wine to Melini, which is how she met her husband, who is an oenologist. Together they decided to build a new cellar and begin bottling their wine, with 2002 their first vintage. It was delicious; part of the Vernaccia had been fermented in oak, to give a discreet hint of vanilla, but it was beautifully balanced and harmonious. The Chianti, from Sangiovese, with a drop of Colorino, had fresh cherry notes and a hint of spice. Then we tried the oil and some delicious *pecorino*. Afterwards Laura showed us the tiny chapel, which had been built in the thirteenth century and restored by her grandfather. Her baby, Andrea, had been christened there a few weeks earlier. There were flakes of snow in the wind, although it was April, and the snow had settled on the mountains north of Pistoia.

San Donato is a small hamlet outside San Gimignano, which dates back to AD 1000. Had we not got lost in the woods near Montenidoli, we would have walked there; instead we went by car. Umberto Lenzi explained that his grandfather had bought the property in the 1930s. There is a tower that was once used to send messages between San Gimignano and nearby Castelvecchio in the days when San Gimignano was of strategic importance. The cellars are scattered around the hamlet in a higgledy-piggledy manner. We sat in the courtyard waiting for Umberto to complete an introduction to the delights of Vernaccia for a coachload of American tourists. They were buying bottles avidly, while we enjoyed the spring sunshine, along with a pair of dogs basking in the warmth, ignoring the attentions of Umberto's two young daughters, Angelica and Benedetta. In the distance we could see the snow-capped Monte Abetoni in the Garfagnana range, a reminder of the chill of a couple of days earlier. We wandered round the hamlet. Just four families live there now, whereas there had been a school until 1978. The church has been bought by *un privato* and is badly in need of restoration. Hopefully that will happen. There were plaits of garlic drying in the barn, and the office walls were covered with old scythes and keys and other pieces of agricultural paraphernalia. A notice advertised *vino rosso superiore di 10 gradi* and *vino bianco superiore di 9 gradi*. Another notice warned: *attenti ai cani; attenti alla suocera*. Beware of the dogs; beware of the mother-in-law!

The Americans departed and Umberto turned his attention to us, offering us a taste of 2001 Vernaccia, which was full and almondy with a slightly bitter finish. He explained how the taste of almonds is characteristic of Vernaccia, as is acidity. Next came the wine named after his elder daughter Angelica, which includes a percentage of barrel-fermented Vernaccia. The oak gave the wine more weight and *rotondità*, but for my taste buds it was a tad clumsy. More elegant was the Vernaccia *riserva* – named after Umberto's other daughter,

Benedetta – even though half of the blend spends six months in barrel. We finished with some rustic Chianti and a Vin Santo, with its characteristic nutty honeyed flavour and firm backbone, not unlike an *oloroso* sherry.

Thus fortified we set off down the lane out of the village, past a couple of farms, Ciliegeta and Voltrona, both advertising *agriturismo*. We exchanged words with a couple of men who were packing up their fishing tackle by a small lake; 'Any luck?', we asked. 'No,' was the disgruntled reply; 'the lake was cleaned out yesterday.' There were vineyards, pruned for quantity rather than quality, with numerous bunches forming, and then we reached another farm, Casavecchia, where a barking mongrel raised the alarm at our arrival. There were sweeping views over the valley, of fields of corn, shimmering in the breeze, with dense woods on the hilltops, and an alleyway of cypress trees forming a large zigzag through the fields to another farm. As we reached a ridge, we were rewarded with more views of San Gimignano. Somehow you never tire of that evocative cluster of medieval towers – there is a timeless quality about it, especially as the colour of the stones changes in the varying light. Dark storm clouds were gathering, creating a more sombre atmosphere, and further along the track the hilltop hamlet of Montauto came into view. There is a cluster of houses around a church, the Chiesa di San Lorenzo, which was firmly closed. A mass was said here on the last Sunday of every month, but the last priest died in September 2002, and there are no signs of a replacement. Just one family lives in the village, at the Podere San Lorenzo, which was advertising wine, oil and saffron.

We had a meeting arranged with Andrea Cecchi, whose family own the Castello di Montauto. We chatted over a reviving *cappuccino* as Andrea explained how his family had been involved with wine since 1893. It all began with his great-grandfather, so that he is the fourth generation, with his brother Cesare. Altogether they own 290 hectares of vines, on four estates, here at Montauto, which was purchased in 1989, Villa Cerna at Castellina-in-Chianti, Villa delle Rose in the Maremma near Grosseto, and at Montefalco in Umbria. In addition, as merchants they buy grapes, mainly for Chianti and Chianti Classico. Their best wines come from their own vineyards. Andrea took us for a drive, making interesting observations as we went. The soil is quite sandy, which is good for white wine, and the vines face both north and south, resulting in two different styles of wine, and a complementary blend, for the warmer southern aspect will make for more alcohol in the wine, while the north-facing slopes produce a more delicate flavour. A scattering of red flags amongst the vines indicated new plants. He pointed out the experimental vineyard we had passed the previous day; they are working with the University of Florence, looking at new clones of Vernaccia, and in particular less vigorous vines. There are two styles of pruning, a single *guyot*, which can cause problems with humidity but gives more concentrated flavours than the *cordone speronata*, which requires less work in the vineyard but can prematurely age the plant. It also produces fewer grapes. The density is now at 5000 plants per hectare. On the steepest slopes they have problems of erosion, but everything looked beautifully tended, with the surrounding fields manicured 'like a garden', suggested Andrea. We had a quick look at the cellar, which was empty, for it is only used between August and February. There were rows of stainless-steel vats and barrels. A couple of barrels have transparent ends, so that you could follow the progress of the fermentation. They make three wines here, Castello di Montauto, Cecchi Vernaccia and Sagrato, a Chardonnay *cru* for the international market, coming from a tiny 1.8-hectare vineyard. Really it is Tuscan grape varieties that interest them. We tasted 2001 Castello di Montauto; about a third of the wine is fermented in oak, so that it was quite nutty in taste, with the biscuity notes of oak, with some firm acidity.

Ricardo Falchini at Azienda Agricola Casale is one of the more opinionated and outspoken producers of San Gimignano, and all in fluent English, as he has an American wife and his two sons are American citizens. It comes from arriving here as an outsider, from Prato, back in 1964; construction engineering is his real expertise. 'There were no cars in San Gimignano then, just one policeman; at Casale, there were twenty-two cows and we kept the hay, here, in what is now the office. The first thing I did was to buy a tractor.' Then in 1976 a meeting with Giacomo Tachis resulted in some useful consultancy advice; Tachis came and saw the old *botti*: take them away, he said. Then they bought an insulated tank for cooling the wine, 'for that crazy guy from Prato who's spending money on electricity'. We wandered round the cellar; the *barricaia*, built in 1986, is earthquake proof. 'Can I talk about the bricks now?' Ricardo was keen to tell us that they were hand-made, from a specialist furnace on the Adriatic.

They make an extensive range of wines, with numerous highlights. As we tasted, Ricardo talked with enthusiasm and energy about Vernaccia, and its appeal, with amusing indiscretions aside about the local politics of the growers' *consorzio* – the presidency alternates between the prince and the communist. We began with a sparkling wine, Falchini Brut. It is not a DOC, but a blend of Vernaccia, Chardonnay and Pinot Noir, with some attractive, rounded fruit; Vigna a Solatio was delicately rounded, the result of overripe grapes, while the *riserva*, which requires an extra twelve months in the cellar – in bottle will suffice, but this was kept for longer in vat – was almost honeyed, with some rich leafy fruit. The blend is slightly different with a rigorous selection of grapes, a higher alcohol level and 10 per cent of Chardonnay, which Ricardo considers complements the Vernaccia, softening it. As for red wine, a pure Sangiovese, Paretaio, was nicely structured, with some rounded fruit, after twelve months in oak, while Campora, which is almost pure Cabernet Sauvignon with a drop of Merlot, was firm and cedary, with a backbone of tannin. We finished with Vin Santo, which tasted of liquid *biscotti*, and firmly refused an invitation to lunch, in deference to punctuality for our afternoon appointments.

Luigi Vagnoni is a bubbly, energetic man, with a friendly smile. He related how his parents had bought their land here in 1953; they came originally from the Marche, but with the rural depopulation of the 1950s, land was going cheap. Hs father paid one and half million lire for a house and 10 hectares, which he gradually increased to 43 hectares, before he died in 1972. No one was planting vines in the 1950s, but his father did. His son never did any formal studies, but learnt from his parent, and now makes a variety of different wines, a delicate minerally Vernaccia, a heavier oak-aged Vernaccia, called Mocale, some fresh Chianti and a San Gimignano Rosso, called San Biagio, from Sangiovese, and Merlot that was first planted in 1996. It was ripe and plummy with soft tannins.

The Cesani family, just down the road, near the church at Pancole, are cousins. We met Maria Luisa, who explained how the family had also seized the opportunity to buy land here in the 1950s. They now have 13 hectares of vines, as well as olive trees, and also produce saffron, reviving a medieval tradition of San Gimignano. Saffron was important for trade in the thirteenth and fourteenth centuries, when it was used as the *moneta di scambio*, for barter, and then the crop disappeared when disease affected the plants. Now it is returning, under the impetus of the Associazione Il Croco. The harvest takes place in October and November, between the grape and the olive harvest, and lasts about a month. It is extremely hard work, for you have to be meticulous and dexterous, picking the flowers early in the morning, and separating the three red stamens from the three yellow ones, so that they can be dried over a wooden stove for three or four days. Apparently the flowers are an intense, almost violet blue, and each plant will give you a maximum of three flowers, which can grow very quickly, almost from one day to the next. One hundred square metres of plants will provide a good crop.

We liked Maria Luisa's Vernaccia too, with its fresh herbal notes. They also make a barrel-aged Vernaccia, called Sanice, which crossword addicts will recognize instantly as an anagram of Cesani. The oak, which allows for longer ageing, was well integrated but I preferred the fresh appeal of the *normale*. There is a Chianti Colli Senesi as well as an IGT, Luenza, from Sangiovese and Colorino, which spends two years in *barriques*. It was nicely balanced with ripe cedary fruit. Maria Luisa admitted that although they are more interested in local varieties, they would like to try Merlot, mainly 'because everyone is doing it', and they will probably produce a San Gimignano Rosso in due course.

Andrea Vecchione at San Quirico is also a saffron producer as well as a winemaker. His saffron bed is close to the house. In late spring it looked like a bed of untidy grass, or maybe chives. Soon they will cut it and it will remain dormant until the beginning of the growing season in September. The bulbs of *Crocus sapidus*, to give its Latin name, are prolific and you often have to separate them in August. A DOP, *Denominazione di Origine del Prodotto*, for saffron from San Gimignano came into effect in 2003, and while there is a DOP for olive oil, Terre di Siena, the oil producers of San Gimignano feel that this is too broad an area, covering the whole of the province of Siena, and would also like a more limited DOP di San Gimignano for their oil.

Signor Vecchione is a gentle, quietly spoken man; you sense, as he talks, that he is a man of the land. His great-grandfather bought the estate in 1860 and his grandfather built their house forty years later. Vecchione talked of the improvements that have taken place over the years; the newer vineyards have a much higher density; and nowadays they consistently debud and carry out a green harvest in order to keep yields low. He is gradually converting his estate to organic viticulture, which means no more chemical fertilizer, anti-rot sprays or insecticides. Techniques in the cellar have improved too. The vinification of Vernaccia entails a very gentle pressing and a controlled fermentation, in stainless steel, with great care taken with the grapes, picking them into small boxes. The result is a delicately flavoured wine. The *riserva* I Campi Santi necessitates a strict selection of the grapes, and eighteen months' ageing in vat followed by at least four months in bottle, making a wine with a firm mineral flavour, and more body and substance than most. A second *riserva*, named after his daughter Isabella, is fermented in oak and given six months' ageing with lees stirring. For my palate the oak was too dominant; I much preferred I Campi Santi. As for red wine, there is a Chianti Colli Senesi and a San Gimignano Rosso, mainly from Sangiovese, with some Cabernet and Merlot. Vecchione explained how the *alba* or register for Vernaccia and Chianti is closed, but if you have planting rights, you may plant for an IGT or San Gimignano Rosso. We agreed that wine in Tuscany is not born for clinical wine-tasting, but is above all meant to be enjoyed with food. It was the end of the afternoon and I was beginning to anticipate a good bottle for dinner.

Vasco Cetti at Il Paradiso is one of the characters of the region. He is lively, energetic and opinionated, with a mop of white hair and purple-rimmed glasses, and although he runs a very successful family estate, he also works as a doctor. However, his son Davide is gradually taking over the estates. Cetti has worked on the new DOC of San Gimignano Rosso. The initial DOC was first discussed some ten years ago and now they want various modifications, as a confirmation of the particular quality of the red wines around San Gimignano. The trouble is, sighed Cetti, there is too much bureaucracy; all the politicians want to interfere; it should be left to the producers. The name will change from Rosso di San Gimignano to San Gimignano Rosso – I was uncertain as to the advantages of that – and the so-called alternative grape varieties, Merlot, Cabernet Sauvignon, Syrah and Pinot Noir, will be allowed, as well as Sangiovese. 'We don't want any *impedimenti*,' he said. 'Otherwise we can just carry on making IGT.'

Cetti was in fact one of the first to plant varieties like Chardonnay, Merlot and Cabernet Sauvignon. 1992 was the first vintage of his Saxa Calida, a blend of equal parts of Merlot and Cabernet Sauvignon, and the 2001 vintage had some firm cassis fruit and sturdy tannins. I preferred Paterno II, which Cetti described as *la nostra Ferrari*; it is a *cru* of Sangiovese and spends two years in wood, with the 2000 vintage showing some lovely rich fruit and the firm backbone of Sangiovese. It could be San Gimignano Rosso, but illogically Cetti feels that his wine is better than that. His Vernaccia di San Gimignano *normale* had a fresh herbal tang, while the *cru* Biscandolo was more substantial, with a proportion of oak ageing.

The Fattoria di Cusona is the property of the Strozzi Guicciardini family, and is known in the British tabloid press as the Tuscan estate where Tony Blair and his family have holidayed. There are photographs of the two families in the tasting room. As for the link between the Strozzi and Guicciardini, these two families came together when the Strozzi had no more heirs and the property passed to a young Guicciardini brother. They are cousins of the Guicciardini at the Castello di Poppiano in the Colli Fiorentini. The estate has been in the family since about 1400, but there are records that wine was produced here as early as 994, providing the excuse for a millennium celebration in 1994. It is a rare estate that can claim one thousand years of winemaking. The Guicciardini were of German origin and came to Italy with the Emperor Frederick I in the twelfth century. Their name is derived from *guardia di caccia* or gamekeeper, so there are hunting horns on their coat of arms. The Strozzis originated from Fiesole. The present incumbent, Principe Strozzi Guicciardini, is a university professor, specializing in international law, and the estate is run by his very able *fattore*, who is also a qualified oenologist. There is an elegant fifteenth-century yellow sandstone villa built around a large courtyard, with gardens that were laid out in the early 1800s, with heavily laden orange trees and neatly trimmed box hedges, as well as a 500-year-old oak tree. The cellars date from the middle of the nineteenth century and still retain the original floor tiles, made on one of the farms on the estate, appropriately called Le Fornace. There are various old artefacts: large *botti*, kept for *la memoria*, cement vats and solid presses, and, best of all, a very early Fiat tractor from 1919.

As well as Fattoria di Cusona, they have invested in land near Grosseto for

Morellino di Scansano, with the first vintage in 2002. Twenty-five hectares have also been planted near Montemassi, in the DOC of Monterregio di Massa Marittima, mainly with Sangiovese and also some Syrah, and they have 10 hectares of Bordeaux varieties in Bolgheri, at Castagneto Carducci, which will come into production in 2004. The wines in San Gimignano impress, and they had undoubtedly improved since earlier visits. Perlato includes 10 per cent of Chardonnay with the Vernaccia, for the Chardonnay reinforces the aroma and maintains freshness in wine, counteracting the tendency of Vernaccia to flatten after a few months. The *riserva* is oak-aged, and for red wine, we sampled Sodole, a selection of Sangiovese, first made back in 1982, which was sturdy and concentrated. Millanni, first made in 1994 for their millennium, from 60 per cent Sangiovese with 30 per cent Cabernet and 10 per cent Merlot, had balanced fruit and firm tannins. Finally there was Selvascura, named after the particular farm, a pure Merlot first produced in 1997, which could comply with the *disciplinari* of San Gimignano Rosso. It had the ripe sweetness and a certain international flavour of the grape variety.

Altogether there are thirty-five producers of San Gimignano, cultivating between them some 750 hectares. Some sell grapes to the big Tuscan merchants, while others sell to larger producers within the *comune*. Teruzzi & Puthod is an example of a business which has expanded exponentially over the last few years, and to my mind lost its quality edge in the process. Enrico Teruzzi was a pacesetter, the first to use barrels, and one of the first to make sparkling wine. Now he is the biggest with a vast state-of-the-art cellar, but for my taste buds his wines no longer provide their previous excitement. However, there is no doubt that San Gimignano has not taken the easy route of catering for undemanding tourists, but is keeping pace with modern developments. Its established reputation for white wine may well be matched by its red wine, with the new DOC of San Gimignano Rosso.

Montecarlo
· *October* ·

East of Lucca; from Fattoria Wandanna to Montecarlo and round the
village; Montechiari, Fattoria Buonamico

THE HILLTOP TOWN of Montecarlo, to the east of Lucca, above the broad
valley of the Arno, gives its name to one of the more original white
wines of Tuscany. Although Trebbiano provides the base, as it does almost
everywhere else all over the region, there is also Roussanne, Sémillon,
Sauvignon, Pinot Grigio and Pinot Bianco, which are no mere new
introductions with the spread of international varieties towards the end of the
twentieth century, but have been here since the middle of the nineteenth
century, when vine cuttings were brought from France. Montecarlo Bianco was
recognized as a DOC in 1969; Montecarlo Rosso came much later in 1985.
However, the area has a long viticultural tradition. The earliest written
references appear in a document dated 846 when the place was noted 'for the
abundant return provided by nature, including a substantial output of pure
wine from grapes pressed three times according to the rule, and then racked'.
The town's Latin name was Via Vinaia, deriving from the Roman road, the Via
Vinaria, which crossed the hill of Montecarlo, linking the Via Cassia near
Buggiano and the Via Romea near Altopascio.

Local tradition has it that a Giulio Magnani, the proprietor of the Fattoria
Marchi-Magnani, which is today the Fattoria Mazzini, returned from a visit to
France in 1870 with cuttings of several different grape varieties. The phylloxera
crisis at the end of the nineteenth century resulted in considerable replanting,
so that the French grape varieties became well established in preference to
Trebbiano. Red varieties such as Merlot, Cabernet Sauvignon, Cabernet Franc
and Syrah were also brought to Montecarlo at that time, but they did not have
the same impact on the region's wines. In the early twentieth century,
Montecarlo was known as *lo Chablis di Montecarlo*; it was drunk at the last king
of Italy's wedding in 1930, and 1933 Marchi Magnani's white wine was

described as 'the best and most appreciated in all Italy'. A decline set in after the Second World War. Today the vineyards of Montecarlo are mainly on the hillsides around the town, spreading a little into the adjoining *comuni* of Altopascio, Capannori and Porcari. The tower of the church of Sant'Andrea Apostolo stands on the skyline for miles around, providing a landmark over the surrounding countryside.

Fattoria Wandanna is at the bottom of the hill outside the village. Apparently, at the beginning of the twentieth century the property belonged to a Canadian, whose wife was called Wanda, and his daughter Anna, and so he changed the name from Fattoria Gioiosa. The estate has had a chequered history, at one time belonging to the singer Luciano Taioli, who was popular in Italy in the 1950s. Vivaldo Fantozzi, who was described to us as one of the characters of Montecarlo, bought a bankrupt property in 1988; he has a clothing business, but 'now everything comes from the Far East' so he is diversifying into wine, with a second property in San Gimignano. We sat in a sombre dining room, with heavy oak furniture, on a rather grey day, and Fantozzi talked. He sports a magnificent walrus moustache and to my mind bore a distinct resemblance to Leo McKern in *Rumpole of the Bailey*. You sense that he really enjoys what he does; he never takes holidays, just one day a year to have lunch in Nice, as he does not want to leave this place – *io amo questo qui*; then his son appeared, a young student 'who doesn't know the meaning of the word stress', according to his father.

We sat and tasted his wines; in his 40 hectares he grows a mixture of different grape varieties, even including some that are not allowed, such as Tannat and Alicante Bouschet, as well as the indigenous Tuscan varieties, and more obvious international varieties, from which he produces an eclectic range of wines, some DOC and some IGT. There is a pure Chardonnay, Labirinto; Virente is a blend of Syrah, Cabernet Sauvignon and Merlot, which is particularly successful in nightclubs in Shanghai, as Fantozzi laughingly explained: the Chinese pay US$400 a bottle for it, in the belief that it comes from the better-known Montecarlo in France. We finished with a pure Pinot Noir, Nero di Taccone, named after his grandfather, whom he described as a '*socialista anarchico*', with his photograph on the label. The vines are young but there was a whiff of a hint of Pinot Noir about the palate; Fantozzi said how much he liked the wine, but curiously he had never tried a Burgundian Pinot Noir, which goes to show how insular some wine regions can be. Before setting off up the hill, we had a quick look around the cellars, a large functional shed, accompanied by Fantozzi's three large dogs.

Our path climbed past a menagerie of birds, with, it seemed, every variety of the edible kind, with geese, ducks, turkeys, guinea fowl and chickens. Nearby there were large greenhouses, filled with pots of orange and lemon trees. A worker was spraying them, with music blaring out over loudspeakers. The track took us through an alleyway of olive trees, past a ruined house and along the edge of the vineyards, with their deep red, iron-rich soil. It was muddy, and after so much unseasonable rain, the vineyards were full of weeds and thick with grass. The roses at the ends of the rows were blown over, but there was cheerful yellow gorse in flower. We carried on up a narrow path through the pine trees and bracken and met an elderly lady looking for mushrooms; she was hoping to find enough for a nice pasta that evening, but so far her forays were proving somewhat unsuccessful. Then the path took us past a hunter's lookout, camouflaged with branches, and past an olive grove onto the road at the entrance to Montecarlo and the turning to the estate of Montechiari.

Two of the old city gates of Montecarlo remain, the Porta Nuova and the Porta Fiorentina, as well as a substantial part of the old walls, and the vestiges of the fourteenth-century castle, now in private ownership but occasionally open to the public for exhibitions. Montecarlo was fortified by the Emperor Charles IV in 1333, for it had an important strategic position at a crossroads of the Via Francigena and the Via Cassia. Two small streets run through the town; the church of Sant'Andrea has a simple Romanesque facade and the high bell tower, added at a later date, which dominates the surrounding countryside. By chance the door of the Mazzini cellars was opened as we walked past, and there behind an unassuming red-brick townhouse was a veritable labyrinth of cellars, a series of small rooms, crammed with barrels, vats and cartons, and eventually we emerged into what seemed like a secret garden, hidden behind high walls, including the town walls, which you could walk along as far as the Porta Fiorentina. Everything was slightly dank, but colour was provided by an orange tree laden with fruit, as well as a persimmon tree, whose leaves were beginning to turn colour.

Just down the road is an *enoteca*, with a good selection of the wines of the fifteen producers who put their wine in bottle. On display was a bottle of Marchi Magnani Montecarlo 1932; the colour looked distinctly amber! But had time allowed the *enoteca* would have provided a good tasting opportunity of some of the estates that we were not going to visit. Instead, we were taken to see the tiny town theatre, which holds just 180 people. It was enchanting, with its beautiful painted ceiling and small boxes; and in the foyer a small group were rehearsing a reading for a performance the next day.

The estate of Montechiari is just outside the village of Montecarlo. The name, which translates literally as 'clear mountains', implies that you can see the mountains all round, as indeed you can, with views of the Colline Lucchesi and beyond to the north and to Monte Pisane to the south-east. There are vineyards in the valley, interspersed with pine trees, and the Fattoria del Buonamico, and in the distance the industrial sprawl along the plain outside Lucca. And you never lose site of the bell tower, standing at the highest point, at 140 metres.

Montechiari is owned by Moreno Panattoni, who runs a travel business in Brussels; in his absence the property is managed by the genial Maurizio Pasi, who came originally from Milan. He worked with tropical plants in California and Hawaii, before coming to Montecarlo, to work first for Michi, then Buonamico and now Montechiari, since 2000. He showed us round, explaining how the estate began with just 2 hectares of vines for family consumption. Now there are 10 hectares, as well as olive trees and woods. The old house has been renovated, with neat new cellars that are well equipped with *barriques* and *tonneaux*. Foolishly we thought it would be nice to taste outside enjoying the view, even if the sky was overcast, but our optimism was short-lived, with the rain driving us inside a little while later. They make four wines. A Chardonnay, with a touch of Sémillon, spends twelve months in barrel and is given regular lees stirring in the Burgundian manner. It was rich and mouth-filling with a long leesy, nutty palate. Some Sauvignon is also being planted, to add to the blend. A pure Sangiovese spends eighteen months in wood, with some attractive cedary fruit. The maritime influence here means that the wine is much softer than in Chianti Classico. Nor is frost a problem, unlike on the valley floor.

Nero di Montechiari is Pinot Nero, which is not allowed to be mentioned on the label. It spends twelve months in *tonneaux – barriques* give too oaky an effect – and there was some convincing varietal fruit. They make just 1000 bottles and began producing it in the mid-1990s. Agronomy is Maurizio's forte and he talked about the problems with Pinot Nero in the vineyard; you must not give it too much fertilizer, but it is not as productive as some varieties, and so does not need a green harvest.

Finally, there was a Cabernet from equal parts of Cabernet Franc and Sauvignon and 10 per cent Merlot. It was ripe and structured, with youthful fruit, firm tannins and an elegant finish, and amply demonstrated the quality of the estate. Maurizio is adamant that quality must be maintained; he fears that people have lost their way with the white wine and that the potential for red is now greater. The Prato merchant Francesco Datini, who was known as a wine connoisseur, recommended the wines of Monte Chiaro to a fellow merchant if he wanted 'a perfectly made and good white wine'.

Vasco Grassi at Fattoria Buonamico, down the hill, gave us a friendly welcome. This was once his family property, and although it was sold to a Florentine company in 1992 he has remained as general manager. His family own a restaurant in Turin, and the very first wine they bottled in 1953 was for the restaurant – the name of the estate is a fantasy, to convey a friendly house wine – and there is a photograph in his office of an old-fashioned bottling line with the straw-covered *fiaschi*, with young Vasco as a lad of eight. The first wine they produced here at Montecarlo was in 1964 and in the cellar there is a long row of old bottles, which Vasco described as 'our history', with the 1953 Buonamico al Gatto Nero, the very first bottling. 1964 was the first bottling of their own wine, Buonamico Rosso, and 1975 marked the first bottling of Cercatoja, the IGT which is a selection of the best vineyards, from Sangiovese, Syrah, Cabernet Sauvignon and Merlot. Today they continue to make a convincing range of wines, with the classic flavours of the DOC. Montecarlo Bianco, from Trebbiano, with Pinot Bianco, Sauvignon, Roussanne and a drop of Pinot

Grigio and Sémillon, has attractive mineral notes with a slightly bitter finish. Montecarlo Rosso, from Sangiovese, with Canaiolo and drops of Syrah, Cabernet Sauvignon and Merlot, is redolent of ripe, rounded cherries. Vasco explained how they wanted a combination of freshness and robustness, with a touch of spiciness, which made an eminently satisfying mouthful. Cercatoja, which he described as the first serious red wine to be made in Montecarlo, had the ripe fruit of Cabernet. He talked about the DOC regulations; the percentage of Trebbiano has been decreased to 40 per cent, that is, in the vineyard, rather than in the wine, and they would like to change the regulations to allow for single varietal wines.

Today there are about twenty-five members in the *consorzio*, of whom fifteen bottle their wine, and the division between red and white varieties is 100 hectares of red and 150 hectares of white. A pure Pinot Bianco, Vasario, is named after the Renaissance painter and architect, whose frieze in the Palazzo Vecchio in Florence depicts the fortress of Montecarlo. The wine had some attractive nutty fruit, while Il Fortino, a pure Syrah, had some sturdy, peppery flavours. Those vines are now over forty years old, for they were planted in 1962, which may make them the oldest Syrah vines in Italy. After a cheerful lunch at the family-run Villa La Nina outside the village, which finished with a dessert wine, Oro del Re, from *passito* Sauvignon and Sémillon, with a ripe honeyed richness, Vasco took us to see a magnificent 600-year-old oak tree, La Quercia delle Streghe, or witches' oak. He explained that the variety is a *farnia*, which is often used for *barriques*, but instead of being tall and straight like its neighbours, it was wonderfully gnarled, with twisted branches, interwoven, almost like Siamese twins, with an enormous span. It was a fitting note on which to leave Montecarlo and head towards the Colline Lucchesi.

Colline Lucchesi
· October ·

North of Lucca; Fattoria di Fubbiano; walk from the village of San Gennaro to Fattoria Maionchi and Vigna di Gragnano; Valgiano, Fattoria Colleverde, Terre del Sillabo

VINES HAVE BEEN GROWN in the hills to the north of the enchanting city of Lucca since Etruscan times. However, it is olive oil that has been more important to the economy of the region, while wine was usually made merely for family consumption.

We stayed at the Fattoria di Fubbiano, outside the village of San Gennaro, in a tiny house that would have once been the home of a *mezzadria* family on the estate. Giampiero and Lucia de Andreis gave up the world of medical publishing in Milan and arrived here in 1988, since when they have gradually been replanting vineyards and renovating the cellar. The previous owners were absentee landlords, content to leave a *fattore* to manage the estate, in the traditional manner. Giampiero is president of the growers' *consorzio* and well placed to provide an introduction to the Colline Lucchesi. They cover quite a wide area of hills behind Lucca stretching from San Mascario in Monte in the west to San Gennaro in the east, with a greater concentration of estates around San Gennaro. In contrast to neighbouring Montecarlo, red wine has always been more important here, with the creation of the DOC in 1968, initially from the traditional Tuscan varieties, but in 1997 the DOC was broadened to include Merlot in the blend, up to as much as 30 per cent, as well as a varietal, with a minimum of 85 per cent in the wine. Sangiovese may also be mentioned on the label in the same way. The white grapes, for a DOC created in 1985, include the inevitable Trebbiano, as well as Malvasia, Grechetto and Vermentino, but none of the international varieties of Montecarlo. Vin Santo has been added to the DOC, but there is no *rosato*.

Unlike Chianti, white grapes have never been obligatory in the red wine, although Trebbiano and Malvasia were often planted in the traditional vineyards, where all the varieties were mixed up together. The fact that the vineyards around Lucca never became part of the mass of Chianti, unlike Pisa, Arezzo or Siena, may be a tribute to the city's history of independence, for it retained its autonomy until 1799 and was presented as a principality by Napoleon to his sister in 1805, and then in 1815 given to Marie Louise de Bourbon as a duchy. It was the merchant classes who were powerful in Lucca; in the first half of the nineteenth century it was ruled by a commercial oligarchy, occasioning the observation: 'If people have a full stomach, they don't rebel.' The silk trade was important, providing the foundations of many a merchant's fortune, enabling them to build the various elegant villas that are scattered throughout the Lucchesi hills. The villa at Fubbiano was built at the end of the seventeenth century, by the Count and Countess Mugnai; their busts adorn the terrace, but curiously they are not looking at each other, but out towards the hills beyond. The *barricaia* at Fubbiano is in the cellar of the villa, which would have been the original wine cellar, with its stone floor and large arch of thin red bricks, and a stone container for oil instead of the customary *orci*. There were views from the terrace of the villa, which is now used for *agriturismo*, towards the church of Tofori in the hazy sunshine, and large yellow balls, as a variation on a scarecrow, were suspended over the vineyards to discourage the birds. Unusually, the lemon trees are planted directly into the ground rather than in large pots, as it is mild enough here for them to stay outside during the winter. The maritime influence means that it is not impossible to lunch outside in January.

We tasted in a renovated outhouse, which had once housed the bakery, with a large but now defunct oven in the corner. There was a pure Vermentino, also a recent addition – in 1997 – to the DOC; a simple Fubbiano Rosso was a blend of Sangiovese, Canaiolo, Ciliegiolo and, very unusually, a touch of Moscato, making a wine with fresh, rounded fruit and a hint of spice. Villa di Fubbiano, from vines that were planted in 1968, was fuller and more structured, while San Gennaro, from a 2-hectare vineyard planted with Sangiovese, Canaiolo and Ciliegiolo, was rich and rounded after a year in *barriques*. Finally there was I Pampini, an intriguing blend of Sangiovese and Teroldego.

Giampiero talked informatively about the local economy, explaining how

Lucca really means olive oil; wine has never been that important commercially, as the small amount produced was all drunk locally, whereas olive oil continues 'to provide a business card and travel the world'. He regretted that the olive-oil production is dominated by large industrialists, who tend to have little sympathy with the aims of the smaller producers. As for the winegrowers' *consorzio*, currently there are about twenty members, ten of whom have a serious market share, with an average of about 10–15 hectares of vines. The DOC totals about 200 hectares, and there is still land that could be planted. Land is cheaper here than in some other parts of Tuscany; you would pay € 26,000–31,000 (50–60 million lire) per hectare for an old vineyard and it would cost you about € 36,000 (70 million lire) to replant a hectare of vines. Encouragingly, as we saw later in the week, some young people are returning to the land, and there are some newer estates, with energetic owners and projects for the future.

Our walk began in the nearby village of San Gennaro, a long thin village with a single street of sombre, shuttered houses. The *alimentari* was firmly closed, and so was the church, but there was a notice giving about ten telephone numbers to ring if you wanted to visit the church. The third number replied and told me to ring the last name on the list; after about a ten-minute wait, Marco, an elderly man who is one of the church wardens, appeared with a key. It was well worth the wait. The church has a Romanesque facade, with solid rounded arches and carved capitals, a beautiful ornate pulpit, and best of all an

enchanting terracotta angel, originally thought to be by Verrocchio, the teacher of Leonardo, but now considered to be the work of Leonardo himself.

Then we set off down the hill, following an old mule track, past terraces of olive trees, and over a babbling brook and into the vineyards of Fubbiano. The rain of the previous night emphasized the smell of herbs underfoot, of wild fennel and pungent *nepitella*, a variety of wild mint. Giampiero keeps horses in his olive grove as they keep the grass down and also perform a useful function in providing natural manure. There were eco-traps hanging from some of the trees, designed to trap the males of the olive fly, a pest which lays eggs in the young olives, especially during wet weather when the olives are softer. They are more of a problem at a lower altitude of 200 metres; at 400 metres it is far too cold for them.

From Fubbiano we took the path down through an alley of cypresses on one side and young olive trees on the other side, on to a road. Fattoria Maionchi was just round the corner and well worth the detour, for its elegant late-eighteenth-century villa, with a yellow facade and beautiful garden, dating from the same period. A double staircase around a fountain took you up to a terrace, with views across the valley towards Monte Pisane. Here the lemon trees were in pots; there were roses, some still in flower in early October, as well as oleander bushes, and a 200-year-old Japanese cherry tree.

Maria Pia Maionchi explained how her family had bought the villa in the middle of the nineteenth century. There is a story of five sons, who came from a farm on the estate and left to make their fortune. One became a general; another, who was Maria Pia's grandfather, ran a successful restaurant in Lucca; it was he who bought the villa, but he never slept in it. The general is said to haunt the villa. Once a year – some time in February, during the night – they regularly hear the sounds of a cheerful party up in the attic. The cellars are delightfully old-fashioned, epitomizing the traditional Tuscan cellar, with chestnut barrels, as well as some new *barriques* and a tiny *vinsantaia*, exuding the delicate aroma of wood and wine, in slightly damp surroundings. There is also a modern cellar with stainless-steel vinification vats, which we did not see and which Maria Pia described as *una cosa orribile*; it made her feel very sad. A small restaurant, open on Friday and Saturday evenings, is also used for tastings. The walls are hung with all manner of collections, of pipes, keys, corkscrews and stirrups. The wines are cheerful, but with no great depth or complexity. Then we went to see the villa, with its late-eighteenth-century frescoes. The entrance hall has an Egyptian theme, while the drawing room is decorated with rural scenes, including the grape harvest. Upstairs there are floral motifs on the ceilings and walls. It was all very elegant and charming.

From Fattoria Maionchi, our path took us towards Gragnano. There were views back over the valley toward Fubbiano, with the skyline dominated by the church tower of San Gennaro. We could discern the vineyard of I Pampini, in its sheltered position in the valley. The vine leaves were just beginning to change colour, but nonetheless the vegetation was extraordinarily green for the time of year, a reflection of the unseasonable quantity of rain. Olive trees seemed to dominate the scenery, reflecting their importance in the region, in relation to vines. At the top of the ridge we could make out the church towers of Lucca, and in the opposite direction the villa of Valgiano. One small vineyard had already been pruned, at the beginning of October, and there were small piles of grapeskins waiting to be dug into the soil. The hamlet of Gragnano has no café or shop, just a large cemetery and an imposing church with a yellow-stuccoed front and a tower in red brick. A dog showed signs of wishing to join our walk; we firmly discouraged him and continued on through the village to the villa of Gragnano, where we peered in through wrought-iron gates at what looked to be an imposing edifice.

However, our destination was the new, adjoining estate, Vigna di Gragnano. Signor Lenzini is an astonishingly youthful 80-year-old, who bought his vineyards some ten years ago as a retirement project. He had sold his share in a paper factory, and found that he got bored in a couple of weeks and needed something else to do. As he said, he didn't know anything at all about making wine, so he bought some books and began to read, and made every mistake under the sun, for his first vintage. Then a friend suggested he consult an oenologist, Stefano Chioccioli, and now things are decidedly on track, to the extent that his granddaughter is just finishing her oenology studies at Pisa University and will be taking over the estate in due course, when her grandfather finally decides to retire.

The vineyards were more or less abandoned, so he started from scratch, planting 13 hectares of Merlot and Cabernet Sauvignon, but no Sangiovese, from which he makes two wines, a DOC that is Merlot based, and an IGT called Poggio dei Paoli, which is a Cabernet Sauvignon and Merlot blend. We tasted the 2000 vintage of Poggio dei Paoli, from barrel. It promised well with some plummy fruit and long rich flavours, albeit with a certain international note, while the Colline Lucchesi was more elegant, with cedary fruit and firm tannins.

Setting off back towards Fubbiano, we encountered Beppi Bonelli, the local shepherd, with his flock of *massese* sheep – in other words, a breed from the nearby town of Massa. They were eagerly dining off vine leaves in a roadside vineyard. Later in the week we went to visit him. He is a man of few words, but when he smiled, his face lit up. You sense that he is more at ease with his sheep than with people, but he explained how he has about eighty in his flock. The oldest is about seven years old; they are deep black with long tails and long ears, very lean and agile with long legs and short coats, looking more like goats than sheep to my inexpert eye. They are shorn a couple of times a year, in April and September, but their coats never grow that long. He takes them out each morning up into the hills after milking, and produces *pecorino*, which he usually sells on to someone else for ageing, and *ricotta* from the remains of the *pecorino* process, once it has been boiled, hence the term *ricotta*, or twice-cooked. We treated ourselves to a twenty-day-old pecorino, which proved to be delicious back in London. Back at Fubbiano, the heavens opened, as they only can in Tuscany.

Laura Petrini, and her winemaker Saverio Petrilli, gave us a friendly welcome at Valgiano. She and her husband Moreno had bought Valgiano in 1993. The elegant villa originates from the sixteenth century and they are just the third family to own it, buying it from the Vidau family who were of French origin, as they came to Lucca when Napoleon's sister was there at the beginning of the nineteenth century. We walked round the gardens in a gentle drizzle; the old chapel has been restored and there is a glass conservatory which the previous owner had used as an aviary. Roses and plumbago were in flower and there were views over the valley towards Montecarlo with its distinctive bell tower, in the mist, and Monte Severa, the mountain between Pisa and Lucca.

Saverio has a broader experience than some of his fellow Tuscan

winemakers; before coming to Valgiano he had spent eight years at Volpaia, but before that had worked in Australia, and also New Zealand. You could taste a New World influence in the white wine of Valgiano, for they also have had an Australian winemaker helping with the vintage, who had suggested a long cool fermentation, without any racking until February. The blend of Trebbiano, Malvasia and Vermentino had an extraordinary depth of character, so it was quite full and leesy, with fresh acidity and a mineral finish. Quite simply, it was a revelation. There are three red wines. Palestorti is a blend of 70 per cent Sangiovese with Syrah and Merlot, producing some lovely ripe smoky fruit. Amusingly, Palestorti means tilted poles, a reference to the posts in the vineyards that would not go in straight as the ground is so stony. Tenuta di Valgiano is a similar blend, but from higher vineyards and spends eighteen months in wood, as opposed to twelve for Palestorti, including some new oak. It was altogether more structured. Cesari, an almost pure Sangiovese, comes from an old vineyard, planted in the mid-1960s by a Signor Cesari, one of the old *mezzadria* farmers. They find that it ripens later than the new plantings, making wines with higher acidity. For my taste buds, it seemed more rustic, with rich smoky fruit. In the cellar some small wooden vats were still fermenting, and I tasted a berry from the vat; it was ripe and alcoholic, almost like a liqueur. Saverio took us to see the vineyards, explaining how Valgiano is on a ridge of limestone and *albarese* soil, lying at between 250 and 300 metres, above which nothing is cultivated; there is just woodland. Altogether they have 16 hectares. In the middle of Cesari's vineyard there is a sculpture, a large stone head, which Saverio laughingly said was Lucca, facing Pisa, referring to the ancient rivalry between the two city states. You sense an intense commitment to quality at Valgiano. At a dinner on an earlier visit, we tasted some wines blind, to find that Moreno had set his 1999 Tenuta di Valgiano alongside 1999 Château Latour, a first growth from the Médoc. That takes nerve, and a fellow guest, a French wine writer, was speechless at the effrontery, but in fact the difference between the two wines was not so startling, possibly as new oak dominated the palate of both. It will be fascinating to observe the progress of Valgiano under new young ownership.

Fattoria Colleverde is down a winding road from Valgiano. The estate was originally part of the larger property of the Guinigi family, who were silk traders and bankers in Lucca. They built the Guinigi tower, which dominates the skyline of the city and is easily recognizable for the trees growing on its roof. For those who climb to the top, it offers extensive views of the terracotta roofs of the city. Paolo Tartagni, elegantly dressed in designer denim, with a thick mop of hair that most men would envy, warmed to his subject as he talked, with some amusing and shrewd observations. He explained how both he and his wife, Francesca Partini, had worked in television and then decided to buy some vineyards from her family to create a new estate, Colle Verdi, which would be quite separate from the Villa Guinigi on the hill behind. The new name dates from 1989 and they now have 6.5 hectares of wines and 3500 olive trees, planted with Sangiovese and Syrah for red wines and Trebbiano and Chardonnay for whites, from which they produce a variety of different wines.

There is a pure Chardonnay, half fermented in stainless steel and half in barrel to make a rich rounded blend, with some intriguing lees fruit. 'Chardonnay is a stupid vine; people plant it when they don't know what else to plant, and it always grows.' Brania del Cancello from Trebbiano and Chardonnay, both fermented in barrel, was light and buttery with soft fruit. Brania is an old term describing a terrace, a reference to the terraced hills behind Lucca. Brania delle Ghiandaie, from Sangiovese with a little Syrah, had a firm smoky flavour with peppery Tuscany notes, while Nero della Spinosa, from Syrah that spends two years in barrel and *botti*, was ripe and rounded. Paolo is critical of the DOC; he feels strongly that they did not take advantage of the recent changes to tighten up the regulations, for they still allow white grapes, which is crazy for a red wine; and they should have reduced the yield. No modern vineyard should produce 120 quintals a hectare; it simply encourages people to buy in wine from elsewhere to supplement their own – a throwaway remark suggested that a quarter of all Chianti is really Cannonau from Sardinia. As for the Colline Lucchesi, he does not feel that it has a great future, for at the moment there is no real leader. The biggest estate only has about 10 or 15 hectares, but it is impossible to have a large vineyard in this area of small properties. Certainly volume will not provide the future; the opportunity lies with creating a prestige product and hopefully some of the new producers are more marketing orientated. But for the moment sales really depend on Lucca and the tourist trade. We finished with a pure Grechetto, Greco delle Gaggie, *gaggie* being another name for mimosa, officially a Vin Santo but in practice a *passito*, but you are not allowed to make *passito* here. The colour was golden amber with a rich honeyed flavour and a dry finish. Then at Paolo's suggestion we headed off to the other side of the DOC, the far western edge, across the Serchio river to the new estate of Terre del Sillabo.

Giovan Pio Moretti comes across as serious and committed and an articulate exponent of his ideas. He is now in his mid-30s, and explained how wine had gradually become an obsession. His grandfather had bought 30 hectares of land here, back in 1929; it was an old Tuscan farm, producing *un po' di tutto*. There was wheat and maize, some vines for *vino sfuso*. The peasant farmers left as the *mezzadria* system was dismantled in the 1970s, and his grandfather finally died at almost 100 in 1984. This was the time that Giovan Pio began to take an interest in wine, first as a consumer, and then he started to do tasting courses, and then looked at what was happening in the cellars, which were run by the *fattore*. He began to visit other estates, and form ideas with which his family did not always agree. He did not say so, but you sensed that things have not been easy, but now he has a measure of independence and is responsible for 7 hectares of vineyards, a cellar and some olive trees.

He took us for a walk up the hill through the vineyard, with views across the valley. We were followed by his eager Jack Russell, called Matisse because his large brown spots on white look like a Matisse painting. He explained how the area has a particular microclimate; the valley begins above Camaiore where the sea air and the mountain air from the Apuanian Alps meet; at one point the mountains meet to form a semi-circle, protecting the vineyards, and then the valley opens up again nearer Lucca, where it is called Val Freddano, a reference to the cold nights. The days may be hot in July and August, but even then the temperature drops at night, which is excellent for white grapes. He has planted Chardonnay and Sauvignon, as he feels that the indigenous white varieties, not even Vermentino, do not produce an interesting flavour here. Some of the original terraces have been restored, so that Chardonnay is on the hillsides and Sauvignon on the valley floor. There is also Cabernet Sauvignon and Franc, Merlot and Sangiovese.

Back at the cellars we settled down to taste an intriguing array of wines, as Giovan Pio expounded his thoughts and ideas. A pure Sauvignon had some attractive mineral flavours, with some pithy juicy fruit. An oak-aged Chardonnay was rounded and powerful. Most intriguing was Gana, meaning *voglia*, or wish, in Sicilian dialect, and a selection of the best Sauvignon that was fermented in oak. The oak was well integrated, making a harmonious whole, of fruit, oak and acidity, with an intense flavour, which would age well. A comparison with a fine Graves would not be out of place. The customary view is that Italian white wines should be fresh and simple, without the power or potential of red wines. Giovan Pio wants to challenge this, and produce white wines with complexity. It all depends on what you do in the vineyard. Spante, a griffon, is his selection of Chardonnay, mainly from the terraced vineyards, with some attractive nutty flavours. Finally there was Niffo, a Lucchese word meaning 'absolutely furious', which is a blend of his four red varieties, which spend eighteen months in wood. It had a dense tight palate, with firm tannins and ripe fruit and held great promise.

For the moment it seems that the Colline Lucchesi lack cohesion, but comprise a group of producers of considerable individuality and talent, as well as future potential, but they do not have a collective voice. From Terre di Sillabo we went into Lucca to walk round the city walls, which are still very much intact, offering views over the city, and into gardens and courtyards at our feet, and then to dine at the Bocca di Sant'Antonio, which remains one of the most delicious tables of the city.

Candia dei Colli Apuani, Colli di Luni and the Val di Magra

· *Late September* ·

On the border with Liguria. Walk in the Colli Apuani from Podere Scurtarola, past Franco Giusti to Aurelio Cima, Cesare della Tommasina, La Caloma. In the Colli di Luni: Nanni Barbero, Il Canniccio, Terenzuola, Boriassi. In the Val di Magra: Noceti Ruschi and the hamlet of Oppilo

THE TWO ADJACENT DOCs of Candia dei Colli Apuani and Colli di Luni are tucked into a lost corner of Tuscany, right on the border with Liguria. In fact, the greater part of the Colli di Luni is in the province of Liguria, and both have more in common with the wines of the Cinque Terre than with the rest of Tuscany.

The DOC of the Candia dei Colli Apuani was created in 1981 and covers vineyards around the three towns of Massa, Carrara and Montignoso. Candia is the name of a tiny vineyard in the hills behind Massa, which belonged to the church of San Lorenzo at the beginning of the sixteenth century; the monks are said to have made a particularly fine wine at a time when there were few vineyards in the area. On the map the vineyard area of the Colli Apuani looks like a large salamander as it sweeps round the towns of Massa and Carrara. The landscape is dominated by the Apuanian hills, the foothills of the Apennines which separate Tuscany from northern Italy. The atmosphere is alpine and quite different from the rest of Tuscany. The hills are famous for their marble; Michelangelo carved marble from Carrara and today the quarries are still a flourishing industry, but the enormous cuts in the mountainside leave ugly white scars, so that the mountains look permanently snow-capped. The vineyards are quite dramatic, and again quite different from any in other parts of Tuscany, with narrow terraces on steep gradients. We left the urban sprawl of Massa and Carrara on the coastal plain and took a narrow winding road up into the hills, appropriately named the Via dell'Uva, and there we found Pierpaolo Lorieri at Podere Scurtarola.

It was late September and the harvest was drawing to a close. Pierpaolo talked about the peculiarities of the year, what he called *un'annata particolare*. June had been hot and humid, with rain in July and August, so that a lot of people had problems with rotten grapes. 'So much depends on us; you need to know how to wait, to have the courage to wait. The decision to pick is a balance of analysis, intuition and a large dose of good luck. Two days can make all the difference; it can be very stressful' – even if you look very relaxed, as he did, sipping a glass of his *spumante*, a delicate blend of Vermentino and Chardonnay.

We were in time for the harvest lunch. They had finished picking that morning and twenty people sat down to celebrate, under the shade of a fig tree. Pierpaolo was cheerful: 'We've been lucky and got some nice grapes,' but he had also had the courage to wait. The conversation flowed in voluble Italian, as we consumed ravioli, followed by gamy sausages, and a succession of bottles, some local, some from further afield. Their friendly hound sat looking hopeful as only dogs can, especially when the sausages appeared. Pierpaolo talked about his various experiments; he is working with the University of Arezzo, looking at various indigenous vines, for which he carries out microvinifications. He has just 6 hectares of vines, from which he makes seven wines: a *spumante*, Candia *secco* and *amabile*, Vermentino Bianco, Vermentino Nero, a simple red from a blend of grape varieties and, finally, a *passito* dessert wine. We later saw the grapes drying in the attic, where they remain for several weeks. Pierpaolo drew a comparison between the *amabile* and tea in England; it's the wine you give to a guest as a gesture of hospitality, whatever the time of day. Very little is made, as it is quite complicated, with some sugar remaining in the wine, which may start fermenting again to turn slightly fizzy. He first began experimenting with *barriques* in 1989; and fermented his first Vermentino Bianco in *barrique* in 1996; 'I like inventing things.' And others have followed his example with the Vermentino. This year he is trying some *ripasso*, a technique sometimes used in Valpolicella, but with white skins; we saw bags of white skins being put back into a fermenting vat, where they would stay for four or five days. It is all indicative of an intensely enquiring mind. Nothing stands still at Podere Scurtarola.

Further down the Via dell'Uva is young Franco Giusti. He was busy in the cellar with his cheerful *cantiniere*, Giulio, loading a small mechanized basket press with red grapeskins. It seemed rather like making a lasagna: between each layer of grapeskins you need what is best described as a large straw mat to help the drainage of the juice. Once the press is full, it is put into position and programmed to the desired pressure, and away it goes, with the juice gradually trickling out into a vat. We left Giulio looking after the press, while Franco took us for a walk through his vineyards. He has just two hectares, planted with Vermentino, Albarola and a little Malvasia and Trebbiano for white wine, and Merlot, Montepulciano, Vermentino Nero and Sangiovese for red wine. Vermentino Nero is typical of this particular part of Tuscany; there is a little on Sardinia, but none in nearby Liguria. The vineyards are in terraces, starting on the valley floor and rising to about 240 metres. A kind of mini-funicular hauls up baskets with the help of a small motor that you can move round the vineyard, which makes things much easier. Before that everything was done by hand. The slope here is about 25°, but as steep as 40° is not unusual.

Franco explained how it was his grandfather who had built the terraces; he had worked on the railways but also had animals, and olive trees, as well as some vines, all for family consumption. The roots of the grass keep the soil in place, but nowadays any new terraces are built with dry-stone walls. The vines are close together, about 80 centimetres apart, with as many as 10,000 plants per hectare. Any dead vines are replaced individually so that the average age of Franco's vines is about 50–60 years. A thin brown snake slithered through the grass and disappeared into the undergrowth. Sometimes wild boar can be a problem. Back in the cellar we tasted the juice for the *amabile*; essentially it is the same as for the dry wine, as the climate here, with its maritime influence, does not allow for noble rot. Instead, the fermentation is stopped, to leave some sugar in the wine, and the fresh juice was lightly sweet and honeyed.

We carried on down the narrow road and stopped to talk to an old man in his vineyard. How's the harvest? we enquired. Oh, it's been difficult this year, what with the rain and rot. It's back-breaking work, working on the terraces, he said, giving his back a rub. Further on a small group were picking grapes, providing some colour on a rather grey day. We skirted past a hill where Pierpaolo had told us there were the remains of a prehistoric temple.

Apparently there's nothing much to see, but on a fine day, the view would have merited the climb. Instead we carry on down the road, past a neat little vineyard with vegetables in between the vines, with manicured rows of carrots, lettuce and chard. There were wild flowers and herbs, thyme and mint, on the roadside. The next vineyard had tall bamboo canes providing support for the vines. Next we passed a quarry and met a couple of hunters. They told us that they were after the migrating birds, *tordi*, which is a type of blackbird, and also *storni*, a variety of dove. Every now and then the sound of guns shattered the peace, and then the church bells started chiming. We cut down through a terraced vineyard to emerge near the cellars of Aurelio Cima.

This is now the largest estate in the area, thanks to the energetic vision of Aurelio. The family began with 4 hectares, from which they produced *sfuso* wine for their restaurant; now they have 26 hectares and make a wide range of different wines. We tasted as we talked. Aurelio Cima is confident and opinionated, a man who is going places. He described himself as *scorbutico*, meaning cantankerous or querulous in Italian, and you could see that he takes nothing for granted. *Sono nato un po' tribuloso.* I was born a little prickly. He did not begin to appreciate wine until he was in his late 20s; he is now in his mid-30s. For his first taste of fine wine, he mentioned some of the great names of Tuscany, Solenga from Argiano, another Brunello, Case Basse, Alceo from Rampolla. It sounded something like the conversion on the road to Damascus.

Aurelio's Candia Vigneto Alto is a pure Vermentino, with an exotic nose and delicate rounded fruit. He is fairly dismissive of any of the other white varieties in the area; nor does he believe in Candia *amabile*. However, he wants to get Candia dei Colli Apuani better known outside the region, as for the moment it remains very much a wine of local interest. Unlike his fellow winemakers, Aurelio is already selling to the United States and the United Kingdom and he firmly believes that it is much easier to create a following in Italy once you have established a reputation abroad. He is also convinced that there is potential for a great red wine in this area, as the soil is suitable and very stony. With this in mind, he has been working on another local grape variety, which is unknown anywhere else, Massaretta, seeing it as his challenge and cause. The 2000 pure Massaretta was quite intriguing, with some distinctive ripe fruit, and a certain sturdiness, after twelve months in new oak. He has also blended it with Sangiovese in Romaldo, which spends sixteen months in wood, with some berry fruit and a sweet ripeness. There was also an appealing Vermentino Nero and a barrel-aged Merlot, and he has recently planted some Syrah, of which the first vintage was highly acclaimed. Aurelio is adamant that the word tradition does not exist; you should constantly be trying to improve your wines and certainly not use tradition as an excuse to rest on your laurels. He should go far. And from Cima, it was a steep climb up through the terraced vineyards back to Podere Scurtarola at the top of the hill.

The other estate of any size in the Colli Apuani is Cesare della Tommasina, which is run by two brothers, Alberto and Pierpaolo. Cesare was their grandfather, who first planted vines on the family land. They began bottling their wine in 1982; until then it was sold *sfuso*, but now they make four wines, a *secco*, an *amabile*, a *passito* and a Rosso della Toscana, from a veritable mishmash of grapes, Massaretta, Sangiovese, Vermentino Nero, Merlot, Ciliegiolo and another local variety, Buonamico. It could not be deemed a super-Tuscan, as you need good wood for that, so they would have to get rid of their traditional chestnut barrels. We tasted the Candia *secco*, which was rounded, with a slightly bitter finish. The *amabile* was softly sweet, and lightly fizzy. They explained that the riper grapes are better for the *secco*, while grapes with higher acidity make a better *amabile*, which needs 12–45gm per litre of residual sugar; they favour the higher level, so that the wine goes beautifully with a deliciously calorific rice cake, a local speciality, which requires at least twenty eggs. The brothers talked about the need to update the style of the local wines, that they needed to become more refined. Certainly they are fine-tuning their vinification methods, with the purchase of a new membrane press for the 2002 vintage. They are aware of the surge of interest in the region since the mid-90s, with the ensuing rise in land prices, with a hectare of vines now costing € 155,000 (300 million lire).

Our day in the Colli Apuani finished with supper with Cesare Canavesio at his estate, La Caloma, outside Montignosa. In fact, the meal was a feast of local specialities, a never-ending array of delicious flavours, culminating in some tasty sausages grilled over an open fire. But first we tried *lardo di Colonnato*, salt-cured pork fat, which is seasoned with herbs and kept in a marble container for several weeks. There was spicy black pudding and some *pane marocco*, a bread studded with black olives, all washed down with a Tuscan red, made from Vermentino Nero, Merlot and Barsaglino, another name for Massaretta. It had a wild untamed flavour, which offset the sausages to perfection. Next came a succulent gorgonzola to accompany sweet Vin Santo, which had spent ten years in small barrels. It was the perfect combination. Cesare enthused about the diversity of the Colli Apuani: 'Except for Cima, we are all small producers; each of us is different and that creates variety; what we do in the cellar is an adventure; and our wine remains a work of art.'

The DOC of the Colli di Luni was created in 1989, and covers fifteen *comuni*, three in Tuscany, namely Fosdinovo, Aulla and Podenzana, with the greater part of the DOC in neighbouring Liguria. The Tuscan producers are mainly centred round the village of Fosdinovo. From the coastal road, the Aurelia, you take a winding road past the Villa Malespina, with its pink facade and elegant proportions, up to the village. In 1340 Fosdinovo became the feudal stronghold of the Malespina family, who remained here until 1820. The castle on the edge of the village was firmly closed, apart from allowing a brief glimpse at a courtyard built of solid blocks of stone. Apparently it has associations with Dante, who is supposed to have stayed there in 1306. The Oratorio dei Bianchi is worth a visit, for its ornate white marble facade and a rich baroque interior.

It was the old Roman port of Luni, at the mouth of the river Magra, which gave its name to the region of the Lunigiana and to the wine, Colli di Luni. Founded in 177 BC, Luni was an important trading centre until the Magra river silted up. Today you can see some of the wall paintings and mosaics, as well as the remains of the amphitheatre.

Somehow the Colli di Luni suffers from its split personality, not knowing whether it is Tuscan or Ligurian, and its growers seem to lack a sense of cohesion and unity, although in some respects it is not so different from Candia dei Colli Apuani, with vineyards on the continuation of the same hills. Nanni Barbero is wonderfully opinionated, an older man who has had a successful career in other fields. He was very dismissive of the DOC. 'I don't believe in it; the permitted yields are far too high to be taken seriously and there are no real controls that would encourage quality.' The harvest was in full swing, with a trailer of white grapes arriving, which were being put through the crusher and then into a vat for twenty-four hours of skin contact. The wine of the previous vintage had a full-bodied almond flavour, with a nutty finish, making a satisfying mouthful of wine. Nanni is distinctly disapproving of modern techniques. 'Chilling equipment ruins the wine and massacres the yeast.' He likes a white *vino da meditazione*, but is quite adamant that you should not put white wine in a barrel: 'After all, you don't want tannin in white wine.' He would, however, like to try oak ageing for his red, if he had the money to afford the barrels. Nor is he very optimistic about the condition of the Italian wine trade. 'Wine is failing in Italy; there will be bankruptcies, whereas olive oil is something special.' His cellar was simple and functional with small concrete vats gurgling with fermenting wine and a couple of large salamis hanging up in the corner.

Cesare Mosignori at Il Canniccio explained how his grandfather had worked his land as a *mezzadria* and then had been able to buy it in 1967, helped by low interest rates. He has a neat little cellar, with barrels and vats, a basket press and a tiny bottling line. The vats were fermenting, emitting a gentle *musica della cantina*. Signor Mosignori explained that *canniccio* described the place where chestnuts were dried in preparation for being ground for flour; a fire smoked for forty days, but nowadays it houses a bread oven. His red wine was a blend of Sangiovese, Merlot and Ciliegiolo and had some fresh cherry fruit and tight tannins. There is also a Vermentino, all from just one and a half hectares of vines.

Further up the hill toward Fosdinovo we came to Terenzuola, where Ivan Giuliani is making a satisfying range of wines. We had eavesdropped the conversation when Pierpaolo was making our appointment. 'If I send you an English journalist, will you give me 2000 bottles? Of water? No, of wine!' Ivan is young and keen, highly motivated and well informed about his region. He initially studied economics at Stresa on Lake Maggiore, but came here where an uncle was already making some wine to help develop the estate. It has grown from just 2 ares of vineyards in 1995 to 20 hectares today. There are three different areas of vineyards, each at a different altitude, from which Ivan makes four wines, two white and two red. The lowest, at 80 metres, is planted with various indigenous varieties such as Merla and Tintoria, then there is a hectare of Merlot at 250 metres, and 12 hectares of Vermentino on sandstone at 350 metres. Ivan explained how Vermentino does best in the higher vineyards, as it benefits from the exchange of day and night-time temperatures. He keeps the wine on its lees, with regular stirring, to make a wonderfully satisfying wine with delicate, understated flavours. The red is a blend of Merla and Merlot – they complement each other, with the Merlot providing body and roundness and the Merla spice and tannin. Ivan's first serious vintage was 1996, and he admitted that wine has become an obsession, 'a drug', and he undoubtedly has a wider vision than his colleagues, who are content to sell to the local restaurants and *agriturismi*.

Signor Boriassi has a couple of hectares of vineyards just outside Sarzana, almost in Liguria. He took us to see his vineyards, which are in the shape of a half moon, planted round the hillside. There were olive and chestnut trees too. Again this was land that had been in the family for three generations or more, but he only began to develop the vineyards more seriously when the DOC was created in 1989. His is the only organic estate in the province of Massa Carrara. We tasted the Vermentino from the Vigneto Mezzaluna, with its delicate nose and fresh acidity on the palate. It was a *simpatico* note on which to finish, before heading up the motorway to Pontremoli and the wines of Val di Magra, which runs from Pontremoli to Aulla and Fivizzano.

The scenery here is quite different from the hills of the Colli di Luni. Here you are further inland, in the foothills of the Apennines, and the atmosphere is even more alpine, with sweet chestnut trees and lush green pastures for contented cows, interspersed with the occasional vineyard. Pontremoli itself is an attractive little town, with a magnificent baroque cathedral and the tempting *salumeria* Angella in the main street, with its old-fashioned shop front and wood-panelled interior. Apparently, salamis and hams are matured in the cellar below the shop.

We went to see the estate of Noceti Ruschi, and tracked down Francesco Ruschi Noceti in an old farmhouse on the outskirts of the town. Sadly, it is now an oasis in the middle of factories for light industry, as the surrounding land was expropriated in order to develop an industrial estate. Here he retains the vestiges of rural tranquillity, with vats and barrels housed in an old barn. It was also rather cramped so he has plans to develop another part of the family property, the remains of an old monastery, also on the edge of the industrial estate, which once provided lodgings for pilgrims on the Via Francigena, which passed through Pontremoli.

Signor Ruschi has 6 hectares of vineyards up in the hills behind Pontremoli, from which he makes a variety of intriguingly original wines from grape varieties I had never heard of. Pollera is a local red grape that was grown extensively around Massa Carrara until the Second World War, which he is now eagerly reintroducing to the area. He described it as being similar to Trebbiano in character, without much colour, but high in sugar and rich in polyphenols, giving alcohol and tannin. The example we tasted later, Podere la Costa Uva Pollera, had some intriguing ripe fruit, the fruit of cherries, but not the sour cherries of Sangiovese; these were ripe, with soft tannins. Archives have described it as *la dolce pollera*, or sweet Pollera, and there are records that it was sold to France at the beginning of the eighteenth century. Marinello is another local red grape, which is also giving some good results in experimental microvinifications, and there is also Merlarola, Corlaga, Monfrà, Vermentino Nero and Morone, all in the hilltop vineyard of Castangiola. As for white wine, this was my first encounter with Durella and Luadga; the resulting wine had an old-fashioned nuttiness, and there was also Verdarella and Pinzamosca. In the old vineyards the different varieties are all mixed up together. The red wine from Podere Castangiola, with all the different varieties, had some attractive berry fruit with a slight pepperiness, with an appealing freshness, some acidity and tannin. Signor Ruschi explained how there used to be many more vineyards here, but rural depopulation has taken its toll, and now there are woods of sweet chestnut trees instead. This is not an area that attracts investment; there is no DOC here, only the IGT of Val di Magra, after the river that flows through Pontremoli. Just eight or nine producers put their wine in bottle, and almost exclusively for the local market. And the final wine in the range was a *passito*, with an intriguing firm nutty bite.

Next we went to meet Signor Benelli in the tiny hamlet of Oppilo. He explained how it was a fourteenth-century *borgo* and that the wine of the area had a reputation at the time of Barbarossa, the twelfth-century Holy Roman Emperor. Now Oppilo has just ten permanent inhabitants, as well as twenty-two dogs and a fluctuating population of people staying in the *agriturismi* during the summer months. None of the buildings looked newer than about 1600 and we felt that we had walked into a medieval stage set. Signor Benelli was the personnel director of a large Milanese company and took early retirement some ten years ago, returning to his roots, for his parents had vines near Pontremoli. He too is very enthusiastic about the originality of Durella, praising it for its distinctive perfume and flavour. As we talked, we sipped a *spumante* made from Durella, which was firm in flavour with hints of almonds and a dry finish. Benelli's enthusiasm is infectious; people were coming for a tasting; there were tempting aromas exuding from the kitchen; *crostini* were being prepared and we were given some *ai funghi* to enjoy with our sparkling Durella. As well as a dry wine, Benelli also makes a sweeter version, not unlike a Candia Amabile, for the fermentation is blocked, while some sugar remains to make a soft dessert wine. He is enthusiastic, too, about Pollera, which he blends with Ciliegiolo and Merlarolla, explaining the origin of the name as *uva di merla* or the blackbirds' grape, for they peck at it when it is ripe. It gives some backbone to the Pollera. The original cellars were built in about 1530. Today there are old cement vats and a basket press, with old vineyard tools hanging on the wall. You really sense that you are off the beaten track in a lost corner of Tuscany, where time has almost stood still.

An Introduction to the Maremma

THE MAREMMA COVERS a large part of southern Tuscany. Originally the name described the coastal plain, which stretches from Cecina to Monte Argentario and the boundary with Lazio, an area that was usually rife with malaria in the summer months. Nowadays the malaria has gone and the term has extended to include the Maremma Pisana, the coast between Pisa and the Colline Metallifere behind Piombino, taking in the DOCs of Bolgheri, Montescudaio and Val di Cornia. Further south the Maremma Grossetana, covering most of the province of Grosseto, stretches from Piombino down to the border with Lazio and as far as Monte Amiata in the west.

The Maremma is suddenly opening up. Ten or twenty years ago it was relatively unimportant for wine. There was Sassicaia and a couple of other estates in Bolgheri, while the twin DOCs of Morellino di Scansano and Bianco di Pitigliano were dominated by their cooperatives, with very few independent producers. Parrina was an early and tiny DOC, consisting of just one property, while Meleta was an isolated estate, in the middle of nowhere so it seemed. How things have changed. A wave of investment has swept through the region, prompted by various factors. Land prices have been relatively cheap compared to those in the more established parts of Tuscany, although they are rising fast fuelled by the intense interest and investment in the region. A whole host of new DOCs have been created in recent years, notably in the province of Grosseto, such as Montecucco, Capalbio and others. Where once the Maremma seemed very much a lost corner of Tuscany, it has been brought into the mainstream of Tuscan viticulture. Conditions in the Maremma are generally different from the rest of Tuscany. The climate is milder, with a strong maritime influence, so that there are less extremes of summer heat or winter cold, with the result that the wines tend to be more accessible, riper, more rounded and with softer tannins than those from the more traditional areas of Tuscany. With so few long-established DOCs, it is an area that offers great scope for experimentation, with a sense that anything is possible, as will be seen in the ensuing chapters.

Bolgheri

· *May* ·

Around Bolgheri, and a visit to Sassicaia. Walk to Castiglioncello, Grattamacco, Ornellaia, Guado al Tasso, Ca' Marcanda. Walk to the tower of Donoratico; Le Macchiole, Michele Satta, Enrico Santini

THE TRANSFORMATION IN Bolgheri over the last ten years has been nothing short of breathtaking. When I first visited this small wine area on the Tuscan coast in the late 1980s there were just two producers, Sassicaia and Grattamacco, while a third, Ornellaia, was little more than a building site. Since then Bolgheri has developed an international reputation for wines based on the grape varieties of Bordeaux. Sassicaia was the pioneer, with the Marchese Mario Incisa della Rochetta planting the first Cabernet Sauvignon here towards the end of the Second World War, choosing a French grape variety for the simple reason that he liked claret. His example was followed several years later by Pier Mario and Paola Cavallari at Grattamacco, and then Ludovico Antinori at Ornellaia, and since then there has been a steady influx of new producers, some on the grand scale, like Angelo Gaja of Piedmont fame, and others more modest, like Enrico Santini.

The village of Castagneto Carducci is the centre of the area, a classic Tuscan hilltop town, with narrow streets winding their way up to a castle at the top. Castagneto takes its name from the Italian for a sweet chestnut, which were grown extensively in the area, for flour. The castle was built by the Gherardesca family, who were landowners here for many generations. Piero and Ludovico Antinori's mother is a Gherardesca, while her sister was the mother of the Marchese Nicolò Incisa della Rochetta, with these two women dividing the Gherardesca inheritance at Bolgheri. Amongst the younger generation, Count Gaddo della Gherardesca has featured in the tabloids for his relationship with Sarah Ferguson, the ex-Duchess of York, with whom he now has a project for *agriturismo* and maybe even a vineyard at nearby Poggio Cerretello. This old Tuscan family also features in Dante's *Inferno*, and the poet Giosuè Carducci spent his childhood in Castagneto, since when the village has taken his name.

It was Michele Satta who set the scene for us, taking us for a drive through the vineyards and explaining the topography of the area. The hills form an amphitheatre, protecting the vineyards from the prevailing winds. The village of Castagneto Carducci perches on one hill, and nearby there is the tower of Donoratico, and further along the coast the hamlet of Bolgheri, with its long alleyway of cypress trees. The air is mild for the sea is very close, separated from the vineyards by the coastal parasol pines. The proximity to Elba creates a wind channel, so that there are always sea breezes, and less rain than in the surrounding areas, as well as a big difference between day and night-time temperatures. The hillsides are covered with *macchia*. Unusually a hillside vineyard is not considered an advantage here, as it would suffer too much from drought so that the grapes would not always ripen; you need underground supplies of water, which the low-lying vineyards have. However, there are exceptions to that rule. Pier Mario Cavallari at Grattamacco has planted a vineyard in the hills, and there is another startling new vineyard, representing a considerable investment, high up in the middle of the *macchia*.

The soil is a mixture, with sand and clay. It is fertile and very rich in minerals, with the deep red soil showing the presence of manganese. Some 800 hectares of vines have been planted over the last three years, representing an enormous investment, mostly by newcomers to the area. The differences between the old and the new vineyards are marked. The farmers who originally had vineyards here grew all sorts of other vegetables, as well as a few rows of Sangiovese and Trebbiano and so on. Michele explained how his oldest, 30-year-old vineyard had once produced a breathtaking 350 quintals per hectare; now, by changing the pruning system, the yield is down to a far more modest 60 quintals.

It was in Bolgheri that we discovered that a footpath is not always a public footpath. Apparently we were quite unwittingly trespassing on the Marchese Nicolò's land, for we had innocently thought that a *strada privata* sign meant simply no cars. Not so; it means nobody at all, as we realized when one of the Marchese's *guardia* indignantly asked us what we were doing, convinced that we would disturb some of the Marchese's stallions, which were grazing in a nearby field. He insisted on driving us off the Marchese's property, which turned out to be timely, as we would otherwise have reached a firmly locked gate, with no means of access to the road. Unceremoniously evicted from the Marchese's land, we continued our way along the road and into the little hamlet of Bolgheri, where the church bells were ringing loudly. It is a pretty place, with compact little streets, a couple of restaurants and a few tourist shops. There were swallows diving in and out of nests under the eaves, and a surprising number of churches for such a small place. The Enoteca Tognoni, just inside the walls, is worth a stop for cooling glasses of local white wine or more substantial reds, accompanied by Tuscan cheeses and salami.

We took a route out of the village, past a pretty arched *lavatoio* and an old fountain, with a coat of arms, and a verse commorating the Count Walfredo della Gherardesca, covered in overgrown vegetation. The vineyard workers were having a picnic in a shady olive grove and we fell into conversation with one of them. He told us that he came from Senegal and that he was working in a vineyard belonging to Ornellaia, and that the adjoining plot belonged to Antinori. It was time for our own picnic, and we found a shady spot, looking at a vineyard of Cabernet Franc, thoughtfully labelled for ease of identification. The path ran parallel to the village, with views of its roofs, broken up by olive trees, with carpets of brilliant red poppies. Then we followed the road along the avenue of cypress trees, immortalized by Giosuè Carducci in his poem 'Davanti a San Guido'. It seemed a long 5 kilometres of straight road, with cypress tree after cypress tree on either side. Some of the old, diseased trees have been replaced with young trees, supported by a construction that resembled a wigwam of poles, surrounded by a small ditch to contain water. At the end of the road is the Oratorio di San Guido, an elegant six-sided building, built in 1703 by the Gherardesca family, to commemorate one of their ancestors, a certain Guido who was a hermit in the twelfth century. The coast close to Bolgheri is also the home of Italy's largest bird sanctuary, a large area of woodland and coastal marshland, covering some 2000 hectares, created in 1958 and now part of the World Wildlife Fund. Mario Incisa della Rochetta was the first president of the Italian branch of the WWF, prompting his son to observe that as a young man his father shot birds, and then spent the latter part of his life protecting them.

Our visit to Sassicaia was set for the next day. The Marchese Nicolò gave us a gracious welcome and we apologized for our misdemeanour of the previous day. 'Oh,' he said, 'I'm so sorry; they always pick up the wrong people.' Sassicaia is the wine that placed Bolgheri firmly on the international wine map, and yet it really all began by accident. It was the Marchese Nicolò's father who first planted Cabernet Sauvignon here in 1944, and for the first twenty years or so his wine remained fairly unsophisticated, destined for family and friends. Then they started to collaborate with their Antinori cousins, benefiting from the advice of Antinori's oenologist, Dott. Giacomo Tachis. His experience at Sassicaia was to provide the inspiration for Tignanello, which he subsequently created for Antinori. Sassicaia was the very first Tuscan wine estate to use French *barriques* for ageing a red wine, and was indisputably a pacesetter in its use of Cabernet Sauvignon. It was the 1968 vintage that brought Sassicaia into the international limelight. The production at that time was just 7000 bottles and the Marchese laughingly observed in his impeccable English that it was a garage wine before its time. (This is a reference to the current fashion for a tiny production of very expensive wine in Bordeaux, often referred to as *vin de garage*, or *garagiste*.) In contrast today the production is some 200,000 bottles a year, and although Dott. Tachis no longer works for Antinori, he continues to consult for Sassicaia, while his main interests now lie in Sicily and Sardinia.

The Marchese is president of the *consorzio* of the DOC of Bolgheri and he talked about its development. Curiously, for the region is known above all for red wine, the DOC was first created in 1983 for white and pink wines, with red coming eleven years later, in 1994, along with the recognition of Sassicaia as a separate *cru* of the DOC. The DOC of Bolgheri lays down various rules regarding the blending of grape varieties; a pure Sangiovese is not allowed; there must be a minimum of 10 per cent of Cabernet Sauvignon, and in some instances 70 per cent is the maximum for Cabernet, Merlot or Sangiovese. Syrah is allowed up to 30 per cent, and when we were in Bolgheri, there was much whispering about Petit Verdot, which not only was not allowed in the DOC, but was not even permitted to be planted in the vineyards. That restriction has now been lifted – Petit Verdot has been officially allowed in the vineyards of Tuscany since the spring of 2003. One third of the DOC remains white wine, even though the reputation of Bolgheri is based firmly on red. However, there is an underlying feeling that the producers who are really committed to the region pay little attention to the requirements of the DOC. Bolgheri may enjoy an international recognition, but it is the reputation of individual estates that counts, with little regard for the precise demands of the DOC regulations, even though they allow for the use of the more international grape varieties.

The growth in Bolgheri has been phenomenal. Eight hundred hectares of vines have been planted since 1994, so that the DOC now totals some 900 hectares, with Antinori alone responsible for 200 hectares of new vineyards at Guado al Tasso, in the space of three years. The majority of the new plantings are by newcomers; there are few local producers, and few small producers. For the moment the decision has been taken not to allow any more planting, for they are concerned that the market success should not run away with them. There may be a large demand, but a considerable number of vineyards are not yet in production. Quality must be maintained, so what is needed now is a period of consolidation.

And at Sassicaia itself, what had changed? Really, very little; the vines are older, and the estate has grown so that there are now 52 hectares in production. The wine consists of at least 80 per cent Cabernet Sauvignon, blended with some Cabernet Franc, fermented in stainless-steel tanks and given a minimum of eighteen months ageing in barrels, one third of which are new, with a further six months in bottle before release. The cellar is very simple and efficient; the winemaking likewise, and it works. Sassicaia has consistently retained its quality over the years, producing harmoniously elegant wines, with supple tannins. They may be accessible in relatively early youth, but they will evolve into deliciously mature bottles, with elegant cedarwood fruit that is the hallmark of fine Cabernet Sauvignon. There is no Merlot; maybe Petit Verdot might be an option in the future, for it would certainly ripen better here than in Bordeaux. Although the Marchese cares passionately about his wine, you sense that his first love is really horses, for the breeding of Arab stallions for racing is another important activity on his estate, as it was in his father's time. His great success was Ribot, who won, amongst other races, the Arc de Triomphe at Longchamp in both 1955 and 1956.

The Marchese also talked about a new wine, Guidalberto, which is being produced in association with his cousin, Federico Zileri, partly from some vineyards on the Sassicaia estate and partly from vineyards planted by Zileri. Its name, Guidalberto, recalls Guidalberto Gherardesca who planted the avenue of cypress trees at the very beginning of the eighteenth century. The wine is made in a separate winery in the village, and will be quite distinct from Sassicaia, with a blend of 40 per cent each of Merlot and Cabernet Sauvignon and 20 per cent Sangiovese, given one year in wood, both American and French new barrels, as well as old Sassicaia barrels. The first, 2000 vintage seemed very approachable, ripe and rounded with well-integrated oak and harmonious fruit.

Then the Marchese very kindly agreed to allow us to walk up to the original Sassicaia vineyard at Castiglioncello, so the next morning we had a *rendez-vous* with another *guardia*, Giorgio, who was quite surprised at our energy. 'You really want to walk to the top? It's a long way.' We followed his small truck down a track, through a high gate designed to deter trespassers, or to keep animals in, for this is also a hunting reserve, to a clearing in the woods where there is a tiny shrine dedicated to La Madonnina. And off we set uphill. It was a gentle climb through the woods, which provided welcome shade. The cistus bushes were in flower, shades of pink and white, with some brilliant yellow broom providing a dramatic contrast to the deep green shrubs. The first vineyard we reached was being sprayed and there was a smell of sulphur in the air. The second vineyard was securely fenced, as protection against the wild boar. We passed a small walled cemetery, with a memorial to a priest who had converted 120 children, and then we reached the Castello di Bolgheri at the top of the hill, a solid building built on rock, surrounding a courtyard and in the process of renovation. A small alleyway of cypress trees leads up to a gate, with substantial stone pigsties and cowsheds outside the gate. Some seventy or eighty families once lived on the estate, with enough children to warrant a school. We sat in the shade of a cypress tree for a picnic and then, with the help of binoculars, identified landmarks amidst the patchwork of vineyards, olive trees and woods at our feet. The flatter land is virtually a carpet of vines, with the large plantings of the Guado al Tasso, with its stylish winery, somewhat camouflaged by trees, and on the hill to our north we could make out the outline of the cellars of Grattamacco. In the distance, if it were not for the haze, we would have been able to see the coastline of Cap Corse, for opposite Bolgheri is the town of Bastia on the coast of Corsica.

We retraced our steps back down the hill, detouring to look at the site of the very first Sassicaia vineyard, a small vineyard planted high up at some 300 metres. There was a tractor at work, for the old vines were being pulled up. It was very overgrown and looked rather sad and forlorn, but will be replanted in a year or two. We passed our car in the clearing and took a track into Bolgheri, a sunken track that felt as though it had been eroded by water, and we also spotted traces of wild boar. Giorgio had lent us a key so that we did not have to climb over a gate, but we did have to squeeze through a hole in a fence by the next gate. There were signs forbidding the collection of mushrooms, truffles or any other *prodotti agresti*. Later, on the way back to collect our car, Giorgio told us that there were very few wild boar, as the present Marchese, unlike his father, is not keen on hunting, and he added as an aside that he probably prefers horses to wine.

Pier Mario Cavallari, at Grattamacco, planted the second vineyard in Bolgheri, but a long time after Sassicaia, and Pier Mario jokingly admitted that he did not know that Sassicaia was here when he arrived in the area, by way of Bergamo and Milan. He knew the name, but as Sassicaia was a humble *vino da tavola* at the time, no precise origin was given on the label. He had an idea that he wanted a vineyard, and he did not want to be too far from the sea as he thought he could go fishing as well as make wine. The origin of the name Grattamacco is intriguing: *macco* describes pieces of iron ore from mining, while *gratta* refers to scraping the pieces of ore, and recalls the early mining activities in the region. Pier Mario has the highest vineyards in the region, 10 hectares in all, planted around his hillside cellar. It is reached along a winding dirt track, offering views towards the hill of Castiglioncello.

A stylish barrel cellar has recently been built. Pier Mario talked about the need for natural insulation rather than artificial air conditioning, so there are six 'windows' that open out onto bare earth, which helps maintain the correct humidity level, with a fan to circulate the air and prevent the development of any mould. At the entrance to the cellar there is a beautiful stained-glass window in deep blue, red and yellow, designed by Michael Zyw. Unusually, Pier Mario uses wooden vats for fermentation, which he prefers to stainless steel.

Pier Mario and Paola are welcoming hosts and we talked over a friendly dinner. His white wine is now a pure Vermentino, of which a quarter is fermented in barrel, to make a nicely rounded, harmonious wine, which accompanied some delicious anchovies with sage leaves fried in batter. Vermentino has a good future in Bolgheri; before Pier Mario had the traditional Trebbiano and also Sauvignon, which was 'a disaster' as it ripened far too early. Vermentino, in contrast, ripens late and does not suffer in drought. Then there are two red wines, one made from young vines, a simple Bolgheri Rosso, while the Bolgheri Superiore, which denotes a higher alcohol and a lower yield, as well as a year in barrel and six months in bottle, is a blend of Cabernet Sauvignon, Merlot and Sangiovese. Pier Mario's wine in fact spends twenty months in wood, most of which is new; it was delicious with spring lamb. We finished with some Aleatico, with its distinctive fruity orange flavours. The estate is in a state of transition, for Pier Mario has rented the property, both cellars and vineyards, for ten years to Claudio Tipa, who already has a vineyard, Colli Massari, in the new DOC of Montecucco. Meanwhile, Pier Mario's son has taken over 3 hectares of vines of his own at nearby San Vincenzo.

After Grattamacco came Ornellaia, the creation of Ludovico Antinori. Things may well change here too, as a large share of the estate was sold to the California producer Robert Mondavi in 2001, and early in 2002 Frescobaldi bought Ludovico Antinori's share, so that the ownership is now divided equally between the two companies. When I first went to Ornellaia back in 1989, the cellar was a building site. Nowadays you take a long vineyard-lined drive to a discreet, half-sunken building. The entrance hall with its marble floor and murals is a blend of California and Tuscany, and from there you go through a discreet door into a forest of stainless-steel tanks, of varying sizes, as well as a large barrel cellar. No expense has been spared here.

Ornellaia – the name comes from *ornello*, an ash tree – established an early reputation for its Sauvignon, Poggio alle Gazze – the name means a hill of magpies and there did indeed seem to be an unusually large number of magpies in the vineyards – but as the red wines of the estate have grown in stature, the decision was taken to discontinue Poggio alle Gazze, from the 2001 vintage, so that the former Sauvignon vineyards are either being replanted or being grafted with Cabernet Sauvignon or Merlot. The very first vintage of

Ornellaia was 1985, and the blend is now 65 per cent Cabernet Sauvignon with 30 per cent Merlot and 5 per cent Cabernet Franc. Although Ornellaia is often compared to Sassicaia, there is a significant difference in the composition of the two wines. Currently there are 70 hectares in production, with a total of 100 planned for the 2004 vintage, in an extensive replanting programme, making some thirty-two different vineyard components, based on soil and grape variety variations.

In the *bordelais* manner, a second wine has been produced, since 1997, Le Serre Nuove, which is aged like Ornellaia for eighteen months in wood, but with a lower proportion of new barrels, 40 as opposed to 70 per cent. A third red wine, Le Volte, is not an estate wine, but comes from grapes bought in the Maremma towards Grosseto, and includes Sangiovese, with some Cabernet Sauvignon and Merlot, which are given just six months in wood.

Finally there is Masseto, a pure Merlot, from a single 8-hectare planting, which was first produced in 1987 and since then has established a reputation as one of Italy's finest Merlots, with a price to match. It spends two years in new oak barrels, and enjoys careful blending of the different components in the vineyard; the soil is predominantly clay, with varying quantities of gravel and sand, each contributing a subtle nuance. We tasted barrel samples, with the winemaker, Thomas Duroux from Bordeaux, imitating Spiderman as he climbed three barrels high with his *pipette*. I quizzed Thomas about the similarities, or otherwise, between Bordeaux and Bolgheri; they may both enjoy a maritime influence, but the vegetation is quite different. However, the Mediterranean influence explains why Cabernet Sauvignon performs so well here. He also feels that Petit Verdot would also be successful, maybe better than Syrah, which is grown in the region.

Ludovico Antinori is now embarking on a new project with his brother Piero, and their nephew, Niccolò Marzichi Lenzi, in a putative DOC, Terratico di Bibbona, that will cover vineyards between Montescudaio and Bolgheri, on an estate called Campo di Sasso. Their plan is to plant 60 hectares of Merlot, Cabernet Sauvignon and Cabernet Franc and produce a wine that will rival Ornellaia and Sassicaia in quality.

Originally Piero Antinori produced a simple *rosato* called Scalabrone from his family vineyards in Bolgheri, but over the last few years a dramatic transformation has taken place, with the first vintage of Guado al Tasso produced in 1990, accompanied by a vast planting programme. Of a total of 300 hectares planted, just half were in production in 2002, covering a vast expanse of flattish land between two parallel roads. An elegant cellar has been built, with a pretty pink facade and a magnificent barrel room, five barrels high, where the wine is given eighteen months' oak ageing. It was quite awe-inspiring. Piero Antinori explained how the composition of Guado al Tasso has changed over the last ten years; first it was a Cabernet blend not dissimilar to his cousin's wine at Sassicaia, but now it includes tiny amounts of Merlot, Syrah and Petit Verdot, while Cabernet Sauvignon remains the most important constituent. The 1999 vintage, drunk with some local pheasant and asparagus, had supple tannins with a harmonious balance; it was already an enjoyable glass of wine, but with further potential. *Guado* is the name of a nearby ford, while *tasso* is a local animal similar to a racoon. Piero explained how Petit Verdot was not yet allowed, but that has never stopped an Italian winemaker in the past. He also admitted that Sangiovese did not give the quality he would have expected from the region, and that is an opinion voiced by other producers. The white wine is a pure Vermentino, with that delicious fresh sappy fruit, typical of Vermentino from the Tuscan coast. We sipped it as an aperitif, sitting on the terrace of the house that Piero's parents built after their marriage in the 1920s, with views out to sea through the dense green parasol pines. The *rosato* has also improved enormously over the years, benefiting from new technology, to make fresh fruity wine.

The other big name in Bolgheri is Angelo Gaja, the renowned Piedmont producer of Barbaresco and Barolo, who in recent years has ventured into Tuscany, first to Montalcino and then to Bolgheri. In 1996 he bought a traditional estate, with fruit trees, olive trees and animals, as well as vines. It was called Santa Teresa, and the Pavoletti family, two brothers and a sister, were very reluctant to sell. Consequently Gaja renamed the property Ca' Marcanda, an expression which describes a long discussion in Piedmontese dialect. Indeed, the family had taken much persuasion to finally agree to part with their property and Gaja's own account of the lengthy transactions, stretching his tenacity and powers of persuasion to the limit, is quite hilarious. The first vintage was 2000, with three wines, Ca' Marcanda, Promis and Magari. Sixty hectares have been planted, with Cabernet Sauvignon, Franc and Merlot, and a little Syrah. Any Sangiovese in the blend is brought from Montalcino, so that Promis includes 10 per cent Sangiovese, as well as 55 per cent Merlot and 35 per cent Syrah, given twelve months' ageing. Magari, an all-embracing word in Italian to cover a multitude of reactions to a situation – if only, you bet, no such luck, of course, and how, to mention but a few – is a blend of 50 per cent Merlot and 25 per cent each of Cabernet Sauvignon and Cabernet Franc, while Ca' Marcanda is 50 per cent Merlot, 40 per cent Cabernet Sauvignon and 10 per cent Cabernet Franc, with eighteen months' ageing, like Magari. First impressions are of wines that are stylish, as one would expect from Gaja, but also expensive.

A state-of-the-art cellar has been built, partially underground, which was not yet complete in the spring of 2002. The design is original, but meets the requirements of modern winemaking, with light relief provided by various sculptures – what our guide described as *libera interpretazione*. One was a rather splendid wooden hedgehog – at least I think it was a hedgehog – and it added a splash of humour to an austere cellar setting with black floors and metal columns. They have used bronze, copper, local stone, black basalt and some extraordinary varnished rusted steel. The two vast floors of barrels are splendidly spacious, avoiding the need to stack the barrels.

The ruined tower of Donoratico provided a fitting destination for a walk. We left our car by a clump of olive trees, all with their roots confined to sacking; about to be planted, we thought, but we later met their owner, who said no, on the contrary, for some reason they were not producing any olives, and so he was selling them as ornamental trees. He also told us that he had climbed to the top of the tower of Donoratico as a small boy. We passed some vineyards; a hawk was hovering overhead, doubtless looking for its lunch, and then the road began to climb, past cistus and wild honeysuckle and delicate pink wild gladioli. There were countless butterflies, some a tiny brilliant blue and others bright yellow. The tower was built in the ninth century by the Counts of Donaratico, the Gherardesca family, to defend the coast from enemy incursions, namely the Saracens, and the enemies of the republic of Pisa. It was partially destroyed by Alfonso of Aragon when he invaded the Maremma in the middle of the fifteenth century, and Ugolino Gherardesca was starved to death here with his sons and nephews, as described by Dante in Canto 33 of the *Inferno*. We picnicked at the foot of the tower, enjoying views of the sea, with some rather sinister black crows circling overhead.

I shall always remember my visit to Le Macchiole. We had been told that Eugenio Campolmi was suffering from cancer and indeed he was wearing a baseball cap to disguise the effects of chemotherapy, but his mental attitude was astonishing. He was so positive and full of enthusiasm, discussing projects for the future, such as rebuilding his cellar, and cheerful almost to the point of ebullience. It was therefore with great sadness that I read of his death a couple of months later. He will certainly be remembered as one of the pioneers of Bolgheri, and his wife, Cinzia, together with their oenologist Luca d'Attoma, plans to continue his work in the vineyard and cellar.

Eugenio's beginnings were modest. His family ran a bar on the Aurelia, the main road to Rome, which runs along the coast, and had vines for their simple house wine. But Eugenio wanted to do something more serious, even though he had never studied winemaking, and began planting Cabernet Sauvignon, initially just three experimental rows, and then gradually he included Cabernet Franc, Merlot and Syrah, as well as Chardonnay, Sauvignon and Vermentino. At the beginning he had Trebbiano and Sangiovese, but had come to realize that Sangiovese simply does not perform well in Bolgheri; the soil is too fertile and the climate too sunny, so that the wines become too fat. We wandered round the cellar, glasses in hand, tasting from barrels, while Eugenio talked about his wines and his plans. He has a large underground barrel hall, with a window to the bare earth, to show the very stony soil, mixed with clay. The stones provide good drainage while the clay maintains humidity, and you could see thick vines roots at 5.5 metres deep, making their way between the stones.

Eugenio's range has evolved over the years. Paleo Bianco, after a weed from the nearby marshes, is a blend of Sauvignon and Chardonnay, but no longer includes any Vermentino, while Paleo Rosso has also developed from a blend of Cabernet Sauvignon and Cabernet Franc to become a pure Cabernet Franc, which was one of Eugenio's particular enthusiasms. He had worked with Cabernet Franc for twelve years and was the only producer to make a pure example. He compared it with Cabernet Sauvignon; it ripens well eight years out of ten, as opposed to two years out of ten for Cabernet Sauvignon. The bunches are looser, giving good aeration of the grapes, and although it may produce less juice than Cabernet Sauvignon, the flavours are delicious, with lovely smoky berry fruit, balanced with tannins. You don't get the vegetal flavours in Bolgheri that you can get in the north, in Trentino. On the other hand, Cabernet Sauvignon he decries as *un fratello scemo, un cavallo pazzo*, 'an idiot brother, a mad horse', as it is so unpredictable so that you can never tell how it is going to age in barrel, and it varies each year. Syrah is another enthusiasm; a 3-hectare vineyard of Cabernet Sauvignon has been replanted with Syrah, with an increased density of 10,000 plants per hectare. It was too soon to see much effect, but so far he thought that the vines produced smaller berries in smaller bunches, but with more intense flavours, but with the proviso that they are still young vines. For Eugenio, Australian Syrah was too sweet and French Syrah could be too acidic, while Scrio, as he called his wine, is ripe and perfumed, with old-world elegance. The pure Merlot is called Messorio, and that too has a fine concentration of fruit. However, Eugenio was firmly against what he called *vini americani, bomboloni*, which are too heavy and overripe. He was very much his own person, making wines with their own individuality; he criticized some of his fellow growers, suggesting that everyone was copying everyone else. 'Now they are all trying Petit Verdot.' Hopefully Cinzia and Luca d'Attoma will maintain the reputation of Le Macchiole and the memory of Eugenio Campolmi.

Michele Satta comes from Varese, near Milan, and studied agriculture at Milan and Pisa universities, and then, as he put it, he fell in love with wine. His first vintage, in 1984, was a typical *contadino* wine sold in glass demijohns; then in 1988 he built a cellar, began bottling his wine and did a course at the leading oenology school of San Michele in the Alto Adige. Things have progressed enormously over the last fifteen years. He now owns 15 hectares and rents a further 15. His oenologist, Attilio Pagli, who has known Michele since 1985, sees his role as helping Michele, and his other clients, to develop their own idea of their wines. He is adamant that Michele's wine is his alone, and that he simply helps him to understand his individual style.

Michele's cellar is impressive, not on the scale of Gaja or Antinori, but one wall is a rock face, providing a dramatic backdrop to tanks and barrels, including a row of wooden fermentation vats. For Michele it is *una cantina viva, una famiglia,* a living cellar and a family. The tasting area is welcoming, with a counter made from old barrel ends and staves, as are the tables, with light fittings in old barrel hoops, which is all very atmospheric and effective. His white Bolgheri is a blend of Trebbiano with Vermentino; the Vermentino gives a touch of class to the Trebbiano, making an easy-to-drink, sappy dry wine. Costa di Giulia – Giulia being the lover of a Gherardesca count – Michele considers to be less technological, with more character. It is a blend of Sauvignon and Vermentino, with some delicate herbal fruit with fresh acidity. Sauvignon is difficult as it can overripen in three days and become almost *passito* and raisined. However, the 1994 Costa di Giulia had aged beautifully, to develop mature leafy notes.

Viognier is a challenge; the second vintage, the 2001, was fermented in wood and stayed in oak for six months, to produce some ripe peachy fruit with hints of bananas and cream, with a touch of tannin. It is called Giovin Re, which means young king and is also an anagram for Viognier. It is much more difficult to produce great white wine than great red wine, especially in Italy, which does not lend itself to international white wines. The Viognier may also be used to add more character to Costa di Giulia, and Michele's exploring mind is also considering Biancolella from Ischia or maybe Greco or Fiano from Campania.

As for his red wines, Michele is looking above all for elegance. He criticizes some of his fellow growers for concentrating on power. He is adamant that a wine must be elegant, even if it is simple; nor does he like the taste of wood. His best red wines are fermented in wood and then aged in barrels, but any taste of oak must be well integrated. Piastraia is a blend of equal parts of Syrah, Cabernet Sauvignon, Merlot and Sangiovese. Although it has spent twelve months in wood, the oak was not at all obvious, with attractive fruit and harmonious flavours. Cavaliere contradicts the prevailing view that a pure Sangiovese does not do well in Bolgheri, for it is pure Sangiovese, which has spent twelve months in wood, with some cedary fruit, in the 1998 vintage. Michele mused: 'It doesn't give itself airs, it doesn't have a jacket or a tie, but it is multi-faceted.' And of the 2000 Cavaliere: 'Perhaps this is my best wine,' with some firm cherry fruit. Then there is a new *cru*, I Castagni, from a nearby vineyard, which is a blend of Cabernet Sauvignon, Syrah, Sangiovese and Teroldego. His enthusiasm for Syrah was prompted by a meeting with Auguste Clape from Cornas in the Rhône Valley. But why Teroldego, a grape from the Alto Adige? He explained that he was asked by the research station at San Michele to plant an experimental vineyard, which included Petit Verdot, Tempranillo and Grenache, which have all subsequently been pulled up, and also Teroldego, which he liked and has kept for its complexity of fruit and elegance. It promised well.

Michele Satta is generous with his encouragement and advice, as his neighbour, Enrico Santini, would be the first to acknowledge, for it was Michele who kindled his latent passion for agriculture. Until 1995 he ran a small supermarket and then in 1996 began working with Michele, while planting his own vines in 1998, and then a couple of years later it was the moment to go it alone for the 2000 vintage. For the time being Enrico has a small compact cellar adjoining his house, but he was planning a new cellar for 2003 and has expanded to 14 hectares of vines, from which he makes three wines, an unoaked white Campo alla Casa, with 60 per cent Vermentino blended with 40 per cent Sauvignon; Poggio al Moro, a blend of 40 per cent Sangiovese, 30 per cent Cabernet Sauvignon, 20 per cent Syrah and 10 per cent Merlot, given just four months in barrel, and Montepergoli, from 40 per cent Merlot, 35 per cent Cabernet Sauvignon, 20 per cent Syrah and 5 per cent Sangiovese, given eighteen months in *barriques*. A little black and white kitten called Tornado, after Zorro's horse, tried to mountaineer up my back as we talked, which proved somewhat distracting for note-taking, but none the less I retained the impression that Enrico has been a keen pupil, paying meticulous attention to detail. He keeps the various components of his wines separately to see how they develop, in a variety of barrels from different coopers, all French, and the results were there to taste in the glass, with some ripe fruit and appealing flavours. Enrico Santini deserves to do well.

The changes in Bolgheri over the past few years have been enormous, with the expansion of the so-called international varieties, notably Cabernet Sauvignon, but also Syrah and Merlot. However, Attilio Pagli would suggest that there is a risk of losing not the *tipicità*, but what he calls the *territorialità*, the concept of territory. You must make wines with a recognizable personality and recognizable origins, avoiding above all uniformity. In some ways they are still trying to find out what really suits the region, and that is not something that can be done from one year to the next.

The interest in Bolgheri from outsiders is enormous. New wines are appearing with every vintage – in 2000, not only Enrico Santini, but Caccia al Piano di Franzini, and Guado dei Gemoli di Giovanni Chiappini. Other newcomers include Knauff, Delia Viader from California in association with a Piedmontese, Gianni Gagliardi. A terraced vineyard is being planted high up in the *macchia* at Campo di Sasso by a Milanese, Erika Ratti. And doubtless there will be more to come. However, land values have soared; Angelo Gaja's purchase was enough to cause prices to spiral overnight, but this could well benefit the adjoining regions of Montescudaio and Val di Cornia, as potential investors look further afield. It will be fascinating to watch an area in evolution. But I would like to give the last word to Michele Satta, who attributes Bolgheri's success to the winegrowers' realization of the requirements of the international market, namely a combination of elegance and fruit. That is just what you find in so many of the wines of Bolgheri.

Montescudaio

· *May* ·

La Nocera, Terriccio, Sorbaiano and Poggio Gagliardo

THE UNASSUMING LITTLE village of Montescudaio gives its name to both a red and a white wine. Much of the village was rebuilt after an earthquake in 1846. There is a wide main street and a couple of churches, but nothing much seems to stir there, except in the cheerful *trattoria*, offering pasta and local wine, with views over the surrounding countryside.

The DOC of Montescudaio was created in 1977, separating it from the mass of anonymous Chianti, and covering seven *comuni* in the Val di Cecina, namely Montescudaio itself, as well as Casale Marittima, Castellina Marittima, Riparbella, Guardistallo and parts of Santa Luce and Montecatini Val di Cecina. Initially the permitted grape varieties were similar to those of Chianti, namely Sangiovese and Canaiolo, with Trebbiano the mainstay of the white wine, but in 2000 the rules were changed to allow for more international blends. A simple Montescudaio *rosso* now needs only include 50 per cent of Sangiovese, with *riserva* denoting two years' ageing; the white includes Vermentino and Malvasia, as well as Trebbiano, and the mention of a grape variety on the label denotes a minimum of 85 per cent of that variety, which may be Sangiovese, Cabernet Sauvignon, Merlot, Chardonnay or Sauvignon. The authorities have responded to market demand, but in reality the DOC has no real identity. The producers observe the success of nearby Bolgheri with a certain envy and adopt the prevalent *laissez-faire* attitude towards their local *disciplinari*. Few of the best wines mention Montescudaio on the label and it is the reputation of the estate that counts, of which there are a handful working well, with just fourteen members of the *consorzio*, with 230 hectares in production, and a further 60 hectares planted in the spring of 2002. However, unlike Bolgheri, the DOC has no obvious leader or pacesetter. As Signora Picciolini from Sorbaiano observed, the new DOCs, such as Bolgheri and Val di Cornia, follow market demand, while the older ones, such as Montescudaio, hang on to the coattails of Chianti.

Comparisons with nearby Bolgheri are inevitable. The area is that bit further from the sea and therefore slightly higher in altitude at 200 metres, and therefore cooler, with a greater contrast of day and night-time temperatures. There is also a significant difference in the price of land, without vines, in the two areas, namely €20,000 (40 million lire) per hectare in Montescudaio, as opposed to €155,000 (300 million lire) per hectare in Bolgheri, a difference which is attracting some investment in the area, but not necessarily for the wines of Montescudaio itself.

The estate of La Nocera is a case in point. It is just outside the village of Casale Marittima, but as the manager, Stefano Moscatelli, explained, they may be within the DOC of Montescudaio, but they are certainly not intending to make Montescudaio. The property has belonged to a Swiss woman from Lugano, Maria-Pia Pagani, for some thirty years, but it was only recently that she decided to do something with her land. Michele Satta from Bolgheri gave her the initial advice to plant 5 hectares of Cabernet Sauvignon, Merlot and Sangiovese, which produced their first crop in 2000; the first wine was made in 2001 and the barrel samples tasted in the spring of 2002 held plenty of promise. Two wines, or maybe three, are planned, a pure Sangiovese and a Cabernet Merlot blend, or maybe two single varietals. It was too soon to decide.

We walked through the vineyards, with views of the pretty hilltop village of Casale Marittima in the distance. The vines were beautifully tended, with the rosebushes at the end of each row just coming into flower. The vines are planted quite densely, with 5600 or 6000 plants per hectare. The soil is heavy clay and there is no water for irrigation; Stefano described it *una terraccia*, or *brutta terra*; in other words, land on which it is virtually impossible to grow anything. The remains of an Etruscan tomb were found there some fifteen years ago. The original artefacts are now in the municipal museum in Cecina and the tomb itself is a grass-covered mound surrounded by tiny cypresses. There are no other wine producers in Casale Marittima, with the neighbouring hillsides covered with ripening wheat, with hay-making in an adjacent field. The neat cellar is unobtrusively built into the hillside and a lone walnut, recalling the origin of the name of the estate, remains in splendid solitude. It presents a challenging opportunity for someone fresh from studies, as Stefano is, but he deserves to do well.

The scale contrasts dramatically with Terriccio. We met Dott. Rossi, or, to give him his full title, Cavaliere Gian Annibale Rossi di Medelana. He is confined to a wheelchair, following a riding accident a number of years ago, but you cannot help but be impressed by his energy and determination. Nor did the accident destroy his love of horses, which he breeds for show-jumping. He took us for a drive, rather than a walk, around his estate, and maybe this was just as well, for we spent two hours in the Range Rover without even leaving the property, as it totals some 1700 hectares, of which about 50 are vineyards, scattered all over the estate, with new plantings up on the hillsides at 400 metres and older vineyards on flatter land at 25 to 60 metres. It can cost as much as € 77,500 (150 million lire) to plant a hectare of vines. The difficult thing is to prepare the land; you need to excavate down to over a metre to prepare the ground and remove any rocks. There were huge boulders piled up at the side of the vineyards. Dott. Rossi explained how his great-grandfather had bought Terriccio in 1923, after Mussolini's compulsory purchase of his land near Rome as part of his agrarian reform. Terriccio had originally belonged to the Poniatowski family, and when the Italian side died out, the French side inherited, only to have their land sequestered and subsequently sold during the First World War. Dott. Rossi came here twenty-five years ago, and started developing his vineyards to put his first wine in bottle in 1992.

We drove through extensive woodland; at times it felt as though we were on safari, forging our way along narrow, bumpy, overgrown tracks, with branches of shrubs whipping against the windscreen of the vehicle. The traditional *macchia* comprises oak trees, cork oak, heather, juniper and cistus bushes. There used to be iron and copper mines in the hills here, dating from the Etruscans, and an attempt was made to revive the mines during the First World War. The chocolate-brown and red soil indicates the presence of copper. You can spot the remains of the castle of Terriccio on a hillside through the trees; it dates back to the eleventh century. Two large pillars mark the entrance to the estate, which takes you along a long drive, lined with cypresses, pine trees and holm oaks, and then past fields of fresh green wheat, and a reservoir with ducks, to a cluster of houses. Not so long ago some sixty-five families lived on the property; now there are just eighteen people, all of whom are employed on the estate.

Dott. Rossi talked about his vineyards; for red grapes he has Cabernet Sauvignon, some Cabernet Franc and Merlot, and also some experimental Petit Verdot in a south-facing vineyard. It might not be allowed in the DOC, but it seems that for an IGT anything goes. There is also some experimental Tannat and Mourvèdre, which were just coming into production. Dott. Rossi was wondering about blending Syrah with Tannat, thus combining elegance with strength. The young vines are irrigated and he uses no fertilizers or pesticides in his vineyards, but does not claim to be wholly organic. We passed a group of workers, hard at work trimming the vegetation.

Dott. Rossi produces four wines. A pure Chardonnay called Rondinaia after the *rondini*, or swallows, had some light buttery fruit and, refreshingly, not a trace of oak. Tassinaia is a blend of Cabernet Sauvignon, Merlot and Sangiovese, in equal parts, given some thirteen months in oak to make a rounded, accessible wine. Con Vento is a pure Sauvignon, and Lupicaia a Cabernet Sauvignon and Merlot blend, with a drop of Petit Verdot. We tasted on the terrace, while Dott. Rossi's large bulldog sat under his wheelchair and every so often scratched himself energetically. 'Suddenly I think there is an earthquake,' observed his owner, as the wheelchair started vibrating. And the wines were poured by one of several nubile young helpers, all looking as though they had been selected by a Hollywood casting director.

Sorbaiano is on a hill opposite the village of Montecatini Val di Cecina. There are views across the valley to Volterra, the city that is known for its alabaster, as well as to the city's salt works, with their unsightly grey slag heaps of salt. Signora Picciolini explained how her mother had bought the property, with an elegant eighteenth-century villa, from an old Volterra family back in 1958. As well as vines, there are olive trees and fields of wheat. She makes five wines, under the guidance of Vittorio Fiore, which mostly conform to the DOC. Montescudaio *bianco* is mainly Trebbiano, with some Vermentino and Chardonnay; Lucestraia *bianca* consists of the same grape varieties, though with less Trebbiano, and both the Chardonnay and Vermentino are fermented in oak. Sorbaiono *rosso* is a blend of Sangiovese and Malvasia Nera, with the classic sour cherries of Sangiovese, while Pian del Conte is a partially oak-aged pure Sangiovese, and Rosso delle Miniere a blend of Sangiovese, Cabernet Sauvignon and Malvasia Nera, all aged in oak to give some rounded ripe fruit. The name refers to the old copper mines nearby, which functioned until the beginning of the last century. As president of the growers' *consorzio*, Signora Picciolini is very aware that Montescudaio needs what she called 'greater visibility', and also as much flexibility as possible within the *disciplinari* for the DOC.

Poggio Gagliardo, in contrast, lies on the western edge of the DOC, in the suburbs of Cecina. The estate has belonged to a Piedmontese family, Surbone, since 1969, and is managed by Silvia Menicagli, who took us for a drive through the vineyards. With its proximity to the coast, the terrain here is quite different. Altogether they have 450 hectares, including 60 of vines, with olive trees, wheat and barley, sunflowers, as well as woods, and Chiana cattle, the large creamy Tuscan cattle, including a couple of light beige calves, who will turn cream with age. They were confined to the cowshed the morning of our visit, as they had escaped the previous day. A cluster of buildings includes the cellars, all painted an attractive dark yellow, and they have plans to encourage more visitors, with a shop and a little museum.

They have bottled wine at Poggio Gagliardo since 1969 and now make some ten different wines, based on traditional varieties like Trebbiano, Malvasia and Vermentino, as well as Chardonnay for whites, with reds from Sangiovese, Canaiolo, Cabernet Sauvignon and Cabernet Franc and Merlot, with variations of different blends and barrel ageing. The simple Montescudaio *rosso* had a pleasing cherry fruitiness; Rovo from Tuscan varieties, with just a drop of Cabernet Sauvignon, was rounded and smoky; Gobbo ai Pianacce, from Merlot, with some Sangiovese and Cabernet Sauvignon, given eighteen months in wood, was firm and smoky, while Anonimo, mainly Cabernet Sauvignon with some Merlot and Sangiovese, also given eighteen months in wood, had some stylish elegance. Lastly there was an oddity, Rovo *chinato*, picking up the old Piedmontese tradition of adding quinine to Barolo, with herbal overtones. It all served to illustrate the diversity of the area, both its originality but also its lack of direction.

Luca Noti at La Regola, another emerging estate, may insist that

Montescudaio has nothing to be jealous of compared to Bolgheri, but however good the *terroir* is, the region has no reputation as yet. Sangiovese in Montescudaio makes attractively elegant but not powerful wines, while the Bordeaux varieties perform differently here from Bolgheri, an inevitable result of the differences in *terroir*. But within the DOC there is a world of difference between Cecina and Montecatini, and no obvious leader amongst a group of emerging estates, all intent on establishing their own individual reputations irrespective of their local DOC.

Val di Cornia and Suvereto

· May ·

Walk around Suvereto and to Belvedere; visits to Tua Rita, Gualdo del Re and Ambrosini in Suvereto; Petra; Jacopo Banti at Campiglia Marittima; Pierluigi Bonti in Piombino; Populonia

VAL DI CORNIA IS ONE of several emerging denominations of the Maremma, lying to the south of Bolgheri and following closely in its wake. The DOC was created in 1990 and covers vineyards in the villages and towns of Piombino, Campiglia Marittima, San Vincenzo, Suvereto, Monteverdi and Sassetta, all touching the valley of the river Cornia, which flows into the Mediterranean at Piombino. Then in 2001 Suvereto was recognized as a separate sub-zone. It is just south of Bolgheri and you cannot help sensing that the producers there are influenced by the success of that particularly international DOC. As in Bolgheri, Sangiovese is not very important, while the so-called international grape varieties are much more highly considered; *barriques* rather than *botti* are the order of the day, and although the wines are not yet as well known as the great names of Bolgheri, they undoubtedly benefit from their proximity to Bolgheri and are following fast in its footsteps.

San Vincenzo is a smart seaside resort, with one of the region's finest restaurants, Il Gambero Rosso; sadly it was closed the week we were there. As an industrial town, dominated by now defunct steelworks, and an important port, with boats leaving for the island of Elba and further afield, Piombino seems an unlikely situation for a vineyard. However, it boasts an unexpectedly attractive historical centre, a rewarding archaeological museum and vineyards in the outskirts. Sassetta is a pretty little village perched on the side of the hill, with narrow alleyways and a profusion of flowerpots crammed into every spare nook and cranny, not just the statutory geraniums, but herbs such as basil and parsley, and even some tomatoes. The road to Suvereto followed the hillside from Sassetta past a ruined twelfth-century church, the Chiesa della Santissima Annunziata, that now looks sadly neglected, and then on through forests of

cork oak. They had recently been harvested and their smooth dark brown trunks looked like naked poodles.

The little hilltop town of Suvereto merits a detour, as the guidebooks would say. The city walls remain intact; the Romanesque church, San Giusto, at the entrance to the town has an elegant facade, adorned with columns and lions, and the former convent of San Francesco, which was built in 1288 and suppressed in 1808, now houses flats for *agriturismo*, around attractive cloisters in soft red stone. The adjoining Church of the Crucifix was built in the sixteenth century to house a sculpture of Christ, which is processed through the town each year on 15 September. A ruined castle, La Rocca, was firmly closed, but from the viewpoint just below, we looked over vineyards that we would later visit, those of Tua Rita and Gualdo del Re. Suvereto's only restaurant of note, L'Ombrone, is suitably characterful, and owned by someone who could only be described as obsessive. Giancarlo Bini has written a book on the olive, *L'olivo, albero degli dei*, and offers a choice of 178 different oils, listed not unlike a wine list by origin, and also according to flavour and style, with the olive varieties used for each oil. It made dressing a salad distinctly complicated. When we finished our meal with an *espresso* coffee, he offered us a choice of twenty-two different coffees, not to mention fifty-one different sugars. Outside we glanced in an estate agent's window; 240,000 Euros would have bought us 8 hectares of land, described as an ideal position for a vineyard, or for 170,000 Euros we could have purchased 6 hectares, including 150 olive trees, again in an ideal spot for a vineyard. Since my previous visit to Suvereto some six years earlier, there is a definite feeling that wine is gaining in importance in the local economy.

We headed towards Belvedere, a little village on a hill outside Suvereto, which indeed lives up to its name, offering broad vistas over the surrounding countryside. The roadside was a profusion of wild flowers, brilliant red poppies, white and yellow daisies, ladies' slipper, borage and serapia orchids. We passed an old *lavatoio*, with two large and two small basins, still fed by a running stream of refreshing water. Then the path turned off the road, up through the woods and alongside a small vineyard with a little stone hut and, outside it, a swivelling office chair, but there was no one to be seen. Did someone come here for a siesta, or to sit and admire their vines?

Belvedere was originally built as a summer refuge, for people escaping the malaria that was rampant on the coast. The simple little chapel of San Tommaso was built by the local Appiani family, with their crest above the door, dated 1560. We continued down the hill back to Suvereto, past a tiny vineyard, with vegetables growing under the vines, carrots, lettuce and rocket. There are views over the vineyards of Suvereto, with the perfume of wild roses and the scent of pine trees in the air after the rain of the morning.

Tua Rita is the estate that has done much to establish the reputation of Suvereto as a vineyard area, but in true Italian manner without paying much attention to the DOC regulations of Val di Cornia. Rita Tua explained that she preferred to sell her wines as IGT; for her the DOC was no guarantee of quality; that only came from the reputation of the producer. The estate has grown considerably in size and reputation since my first visit in 1996. Their beginnings were quite modest. Rita explained how she and her husband were living and working in Piombino, as distributors of video games and jukeboxes and so on. Her husband, Virgilio, was born in nearby Follónica and had always wanted to return to the countryside, and so they made the move inland, buying their first vineyards in 1984, planting Cabernet Sauvignon and Merlot in 1988, and bottling their first wine in 1992. Until then they had sold their wine *sfuso*. Nowadays they have 12 hectares in production, with another 8 planted, concentrating mainly on Cabernet Sauvignon and Merlot, with a little Sangiovese. Rita explained how the land around Suvereto had originally been planted with wheat and olive trees. A new cellar was under construction, with the stainless-steel vats in place and a barrel cellar taking shape, with prefabricated arches and columns, designed to house two years' wine. Rita explained how they will be able to heat under the floor to encourage the malolactic fermentation. The bottling line was already functioning, with a bright orange bouncy castle in the corner for the benefit of her grandchildren. For the moment the barrels are accommodated on the ground floor of their house, in what were once the old stables. Any new cellar is an enormous investment, but the local banks are more sympathetic to wine producers than ever before.

Rita's wines are made with the guidance of Stefano Chioccioli; they are all IGT rather than DOC, each with a fantasy name. For Rita, Suvereto as yet has no tipicity; ten years ago nearly everything was sold in bulk, so there is very little history of bottling, or experience of how the wines age in bottle. Her white wine, Lodano, after a nearby stream, is a blend of Riesling, Gewürztraminer and Chardonnay, which spends twelve months in new oak. The aromatic varieties were originally planted to add flavour to Trebbiano, which was once the only white variety here. However, although they do enhance the wine, which promised well, they are problematic as they ripen unevenly, and often much too early, even as soon as 10 August.

Perlato del Bosco, after the marble quarry on the adjoining hill, is a pure Sangiovese, given twelve months' oak ageing, and could be a DOC. Giusti di Nostri – Nostri is the address of Tua Rita, and Giusti the church of Suvereto – consists of 60 per cent Cabernet, both Sauvignon and Franc, with some Merlot, giving some rounded fruit and good tannins. Merlot grows well here as illustrated by a pure Merlot, Redigaffi, named after another stream, which exuded ripe plummy fruit. Rita then took us for a drive through her vineyards – this proved to be a mistake as we very nearly got stuck in the mud. Her skilful driving extricated the car, after we had got out in order to lighten the load, and then it took another fifteen minutes to remove the sticky red clay from our shoes!

Gualdo del Re is just down the road and Teresa Rossi, a vivacious blond curly-haired woman, gave us a friendly welcome. She explained how her husband Nico's grandfather had bought their land back in 1953, just 7 hectares, of which 5 were vineyards, while the rest was cultivated for wheat or used as grazing land for animals, with some olive trees. Now they have 40 hectares, for vineyards and olive trees, and have just bought another 12 hectares. Their first vintage was 1989. Teresa explained how Suvereto is now a sub-zone of Val di Cornia, allowing either a Bordeaux blend, following the example of Bolgheri, or a varietal wine. They want to keep Sangiovese, as it is part of the region's history, but she considered Cabernet and Merlot to make the better wine. Suvereto requires thirty months' ageing, of which eighteen must be in wood, while Val di Cornia does not have any ageing requirements. Teresa has abandoned the old *botti*, so that her neat cellar has *barriques* and 500-litre *tonneaux*, as well as stainless-steel vats. Sangiovese does better in the larger wood, while Cabernet needs something stronger. The *terroir* of Suvereto is quite distinctive, for the vineyards are protected by an amphitheatre of hills, and the soil is quite different from elsewhere in the DOC, for it is based on clay that is often red in colour, and some vineyards are very stony. There are about 500 hectares of vines, but not all are in production yet, and there is still scope for further planting.

We sat in the tasting room and talked. There was a word of warning to potential teetotallers: *A chi non beve vino, Dio neghi anche l'acqua.* To him who does not drink wine, God also denies water. Eliseo is a simple white wine, from Trebbiano, with some Clairette, Vermentino and Malvasia, the old white varieties of the area. Valentina is a pure Vermentino, of which a tiny amount is aged in wood. The white Gualdo del Re, fermented in new *tonneaux*, comes from Pinot Bianco, which the vine nursery had sent instead of Chardonnay. It seemed a happy mistake. Eliseo Rosso is a simple red, from traditional varieties, Sangiovese, Canaiolo and Malvasia Nera, while Gualdo del Re *rosso*, from Sangiovese, is given two years in *tonneaux* and is more serious in stature. Federico Primo, a pure Cabernet Sauvignon, with eighteen months in oak, certainly illustrates the potential of the Bordelais varieties, as did Il Rennero, a pure Merlot, also given eighteen months' oak ageing. The Merlot was plummier and fruitier, while the Cabernet was more elegant.

In some ways this is a wine area that is still searching for a direction, with a broad choice of grape varieties. Take the example of Lorella Ambrosini and Roberto Fanucci at Ambrosini. They have 2 hectares to plant and want to create a new wine, but are not sure what to plant. Roberto explained that they are considering Cabernet Sauvignon, but maybe also Montepulciano or Syrah. They also believe in Sangiovese, 'but it is a difficult variety. You need a good clone, with small bunches, not the traditional large-bunched Sangiovese.' Their Tabarò is a cheerful, fruity Sangiovese, with sour cherry fruit and not a trace of oak. They have grafted some Petit Verdot onto Trebbiano, just one experimental row, which produced just 50 litres in 2001. Grafting is a successful and efficient way of changing the composition of your vineyard, as the climate is sufficiently mild on the Tuscan coast.

The Ambrosini family originated from the Abruzzi and Lorella's father bought the estate back in 1953, but they did not bottle their first wine until 1983, and now have a neat little cellar adjoining the house. Trebbiano and Malvasia have disappeared from the vineyards, replaced by Vermentino and Ansonica, and for red wines they have Sangiovese, Merlot and Syrah, as well as Montepulciano, in deference to their Abruzzese origins. Apparently it is related to Sangiovese. Reflesso Antico is a pure Montepulciano, which spends twelve months in *barriques* and *tonneaux*, with some ripe sturdy fruit. Subetum, recalling the old name for Suvereto, with a reference to the cork oaks in the woods, carries the coat of arms of Suvereto on the label, with the lion, an *orcia* and a cork oak. As for the wine, it is a blend of Sangiovese, Merlot as well as Syrah, of which just 10 per cent is allowed in the DOC. For the moment they are alone in having Syrah, having begun with just 400 vines and now have one and half hectares.

Just within the confines of the *comune* of Suvereto, almost closer to Massa Marittima, is the brand-new estate of Petra, the creation of the Moretti family, who produce sparkling wine at Bellavista in northern Italy in the DOC of Franciacorta. The family money was made in the construction business and the locals have watched the building of the new cellars with a certain fascination. These are no ordinary cellars. I was told that they look like an Egyptian pyramid. The design is the work of the Ticino architect Mario Botta; this was his first wine cellar and there is no doubt that the external design is like no other wine cellar, with its soft red stone, *pietra di Verona*, and circular and pyramidal shapes. The building materials are those produced by the family business. Inside the design is entirely appropriate to a streamlined modern wine cellar. It all works by gravity; both temperature and humidity are carefully controlled in the fermentation cellars and the barrel rooms. A wonderful sense of space pervades the cellar, a rare luxury in many functional wineries.

We met Francesca Moretti, who explained that after his success with sparkling wine, her father, Vittorio, wanted to try his hand at red wine. They approached the project very seriously, examining the soil in different areas, including Bolgheri and Elba, under the guidance of an acknowledged expert, Attilio Scienza, who is a professor at the University of Milan. Then this opportunity presented itself, a small cellar and 16 hectares of 25-year-old Cabernet Sauvignon, Merlot and Sangiovese. They have subsequently bought more land and now have a 300-hectare estate, including 93 of vines, of which 40 are in production. You sense that Vittorio Moretti is not a man to do things in half measures. His daughter admitted that her father's ambition was to *revalorizzare* the image of the Val di Cornia. He certainly succeeded with Franciacorta, so there is no reason why he should not meet this challenge either.

The new cellar was used for the first time in 2002, although the first wine was made from the old vineyards in 1997, in the old cellar, really just to assess the potential. Things really got going in 1999. For the moment they make two wines, an IGT Petra, from Cabernet and Merlot, and a DOC, with 70 per cent Sangiovese, and there are plans for a third wine, a pure Merlot. The best grapes are fermented in 100-hectolitre Allier vats, but not everything will go into wood, only the most suitable batches, as they do not want the wood to become too invasive. We tasted the 2000 Suvereto, with Sangiovese from the original vineyard, and 15 per cent each of Merlot and Cabernet Sauvignon from new vineyards. The wine had spent twelve months in old wood, and has some attractive ripe fruit and supple tannins, but with a firm backbone. Francesca explained how she found Sangiovese here quite different from the rest of Tuscany; there is a freshness, with more acidity, but the wine is delicate and not so structured. I still thought that it had the energy I associate with Sangiovese. Petra, of the same vintage, with 45 per cent Cabernet Sauvignon and 55 per cent Merlot, from the original vineyards – 'the vineyard that made us buy the estate' – was aged for fifteen months in *barriques* of which one third were new. The mouth feel was quite different, with ripe cassis fruit, and long firm finish, but nonetheless an underlying elegance. And why the name Petra? It was obvious, really – a reflection on the enormous quantity of stones in the vineyard. Again, it will be fascinating to observe the development of a recently created estate.

From Suvereto we took the road back to the coast, past the entrance to the old Etruscan mines in the park of San Silvestro, to the estate of Jacopo Banti, outside the village of Campiglia Marittima. I had met Jacopo some fifteen years earlier; now it is his son Lorenzo who runs the estate, a rather shy man, with a thick Tuscan accent that stretched our Italian almost to its limits. He has 12 hectares with a further 6 just planted, with Cabernet Sauvignon, Ciliegiolo and Aleatico. The soil is very varied; here in the hills, at 200 metres, it is a rich mixture of schist and clay, in contrast to Suvereto, which is more alluvial. Once again, it seems that anything goes. Cent'omini is a blend of Clairette, with Ansonica. Clairette has always been grown here, but the wine can age too quickly and it is a vigorous vine that suffers from drought, which can result in bitterness in the wine. However, Lorenzo has found that by pruning it very hard to reduce its vigour, the bitterness disappears. Poggio Angelica is an oak-aged Vermentino, and Ceragiolo, created by his oenologist, Attilio Pagli, is a pure Ciliegiolo, with some cherry fruit, while Il Peccato is a blend of Cabernet Sauvignon with 15 per cent Merlot, and Di Campalbo the reverse. We finished with some Aleatico, a dessert wine, which is more commonly found on the nearby island of Elba. The raisined grapes produce some intense orange flavours. At least I thought that I detected oranges, while Lorenzo said that the 2000 vintage smelt of roses, and this, the 2001, reminded him of chocolate.

Nearby Campiglia Marittima is another little hilltop town, with an attractive medieval quarter and a climb to the fortress at the top, which challenges legs and lungs. The fortress, which was built by a Gherardesca, and subsequently captured by Alfonso of Aragon, is now in private hands and undergoing an extensive restoration. The church of San Lorenzo merits a visit for its painted ceilings and elegant architecture, and the central square offered a friendly café and an opportunity to watch the theatre of the Italian street.

Piombino is an unlikely destination for a vineyard walk, but preconceptions can prove surprisingly wrong. We tracked down Pierluigi Bonti at San Giusto on the outskirts of the town. He explained how his grandfather's family came from Elba, and before that Corsica, where they had had vines, before deciding to move to 'the continent', as the islanders call mainland Italy. So his grandfather bought land and sold wine *sfuso* successfully to the local restaurants, with his father establishing a reputation for their wine, especially their white wine, as far afield as Milan. Then in 1987 Pierluigi took the decision to concentrate on quality, which meant bottling his own wine for the first time. It proved a learning experience, but gradually he has developed a fine range of wines. First we talked in the rather formal sitting room and admired a crocheted tablecloth, the handiwork of his mother-in-law. He was more at ease in his cellar, a rather chaotic vinification cellar, and a neater barrel room under the house, with elegant brick arches, built in the eighteenth century. He first began working with oak in 1990, buying his first barrels from Ornellaia.

Although he has planted some Cabernet and Merlot, he describes himself as a traditionalist. You must have the Tuscan varieties; Sangiovese is compulsory, even if it is more temperamental than Cabernet Sauvignon. For the moment he makes five wines: Bontesco *bianco* is based on Trebbiano, or rather the Elba clone, Procanico, with some Biancone and Malvasia Bianco. It was a touch salty, with fresh acidity, conveying a taste of the sea. His best white wine is a pure Vermentino, which performs well on the Tuscan coast. Rosso degli Appiani recalls the name of the local lords of the fourteenth and fifteenth centuries and the family who also owned part of Elba. The wine is a blend of Sangiovese, with 30 per cent Montepulciano, which is not allowed in the DOC, but Pierluigi likes it for its deeper colour, while San Giusto is an oak-aged pure Sangiovese.

Pierluigi's vineyards are on the hill near his house, affording wonderful views out towards Elba, with ships leaving the port of Piombino. You could make out the castle of the Appiani close to the port, and in the distance Monte Argentario. Pierluigi talked about the microclimate of the Piombino area, explaining how much warmer it is here, with a difference of as much as 5° just two kilometres away. The plain between Piombino and Campiglia, although technically part of the Cornia valley, is not included with the DOC, while

Piombino may possibly have been linked to Elba centuries ago. We admired the neat new plantings of Cabernet Sauvignon and Merlot, their young green leaves forming a contrast with the deep red of the soil, and the surrounding *macchia*, with cistus flowers galore. Apparently the leaves of the cistus were once used for scouring plates. Then Pierluigi led us through the thick green *macchia*, so dense that it eliminated any sunlight, to his hunting platform which offered views over the sea, with Elba and other islands in the distance. The contrast of the deep green *macchia* with the brilliance of the blue sea in bright sunlight was breathtaking.

There is a track that leads to the Etruscan remains at Populonia, but time prevented us from taking it. Instead we went by car, on another day, to meet Carlo and Francesca Gasparri. Carlo explained how his grandfather had bought the estate of Populonia back in 1936 when it included hectares of farmland, as well as the archaeological sites and the castle and village of Populonia. The farmland was expropriated as part of the agrarian reform of the 1950s and now Carlo and his family run the castle as a tourist attraction. It was a sunny Saturday morning and Carlo proved to be a willing and informative guide to the excavations taking place on the hillside by the castle. There are extensive necropoli on the coastal plain by the little port of Baratti, but now the acropolis is being excavated. We learnt that in the sixth century BC, the golden age of the Etruscans, Populonia was one of the biggest ports of the Mediterranean, with a flourishing trade in iron ore from Elba. At that time as many as 25,000 people lived here. Subsequently the Romans arrived, and when a vineyard was pulled up some years ago, a Roman road came to light. We walked through the *macchia* past the various excavation sites, stamping our feet loudly to frighten away snakes. There were remains of walls and arches; Carlo pointed out a spot where there had been a magnificent mosaic, a pattern of various Mediterranean fish, which is now in the archaeological museum of Piombino.

The village of Populonia is dominated by the remains of the castle and its tower, which offers views across the sparkling water to Elba. There is a small museum boasting the largest private collection of Etruscan artefacts, pieces of pottery, jewellery and amphora, and the single street, running the length of the village, houses shops of tempting craftwork. In winter the population is just fourteen, with many more in the summer, including some 100,000 visitors to the tower each year. In the Middle Ages Populonia merited its own bishopric and the title still exists today, as an honorary post held by a member of the Curia, even though the village is a shadow of its former self. Suddenly it was time to leave and head further south into the Maremma.

Monteregio di Massa Marittima and a Detour for *Grappa*

· *September and June* ·

Moris Farms; a walk from Moris Farms; Massa Vecchia and Serraiola; Nannoni

MASSA MARITTIMA IS A jewel of a town and gives its name to one of Tuscany's newer DOCs, Monteregio di Massa Marittima, with Monteregio recalling an old fortress in the town. It was at the height of its splendour as an independent republic between 1245 and 1335, when the magnificent cathedral was built with its breathtaking facade which dominates the main square. Carry along the lively main street of the *città vecchia* and you will come to one of the best *pasticcerie* in the whole of Tuscany, Le Logge, owned by the Schillaci family, who have perfected their recipe for the classic Sienese cake, *panforte*. They make a lighter *bianco* version with a high proportion of almonds and with candied citrus fruit, while the darker, *nero* version includes spices and toasted hazelnuts. Both are sublime.

As for the wine, the DOC of Monteregio di Massa Marittima was created in 1994 and includes all three colours, including a *riserva* for the red wine, as well as a *vino novello* and Vin Santo *occhio di pernice*. The area covers the seven *comuni* of Massa Marittima, Follónica, Roccastrada, Gavorrano, Castiglione della Pescaia, Monterotondo and Scalina. In the north it touches Val di Cornia and Suvereto and to the south the vineyards of Morellino di Scansano. As for grape varieties, the regulations for white wine allow for Trebbiano, with some supporting Sauvignon and Chardonnay, or for Vermentino as a single variety, while the red demands a minimum of 80 per cent Sangiovese, which may be complimented by any of the varieties allowed within the province of Grosseto. These may be the traditional varieties such as Malvasia Nera, Ciliegiolo and Alicante, the local name for Grenache Noir, or the international newcomers, Cabernet Sauvignon, Merlot and Syrah.

Our first visit was to Adolfo Parentini at Moris Farms. His vineyards cover a splendid south-facing slope, which you glimpse as you speed up the Aurelia. You approach his estate along a long alley of cypress trees, even longer than the famous avenue at Bolgheri, with some 3600 trees planted by his father-in-law in 1937. We continued up the hill to an attractive eighteenth-century house, with a winery adjoining. The harvest had started a couple of days earlier; we stood hypnotized by bunches of grapes ascending a moving carpet into the destemmer. They were Syrah, and a few minutes later we were tasting the juice, with its deep-staining red colour and concentrated sweet fruit, with a pip or two floating in the glass. To my inexperienced taste buds it promised well.

Adolfo then took us to see his vineyards. He explained how the property had belonged to his wife's family since the eighteenth century. Originally there had been 6000 hectares; now, following various land divisions, there are 320 hectares, including 100 of woods, as well as olive groves, fields of wheat and animals, and 40 hectares of vineyards. Adolfo described the woods as the petroleum of the nineteenth century, for the charcoal obtained from them provided the energy of the period. His father-in-law had planted vines, first to sell the grapes, and then to make wine in bulk, and then they took a decision to bottle their wine, with the realization that this was the only way to render the vineyards remunerative. Attilio Pagli, who has done so much to improve the quality of the Maremma wines, is his consultant oenologist. As well as vineyards here, Adolfo has land in Scansano, with 30 hectares of vines, mainly Sangiovese, and a hectare each of Syrah, Cabernet Sauvignon and Merlot.

At Massa Marittima Adolfo makes two wines, a pure Sangiovese, half of which is aged in new oak for six months to make for some firm tannins and ripe fruit, and instead of a *riserva*, there is Avvoltore, the *cru* from the vineyard above the Aurelia, which was planted in 1990, with Sangiovese and some Cabernet Sauvignon and Syrah. With 25 per cent of complementary grape varieties it does not conform to the DOC regulations, but who cares? After twelve months in barrel it was long and cedary, with some elegant fruit and firm tannins. Avvoltore is the *maremmano* name for the falcons you can see hovering above the vineyards, while Moris is Spanish in origin, recalling the Spanish incursions of the seventeenth century. The family crest, which features on the labels of Moris Farms, depicts a dark-skinned Moor holding the head of a pale-skinned Christian, recalling the earlier wars and the origins of the name. A comparison with Morellino di Scansano was intriguing; the young Morellino, with a touch of Syrah, Cabernet Sauvignon and Merlot, had some appealing cherry fruit, while the *riserva*, which has spent time in both small and large barrels, was ripe and smoky. The wines were more accessible than the more structured and powerful Monteregio di Massa Marittima. After a convivial lunch we went to meet the domesticated herd of wild boar, and some particularly endearing little boarlets, who came running over in eager anticipation of some food. We were warned that their docile appearance quite belies their character.

Constraints of appointments prevented us from walking in Massa Marittima in September; instead we returned the following June to explore the town at greater leisure. The cathedral facade is enchanting in the evening light, if you sup at one of the restaurants in the square – sadly they cannot be recommended for their cuisine, nor for their extensive wine lists, but they do provide an opportunity to savour one of the most enchanting of Tuscany's squares at leisure. The swallows wheel around the square in the evening light and as the sun sets the colour of the marble turns a delicate pink to subtle grey. You can indulge in that never-ending spectator sport of people watching, following the theatre of the street, the evening *passeggiata* beloved by Italians, with children enjoying ice cream and playing hide-and-seek while their parents chat to their friends.

Adolfo Parentini's alley of cypress trees seemed the perfect start for a walk, providing welcome shade on a warm June day; lizards darted across our path and we found wild asparagus and fennel, and then passed a small lake with tall reeds. Between the trees, there were views up to the cellars of Moris Farms. We picnicked looking over a field of ripening corn, to the sound of crickets, and continued along the track, past more corn, interspersed with rows of olive trees, in the traditional manner of alternating cultivation. There were vineyards, some recently leaf-plucked, and in the days after flowering tiny grapes were forming, the size of pinheads. Then we came to a smelly factory, with greedy seagulls wheeling overhead. It was the moment to turn back and enjoy views of the cypress alley before we retraced our steps and reached our car just before a fleet of cyclists came thundering down the track at breakneck speed.

*

Fabrizio Niccoliani at Massa Vecchia outside the town of Massa Marittima exudes a passionate conviction in what he is doing on his small estate. He admitted to *un amore profondo di questa terra*, a deep love of this land, explaining how he originates from Massa Marittima. His grandfather on his mother's side had been a charcoal burner, while his paternal grandfather was a farmer, who had planted vines; in contrast, his father had been a diplomat. Fabrizio admitted that he is self-taught, with *una formazione contadina*, and has never studied the theory of winemaking. He is committed to organic viticulture, using very simple methods, with no chemicals and as little sulphur dioxide as possible.

We tasted in a neat little cellar, with Mozart playing in the background. First there was Ariento, a pure Vermentino, which had been given three weeks of skin contact, followed by two years on the lees in *botti*. The result was quite original and intriguing, a golden amber colour, with hints of marmalade on the nose, and dry orange fruit with balancing acidity. A pure Sangiovese, Poggio Venti, came from his grandfather's old vineyard. It had been fermented in wooden open-top vats, and then put into new *barriques* and *botti* for a couple of years, and given no fining or filtering. It was a sturdy mouthful of cedary fruit. La Fonte de Pietrazza, after a short story by Renato Fucini, was a pure Cabernet Sauvignon, with a good concentration of fruit and tannin. Terziere, an Alicante, was very intriguing, with a tannic structure and a certain animal warmth. Then came a blend of Sauvignon and Vermentino, called Patrizia Bartolino, after Fabrizio's partner. It is a late-harvest wine, with the grapes left to dry on the vines until at least mid-October, if not into November, and then the wine is kept in *barriques* for eighteen months. It was amber in colour and on the palate redolent of dried oranges and apricots with a long, rich finish. Finally there was an Aleatico, Il Matto della Giuncaia, meaning a bed of rushes in Italian. The grapes are picked in early September, and left to dry outside – we saw them hanging up in an open shed. Aleatico will not ripen later than September, and will rot if it is left on the vines, unlike Vermentino or Sauvignon. It is given a long maceration, of a couple of months, with the stalks, which are retained to add tannin, which will balance the sugar. It smelt of oranges and prunes, with herbal notes, and on the palate there was some wonderfully intense fruit, balanced with good acidity and a sweet finish. In short it was an original and intriguing range of wines, none of which made the slightest attempt to conform to the DOC regulations of Monteregio. As one of the individualists of the Italian wine trade, Fabrizio is adamant that he wants to do his own thing.

We talked about the future of the vineyards, how he would like to work with oxen rather than tractors, with a return to natural viticulture. He is planting a new vineyard, which returns to the tradition of Tuscan viticulture, what he described as archaic agriculture, reviving the union between vines and trees. The pruning method is *alberello*, with just 600 vines to the hectare, in a system of minimal intervention. He also has a terraced vineyard, of Sangiovese in *alberello*, with just one row per 5-metre terrace, with the vines 30 centimetres apart. Altogether Fabrizio has 38 hectares of land, with just 4.5 hectares of vines, as well as 500 olive trees and some grazing land, while the rest is woodland. He has achieved fine things since his first vintage in 1985, and he deserves to go far.

Fiorella Lenzi is the energetic president of the Strada del Vino di Monteregio di Massa Marittima. For the moment there is no growers' *consorzio*. She used to be a games teacher but then changed direction to work at Serraiola, the estate her father had bought in 1968, when he planted the first vines, the traditional Tuscan varieties of Sangiovese, Trebbiano and Malvasia. In 1991 Chardonnay, Sauvignon and Traminer were added, and then in 1994 Vermentino, Merlot and Syrah, so that there are now 10 hectares of vines, as well as olives, maize and wheat. At Serraiola she is very close to Suvereto and feels that she has more in common with the Val di Cornia than with Scansano. The climate is similar in that it is milder than Scansano; however, the red wine is not as soft as Morellino, and whites do well here too.

Like so many other parts of the Maremma, Massa Marittima has attracted investment by outsiders, including some big names such as Antinori, Zonin from the Veneto, Ezio Rivella, the former winemaker at Banfi, the Rothschilds of Lafite in conjunction with Paolo Panerai from Castellare in Chianti Classico, and Roberto Guldener, from Terrabianca, another Chianti Classico estate, amongst others. The groundbreaking estate of Meleto, near the town of Roccatederighi, with its ruined watchtower, was set up by a Swiss, Max Suter, in the mid-1970s and made an intriguing range of wines. Sadly he has since died and his widow sold the estate in 2003 to Elisabetta Foradori of Friuli fame, and two other partners. The name will change to Ampelaia and the wines are unlikely to conform to the *disciplinari* of Monteregio di Massa Marittima. However, Fiorella Lenzi foresees changes in the DOC regulations to allow for a higher percentage of international grape varieties, more in line with Bolgheri or Suvereto. Again it will be intriguing to observe the progress of yet another region that was unknown a few years ago.

While we were in Massa Marittima, we could not resist a visit to Nannoni. *Grappa*, the drink that originates from the distillation of grapeskins, is an intrinsic part of the Italian wine culture, and there is no better place to see its production than with Gioacchino Nannoni, who is widely acknowledged to be the master of the art, if not in the whole of Italy, most certainly in Tuscany. We found our way to L'Aratrice, a tiny hamlet down a narrow lane outside the town of Roccastrada. There is nothing else in the hamlet but the anonymous premises of Nannoni, without a sign to indicate their presence, in an elegant nineteenth-century villa with a pretty pink facade, and the distillery itself, which to my inexperienced eye exuded an atmosphere of Heath Robinson charm. However, there was no doubt that this was a highly professional operation, but with a homespun charm.

Gioacchino Nannoni is an immediately likeable, welcoming man, with rugged beard and a twinkling eye. He explained how his grandfather had been the first member of the family to distil, and how he had learnt the craft from his father and set up the distillery in 1970. It is very seasonal work, following the harvest. For about three months they work flat out, until the end of November, and then, after a pause, distil Vin Santo *vernacce* from January until March. We were there the day before distilling was due to begin in mid-September. Priscilla Occhipinti, his friendly apprentice, explained how the *vernacce*, or lees, must be absolutely fresh, for Gioacchino has been known to reject *vernacce* that are not up to scratch. In fact, they have three criteria for taking on new clients: their wine must be good; their *vernacce* must be of fine quality, and finally they must be *gente simpatica*, who become good friends. Their client list includes some of the great names of Tuscan viticulture: Sassicaia, Ornellaia, Montevertine, Mantelassi, and so on, with about fifty estates altogether.

The *vernacce* of white grapes consist of stalks, sugar and skins, whereas from red grapes the skins will include alcohol but no sugar or stalks. It is essential that they are fresh, for otherwise the quality of the *grappa* will suffer. The distillation is a three-part process, with the final distillation taking part in a tall copper column. At this point they want the heart, the *cuore*, of the distillate; the smell changes as there is methanol in the head, the first part, and an indication of this is the arrival of clusters of tiny flies, attracted by the aromatic fumes. Once the *cuore* is separated from the head and the tail, it is aged for anything from eighteen months to fifteen years. Each producer sends their own barrels, which must have been used for at least a few months for maturing wine, but must not be too old either. Once in bottle, *grappa* will improve for three or four years, and then the changes become imperceptible, but the quality will never actually decline – until the bottle is opened, when it is best consumed within four or five months.

I must admit to having certain reservations about *grappa*, influenced by the sight of slag heaps of desiccated stalks outside cooperatives of the south waiting to be sent off to an industrial distillery, with the taste of the finished product reminiscent of dry stalks and cardboard. But sip a Nannoni *grappa* and you are in quite another world of finely crafted, elegant flavours.

Montecucco

· *September* ·

*Fattoria di Montecucco; walk towards Colle Massari; Parmoleto,
Perazetta*

MONTECUCCO IS ANOTHER of the new DOCs of the Maremma, separated
from Montalcino in the north by the Ombrone river, while it is limited
by Morellino di Scansano in the south, Monteregio di Massa Marittima in the
west, and in the east there are the forested slopes of Tuscany's highest mountain,
Monte Amiata. It covers the *comuni* of Civitella-Pagánico and parts of
Arcidosso, Campagnático, Cinigiano and Castel del Piano. Montecucco itself is a
small hamlet and it is the Fattoria di Montecucco that gave its name to the DOC.

This is an old property that belonged to the Piccolomini family from the
twelfth century until its sale in 1968 to a Florentine chemist. Until the 1950s
the estate totalled some 2000 hectares, but has since been reduced to a more
manageable 700 hectares, of which 34 are vineyards. Stefano Alessandri
manages the estate for the absentee landowners. He is president of the
consorzio of Montecucco and talked about its development over the last five
years. 1998 is the first vintage of the new DOC; then there were 150 hectares of
vines, with just six people who put their wine into bottle, while others were
simply selling their grapes. But interest has grown, along with the vineyards, so
that by 2002 they had increased to 400 hectares, but only half are actually in
production. Producers from outside Tuscany have invested here, such as Masi
and Santa Margherita, as well as other Tuscan winemakers, such as the Folonari
family. Land prices have risen accordingly. In 2002 a hectare of bare land cost
€ 15,500 (30 million lire), representing a sharp rise from € 2500 (4.5 million
lire) in 1998. How things have progressed; where once people were content to
make what Stefano described as *un vino da contadino*, now they employ
oenologists, with the resultant change in working methods. New cellars are
being built, as witness to some serious investment.

At the Fattoria di Montecucco they still have their historic cellars dating back to the seventeenth century, with attractive brick arches, all newly cleaned, housing *barriques* and *botti*. You approach the estate along a small alley of cypress trees, to reach an attractive cluster of buildings on the top of a hill, with views towards Monte Amiata and the distinctive silhouette of the Banfi property of Poggio alle Mura near Montalcino. There is a tiny chapel, which was rebuilt after the Second World War, and various houses for *agriturismo*. The original vineyards were planted with Sangiovese, Canaiolo and Ciliegiolo, while Cabernet Sauvignon, Merlot and Syrah were added in 1999, with Vermentino the principal variety for white wine. For the moment their wines are based firmly on Sangiovese. Passonaia, with some Canaiolo and Ciliegiolo as well as Sangiovese, is kept in wood for a couple of months, and tastes of ripe cherries and firm tannins; Le Coste, a pure Sangiovese, kept in barrel for twelve months, is sturdier with an obvious impact of oak, which will mellow with age, while the *riserva*, which has spent two and a half years in large *botti*, was altogether more Tuscan in flavour, with mature cherries on the palate. Doubtless there will be more changes as the international grape varieties come into production. The Fattoria di Montecucco also produces olive oil, with a magnificent *orciaia* containing pungent oil; many of the *orci* are signed with the thumbprint of the man who made them.

From Montecucco we set off down the alleyway of cypress trees; the smell of resin was intoxicating in the sunshine. The road took us along a ridge, with views of the wide open countryside, with rolling hills and broad fields of arable land. We passed vineyards, some immaculate, others looking distinctly scruffy, with grass and weeds. Another hillside was being cleared, doubtless for the planting of yet another vineyard. Then two building sites came into view, with high cranes and scaffolding, one a castle undergoing restoration, and the other a brand-new cellar. They are both the responsibility of Claudio Tipa. We had already met Claudio at Grattamacco in Bolgheri; he bubbles with enthusiasm and energy, explaining how he bought his property here, Colle Massari, in 1999. It is a magnificent medieval castle dating at least from the fourteenth century, if not the thirteenth, which dominates the skyline outside the village of Sasso d'Ombrone. It came with 200 hectares of land, some of which is gradually being planted with vines, at the rate of 10 hectares a year, aiming for a total of 70 hectares.

We took a track along the edge of a vineyard to reach a viewpoint looking down on Colle Massari, with its hillside of neatly manicured young vines, and a landscaped driveway lined with young cypress trees. Then we picnicked under a clump of cork oaks, looking across the valley to the village of Poggio di Sasso.

Claudio explained that like all the Tuscan DOCs, the backbone of Montecucco is formed by Sangiovese, requiring a minimum of 60 per cent, with the traditional varieties such as Ciliegiolo, Mammola, Alicante, as well as Cabernet Sauvignon and Merlot. He is convinced of the potential of Sangiovese, but feels that Cabernet, which seems to do better than Merlot here, is also needed to provide a choice. There is no *rosato*, while white Montecucco is based on Vermentino, as well as the ubiquitous Trebbiano. Grape growing is no new activity in this area; traditionally the grapes were sold to Montalcino, just across the valley, but now the wine is set to assume its own importance and reputation.

The 2002 harvest, which will be the first serious vintage of Colle Massari, was in full swing in early September. Claudio was planning three wines, a Sangiovese, a super-Tuscan of Sangiovese, Cabernet Sauvignon and Merlot, and a wine based on Ciliegiolo. The cellar was a building site, and the castle shrouded in scaffolding, all teeming with activity. To show us just why he is so enthusiastic about the potential of this new area, Claudio took us to taste the wines of an associate estate, Salustre, where young Marco Salustre first began making wine, rather than simply growing grapes, in 1996, with the expert guidance of Maurizio Castelli. These were the wines that convinced Claudio to come to Montecucco. The 2001 Sangiovese showed real promise, with ripe refreshing cherry fruit, while the 1999 Santa Marta, from 30-year-old Sangiovese, with a drop of Ciliegiolo, after fourteen months' ageing in wood, was structured with firm cherry fruit. There was no doubt that it had more in common with Montalcino than Scansano.

Parmoleto, just across the valley from Sant'Angelo in Scalo and the vineyards of Montalcino, is an example of an estate that has changed direction, for it is owned by people with modest horizons who are realizing the potential of their land. We talked to Luciana Sodi, while her son struggled with a basket press. She explained how the farm had been bought by her grandparents a century or so ago. They began bottling their wine in 1990; first of all it was plain *vino da tavola*, and then in 1996 it was recognized as an IGT, Rosso Toscano, and finally became a DOC in 1998. Certainly the influence of the proximity of Montalcino was to be felt. Are conditions across the other side of the valley so very different? She thought not. For the moment they have just 3 hectares in production, of Sangiovese and a little Montepulciano, and they planted Syrah and a little Cabernet Sauvignon in 1999. Most of the 70-hectare estate consists of arable land for wheat, as well as some olive trees. For the moment there is a neat little barrel cellar, and as they expand they are planning a new cellar. We tasted the 2000, Sangiovese with just a drop of Montepulciano, which had spent a year in *barriques*; it was structured with firm cherry fruit. Under the guidance of Paolo Vaggagini as their consultant oenologist, it all promises well.

We tracked down Rita Bocci of Perazzeta in her vineyards just outside the hilltop village of Montenero, just down the road from Parmoleto. Family and friends were busy picking grapes, what she called a *prima passata*, or first passage, for the rest would be picked about ten days later. There were views across the valley to Montenero, and a giant digger was preparing land for vines further down the hill. Rita explained how this had been her father-in-law's hobby; he had begun with just one hectare and then things had become more serious as he had bought more land, and bottled his first wine in 1994. They now produce four different wines, all based on Sangiovese; most serious is Licurgo, a pure Sangiovese and a selection of the best grapes, given two years in *barriques*. Rita felt that there was no real difference between their Sangiovese and that of Montalcino. 'They just have thirty years more experience than us. However, we don't want to copy Montalcino; we need to look for something more original.' For the moment Montecucco may lack cohesion and be searching for an identity, but the potential is there and it will be fascinating to observe its progress over the coming years.

Morellino di Scansano
· September ·

A walk from Scansano, in two parts; Mantelassi, Le Pupille, Erik Banti, the cooperative at Scansano, Castello di Montepò, Poggio Argentiera

THE VITICULTURAL LANDSCAPE of Scansano has changed dramatically since my earlier visits at the end of the 1980s. Back then Scansano was a rural backwater, hardly touched, it seemed, by the mainstream of Tuscan viticulture, but in the 1990s the Maremma, and Scansano in particular, was 'discovered' by some of the big names of Italian viticulture, with enormous interest shown in the region, not just from winemakers in other parts of Tuscany, but also from other regions of Italy. Erik Banti, one of the early pioneers of Morellino di Scansano, summed it up nicely when he observed: 'My neighbours used to be sheep, but nowadays they are the likes of Biondi Santi, Bolla, Mondavi, Masi, Frescobaldi.' There has been an enormous expansion in the vineyard area of Scansano, not just for the DOC, but also for IGT wines, and accordingly a considerable increase in land prices. But nevertheless vineyards are still not the main feature of the landscape of Scansano, for the plantings are not as dense as in Montalcino, with fields for grazing animals, olive groves, wheat and other crops and expanses of woodland.

The DOC of Morellino di Scansano centres on the little town of Scansano, stretching into the neighbouring *comuni* of Manciano, Magliano-in-Toscana, Grosseto, Campagnático, Roccalbegna and Semproniano, in the hills between the Ombrone and Albegna rivers. Scansano itself can seem a rather sombre place, especially on an afternoon of torrential rain; traffic manoeuvres, sometimes with difficulty, through the small square, the Piazza Garibaldi, with its statue of the conquering hero, who is reputed to have asked for Morellino when he was recruiting volunteers to his cause. An arched gateway leads into the old town, with houses clustered around narrow streets, and splashes of colour provided by pots of geraniums.

We set off up a steep path out of the town, following a way-marked route in the direction of Montiano. Happily the path soon levelled out to follow a sunken track lined with holm oaks, with their roots exposed by years of erosion. Tiny pink cyclamen nestled in the shade. Abruptly we emerged from this seemingly secret hidden path onto a tarmac road by the large *cantina sociale* and the adjoining sports stadium. We quickly found another shady path, following the edge of fields of ripening maize, and through a small hamlet and then onto a *strada bianca* by the small shrine of the Madonna di Scansano. From there the path continued steadily downhill past various houses and farms; a group of jet-black horses were sheltering from the sunshine under a large oak tree. We passed a tiny cottage with quite the largest chimney, totally out of proportion to its size; vines crept over a trellis, with a garden of olive trees and a fruiting pomegranate. The *strada bianca* petered out and we followed a rocky track, with holm oaks on either side, and found a picnic spot in a field with a view over the valley, with a mixture of olive groves and pasture land, with some ploughed fields and a few vineyards. The vines almost seemed conspicuous by their absence. We crossed a stream, the *fosso* Patrignone, with evidence of wild boar tracks in the mud, and turned uphill to a farmyard, where the dogs barked noisily at us. Suddenly we came out on the road to Montiano at a bar which was empty, apart from a group of elderly men intently playing cards. It was the moment to turn back towards Scansano, with a steep climb back to the town. Once there we realized that there was an afternoon for *cantine aperte*, with various stands in the old town, so we found the medieval cellar next to the church, with its enormous bricked ceiling with fine arches and some antique equipment, an old destemmer and large vats. Then it was time to return to Fattoria Mantelassi.

It was Ezio Mantelassi who gave me my first introduction to the wines of Morellino di Scansano. Nowadays it is his son Aleardo who shoulders a large part of the responsibility for running the estate. It was harvest time, an anxious and exciting moment in the vineyard calendar, especially with the unpredictable weather of that September. Aleardo was much preoccupied, but he still found time to hunt for *porcini* with remarkable success most mornings, which we all appreciated for dinner in the evening. Silvana Mantelassi's *risotto ai porcini* is memorable, not to mention the succulent richness and melting sweetness of plain roasted *porcini*. Aleardo also took the time to show us their cellar and vineyards. They now have 60 hectares of vines, whereas Ezio began with 20 hectares on a 120-hectare estate bought in the 1960s. Once they also had animals, cows until fifteen years ago and sheep until five years ago, but are now concentrating on wine, with plans for a new cellar. The most significant change is the introduction of *barriques*, although they still use *botti* for the *riserva* wines.

Some of their vines are over thirty-five years old, with thick trunks and tiny bunches of berries. The soil is very stony; huge boulders had been taken from the newly planted vineyards, great chunks of travertine, and the nearby woods had a sign telling you not to pick the produce of the woods. Aleardo explained that this meant not just *porcini*, but also asparagus, snails, blackberries, indeed anything remotely edible. Italian country folk have a firmly ingrained culture of free food and it is far from unusual to see people with plastic bags who have stopped their car and are eagerly picking herbs at the side of the road.

The majority of the Mantelassi vineyards are planted with Sangiovese, which is what they call Morellino, and the mainstay of the DOC, as the name would imply. Morello is a derivation from *moro*, meaning brown or a deep colour, describing the colour of the ripe grapes, with Morellino the diminutive. We tasted sitting on the terrace looking out on views of the hills. First came their white wine, Sassobianco, from Trebbiano and Malvasia, with a little Ansonica, with attractive mineral notes and some rounded fruit. Lucumone, after a local Etruscan lord, is a pure Vermentino, with leafy fruit and fresh acidity. The simple Morellino di Scansano, from Sangiovese, with a little Canaiolo and Malvasia Nera, is a classic example of the wine with ripe cherry fruit, some soft tannins and fresh acidity, and all too drinkable with a plate of pasta. More substantial is San Giuseppe, from a selection of the same grapes, but given some barrel ageing. You are aware of the oak influence on the young wine, but it mellows with time. More classic is the *riserva*, which requires a minimum of two years' ageing in the cellar, be it in barrel, vat or bottle. As well as Sangiovese, Malvasia Nera and Canaiolo, it includes some Grenache Noir, which is usually called Alicante Toscano, or Tinta d'Espagna, recalling the time when the Spaniards were at nearby Monte Argentario. This *riserva* is given fifteen months in 15-hectolitre oak barrels, so that the oak influence is subtle and there is some stylish ripe fruit on the palate, with ageing potential. More structured is Le Sentinelle, with a firm cedary palate and structured tannins, made from Sangiovese, with a small amount of Alicante, grown in their highest vineyards and given eighteen months in *barriques*. Querciolaia comes from 35-year-old Alicante vines and is quite different, with warmer, more animal notes, even though it has spent a year or more in *barriques*. Our concentration was interrupted by the noise of a pair of cats spatting on the balcony above our heads.

We wanted to continue the walk to Montiano, so Aleardo took us back to the café where we had turned round earlier in the week, but the encouraging red and white markers indicating our route seemed to peter out. There was no obvious path apart from a hard tarmac road. When we asked at the café about the signs, they said: 'Oh, those are for tourists.' 'But it's marked on the map,' I said, which was a local walking map. This was met with the riposte: 'Oh, Italian maps, you know, they are not always very accurate,' with a wonderful dismissive shrug of the shoulders. As we set off down the tarmac road, somewhat despondently, a car came to a halt beside us and there was Adolfo Parentini from Moris Farms, a knight in shining armour, offering us a lift, which we accepted gratefully, back to our own car in Montiano. From there, we set out following the signs towards Scansano. The track took us past some noisy hunting dogs. With the rain of the previous day the air was heavy with the scent of thyme and pine trees. A rocky track had turned into a stream, so we deviated into a field and followed the path back up the hill, past farms and fields, olive groves and a plot of vines. Across the other side of the valley land was being prepared for yet another new vineyard, and as we reached the top of the hill, there was a view of the coastline, with Monte Argentario and the lagoon of Orbetello in the haze, emphasizing Scansano's proximity to the sea, and a little further along we joined the tarmac road.

Elisabetta Geppetti of Le Pupille has vineyards just up the road from Mantelassi. What was once her grandparents' holiday home has over the years been turned into a serious wine estate, so that with 60 hectares of vineyards in production, Le Pupille is now one of the largest producers. The vineyards have gradually been extended with the purchase of Poggio Valente, a single *cru*, and new cellars were built in 2001, adjoining an elegant villa right on the edge of the DOC close to Grosseto, which houses the barrels in elegantly arched rooms. An underground cellar is impossible here as the water table is too high, with their proximity to the Ombrone river. We wandered round – picking had begun a couple of days earlier, with bunches of Merlot being checked on the sorting table – and then we adjourned to the cellar for some tasting, with Elisabetta's husband, Stefano Rizzi. Unusually, they make a white wine, Poggio Argento, from Sauvignon and Traminer; contrary to my expectations the Sauvignon was more obvious on the palate, while the Traminer provided a lift on the finish. Their Morellino di Scansano is a cheerful blend of Sangiovese and Alicante, with some Malvasia Nera instead of more usual Ciliegiolo. For Stefano, the Malvasia provides more complexity and personality, while the Ciliegiolo is too delicate. He explained how they are looking for ripe fruit, but combined with elegance; the last thing they want is *marmelata*, or jam, in a glass. Next came Poggio Valente, the single-vineyard vine, which they make instead of a *riserva*, from at least forty-year-old Sangiovese and Alicante, which was rounded and harmonious with dense fruit, and some oak influence from twelve months in barrel. Stefano talked about what he called the culture of the Fiat vineyards, which were planted in the 1950s, when people first began to use tractors, so that the width of the rows was determined by the size of the machine, irrespective of what suited the vines. Saffredi is a stylish blend of Cabernet Sauvignon, Merlot and Alicante, made for the first time in 1987. The original idea had been to use Cabernet Sauvignon to improve their Sangiovese, but it was so good, *una cosa strepitosa*, that they made a new wine. We finished with their dessert wine, Solalto, a blend of Sauvignon, Traminer and Sémillon, which are left to dry a little on the vines, but as there is no noble rot, this is not an imitation of Sauternes. It is fermented in stainless-steel vats, not in oak, and has the elegance of a German Auslese, with some delicate, honeyed flavours.

Erik Banti is another early pioneer of Morellino di Scansano, who celebrated his twenty-second vintage in 2002. Originally he had tiny cramped cellars in the little village of Montemerano, but now is expanding into more spacious facilities outside Scansano to accommodate the fruit of some 60 hectares of vineyards, with more to come into production in the next few years. Erik's wines have evolved over the years. He has improved his Sangiovese by planting a greater variety of clones, as well as Cabernet Sauvignon and Merlot, and is also trying out Petit Verdot, Syrah and Zinfandel. His young Morellino di Scansano, with a little Alicante, Merlot and Cabernet Sauvignon blended with the Sangiovese, has the fresh cherry fruit that is the hallmark of Morellino di Scansano. Carato, currently an IGT Rosso Toscano, as the vineyards were not classified as Morellino di Scansano, is a more traditional blend of Sangiovese, Canaiolo, Malvasia Nera and Alicante, but aged in American oak *barriques* as well as Slovenian oak casks. It fulfils a commercial demand, for those who like the oaky flavour of vanilla. There used to be two *crus*, Ciabatta and Aquilaia, but officialdom deemed that Aquilaia could be confused with the Aquileia of Friuli, so Ciabatta remains, as an elegantly smoky Sangiovese, aged in both *barriques* and cask. Finally there is Annoterzo (next year it will be Annoquatro), made from a recently purchased vineyard outside Montemerano, from Sangiovese and a little Merlot, which is richer and fuller-flavoured. Ciabatta tasted more truly Tuscan, but Erik is adamant that you have to be aware of market demands and move with the times. Wine production is a business and you cannot afford to make a mistake.

Erik is also refreshingly perceptive about the influx of newcomers into the area. There is no doubt that they have pushed up the prices of land. Back in the early 1990s you could buy a hectare of bare land for €3000 (£2000); nowadays it costs €30,000 (£20,000), but that compares favourably with €215,000 (£150,000) in Chianti Classico or €285,000–360,000 (£200,000–250,000) in Montalcino, so the attraction of Scansano becomes obvious, and until a couple of years ago land was readily available. Nevertheless, on top of that, you have to buy planting rights, which cost about €10,000–11,500 (£7000–8000) per hectare for IGT, and would be double for Morellino di Scansano, if they were available, which they are not. The vineyard area has increased enormously from 370 hectares in 1998 to 1100 hectares in 2002, which means a huge growth in production, a leap from 3.5 million bottles to 10 million bottles. There are now 160 members of the *consorzio*, twenty-five of whom currently bottle their wine.

However, many of the new vineyards are not yet in production and as yet no one knows if there is a market for so much wine. Some, such as Alessandro Bargagli, the president of the *consorzio*, would argue that 10 million bottles is the absolute minimum in order to make any kind of impact in the world marketplace, but in some markets, such as England, medium-priced Italian wines are notoriously difficult to sell. I have lost count of the number of producers who have observed wistfully, as they admitted that they did not have an English importer: the English market is *molto difficile*. Grape prices have also risen, from 35 Euros per quintale in 1998 to 100 Euros in 2000, and in 2001 they soared to 160 Euros; however, in 2002 a 10 per cent decrease was registered.

If you take the back road from Scansano to Montiano, as we did, to see Erik's new vineyards, there is a plethora of new plantings, such as Guicciardini, Frescobaldi, both alone and in association with Robert Mondavi at La Capitana, Bruna Baroncini's estate at Aia della Macina and others. For the moment the wine must be fermented here around Scansano but can still be bottled outside the DOC, though that will change in 2006, so that the newcomers will have to build cellars within the DOC.

We arrived at the *cantina sociale* just in time to watch a lorry unload its grapes into the crusher. The lorry slowly tilted up its load, triggering a mini waterfall of juice, pressed under the weight of so many grapes, which soon turned into a gushing torrent of grapes. The president of the cooperative, Benedetto Grechi, was on duty at the grape reception line, weighing the arriving grapes and giving each cooperative member a paper slip, recording his crop. This was the last cooperative to be founded in the Maremma, in 1972, and until the mid-1980s it was very much what he called a cooperative *di massa*; now it is a cooperative *di qualità*. Stricter measures were introduced and anyone who did not like them was encouraged to leave, but they also encouraged others to join. For the last five years Attilio Pagli has been their consultant oenologist, with a significant effect on quality. Grechi, like so many, is adamant that quality is produced in the vineyard: *la natura è molto generosa*. Scansano benefits from a good contrast between day and night-time temperatures, which makes for wines with a balanced acidity. There is good ventilation here too, so that problems with humidity are not usually a problem. The mild maritime influence on the climate renders the wines of Scansano so much more approachable than those of Chianti Classico, with its much harsher climate.

The cooperative has three different reception lines, according to the quality of the grapes. They no longer use cement vats, only stainless-steel ones, as well as oak barrels, and there is no centrifuge and no more pasteurization, while longer maceration periods have also improved quality. They make a range of different Morellino di Scansano, from 170 hectares, varying from the light and fresh to the more serious oak-aged, as well as some Bianco di Pitigliano, taking into account the small overlap of the two vineyard areas. Grechi feels strongly that the newcomers will help enhance the reputation of the region, though he recognizes that others might see them as competition. It is a decisive moment as the vineyard area has grown so greatly. Much will depend on the individual producers.

One of the most conspicuous of the newcomers is Jacopo Biondi Santi, of Montalcino fame, who has bought Castello di Montepò. This was the property of Graham Greene, a former chairman of the British Museum and nephew of the well-known author, and before then for some three or four hundred years it belonged to the Sergardis, an old Sienese family. A map of the estate in 1700 shows that it totalled some 14,000 hectares, making it one of the largest Tuscan estates of the time, stretching almost to Grosseto. Today it is a shadow of its former self, with some 500 hectares, of which 50 are planted with vines, while the castle retains the atmosphere of an imposing medieval edifice. The ramparts have long since disappeared, leaving a solid grey stone building with four towers. Standing at 500 metres, it dominates the surrounding countryside, with an amphitheatre of hills enhancing the impression of impregnability. There are views over the vineyards from the terrace, some newly planted, and in addition Jacopo Biondi Santi has vineyards at Poggio Salvi in Montalcino, as well as in the new DOC of Monteregio di Massa Marittima, and also rents vineyards near Greve-in-Chianti in the heart of Chianti Classico.

This makes for an eclectic range of wines. For my taste buds, the highlights included the Rosso di Montalcino from Poggio Salvi with its fresh cherry fruit, which was much more accessible than the traditional Biondi Santi wine, as was the Brunello from the same estate. Jacopo explained that the vineyards of Biondi Santi have more acidity and lower tannins, while Poggio Salvi has the opposite, accounting for its accessibility. Sassaloro is a pure Sangiovese, with soft tannins and lively fruit; Montepaone, a pure Cabernet Sauvignon, which was quite cedary on the palate, with some sturdy oaky fruit; Schidione, with which Jacopo wanted to combine ageing potential and freshness, is a blend of Cabernet Sauvignon, Sangiovese and Merlot which have spent two and half years in Troncais barrels. It is very intense and chocolatey; Jacopo described it as his *peccato di vanità*, sin of vanity. Best of all was the Morellino di Scansano *riserva*, Castello di Montepò, mainly Sangiovese, with a drop of Cabernet, which has a firm smoky nose and rounded cherry fruit, with a long finish.

The heavens opened during lunch, with a dark sky bringing torrential rain, accompanied by thunder and lightning, which triggered the noisy arrival of Tancredi, Jacopo's energetic young son, in distinctly muddy mountain-bike gear, cheerfully disrupting the rather formal atmosphere in the dining room. His mother, Francesca, observed that the muddier he is, the happier he is. The rain ended as abruptly as it had started, and Jacopo insisted on taking us for a drive through the vineyard, fortunately in a four-wheel-drive Range Rover, though I might have preferred the even sturdier American military vehicle that was parked in the courtyard. My vision of remaining stuck in the mud was happily not fulfilled, but the effects of the rain, not just from that day but earlier in the week, were quite startling. The erosion of the soil was visible to see, with gullies filled with silt. Jacopo has carried out a detailed soil analysis and is applying his findings; areas of land are being replanted; huge rocks have been removed and drainage systems added. There were dramatic views of the castle with a lowering grey sky behind. Before we left we had a quick glimpse of Mrs Greene's rose garden, with some 130 different varieties. There was just one delicate white flower in September, with everything looking rather damp and forlorn.

Giampaolo Paglia at Poggio Argentiera is a newcomer too, but on quite a different scale. He bought an abandoned farm a few years ago and began replanting the vineyards so that his first vintage was, like Jacopo's at Montepò, as recent as 1998. We sat outside in the shade, with his English wife, Justine, and their baby son, Oliver, while the black and white spaniel Daisy sniffed our feet. Giampaolo explained how he was born in Orbitello and after a first degree in agriculture had studied molecular biology. It was while he was working in Friuli that he became interested in wine. He has planted various grape varieties, the traditional Sangiovese, Alicante and Ciliegiolo as well as Syrah, Cabernet Franc, Merlot and Cabernet Sauvignon, with the idea of seeing for himself what works in his vineyard. 'You cannot trust the scientific research; you have to find out for yourself.' He is right on the edge of the DOC, closest to the sea and almost at sea level, so that the climate is very similar to Bolgheri and the soil is quite sandy. He has subsequently acquired a second estate, at Arcille, just north-east of Grosseto on the northern edge of the DOC. He reckons that he bought just in time, and that things will become increasingly difficult, not only with land becoming much more expensive, but also with more intense competition. And how do you create a market for your wines? Giampaolo is concentrating on the local market. 'The quality will speak for itself, but you also need patience and an element of luck.' The wines are impressive. His Morellino di Scansano is pure Sangiovese, of which a small part is given some barrel ageing, making a rounded, harmonious mouthful of fruit. Capatosta, from Sangiovese with just a drop of Alicante, spends twelve months in barrels and is more serious, with firm tannins and structure, but equally fine. 'Above all it is what you do in the vineyards that counts; you learn something new each year, and yet you probably only have forty opportunities in your lifetime.'

Pitigliano and Sovana

· September ·

Sassotondo, La Stellata, Tenuta di Roccaccia; a walk round Pitigliano and on to Sovana; Fattoria Aldobrandesca, Sopra lu Ripa, La Busattina

OUR FIRST GLIMPSE OF Pitigliano was breathtaking. We were late and it was dark. We rounded a corner on the winding road and suddenly there before us was the floodlit town perched precariously on a cliff. This is the approach on the coastal road. However, if you arrive from Viterbo in the other direction, you are quite unaware of its dramatic position, as happened on my first visit there, when I opened the shutters of my hotel room to find myself looking down a sheer cliff face.

Pitigliano is virtually impregnable. Its origins are Etruscan, and it was the Etruscans who gave their name to Tuscany. This ancient race occupied an area of Italy, limited by the Arno and Tiber rivers and the Tyrennian Sea, from the ninth to the first centuries BC, but they were unable to withstand the advances of the Romans, and endured numerous disastrous defeats, finally to become Roman citizens in 90 BC. Around Pitigliano there is much evidence of their presence; the soft tufa cliffs below the town are riddled with caves, which were originally dug as burial sites. Nowadays they have a more prosaic use, maybe as a workshop, or even as a wine cellar.

We stayed at Sassotondo, a wine estate a few kilometres out of the town, where Edoardo Ventimiglia and Carla Benini are making an intriguing range of wines, including both the DOCs, of Sovana and Bianco di Pitigliano, as well as various IGT. We walked round the estate in the September sunshine on the first morning accompanied by their two dogs, Mila and Panda. The harvest was about to begin, and after the unseasonable rain of August there was a surprising amount of vegetation. The first hazard was the electric fence, intended to protect the grapes from marauding wild boar. Apparently it is less efficient against porcupines, which also have a predilection for ripe grapes; nor is it unknown for the neighbour's sheep to dine off vine leaves. Carla and

Edoardo grow a variety of different grapes. For Bianco di Pitigliano there is Trebbiano, as the base of most Tuscan white wines, as well as Greco and some Sauvignon, while there is Chardonnay for a new '*super bianco*' Edoardo is planning, with some Greco. They question the validity of the change in the regulations in 1992, which obliges you to have either Sauvignon or Chardonnay in your Bianco di Pitigliano. Riesling Italico, Pinot Bianco, Malvasia, Grechetto and Verdello are also allowed, but Trebbiano remains the mainstay. The more recent DOC, Sovana, created in 1999, allows for an equal diversity of red grapes. Sangiovese may form the backbone, with a blend of any of the grapes allowed in the province of Grosseto, while wines based on a single varietal include Merlot, Cabernet Sauvignon and Aleatico. Edoardo and Carla feel strongly that Ciliegiolo, as an indigenous variety of this particular part of the Maremma, deserves a place in the DOC, as they prove with their San Lorenzo, a pure Ciliegiolo, from thirty-year-old vines. Opinions vary as to the quality of Ciliegiolo; for some it is no better than Trebbiano, the weed of the Tuscan vineyards, while others consider that it not only enhances Sangiovese but deserves a more important role in the DOC regulations of Sovana.

Winemaking represents a complete change of direction for Edoardo; his earlier world was the cinema, and although Carla studied agriculture in Milan, they have come to Tuscan viticulture with the fresh eyes of outsiders. Carla's kitchen proved a cosy venue for a pre-supper tasting, with its large welcoming table and open fireplace. Their Bianco di Pitigliano is based on Trebbiano, enlivened by Sauvignon, Greco and a drop of Chardonnay. Greco provides the body and Sauvignon the perfume, while Trebbiano adds notes of almonds. It was quite textured, with a satisfying old-fashioned feel to it. The Sassotondo *rosso*, from Ciliegiolo and Sangiovese with a dash of Alicante, has some attractive spicy fruit with peppery overtones. This is an IGT, not a DOC, for it does not conform to the regulations for Sovana, but more importantly, with an IGT you can put the word Tuscany on the label, whereas for the DOC the labelling regulations dictate Sovana, Italy. And who knows where Sovana is? Next came Franze, officially a DOC, but with a certain flexibility about the exact proportions of Sangiovese, Ciliegiolo, Merlot and Alicante, with ripe fruit, firm tannins and a long elegantly spicy finish. The pure Ciliegiolo San

Lorenzo is sturdy and structured, again with the characteristic spicy flavours, while the first vintage, 1997, amply illustrated the ageing potential of the wine, with tannin and spice. The labels at Sassotondo are simple and evocative, portraying the mountains, the huge stone after which the estate is named, and the vines.

Sovana comes in three categories: *normale*, which is sold from March following the vintage; *superiore*, which is released in June, and *riserva*, which entails thirty months of ageing, including eighteen in wood. However, the regulations are severely criticized, as the permitted yield is far too high, representing a retrograde step in the move towards quality. There is a distinct suspicion that the Pitigliano cooperative, which dominates the production of both DOCs, is largely to blame, as its members are more attuned to quantity than quality production.

However, things had certainly improved there since my last visit in 1988. The cooperative is a large sprawling building outside the town, and with seven hundred members it is responsible for some 1000 hectares, in both the DOCs of Bianco di Pitigliano and Sovana, including vineyards in the *comune* of Sorana and part of Manciano. While Bianco di Pitigliano spreads into the neighbouring DOC of Morellino di Scansano, Sovana does not. The cooperative cellars are a labyrinth of vats. The old concrete ones have been abandoned in favour of shiny new stainless steel; temperature-control methods have been introduced and small barrels purchased. The harvest was in progress, with boxes of Sauvignon grapes being unloaded into the crusher. Much of the impetus for the improvement in quality comes from Attilio Pagli's arrival as a consultant oenologist in 2000. He has not instigated any dramatic changes, just a persistent fine-tuning of attention to detail, from a greater selection in the vineyard to more care in the cellar. The cooperative, in recognition of the once strong Jewish community in Pitigliano, produces kosher wine, which entails an elaborate process that is followed by a rabbi from Rome, who charges for his services. Finally the wine is blessed and then pasteurized, so that it is purified, and then can be served by a gentile. Until that moment it must not be handled by anyone other than a Jew.

At one time Clara Divizia at La Stellata was the sole private producer of Pitigliano but happily things have changed as more people are seeking independence from the communal vats of the cooperative. She has 5 hectares, with her husband Manlio Giorni, outside the village of Manciano, and makes just three wines, Lunaia red and white, and Selene, a second white wine from younger vines. I have always liked her wines. The white Lunaia, Bianco di Pitigliano, is aged in wood for several months, with the wood serving to soften the acidity, and she follows its evolution closely, tasting each barrel every couple of weeks. The wine is nutty and rounded, with quite firm acidity and intriguing layers of flavour. Clara talked about their life. She and her husband both had earlier careers in Rome, she as an interior designer and he with cars, and then they fell in love with wine. 'It was a romantic choice'; they followed their hearts and not their heads, and have no regrets. However, now she feels that things are changing; that wine has moved away from the winemaker and that people are forgetting that wine is born in the vineyard. She feels strongly that wine should not be a fashion item; so many wines are far too expensive; it costs no more than €6.70 (13,000 lire) to produce a bottle of wine; all the rest is packaging and PR. And some of the newcomers are buying wine estates simply because they think it is chic. She admitted to being more than a little disillusioned with the way things have gone.

In contrast, Danilo and Rossano Goracci at Tenuta di Roccaccia are two young brothers running vineyards which until recently were part of the cooperative. Their father bought the estate in 1965, and in 1998 they decided to go it alone, withdrawing 30 hectares of vines from the cooperative. We sat round a table in the cellar, tasting and talking. Their Bianco di Pitigliano is a blend of Trebbiano, Chardonnay, Sauvignon and a touch of Vermentino, with delicate, understated but satisfying fruit. A basic Sovana is a blend of Sangiovese, with Ciliegiolo and Alicante, showing ripe fruit and a streak of astringency on the finish. Fontenova, from Sangiovese and Ciliegiolo, given a year or so of wood ageing, was more substantial with peppery fruit and firm cherries, and promised well. Like Edoardo and Carla at Sassotondo, they too believe in Ciliegiolo, as illustrated by their Poggio Cavaluccio, from a one-hectare vineyard of thirty-year-old vines, with soft tannins and peppery fruit. The brothers are full of enthusiasm; they are adamant that the most important thing is the vineyard, and they deserve to do well.

*

Pitigliano itself rewards an exploration. On a sunny morning in early September there was a gentle animation in the *centro storico*, not just from the handful of tourists, but also from the locals, going about their daily business. An old man was sitting on a chair in the street outside his front door and watching the world go by. It was late morning and tempting smells of lunch, of roasted meat and pasta sauces with hints of garlic, assailed our nostrils, whetting our appetites. Pitigliano essentially consists of one main street, with numerous *vicoli* and narrow passageways leading off it, all of which finish in a dead-end at the edge of the cliff. Pots of geraniums provide welcome colour in the sometimes sombre, shaded streets. A woman was sweeping the street outside her front door with a traditional broomstick of uneven twigs. Washing hung from several windows. By the square at the entrance to the old town is the Palazzo Orsini, with various ecclesiastical relics and some attractive painted wooden ceilings, and solid beams and thick walls. Francesco Zuccarelli, who became a founder member of the Royal Academy, was born in Pitigliano in 1702. Pitigliano has had a Jewish community since 1570 and the synagogue has been recently rebuilt. The cooperative also has an old cellar in the *centro storico*, cut out of tufa and hidden behind a discreet old wooden door, with a new shiny brass lock. They think it dates back to the eighteenth century. Wine was made there once, and there was an old wooden vat in the corner, but today it is used for storing bottles, and also for tastings. Another fine example of the tufa rocks of Pitigliano is to be found in a cheerful restaurant, Osteria il Tufo Allegro, which is run by the genial Domenico Pechini. The basement room of the restaurant is carved out of tufa, and below that there are three cellars, with the tufa maintaining ideal storage conditions. Finally you emerge onto a terrace with vines growing up a pergola, as was the traditional practice in Pitigliano. The town has changed enormously over the last thirty or forty years. As a child Domenico remembers elderly ladies doing their washing at the public *lavatoio*, an indication of the prevailing poverty, but now wine and tourism have brought prosperity.

At the end of the Via Roma there are views over the surrounding countryside, the woods on the opposite side of the valley, and below the city walls the carefully tended vegetable gardens. We took the steps down to the Porta Sovana and followed an old Etruscan track, the Via Cava Poggio Cani, which was cut out of the tufa, forming a deep alleyway with cellars in the walls. It seemed very much a hidden trail, with vegetation growing high above our heads, keeping out most of the sunlight, with smells of damp moss. There was a sign, Cantina San Giuseppe, with a little shrine and green painted door. We squinted through a crack in the door and could just make out rows of glass demijohns in the gloom. The Via Cava, as these Etruscan tracks are called, led down to a road and we crossed the river Lente to take another Via Cava. This one was hidden in the undergrowth and a man from whom we asked directions tried to dissuade us: 'You will get wet and dirty.' But we persisted. It was a bit of a climb, but quite exhilarating, and soon we were at the top of the cliff on the other side of the valley, and took the *strada bianca* towards Sassotondo, where Carla and Edoardo were taking advantage of a sunny day to pick their Sauvignon. A pen of hunting dogs barked loudly as we passed.

Everything seemed very green, unnaturally lush for the end of summer, but evidence of the unseasonable rain of August. There were more flowers than you would expect, delicate pink autumn crocuses and ripening red hips. The path took us across a field, but with layers of bare rock, little was growing, and then we followed the stony track down to a stream, past the remains of an old bridge, and then across another field to join a road. Sovana came into view, with its fine cathedral tower, and the bells were chiming. Like Pitigliano, Sovana is Etruscan in origin. Its greatest claim to historical fame is as the birthplace of Hildebrand, better known as the eleventh-century pope Gregory VII. There is a wide stone-paved street, with a few tourist shops and a café, with the remains of the Albrandeschi castle at one end and the cathedral at the other, with a beautifully carved doorway, with stylized figures, animals and plants. We refreshed ourselves at the bar and then went to wait for the bus back to Pitigliano, having been informed, reliably we thought, by the café, which had even provided us with bus tickets, that one was due shortly. A bus did duly appear, but not for Pitigliano. It was going to Grosseto; the next bus to Pitigliano was not until seven that evening, in another four hours. It was far quicker to walk, so we retraced our steps and were rewarded with spectacular views of Pitigliano, straggling the length of the rocky spur, with its medieval houses dominated by the impressive cathedral bell tower and two other towers. They seemed like a natural continuation of the rocks.

*

The next day we had arranged to meet Piero Antinori in the one and only bar in Sovana. Piero had persuaded a friend with a small plane to fly him over from Bolgheri; they had landed in a field outside the village, to be retrieved by Piero's estate manager, Walter Guerrini. After reviving cups of *cappuccino* in the sunshine, we set off for a drive round the vineyards, or in some instances the vineyards-to-be. The 200-hectare estate, the Fattoria Aldobrandesca, named after the noble Tuscan family that dominated this area in the Middle Ages, had been bought by Antinori in 1995, initially for the planting rights that it would provide, but Piero and his agronomist had quickly realized the potential of the area for red wines of a certain structure. Land was being prepared for planting on a steep hill overlooking Sovana, forming part of an amphitheatre of hills, exposed towards the sea, with Monte Amiata protecting it from the north winds. The soil is volcanic tufa, in some places very stony, with great variations in colour, sometimes black, sometimes red, and all shades in between. There was evidence of erosion, deep gullies in the tufa formed by the heavy rainfall of a week ago. Cabernet Sauvignon has already been planted, and also some Malbec – Piero admitted to being inspired by a visit to Argentina – and probably there will be Sangiovese too. The cooperative of Pitigliano was the prime instigator of the new DOC of Sovana and it was they who were responsible for the inclusion of Cabernet and Merlot at the expense of Ciliegiolo. Walter was less than enthusiastic about Ciliegiolo: 'It's a Trebbiano *rosso*' – but Piero thought it a pity not to include it within the DOC. The real shame is the failure to limit the permitted yield. At 110 quintals per hectare, how can you make a serious red wine? Doubtless the cooperative pandered to the demands of its members, who as grape growers are still much motivated by quantity, not realizing that it is often at the expense of quality. A neighbour's vineyard was laden with fat Trebbiano grapes: an example not to be followed, observed Walter. We drove on to a nearby vineyard where a group of workers were busily carrying out a green harvest, reducing the yield to more modest proportions. There is also potential for Aleatico here, a red grape that is distantly related to Muscat, with similar sweet orange overtones. As will be seen, it grows well in the volcanic soil of Elba, and also for the nearby DOC of Lazio, Aleatico di Gradoli. Here at Sovana there was already one vineyard of old vines, from which cuttings have been taken to extend the vineyards. The grapes are picked as late as possible, when they are almost overripe and a little *passito*, to make a sweet dessert wine with orange Muscat overtones.

Francesca Ventura, who owns the estate of Sopra la Ripa with her brother Michele, lives in the Bourbon *palazzo* opposite the bar in Sovana. We pushed open the heavy iron gate and then there was a second, wooden gate which led into a secluded garden, with an energetic dog and three basking cats. Stone steps took us up to the first floor of the *palazzo*, to a magnificently proportioned room with a painted frieze. Francesca was bubbly and enthusiastic, and gave us their wine, Ea, to try. Named after the mother goddess of the Etruscans, it is a blend of Sangiovese and Ciliegiolo, aged in *barriques* for eighteen months. The vineyard is now thirty-eight years old, for it was planted when her brother was born. First made in 1999, this wine is serious, with good fruit and well-integrated oak, promising a long future. Ripa, their second wine, is more accessible with riper, more upfront fresh red fruit.

Michele was a journalist until he realized that he could not be an absentee landowner, unlike their father, who had been a lawyer and simply made wine for fun on a property that had been in the family for generations. He took us to see his vineyards; he began with just a hectare and a half and has been gradually planting so that he now has 8.5 hectares in a 70-hectare property, which includes Etruscan tombs. Sadly it is too wet and muddy for us to go and see them. One vineyard was looking distinctly retarded in its growth; apparently the neighbour's sheep escaped from their field and supplemented their diet with young vine leaves, but fortunately the damage will not be lasting. Michele is intensely passionate about his wine, and at times stretched our comprehension of Italian to its limits. He described Ciliegiolo as capricious. It is thick-skinned, which presented problems with the excessive rain of 2002, and very little has been done in the way of clonal selection for it. Outside his compact little cellar were a pair of ferocious geese acting as guard dogs, and just as aggressive, while inside we tasted a barrel sample of the 2001 Ciliegiolo; it was supple, spicy and immensely appealing. 2001 was his first year of production for Merlot and Cabernet Sauvignon, and the barrel samples of these promised well too. In short, Sopra la Ripa is an emerging estate, which deserves to go far.

La Busattina is another new Sovana estate. In 1990 Emilio Falcione bought an abandoned estate with 7 hectares of vines outside the adjacent village of San Martino sul Fiora. He explained how he had managed to recuperate some of the vineyards. The previous owners only had white varieties and took their grapes to the cooperative, whereas he has planted Sangiovese and Ciliegiolo and made his first wine in 2000, following biodynamic precepts in the vineyard. At 500 metres these are the highest vineyards of the area and, like the Antinori vineyards, they face west, towards the sea, and are protected from the north winds. Frost is not a problem, even though the grapes ripen later. As well as vines, Emilio and his girlfriend, Elisabetta, have animals, such as a rare breed of donkey, *asino dell'Amiata*. They were handsome beasts, grey with elegant black markings outlining their ears and striping their backs. There were *cinta senese* pigs and a pair of goats, answering to the names of Wanda and Ortese, with the most extraordinary twisted horns, which can grow to 70 centimetres in length. All around us were spectacular views. On a clear day you can see the islands of Giglio and Montecristo, and even Gran Sasso in the Abruzzo; we had to content ourselves with Monte Amiata, Pitigliano and Monte Argentario, while thunder rumbled ominously in the distance. Emilio has a neat little cellar under the house, with a few *barriques* and some stainless-steel vats. We tasted his Terre Eterea, from Sangiovese, with Ciliegiolo, which softens the Sangiovese, resulting in some attractive peppery cherry fruit. It was a good flavour on which to leave Sovana.

Capalbio and Ansonica Costa dell'Argentario

· September ·

Cooperative of Capalbio; a walk from the village of Capalbio; visit to Santa Lucia

TWO NEW DOCS HAVE recently been created in southern Tuscany, namely Capalbio and Ansonica Costa dell'Argentario, in 1999 and 1995 respectively. Capalbio takes its name from the hilltop village, which has become very fashionable in recent years amongst Roman left-wing intellectuals, so we were told, and it is also known for its wild boar festival, *La Sagra del Cinghiale*, in early September. The DOC covers the entire *comune*, with the vineyards of La Parrina forming a small oasis in the middle, but also producing Capalbio and Ansonica, as well as their own DOC. Capalbio is a tricolour DOC, based on the usual grape varieties, while Ansonica Costa dell'Argentario singles out Ansonica as an original grape variety worthy of individual recognition.

The cooperative of Capalbio plays an important role in both, comprising 300 members, cultivating 450 hectares of vines, not just in the *comune* of Capalbio but also in Orbetello and Magliano, including about 130 hectares of Capalbio and 60 of Ansonica. It is far and away the largest producer of both. The creation of the two DOCs has spurred moves towards an improvement in the wines with what they called a quality project, which entails much stricter procedures in the vineyards, notably working on lower yields. None the less I found that the wines, both red and white, still retained a certain rustic quality. As in the other vineyards of the Maremma, there is much talk of new investment by outsiders.

The hilltop village of Capalbio merits a detour. We walked round the old walls enjoying views over the surrounding countryside towards the sea. The old castle tower dominates the village and the church of San Nicolò contains the remains of frescoes from the fifteenth and sixteenth centuries. There is a maze of narrow alleyways and steep passages, often ending in a stone wall. We found the beginning of a way-marked path to Manciano, one of the villages of Morellino di Scansano. The path started at the foot of the hill outside the village and soon began to climb, quite steadily, offering satisfying views back towards Capalbio and the Lago di Burano beyond. We walked through thick *macchia*, in one spot cleared to reveal the vestiges of old stone terraces. There were woods of ilex and cork oak, with a profusion of white roses and yellow broom. Suddenly we became aware of loud rustling in the undergrowth and there, as we turned a corner, was a small wild boar on the track in front of us. He sniffed the air as if he could sense our presence. Then there was more rustling and another small boar scampered out onto the path and back into the dense *macchia*. We waited, and heard yet more rustling, but the boars never appeared again. On the track there was a large muddy puddle, where they had obviously been looking for water. Bright yellow butterflies flitted in the sunlight and we walked on downhill until we came to a fork in the paths, but no reassuring sign guided us towards Manciano. This was the moment to turn back and enjoy more views of Capalbio and the silhouette of Monte Argentario in the heat haze, as we retraced our footsteps.

Our next encounter with Capalbio and Ansonica came from Lorenzo Scolti at Santa Lucia on the Aurelia just north of La Parrina. He is young and keen, having studied oenology, and is helping to develop the family estate, which his parents bought in the 1970s. They first began bottling wine in the early 1980s. He explained how they have vineyards in four different areas. At Santa Lucia they are within the new DOC of Capalbio, where the vineyards are planted with traditional varieties, Sangiovese, Colorino, Canaiolo and Alicante, as well as Vermentino, and also some Cabernet Sauvignon and Merlot. However, Lorenzo said firmly that he preferred the indigenous varieties. Then they have a hectare of vines on the Monte Argentario above Porto Ercole, planted with Ansonica for the DOC of Ansonica Costa dell'Argentario. This is very much the historical heart of the estate, with vines on old terraces, which are very difficult to cultivate, as mechanization is well-nigh impossible. Outside Magliano-in-Toscana, they have 20 hectares of Sangiovese, planted over the last three years, from which they make Morellino di Scansano, in a separate cellar.

Finally there are 2 hectares in the national park of the Maremma, planted with Sangiovese, Merlot and Cabernet Sauvignon, producing IGT Maremma Toscana, for the park lies outside any DOC. Here the vineyards need protection from the ravages of the animals in the park, with high wire fences.

We chatted as we tasted. Capalbio Vermentino was dry and nutty; it would be possible to include Ansonica or Trebbiano and Malvasia too, but Lorenzo prefers a pure Vermentino. Ansonica Costa dell'Argentario provided an intriguing contrast. Ansonica is not necessarily more aromatic than the Vermentino, but more characterful, with intriguing layers of flavours, and unusual in that this is the only DOC based on Ansonica. Apparently Ansonica originated in Greece and arrived in Sicily as Inzolia, and from there came to the Monte Argentario. They have also experimented with late-harvest and *passito* wines, as well as oak ageing. Nothing is fixed. Lutoscolo, a pure Sangiovese from the vineyards in the park, had some rounded cherry fruit, with a backbone of acidity. These are old vineyards, some as much as fifty years old. They were quite sold out of the red Capalbio, Losco, so there was none to taste, but Lorenzo explained the differences in the vineyard; the vines are less vigorous, giving lower yields so that the wine would be more structured. Finally there was Betto, a blend of Sangiovese, with a little Merlot and Cabernet Sauvignon from the vineyards in the park. The international varieties were planted ten years ago, and they are given a long maceration and then twelve months' barrel ageing to make for a rounded palate, with some oaky overtones. Lorenzo explained that he was looking for harmony between the fruit and the wood, aiming to make supple wines that are both ready to drink and also allow for some bottle ageing. He has plans for the future; they are gradually renovating their vineyards; he would like a new cellar, and also to make more Capalbio *rosso*, planting more Sangiovese and Ciliegiolo, and maybe a little Cabernet. Finally he would love to try out a barrel-aged Cabernet, what he called *un vino di grande struttura*. Lorenzo's enthusiasm promises well for the future.

Parrina

· *September* ·

THE ESTATE AND THE DOC of Parrina are virtually synonymous, with the DOC created in 1971 far ahead of most of the other DOCs of the Maremma, thanks to far-sighted owners, who realized the potential importance of a DOC. The estate was a wedding present from a Strozzi to a Giuntini, the great-grandfather of the present owner, Franca Spinola Malfatti, in 1830. Her uncle is Francesco Giuntini of Selvapiana in Rufina and on a wall in the courtyard a plaque commemorates Guido Giuntini, who invented a threshing machine in 1854. The name Parrina illustrates the Spanish influence in the region, for *parra* means a pergola for vines in Spanish. This is virtually the most southern vineyard of Tuscany, almost bordering Lazio.

In Signora Malfatti's absence, we were shown round by the manager, the amiable Rolando Bernacini, who took us on an extensive drive through the vineyards. Altogether they have 55 hectares of vines and, as well as Parrina, produce Capalbio and Ansonica Costa dell'Argentario, and also Morellino di Scansano on a nearby property, Colle del Lupo outside Magliano-in-Toscana, which is run by Signora Malfatti's daughter, Costanza Malfatti. Altogether the estate totals some 530 hectares of which over half is *macchia*; there are fruit trees, peaches, apples, apricots, kiwis; land for vegetables, 70 hectares of pasture land for eight hundred sheep, as well as 3000 olive trees, and also a flock of goats who produce delicious cheese. This is a very varied property, with houses for *agriturismo* and a tempting farm shop selling all the local produce.

The most noticeable aspect of the vineyards is the deep red volcanic soil, which forms a dramatic contrast with the green of the vegetation. We drove past an avenue of eucalyptus trees to a viewpoint overlooking the vineyards, and the coastal *pineta* beyond, to the lagoon of Orbetello and Monte Argentario. The altitude here is just 40 metres and the vines enjoy the influence of light and heat from the sea. In the early-evening sunshine, there was a wonderful luminosity. With the maritime influence, it is never very hot, nor very cold, and frost is unknown. Then we stopped to look at some Ansonica grapes. In early September they were almost ripe and golden amber in colour, with crunchy skins and a lightly aromatic flavour. Ansonica tends to produce large bunches, so that you have to prune it quite viciously. They have a certificate dated 1953 showing that Ansonica del Littorale (of the coast) was made at La Parrina.

Then we returned to the cellars to taste an impressive range of wines showing the diversity of the estate. Vialetto, their Capalbio *bianco*, is a pure Trebbiano, but quite unlike any other Trebbiano I have ever tasted. It was almost peachy, with great depth of flavour. Roberta Babini, the young assistant winemaker, explained. You have to work in the vineyard and the secret is two separate harvests, the first in early September when the grapes still retain their acidity, and then again in late September when the grapes are much richer and almost overripe. The two wines are blended together to make a magnificently balanced whole. In contrast, Parrina *bianco*, although based on Trebbiano, includes some Sauvignon and Chardonnay and is lightly buttery and rounded. Ansonica, which was described as a white grape, but with the character of a red grape, requires what they called *un lavoro strepitoso*, both in the vineyard and in the cellar, as it oxidizes easily. They look for very ripe grapes that give a wonderful herbal character to the wine. Altogether there are seven bottlers of Ansonica but not all are up to this high standard. Sadly the only producer on the island of Giglio makes a wine that is earthy and oxidizing and does a gross disservice to his island and the DOC.

As for red wine, Parrina has the fresh cherry flavours of young Sangiovese, while Muraccio, the *cru*, named after the nearby Etruscan remains, consists of Sangiovese with a little Merlot and Cabernet Sauvignon, which spend ten months in *barriques*, to make it much more substantial and structured, while the *riserva*, included in the DOC since 1985 and comprising Sangiovese with more Cabernet and Merlot and a longer period of oak ageing, is rich and smoky with concentrated fruit and tannins. Finally, the Morellino di Scansano provided an intriguing contrast of *terroir*, for the soil around Magliano is less volcanic, with more clay, with vineyards at a higher altitude. The wine is largely

Sangiovese, with just a little Cabernet Sauvignon, and after a period of barrel ageing has a deliciously smoky cedary palate with firm tannins and ripe fruit. It was a good note on which to leave the Tuscan mainland and head for the island of Elba.

Elba

· June ·

ELBA IS THE LARGEST island of the Tuscan archipelago, which also includes Giglio, Gorgona, Capraia and Montecristo. Since 1996 the creation of a national park has protected large parts of these islands, preventing the excessive development of unsightly modern buildings. This is particularly fortuitous on the island of Elba, which is a tourist's delight, especially in the summer.

The first time we visited Elba, we flew in a tiny eight-seater plane from Pisa. Our altitude was barely 500 metres, so that you could follow the initial route over land with a road map, as the plane bounced in the wind. This time we travelled more sedately, taking the car ferry from Piombino to Portoferraio in a calm sea on a sunny day in early June.

The ugly remains of the steel plants with their ghostly chimneys form a backbone to the port, with the Colline Metallifere behind, so-called for their wealth of ore. But soon the boat was following the coastline of Elba into the large bay of Portoferraio.

Most of us automatically associate Elba with Napoleon, who spent ten short months here from May 1814 to February 1815, as Prince of Elba, a position that left him with a mere shadow of his former power and authority. You can visit the Villa dei Mulini in the old centre of Portoferraio, a gently decaying town house with oddments of Napoleonic memorabilia. Rather grander is the so-called Villa Napoleone di San Martino in the hills behind the town. There is a modest villa, described as Napoleon's summer residence, alongside a neoclassical palace, built by Prince Demidoff several years later after the emperor's death, which houses a display of Napoleonic pictures.

Today the island's greatest attractions are its sandy beaches and rocky coves, with a warm clear sea. Italians love it for summer holidays; as do the Germans. For us it offered wonderful walking opportunities, with some marked footpaths along clear tracks up into the hills, with views over the island. And there is wine, but, it has to be said, of dwindling significance.

Fifty years ago, we were told, there were over 3000 hectares of vines on the island. Whole hillsides were covered with terraces of vineyards as recently as twenty years ago. Today there are barely 130 hectares, with just a dozen producers bottling their wines. At the peak of production, virtually all the wine was white, and sold *sfuso* to Liguria for use in the production of vermouth.

The DOC of Elba was created in 1967 and has been amended over the years. It covers all three colours. The white is inevitably based on Trebbiano, known as Procanico on the island, which can be blended with the more characterful varieties such as Ansonica and Vermentino. Ansonica can also stand alone, as Ansonica dell'Elba, with a minimum of 85 per cent of the variety. Elba *rosso* is inevitably based on Sangiovese, along with the other usual Tuscan varieties, as well as some Cabernet and Merlot, and more surprisingly some Syrah. The *riserva* demands twenty-four months of ageing, with a minimum of twelve in wood, while Elba *rosato* comes from the same grape varieties as the red wine.

More original are the *passito* wines, from Aleatico, Moscato and Ansonica. The island's climate is particularly suited to this type of wine, with the prerequisite warm sunshine and drying winds after the harvest. Originally the *passito* wines were not part of the DOC, as production was simply too limited, and more often than not they were made by people with just a few rows of vines in their vegetable patch, for family and friends. Nowadays they have a more official footing, with the recognition of their individuality.

Dimitri Galletti at Montefabbrello explained the intricacies of the production process. The grapes are left to dry on straw mats, outside, subjected to sunshine and wind, and protected from any unseasonable rain. In the right conditions the *appassimento* or drying process takes about ten days, reducing the grapes to the consistency almost of raisins. The grapes are checked regularly to ensure that none have any rot or damage. Fermentation, in vat or barrel, is slow and lengthy. The Aleatico stays on the skins for about a week, while the Moscato and Ansonica are pressed immediately after *appassimento*, and the results are highly individual. Unfortunate is the way that less scrupulous producers have chosen to take advantage of the popularity of these wines to sell Aleatico and Moscato as *vini liquorosi* or fortified wines. The grapes will almost certainly have come from southern Italy and the fermentation will have been arrested by the addition of grape spirit. The difference in price is significant; as is the taste. The real thing is expensive and delicious.

It was Dimitri's *nonno*, a distant grandparent, who bought the estate in 1880, and today it comprises some 14 hectares, of which just 3 are vineyards, on terraced hillsides. The dry-stone walls require careful maintenance. The wild boar damage them, looking for snails, and in September 2002 there was the heaviest of rainstorms lasting over twelve hours, which left a trail of destruction in its wake. Dimitri is daunted by the work involved; he spoke of *una viticultura eroica*, as so much has to be done by hand. With just two or three rows per terrace, there is little opportunity for mechanization. In labour terms, 3 hectares here equate to 10 hectares on flatter, easier terrain. Dimitri is one of a new generation of young innovative producers; he only began bottling his wine in 1999. Until then it was all sold *sfuso*; now it is all sold in bottle, taking advantage of the ready market of the tourist trade.

Dimitri's white wine, Bianco Contessa Castori, after the lady who sold his grandfather the land, is mainly Procanico with a drop of Ansonica, with a firm nutty flavour. The red Poggio le Lenze, from Sangiovese, with 10 per cent Merlot, is ripe and rounded with oaky tannins. Dimitri explained that there was Merlot mixed up in his old vineyard, while 2002 was also the first harvest of his new Merlot vineyard.

Very few of the island's producers make an Ansonica *passito*, but Dimitri does. In 2002 the grapes were picked in October, which is later than usual. Some had even developed noble rot; once dried, they were pressed on 2 November and the juice was given forty hours of skin contact and then left to ferment in barrel until the end of January. The fermentation stopped slowly of its own accord. Tasted from vat in June, the wine was amber in colour and redolent of apricots on both nose and palate, with a firm acidity to balance the sweetness. Dimitri suggested drinking it with gorgonzola, with the saltiness of the cheese balancing the richness of the wine. As for his Aleatico, for which 24 quintals of grapes produced just 350 litres of juice, it was intensely sweet and rich, with fresh red fruit and herbal notes. It could accompany a fruit tart, or a more original suggestion was *pecorino* cheese, with some *miele di corbezzola*, the intensely perfumed honey of the strawberry tree. And it worked, with the slight saltiness in the cheese providing an intriguing contrast with the sweet honey.

A walk on our first morning gave us some splendid views of the surrounding vineyards. We set off from Montefabbrello, passing the estate of Acquabona to take a track that climbed steadily uphill. The town of Portoferraio stretched out at our feet – the old town around the Medici fortress is perched on a promontory, while the newer town has sprawled along the bay. There was a large cruise ship in the port, with a couple of smaller car ferries and a cluster of private yachts at the smarter end of the waterfront.

Our path took us past various holiday houses, most firmly shuttered, with signs warning you to beware of the dog. There were wild flowers in profusion, red poppies, yellow daisies, and sweet peas and vetch in shades of pink and purple, combined with the scent of herbs, mint and fennel in the warm sunshine. After a steep climb we came into the cool of the pinewoods, with the intoxicating scent of resin. This was the spot for a picnic, with views over the bay of Portoferraio, and in the opposite direction the ruined castle of Volterraio, perched on a steep hill. On the shore we could make out the walled vineyard of La Chiusa, by the hamlet of Magazzini. Our path then took us steeply downhill through woods of ilex and cork oak, interrupted by occasional views through gaps in the trees over the vineyards of Acquabona and the house of Montefabbrello, to emerge onto the road, close to the path leading back to our *agriturismo*.

We were given a rather frosty welcome at Acquabona for it seemed that we had committed the cardinal sin of arriving ten minutes late. Evidently the winemaker, Ugo Lucchini, has fallen under the influence of the vast numbers of German tourists on the island and come to expect Teutonic standards of punctuality. However, Acquabona is a pretty place with a villa, which you approach along an avenue of shady umbrella pines. The remains of an old bunker act as reminder of the German occupation of the island during the Second World War, and in June the gardens were a riot of flowering oleanders, a mass of pink of every shade. The name Acquabona means good water and refers to the springs in the nearby hills above the estate.

Lucchini explained how the estate is run by three partners, Marcello Fioretti, Lorenzo Capitani and himself, while the land belongs to two Milanese families, from whom they have rented the 15 hectares of vineyards, all close to the winery, since 1987. Elba *bianco*, mainly from Procanico, with some Vermentino, Ansonica and Malvasia, which all ripen together, so that they can be fermented together, was lightly herbal with a fresh finish. The pure Vermentino, an IGT, had more depth of flavour, while the pure Ansonica dell'Elba had intriguing nettley notes. Ansonica may have arrived here from the island of Giglio and consequently is also known as Uva del Giglio. Lucchini explained how you have to take great care pressing it, as it oxidizes very easily and any skin contact gives you problems.

The *rosato* is a pure Sangiovese, fresh with good acidity, and a pale orange-pink colour coming from half a day of skin contact. As for reds, they make a Rosso Toscano from Sangiovese and Cabernet; the Cabernet makes the young Sangiovese more accessible, giving it body and colour, with some attractive notes of cassis, and they have also planted Merlot and Syrah, which are not yet in production. Their basic Elba Rosso was sold out; instead we tried an oak-aged wine, but it was not a *riserva* as they only make a *riserva* in the very best vintages. This was a pure Sangiovese that had spent twelve months in 550-litre barrels, making for a rounded sturdy palate. They also make Ansonica and Aleatico *passito* in the island tradition, but quantities are so tiny that the wines were not available for tasting. Fortunately Il Chiasso, in the hilltop town of Capoliveri, and one of the island's better restaurants, offers Acquabona's Aleatico by the glass and suggested an accompaniment of ripe peaches marinated in Aleatico, which was truly delicious. The wine is aged in wood for a few months, which provides more depth of flavour than the overtly fruity young Aleatico.

La Chiusa is the most historic estate of the island. Until early in 2003 it belonged to Giuliana Foresi, whose family had bought the estate in the 1870s. Signora Foresi now lives in Portoferraio across the bay and the estate had been bought by a lady from Rome, Giuliana Bartozzi. It is a beautiful spot. You approach the nineteenth-century villa along an alleyway of olive trees, while a second alleyway of flowering oleanders takes you down to the beach and the tiny port of Magazzini. The gates on the seashore are a reminder of the time when wine left the cellars directly by sea, rather than by road. The name La Chiusa describes a walled vineyard, like the French *clos*, and the original stone wall dating from the eighteenth century still stands, encompassing 9 hectares of vineyards.

We tasted Elba Bianco, from Trebbiano with a dollop of Sauvignon, which was planted about ten years ago. Elba Rosso is pure Sangiovese; Grecale an IGT made for the first time in 2001, from a blend of Merlot and Sangiovese; and the Aleatico *passito* was sweet and raisiny. The tasting and sales room is decorated with old certificates; a bronze medal from Milan in 1881; a silver from Turin in 1884, and there were old labels from the beginning of the twentieth century, including Vermutte di Lacona, Biancone, Sangioveto and Anzonica, produced by Ulisse di Jacopo Foresi.

You can taste the wine of Mola at their tasting booth on one of the rare stretches of straight road on the island, just outside Porto Azzurro. On the hillside opposite is the town of Capoliveri. The estate belongs to the Pavoletti family, who are in the construction business in Piombino, notably at a time when the now defunct steel industry was one of Italy's biggest steel plants. In Mario Pavoletti's absence we were introduced to the wines of Mola by the lively Riccardo Valdini. He explained that there are 12 hectares of vineyards on the 42-hectare estate, in several plots surrounding the cellars.

They make a variety of different wines, red, white and pink, as well as both Moscato and Aleatico *passito*. The highlights included the white Vigna degli Aiali, a blend of Trebbiano, Vermentino and Ansonica, which illustrated the benefits of diluting Trebbiano with other varieties. The Aleatico *passito* had an appealingly spicy fruitcake nose and palate, not unlike a ruby port.

Next door to Mola is the estate of Sapereta. They are well set up for visitors; we coincided with two busloads of German tourists enjoying a tasting in the welcoming shop. Italo Sapere explained how his grandfather had bought the land in 1927. The name Sapereta comes from the addition of his father's initials to their surname. First they grew Ansonica as a table grape – it has hard skins, making it very *croccante* and thereby easy to transport to the mainland. Then they began making wine, selling it *sfuso* and their first customers included the prison in Porto Azzurro. The influx of tourists in the early 1970s encouraged them to begin bottling and now everything has been sold in bottle for the last twenty years. Altogether they have 14 hectares of vines scattered on nearby hillsides. All are cultivated organically, which is relatively easy given the beneficial drying winds, while the sea breezes usually temper any climatic extremes. However, they did not prevent the spring frost that struck the vineyards on the night of Easter Sunday 2002 – it was the first spring frost for over thirty years.

Fifteen years ago nearly all their production was white wine, but since then there has been a distinct shift towards red wines. However, I could not help feeling that Elba *bianco* is so much more successful, especially accompanying the vast array of seafood that forms the backbone of the island's cuisine. Flavours have progressed dramatically with the development of Vermentino, Ansonica and even Chardonnay, along with the overall improvement in vinification methods.

Italo Sapere is well informed on the history of the island. As he took us round his cellars, he talked of the Spanish influence that remains from the time when Porto Azzurro was under Spanish control, providing a safe haven for Spanish ships as one of a series of Spanish ports along the Tuscan coast. The fortress in Porto Azzurro was built by the Spanish; that of Portoferraio was the work of the Medici. You can find Grenache, or Alicante as they call it locally, which was doubtless introduced by the Spanish, as it was in Scansano. There are people with Spanish surnames in Porto Azzurro who cannot speak a word of Spanish, and the Hispanic influence remains in the cooking. At the entrance to the cellar there is a display of various artefacts – some relating to wine, such as old corkscrews and cellar implements; others, oddments of family memorabilia, his sister's toys and his mother's school books.

We wandered through the vineyards. Flowering was over and bunches of grapes were beginning to form. Sapere explained how Aleatico is very susceptible to the *appassimento* process for not all the grapes set so that the bunches are very loose and therefore dry easily. The grapes begin drying on the vines and then they are picked and laid out on straw mats. The tradition for

Aleatico has always existed on the island. There would always be a row of Aleatico in the family vineyards, though no one quite knows how the grape variety came to the island. Elsewhere in Tuscany, we encountered it in the Val di Cornia, at Massa Vecchia, outside Massa Marittima, and from Antinori's estate at Sovana.

The hillside behind Sapereta's cellar was covered with vines some thirty years ago. Often they were tiny holdings, just 20, 30 or 50 hectares, which have gradually been abandoned, usually when the owner was no longer able to cultivate his vines, or maybe a fire played a part. Signor Sapere explained how Italian law does not encourage the renting of land as it is so difficult for owners to reclaim their property later. Tourism has also had a significant effect on land prices. He cited the example of the small adjoining vineyard that was a mass of weeds, with the unpruned vines running amok. The owner has become too old to look after his vineyard, but has refused Sapere's offer to take it over, in the hope that he might just get planning permission for the land and then it would become so much more valuable than a mere vineyard. Although tourism has resulted in the abandonment of some vineyards, it also provides a ready and fairly indiscriminating market for wines on the island.

Although Signor Sapere is a trained oenologist, Attilio Pagli advises, and Sapere admits that his table wines took a quantum leap in quality as a result. Certainly they were amongst the best we tasted on the island. The whites are particularly appealing, delicate and understated. Vigna le Stipe, a blend of Procanico, Vermentino and Ansonica, benefits from a period of lees contact, to develop some attractive herbal fruit. Vigna Thea has a higher proportion of Vermentino, which is also known as Rimanese or Uva di Rimini, as well as some Chardonnay to give it more depth.

The red Vigna Thea is mainly Sangiovese with some Cabernet and aged in oak for twelve months. This was Attilio Pagli's influence, encouraging an experiment with barrels for the first time in 1999. However, for the *passito* wines, Signor Sapere said modestly that Attilio didn't need to suggest any improvements – in fact, he had even learnt something. The fermentation is very slow, as the juice is very syrupy, almost the consistency of jam, and it stops of its own accord. The Moscato was fresh and unctuous, tasting of apricots and intensely sweet, with balancing acidity.

The Aleatico is sweet and raisiny; it ferments very slowly in stainless-steel vats until February, and then needs filtering, which is easier said than done, and can cause oxidation problems. Some people sell their wine the following year, without filtering, or age it in oak for a few months, but for Italo Sapere freshness is the quintessential character of Aleatico. It went deliciously with a traditional Elba cake, *schiaccia*, stuffed with currants and orange peel.

The next day we retraced our drive up to Dimitri's vineyard, but on foot. Missing a turning, we climbed higher up the hill and found ourselves by the yellow ochre house that had belonged to the countess from whom Dimitri's grandfather had bought his land. The next-door neighbour's dog growled unwelcomingly and this was the moment to turn back. We met an old man shuffling slowly down the lane, taking his morning constitutional, and we agreed that it was a bit hot for walking. That day's *Corriere della Sera* was full of the news that temperatures in Italy were 10°C higher than average for the time of year.

There were views across the valley to some neatly terraced vineyards, which belong to Sapereta, and houses scattered randomly over the hillside gave a feeling that building regulations were never strictly enforced. We passed a farmhouse and peered into a rather gloomy dark barn to see a couple of calves with large bright eyes and rabbits of different sizes in countless hutches, doubtless intended for dishes of *coniglio*, at which Italy excels. The occasional palm tree served to illustrate the difference in climate between Elba and the mainland.

Our final walk on the island took us up a track close to Acquabona, past a house with a colourful array of pot plants, geraniums of every shade of pink and red, and through an olive grove, across a field full of blue daisies. We passed an untidy farmyard, with dogs barking loudly as they sensed intruders disturbing the tranquillity of the morning. The path carried on through the *macchia*, with holm oak and cistus. There were butterflies galore, bright yellow ones and vivid black and yellow swallowtails – so many more than you ever see in England, with splashes of yellow broom, as well as wild fennel and rosemary. Italians may have a reputation for shooting small birds but at times the birdsong was almost deafening, and often matched the noise of the crickets.

We felt on top of the world; there were views towards Portoferraio, across the valley to Capoliveri, and then we reached a glade of parasol pines, with a view of Porto Azzurro at our feet. This was the moment to retrace our footsteps, and the next morning we caught the ferry back to Piombino and the mainland.

GLOSSARY

Agriturismo – holiday home on a farm or wine estate.

Albarello – method of vine pruning; the vine stands alone with one supporting post and no wires.

Albarese – type of soil that is particularly rich in calcium.

Alicante – a popular synonym for Grenache Noir in the Maremma; it has absolutely no connection with the inferior Alicante Bouschet of the south of France.

Appassimento – the process of drying the grapes to render them *passito*.

Barricaia – cellar of *barriques*.

Barrique – barrel of 225 litres, the traditional size of Bordeaux and increasingly popular in Tuscany; usually of French oak, occasionally American and often new.

Bianco – white.

Biscotti di Prato – traditional biscuits with almonds, which accompany Vin Santo; also called *cantuccini*.

Borgo – fortified hamlet.

Botrytis – rot, which can be noble or grey.

Bottaia – cellar of *botti*.

Botte(i) – very large cask, usually of Slovenian oak.

Cantina – cellar.

Cantina sociale – the wine cooperative for a village or a DOC.

Cantuccini – see *Biscotti di Prato*.

Caratelli – small barrels used for Vin Santo; traditionally made of chestnut, now usually oak.

Comune – translates literally as a parish; may be a village or town; DOC(G) regulations list the *comuni* where a wine may be produced.

Coniglio – rabbit.

Consorzio (consorzi) – the association of growers and producers which runs a DOC(G).

Contadino(i) – peasant farmer, a member of the traditional *mezzadria* system of landholding.

Cordone speronata – method of vine pruning necessitating supporting wires and slightly different from *guyot*, whereby the main arm of the vine is not replaced every year, but rather the shoots that grow off it.

Cru – usually a single vineyard and often considered the best wine of an estate.

Délestage – French term to describe a method of extracting colour and flavour during fermentation; the juice is run off into another vat so that the grape skins are temporarily without any liquid, and then the juice is returned to the vat, so that the skins rise to the surface through the juice.

Disciplinari – the regulations for DOC(G).

DOC or Denominazione di Origine Controllata – denomination of controlled origin recognizing the origin of a wine, with regulations about grape varieties, yield, precise area and so on.

DOCG or *Denominazione di Origine Controllata e Garantita* – the denomination of origin is guaranteed, as well as controlled, and therefore with stricter regulations than for a DOC.

Dolcezza – sweetness.

Enjambeur – tractor that straddles one or two rows of vines; essential in vineyards with narrow rows and therefore increasingly common in Tuscany.

Enoteca – wine shop or wine library.

Fattore – estate manager.

Fiasco – the traditional wicker-covered dumpy bottle once used for Chianti.

Frantoio – where olive oil is produced.

Free-run juice – juice extracted from the grapes by their own weight, and without pressing them; generally considered to be of better quality than pressed juice.

Galestro – particular kind of very stony soil, which is almost rocklike, and found especially in Chianti Classico. Also used as a wine name.

Governo, metodo all'uso governo – once part of the process of producing Chianti, whereby lightly raisined grapes are added to the fermenting grape juice. Very rarely practised these days.

Green harvest – the practice of reducing the crop in early summer by removing surplus green grapes.

Guyot – method of vine pruning, leaving a trunk and either one or two arms, necessitating supporting wires.

IGT or *Indicazione Geografica Tipica* – the equivalent of a *vin de pays* in France; a wine that does not conform to the local DOC(G), probably because it includes grape varieties that are not allowed, but its producer may well consider it to be of better quality and charge accordingly.

Lavatoio – old-fashioned outdoor communal washing place for laundry with a tap or fountain.

Macchia – the vegetation, particularly of the Maremma, typical of the Mediterranean coast, with plants such as cistus, holm oak, juniper, rosemary, laurel and so on.

Madre or mother – the lees of the previous wine, which are left in the Vin Santo barrel to enhance the new wine.

Malolactic fermentation – the secondary fermentation which converts malic acid into lactic acid and thereby reduces the total acidity level in a wine.

Mezzadria – the old-fashioned system of landholding whereby the landowner supplied the finance and the *contadini* the manpower, and they divided the harvest.

Micro-oxygenation – process whereby a tiny amount of oxygen is gently introduced to a vat of red wine to soften the wine and replicate the effects of barrel ageing.

Monovitigno – describes a wine made from a single grape variety.

Must – freshly pressed grape juice that is about to begin fermentation.

Noble rot – as opposed to grey rot; a fungus that affects grapes causing them to dehydrate and ultimately produce delicious dessert wine. Sauternes is the quintessential example, but examples are also found in Tuscany.

Normale – the basic quality of a DOC(G) wine (as opposed to a *riserva*).

Oidium – also known as powdery mildew; attacks leaves and berries, and spreads in warm dry weather. Can be treated with sulphur.

Orci – large terracotta amphorae traditionally used for storing olive oil.

Panforte – traditional and delicious Tuscan cake, made with dried fruit and spices.

Passito – describes grapes that have been dried by sun and wind, either on the vine or in a well-ventilated place, so that they become raisined and dehydrated, with very concentrated juice. An essential part of the process for Vin Santo.

Pasticceria – pastry shop.

Pecorino – variety of sheep's cheese. The best in Tuscany comes from Pienza.

Peronospera – downy mildew; caused by warm humid summers.

Phylloxera – vine disease spread by aphids in the soil, which affected most of the vineyards of Europe in the second half of the nineteenth century. It was brought to Europe on cuttings of American vines and the remedy is to graft European vines onto resistant American rootstock.

Pigiatura – punching down; a means of extracting colour and flavour from fermenting grape juice or must. Traditionally the grapes were trodden by foot; these days there are various pieces of equipment, even computerized machines and 'feet', for pushing down the grapes skins through the fermenting juice.

Porcini – variety of large mushroom found in the woods in autumn.

Prosciutto – ham.

Quintal – Italian measure for a hundred kilograms. Yields of wine are given in quintals per hectare. In theory one hundred quintals of grapes gives you one hundred hectolitres of juice, but the DOC(G) regulations restrict the amount of juice permitted to a specific percentage.

Rimontaggio – pumping over; a means of extracting colour and flavour from fermenting grape juice or must. This is done mechanically with a pump; the process may be computerized with a timer so that the operation takes place for a predetermined time and a certain number of times during the day.

Ripasso – technique found more usually in Valpolicella, whereby grape skins are added to another fermenting vat to enhance colour and body.

Riserva – better than the basic *normale* quality of a DOC(G) wine; usually denotes an extra year of cellar ageing, in *barriques*, *botti* or bottles, and by implication a selection of better grapes.

Rosso – red.

Sfuso – in bulk; describes the sale of wine in barrel or tank, and not in bottle.

Solera – process used in sherry, but also applies to balsamic vinegar: a series of barrels, the contents of the older one refreshed by the addition of wine or vinegar from the younger one; the younger liquid takes on the characteristics of the older liquid.

Spumante – sparkling wine.

Strada bianca – literally a 'white road'; passable for cars, but untarmacked.

Super-Tuscan – term that commonly describes an estate's best and most expensive wine, which does not usually conform to any Italian wine law, so not a DOCG or DOC but usually these days an IGT.

Tapenade – delicious olive paste, often spread on *crostini*.

Terroir – French word which describes not just soil, but the whole environment in which the vine is grown – the aspect, altitude and so on.

Tipicità – literally 'tipicity', referring to the recognizable characteristics of a wine, originating from the climate and soil, or *terroir*.

Tonneau(x) – usually a 500-litre barrel.

Varietal wine – describes a wine made from a single grape variety.

Vendemmia verde – see *Green harvest*.

Vendita diretta – sale of wine directly from the cellar door.

Vernacce – the lees and skins left after fermentation.

Vertical tasting – tasting of several vintages of the same wine.

Vino da tavola – table wine; in theory the lowest quality, but until the introduction of IGT, wines such as Sassicaia were *vini da tavola* as they did not conform to DOC(G) regulations.

Vino tipico – another term for an IGT wine, but of simpler level than an IGT.

Vinsantaia – place where the *caratelli* for Vin Santo are kept.

DOCGs and DOCs

For each Italian province, there are two lists of authorized and recommended grape varieties. The difference between the two is somewhat blurred, but essentially it means that for the newer DOCs any permutation of grape varieties is allowed, be they the traditional varieties of Tuscany such as Sangiovese, Canaiolo and Malvasia Nera, or the international newcomers, Cabernet Sauvignon, Chardonnay, Syrah, Petit Verdot and so on, provided they feature on one of the two lists.

Brunello di Montalcino, Rosso di Montalcino, Moscadello di Montalcino

DOCG *Brunello di Montalcino* – pure Sangiovese. DOCG since 1980. The ageing regulations have relaxed over the years but must include a minimum of two years in cask, and the wine cannot be released for sale until five years after the harvest, or for a *riserva* six years.

Rosso di Montalcino, also pure Sangiovese, requires a year in the cellar and can be sold from 1 September after the vintage.

Moscadello di Montalcino, from Muscat, comes in various forms, sparkling, *passito*, or simply sweet.

Carmignano, Barco Reale di Carmignano, Rosato di Carmignano

DOCG Carmignano, since 1990, requires a minimum of 10 per cent and a maximum of 20 per cent Cabernet Sauvignon, a minimum of 50 per cent Sangiovese, and an optional 10 per cent of recommended or authorized varieties, such as Merlot. Canaiolo and Trebbiano are also permitted, but rarely used in practice. The *normale* must have eight months' barrel ageing, and the *riserva* twelve. Barco Reale is a lighter version of the same blend, and the Rosato or Vin Ruspo also comes from the same varieties.

Chianti Classico

Separated from the other Chiantis since 1996. The blending regulations have evolved over the years, so that Chianti Classico is firmly based on Sangiovese, now no longer allows any white grapes, and may include a small percentage of Canaiolo and other traditional Tuscan varieties, as well as a maximum of 20 per cent international varieties. The *normale* can be sold on 1 October in the year following the harvest, while the *riserva* demands two years' ageing from 1 January after the harvest.

Chianti, Rufina, Colli Fiorentini, Colli Senesi, Colline Pisane, Colli Aretini, Montalbano, Montespertoli

DOCG since 1984, with the more recent addition of Montespertoli. With the exception of Rufina, these are lighter wines than Chianti Classico. Based on Sangiovese, as well as Canaiolo and other Tuscan red varieties. White grapes are still allowed, but rarely used.

Vernaccia di San Gimignano and San Gimignano Rosso

DOCG since 1993. Vernaccia with 10 per cent Chardonnay or Sauvignon allowed. San Gimignano Rosso is based on a minimum of 70 per cent Sangiovese, blended with Cabernet Sauvignon, Merlot, Syrah or Pinot Noir, or may be a varietal wine from 85 per cent of any of those four varieties, with the grape featuring on the label.

Vino Nobile di Montepulciano, Rosso di Montepulciano

DOCG since 1980. Based on a minimum of 70 per cent Sangiovese; may be pure Sangiovese or include other Tuscan reds up to 20 per cent, and the usual international varieties up to 20 per cent. Requires a minimum of two years' ageing in cellar from I January after the vintage, or three years for *riserva*. Rosso di Montepulciano is a lighter version released from I March after the harvest.

Ansonica, Costa dell'Argentario

Pure Ansonica made around the Argentario peninsula.

Bianco della Valdinievole

Insignificant white from Trebbiano and Malvasia.

Bianco dell'Empolese

Ditto.

Bianco di Pitigliano

White wine from the hilltop town of Pitigliano; mainly Trebbiano; must include a small amount of either Chardonnay or Sauvignon and may also include Malvasia, Greco, Grechetto, Riesling Italico, Pinot Bianco or Vermentino.

Bianco Pisano di San Torpè

Insignificant white based on Trebbiano, grown in the Colline Pisane.

Bolgheri – Bolgheri Sassicaia

Tri-colour DOC on the Tuscan coast; the red is usually based on a Bordeaux blend of Cabernets and Merlot; Syrah and Petit Verdot are also to be found. Also a 70 per cent base of Sangiovese is allowed, but is less common. *Rosato* uses the same varieties as the *Rosso*. Sassicaia is recognized as a *cru* of the DOC. *Bianco* is based on Vermentino, as well as Trebbiano and Sauvignon.

Candia dei Colli Apuani

White DOC from the hills above Massa Carrara, based on Vermentino, Albarola, Malvasia and Trebbiano. *Secco, amabile* or *passito*.

Capalbio

Tri-colour DOC; white based on Vermentino, Malvasia and Trebbiano; red and pink on Sangiovese, Canaiolo, Colorino and Alicante.

Colli dell'Etruria Centrale

Tri-colour DOC covering most of the hills of Chianti, based on traditional Tuscan varieties blended with the international varieties. A relatively new DOC that has never really taken off.

Colli Luni

Part in Tuscany; part in Liguria. White from Vermentino and Trebbiano; red based on Sangiovese.

Colline Lucchesi

Red based on Sangiovese. Merlot also allowed, up to 30 per cent in a blend, and as a varietal with a minimum of 85 per cent. White is Trebbiano, Vermentino, Grechetto, Malvasia.

Cortona

New DOC allowing for international grape varieties, notably Chardonnay, Cabernet Sauvignon, Merlot and Syrah.

Elba

Tri-colour DOC based on traditional grape varieties, but allowing the inclusion of Cabernet, Merlot and Syrah in the red, with a white made from Trebbiano, Vermentino and Ansonica, as well as Ansonica dell'Elba with a minimum of 85 per cent. More original are the *passito* wines, from Aleatico, Moscato or Ansonica.

Montecarlo

As well as Trebbiano, the white includes Sémillon, Pinot Grigio, Pinot Bianco, Vermentino, Sauvignon and Roussanne. Red is mainly Sangiovese, and other Tuscan varieties, with small amounts of Cabernet Sauvignon, etc.

Montecucco

New DOC since 1998. Red a minimum of 60 per cent Sangiovese, blended with traditional Tuscan varieties, or Cabernet Sauvignon and Merlot. White from Vermentino and Trebbiano.

Monteregio di Massa Marittima

DOC since 1994. Red from 80 per cent Sangiovese, blended with traditional Tuscan or international varieties. Also a *riserva* category. White from Trebbiano blended with Sauvignon or Chardonnay. Also Vino Novello and Vin Santo.

Montescudaio

Rosso from a minimum of 50 per cent Sangiovese, plus Tuscan varieties, or Cabernet Sauvignon and Merlot. White from Trebbiano, Malvasia, Vermentino, Chardonnay and Sauvignon. Sangiovese and the international varieties may feature on the label if there is a minimum of 85 per cent in the wine.

Morellino di Scansano

Based on Sangiovese, with Tuscan varieties, including Alicante (the local name for Grenache Noir) and Ciliegiolo, plus small amounts of Cabernet Sauvignon and Merlot; *riserva* category.

Orcia

A recent DOC, sandwiched between Montalcino and Montepulciano; includes international varieties, as well as Sangiovese.

Parrina

White from Trebbiano, with Sauvignon and Chardonnay. Red based on Sangiovese, with Merlot and Cabernet Sauvignon.

Pomino

Red from Sangiovese and traditional varieties, plus Pinot Noir and Merlot. White includes Chardonnay, Pinot Bianco and Pinot Grigio, plus Trebbiano.

Sant'Antimo

A recent DOC; encompasses the international varieties planted in Montalcino.

Sovana

Red wine based on Sangiovese, with international varieties such as Merlot, Cabernet Sauvignon and also Aleatico. *Normale* is released in the March following the harvest, *Superiore* in June; the *riserva* requires thirty months in cellar, including eighteen in wood.

Val d'Arbia

A white from traditional grape varieties, mainly Trebbiano, and of little importance these days.

Valdichiana

The same as the Val d'Arbia.

Val di Cornia; Val di Cornia Suvereto

DOC since 1990, with Suvereto recognized as separate sub-zone in 2001; reds from Suvereto requiring thirty months in the cellar, including eighteen in wood. Sangiovese, Cabernet and Merlot as varietals, or a Bordeaux blend. Syrah also allowed. White from Trebbiano, Ansonica and Vermentino.

Vin Santo

Most of the DOCs include Vin Santo. Made from dried grapes, usually Trebbiano and Malvasia. Minimum of three years' ageing in tiny barrels, but often longer.

THE SUPER-TUSCANS, *RISERVAS* AND *CRUS*

This list is in no way complete, but covers most of the wines I have enjoyed in this book.

Acetone – pure Sangiovese from Vittorio Innocente in Montepulciano.

Aglaia – barrel-aged Chardonnay from Corzano e Paterno in the Colli Fiorentini.

Alte d'Altesi – 70 per cent Sangiovese, with Cabernet Sauvignon and Merlot, from Altesino in Montalcino.

Altero – originally an IGT, now a DOCG; Sangiovese aged in barrel for two years, from Poggio Antico in Montalcino.

Anfiteatro – Vecchie Terre di Montefili's best vineyard; in Chianti Classico. A pure Sangiovese.

Annoterzo, Annoquatro, etc. – Sangiovese Merlot blend from Erik Banti in Scansano; the name changes with the vintage.

Anonimo – mainly Cabernet Sauvignon, with some Merlot and Sangiovese; from Poggio Gagliardo in Montescudaio.

Ardingo – Cabernet Sauvignon Merlot blend from Costanti in Montalcino.

Ariento – pure Vermentino from Massa Vecchia in Massa Marittima.

Asinone – *cru* from Poliziano in Montepulciano; Sangiovese aged mainly in new wood.

A Siro – IGT from San Gervasio near Pisa; Sangiovese with 5 per cent Cabernet Sauvignon.

Avvoltore – *cru* from Moris Farms in Massa Marittima, from Sangiovese with some Cabernet Sauvignon and Syrah.

Badiola – IGT from Fonterutoli in Chianti Classico, from Sangiovese.

Balifico – one-third Cabernet Sauvignon and Cabernet Franc and two-thirds Sangiovese, from Castello di Volpaia in Chianti Classico.

Banditella – single-vineyard oak-aged Rosso di Montalcino from Col d'Orcia.

Belcore – blend of Sangiovese, Merlot, with a little Syrah and Petit Verdot from I Giusti e Zanza near Pisa.

Il Benefizio – *riserva* from Frescobaldi's Pomino estate.

Berardo – *riserva* from Castello di Bossi in Chianti Classico.

Betto – Sangiovese, Merlot, Cabernet Sauvignon blend from Santa Lucia, from a vineyard in the national park of the Maremma.

Birbone – Sangiovese, Canaiolo, Alicante, Merlot blend from Fattoria dei Barbi in Montalcino, but also including grapes from their property in the Maremma.

Bontesco – Trebbiano, Biancone and Malvasia blend from Bonti in Piombino.

Le Borranine – pure Cabernet Sauvignon from Monteverdi in Chianti Classico.

Il Bosco – top Syrah from Fattoria di Manzano; now DOC Cortona.

Brania del Cancello – Trebbiano and Chardonnay blend from Fattoria Colleverde in the Colline Lucchesi.

Brania della Ghiandaie – Sangiovese with a little Syrah from Fattoria Colleverde in the Colline Lucchesi.

Il Brecciolino – IGT from Castelvecchio in the Colli Fiorentini, from Cabernet and Sangiovese.

Briareo – Vino Nobile *cru* from the Vecchia Cantina in Montepulciano.

Bruno di Rocca – blend of 60 per cent Cabernet Sauvignon and 40 per cent Sangiovese from Vecchie Terre di Montefili in Chianti Classico.

Bucerchiale – *cru* of Selvapiana in Rufina, a pure Sangiovese.

Buriano – Cabernet Sauvignon from Rocca di Castagnoli in Chianti Classico.

Ca' del Pazzo – Cabernet Sauvignon Sangiovese blend from Caparzo in Montalcino; now DOC Sant'Antimo.

Ca' Marcanda – top wine from Gaja's Bolgheri estate; 50 per cent Merlot, 40 per cent Cabernet Sauvignon and 10 per cent Cabernet Franc.

I Campi Santi – *riserva* from Vecchione in San Gimignano.

Campo alla Casa – Vermentino Sauvignon blend from Enrico Santini in Bolgheri.

Campo al Sorbo – IGT from Grati in Rufina, Sangiovese with Merlot.

Campolucci – IGT from Manucci Droandi in the Colli Aretini, with Sangiovese and some Cabernet Sauvignon and Merlot.

Campolungo – *cru* from Lamole in Chianti Classico.

Campora – Cabernet Sauvignon with a drop of Merlot, from Falchini in San Gimignano.

Capannelle – pure Sangiovese from the eponymous estate in Chianti Classico.

Capatosta – Sangiovese with a little Alicante from Poggio Argentiera in Scansano.

Capraia – Sangiovese, with a little Cabernet Sauvignon and Colorino, from Rocca di Castagnoli in Chianti Classico.

Carato – barrel-fermented Vernaccia di San Gimignano from Montenidoli. Also blend of Sangiovese, Canaiolo, Malvasia Nera and Alicante from Erik Banti in Scansano; partially aged in American oak.

Carmione – 60 per cent Cabernet Sauvignon and 40 per cent Merlot from Pratesi in Carmignano.

Casalferro – Sangiovese and Merlot blend from Brolio in Chianti Classico.

Cascarilla – *riserva* from Poggio al Sole in Chianti Classico. Sangiovese, with a drop of Cabernet Sauvignon.

I Castagni – blend of Syrah, Sangiovese, Cabernet Sauvignon and Teroldego from Michele Satta in Bolgheri.

Castello di Monna Lisa – *riserva* from Vignamaggio in Chianti Classico.

Casuccia – *cru* from Castello di Ama, a blend of Sangiovese and Merlot.

Cavaliere – pure Sangiovese from Michele Satta in Bolgheri.

Cenerentola – Sangiovese with a little Foglia Tonda from Il Colle in the new DOC of Orcia.

Cent'Omini – Clairette and Ansonica blend from Banti in the Val di Cornia.

Cepparello – pure Sangiovese from Isole e Olena in Chianti Classico; made instead of a *riserva*.

Ceppatello – blend of Sangiovese and Canaiolo from Tenuta di Fibbiano near Pisa.

Ceragiolo – pure Ciliegiolo from Banti in the Val di Cornia.

Cercatoja – blend of Sangiovese, Syrah, Cabernet Sauvignon and Merlot from Fattoria di Buonamico in Montecarlo.

Cesari – almost pure Sangiovese, from very old vines, from Valgiano in the Colline Lucchesi.

Ciabatta – *cru* from Erik Banti in Scansano.

Cignoro – Sangiovese with 25 per cent each Merlot and Cabernet Sauvignon, from Villa Cilnia in the Colli Aretini.

Il Cipressone – blend of Sangiovese and Cabernet Sauvignon from Monteverdi in Chianti Classico.

Coltasala – pure Sangiovese with a drop of Mammola, from Volpaia in Chianti Classico.

Contessa Castori bianco – Procanico and Ansonica from Montefabbrello on Elba.

Contessa di Radda – Chianti Classico from the Agricoltori del Chianti Geografico.

Con Vento – pure Sauvignon from Terriccio near Montescudaio.

Convivio – Sangiovese with 25 per cent Cabernet Sauvignon from Valtellina in Chianti Classico.

Corbaia – *cru* from the Chianti Classico estate, Castello di Bossi, 70 per cent Sangiovese, blended with Cabernet Sauvignon.

Cortaccio – Cabernet Sauvignon from Cafaggio in Chianti Classico.

Corte d'Oro – late harvest Sauvignon and Sémillon from Fattoria del Cerro in Montepulciano.

Il Corzanello – blend of Trebbiano, Malvasia and Chardonnay from Corzano e Paterno in the Colli Fiorentini.

Il Corzano – *rosso toscano* from Sangiovese, Cabernet Sauvignon and Merlot from Corzano e Paterno.

Costa di Giulia – Vermentino Sauvignon blend from Michele Satta in Bolgheri.

Le Coste – pure Sangiovese from the Fattoria di Montecucco.

Crognolo – Sangiovese, with 10 per cent Merlot from Sette Ponti near Arezzo.

Le Cupole – from Tenuta di Trinoro in the Orcia valley; a blend of Cabernet Sauvignon and Franc, Merlot and Cesanese d'Affile.

Dedicato – pure Sangiovese from Montellori near Pisa; replaces Castelrapiti.

Desiderio – Merlot with 15 per cent Cabernet Sauvignon from Avignonesi in Montepulciano. DOC Cortona; replaces I Grifi.

Di Campalbo – Merlot with 15 per cent Cabernet Sauvignon from Banti in the Val di Cornia.

Divertimento – blend of Mammola, Canaiolo and Colorino, from Dievole in Chianti Classico.

Don Tommaso – Sangiovese, with 15 per cent Merlot, from Le Corti in Chianti Classico.

Il Duca di Montechioccioli – pure Merlot from Valtellina in Chianti Classico.

Dulcamara – blend of Cabernet Sauvignon and Merlot from I Giusti e Zanza.

Ea – oak-aged Sangiovese and Ciliegiolo from Sopra la Ripa in Sovana.

Eliseo bianco – Trebbiano, Clairette, Vermentino and Malvasia from Gualdo del Re in Suvereto.

Eliseo rosso – Sangiovese, Canaiolo and Malvasia Nera from Gualdo del Re.

Federico Primo – pure Cabernet Sauvignon from Gualdo del Re, given eighteen months' oak-ageing.

Ferraiolo – blend of Sangiovese and Cabernet Sauvignon, from the Agricoltori del Chianti Geografico in Chianti Classico.

Fiore – blend of Sangiovese, with 15 per cent Merlot from Castello di Meleto in Chianti Classico.

Flaccianello – pure Sangiovese, produced by Fontodi in Chianti Classico.

Folgòre – San Gimignano Rosso from Panizzi; a blend of Sangiovese, Merlot and Cabernet Sauvignon.

Fontalloro – IGT and a pure Sangiovese from Felsina Berardenga in Chianti Classico.

Fontarca – 60 per cent Chardonnay and 40 per cent Viognier from Fattoria di Manzano near Cortona.

La Fonte di Pietrazza – pure Cabernet Sauvignon from Massa Vecchia in Massa Marittima.

Fontenova – Sangiovese and Ciliegiolo blend from Tenuta Roccaccia in Pitigliano.

Fontestina – barrel-aged Sangiovese from Bruno Moos near Pisa.

Formule – pure Sangiovese from Brolio in Chianti Classico.

Fornace – *cru* from Selvapiana, a Cabernet Merlot blend, with 20 per cent Sangiovese.

Il Fortino – pure Syrah from Fattoria di Buonamico in Montecarlo.

Franze – Sangiovese, Ciliegiolo, Merlot and Alicante blend from Sassotondo; DOC Sovana.

Frasca – 60 per cent Sangiovese, plus 20 per cent each of Merlot and Syrah from Varramista near Pisa.

Il Futuro – IGT from Colombaio di Cencio in Chianti Classico, from equal parts of Sangiovese and Cabernet Sauvignon with 20 per cent Merlot.

Galatrona – Merlot from Fattoria Petrolo near Arezzo.

Gana – oak-aged Sauvignon fromTerre del Sillabo in the Colline Lucchesi.

Il Garrulo – light, fruity Rosso Toscano from Montenidoli in San Gimignano.

Geremia – super-Tuscan Merlot and Cabernet Sauvignon blend from Rocca di Montegrossi in Chianti Classico.

Gersemi – Vino Nobile di Montepulciano from Fassati, includes some Cabernet Sauvignon and Merlot, as well as Sangiovese.

Ghiaie della Furba – IGT from Capezzana in Carmignano; 60 per cent Cabernet Sauvignon, 30 per cent Merlot and 10 per cent Syrah.

La Gioia – *cru* of Riecine in Chianti Classico; a pure Sangiovese, aged in new oak.

Giorgio Primo – La Massa's Chianti Classico; Sangiovese wtih 10 per cent Merlot.

Giovin Re – pure Viognier from Michele Satta in Bolgheri.

Girolamo – pure Merlot from Castello di Bossi in Chianti Classico.

Giusti di Nostri – blend of 60 per cent Cabernet Sauvignon and Franc, with 40 per cent Merlot from Tua Rita in Suvereto.

Gobbo ai Pianacce – mainly Merlot with Sangiovese and Cabernet Sauvignon from Poggio Gagliardo in Montescudaio.

Le Grance – Chardonnay with 5 per cent Traminer and 20 per cent Sauvignon from Caparzo; originally an IGT, now DOC Sant'Antimo.

Grato Grati – produced by Grati in Rufina from very old Sangiovese vines, plus Canaiolo, Colorino and even Trebbiano.

Grecale – IGT from La Chiusa on Elba; blend of Merlot and Sangiovese.

Greco delle Gaggie – pure Grecchetto *passito* from Fattoria Colleverde in the Colline Lucchesi.

Guado al Tasso – Cabernet Sauvignon, Merlot, Petit Verdot and Syrah blend from Antinori in Bolgheri.

Gualdo del Re – pure Sangiovese from the eponymous estate in Suvereto.

Guidalberto – new wine made in association with Sassicaia in Bolgheri; blend of 40 per cent Merlot and Cabernet Sauvignon with 20 per cent Sangiovese.

Labirinto – pure Chardonnay from Fattoria Wandanna in Montecarlo.

Leone Rosso – Sangiovese with 30 per cent Merlot, from Fattoria Il Colle in the DOC of Orcia.

Licurgo – oak-aged Sangiovese selection from Perazetta in Montecucco.

Locorosso – IGT from Pratesi in Carmignano, from 90 per cent Sangiovese and 10 per cent Merlot.

Lodano – blend of Riesling, Gewürztraminer and Chardonnay from Tua Rita in Suvereto.

Logaiolo – 70 per cent Cabernet Sauvignon, with Sangiovese, from Aiola in Chianti Classico.

Losco – red Capalbio from Santa Lucia.

Lucestraia – Vermentino, Chardonnay and Trebbiano blend from Sorbaiano in Montescudaio.

Lucumone – pure Vementino from Mantelassi in Scansano.

Luenza – red *barrique*-aged IGT from Sangiovese and Colorino, from Cesani in San Gimignano.

Lunaia – lightly oaked Bianco di Pitigliano from La Stellata.

Lupicaia – Cabernet Sauvignon and Merlot with a drop of Petit Verdot, from Terriccio near Montescudaio.

Lutoscolo – pure Sangiovese, grown in the national park of the Maremma, made by Santa Lucia.

Magari – second wine from Gaja's Bolgheri estate; blend of Merlot, Cabernet Sauvignon and Cabernet Franc.

Manderlo – IGT from Montellori near Pisa; a blend of Roussanne, Marsanne, Clairette, Chardonnay and Viognier.

Manechiara – Brunello di Montalcino *cru* from Tenute Silvio Nardi.

Manero – pure Sangiovese from Fattoria del Cerro in Montepulciano.

Il Marzocco – pure Chardonnay from Avignonesi. Now DOC Cortona.

La Massa – from the eponymous estate; Sangiovese, Cabernet Sauvignon and Merlot.

Masseto – pure Merlot from Ornellaia in Bolgheri.

Il Matto della Giuncaia – Aleatico *passito* from Massa Vecchia in Massa Marittima.

Mesorio – pure Merlot from Le Macchiole in Bolgheri.

Millanni – red from Fattoria di Cusona in San Gimignano; a blend of 60 per cent Sangiovese, 30 per cent Cabernet Sauvignon and 10 per cent Merlot.

Mocale – oaked Vernaccia di San Gimignano from Vagnoni.

Molino delle Balze – Chardonnay from Rocca di Castagnoli in Chianti Classico.

Montepaone – Cabernet Sauvignon from the Castello di Montepò in Scansano.

Montepergoli – blend of 40 per cent Merlot, 35 per cent Cabernet Sauvignon, 20 per cent Syrah and 5 per cent Sangiovese from Enrico Santini in Bolgheri.

Montesodi – *cru* from Castello di Nipozzano in Rufina.

Montosoli – *cru* of Altesino, in Montalcino.

Mormoreto – *cru* from Castello di Nipozzano, planted with Cabernet Sauvignon, Cabernet Franc and Merlot.

Moro – Sangiovese with 10 per cent each of Cabernet Sauvignon and Malvasia Nera from Montellori near Pisa.

Muraccio – *cru* from la Parrina; *barrique*-aged Sangiovese with a little Merlot and Cabernet Sauvignon.

Nambrot – 70 per cent Merlot, with some Cabernet Sauvignon and Petit Verdot, from Tenuta di Ghizzano.

N'Antia – blend of Sangiovese, Cabernet Sauvignon and Merlot from Badia a Morrona near Pisa.

Nemo – pure Cabernet Sauvignon from Monsanto in Chianti Classico.

Nero della Spinosa – Syrah from Fattoria Colleverde in the Colline Lucchesi.

Nero di Montechiari – pure Pinot Noir from Montechiari in Montecarlo.

Nero di Taccone – Pinot Noir from Fattoria di Wandanna in Montecarlo.

Niffo – blend of Sangiovese, Cabernet Sauvignon, Cabernet Franc and Merlot from Terre del Sillabo in the Colline Lucchesi.

Notte – Syrah and Merlot blend from Villa Vestri near Pisa.

Obsession – blend of Merlot, Cabernet Sauvignon and Syrah from Vignamaggio in Chianti Classico.

L'Ora Blu – blend of Trebbiano and Vermentino from Villa Vestri near Pisa.

Oreno – 50 per cent Sangiovese, with Cabernet Sauvignon and some Merlot, from Sette Ponti near Arezzo.

Ornellaia – top wine from the eponymous estate in Bolgheri; 65 per cent Cabernet Sauvignon, 30 per cent Merlot and 5 per cent Cabernet Franc.

Oro del Re – dessert wine from Fattoria di Buonamico in Montecarlo; *passito* Sauvignon and Semillon.

L'Oro di Lamole – Sangiovese with 20 per cent Cabernet Sauvignon, from Lamole in Chianti Classico.

Palazzo Altesi – pure Sangiovese from Altesino in Montalcino, including some carbonic maceration, as well as barrel ageing.

Paleo bianco – Sauvignon Chardonnay blend from Le Macchiole in Bolgheri.

Paleo rosso – Cabernet Franc from Le Macchiole in Bolgheri.

Palestorti – 70 per cent Sangiovese, with Syrah and Merlot, from Valgiano in the Colline Lucchesi.

I Pampini – blend of Sangiovese and Teroldego from Fubbiano in the Colline Lucchesi.

Paretaio – pure Sangiovese from Falchini in San Gimignano.

Pasiteo – Vino Nobile di Montepulciano from Fassati.

Passonaia – Sangiovese, Canaiolo, Ciliegiolo blend from the Fattoria di Montecucco.

Paterno II – Sangiovese *cru* from Il Paradiso in San Gimignano.

Patrizia Bartolino – late harvest blend of Sauvignon and Vermentino from Massa Vecchia in Massa Marittima.

Il Peccato – Cabernet Sauvignon with 15 per cent Merlot from Banti in the Val di Cornia.

Percarlo – pure Sangiovese from San Giusto a Rentennano in Chianti Classico.

Pergole Torte – *cru* from Montevertine in Chianti Classico.

Perlato – Vernaccia di San Gimignano from Fattoria di Cusona, includes 10 per cent Chardonnay.

Perlato del Bosco – pure Sangiovese from Tua Rita in Suvereto.

Petra – blend of Cabernet and Merlot from the eponymous estate outside Suvereto.

Pian del Ciampolo – IGT from Sangiovese with some Canaiolo from Montevertine in Chianti Classico.

Pian del Conte – partially oak-aged Sangiovese from Sorbaiano I Montescudaio.

Piastraia – Syrah, Cabernet Sauvignon, Merlot and Sangiovese blend from Michele Satta.

Pietra Rossa – *cru* from Contucci in Montepulciano.

Il Poggio – *cru* of Monsanto in Chianti Classico; a pure Sangiovese.

Poggio ai Frati – *cru* from Rocca di Castagnoli in Chianti Classico, with Sangiovese and a little Canaiolo.

Poggio al Muro – blend of 40 per cent Sangiovese, 30 per cent Cabernet Sauvignon, 20 per cent Syrah and 10 per cent Merlot from Enrico Santini in Bolgheri.

Poggio al Vento – Brunello di Montalcino *cru* from Col d'Orcia.

Poggio Angelica – oak-aged Vermentino from Banti in the Val di Cornia.

Poggio Argento – Sauvignon and Traminer blend from Le Pupille in Scansano.

Poggio Cavaluccio – pure Ciliegiolo from Tenuta Roccaccia in Pitigliano.

Poggio dei Paoli – IGT Cabernet Sauvignon Merlot blend from Vigna di Gragnano in the Colline Lucchesi.

Poggio Golo – pure Merlot from Fattoria del Cerro in Montepulciano.

Poggio le Lenze – Sangiovese with 10 per cent Merlot from Montefabbrello on Elba.

Poggio Rosso – *cru* from San Felice, Sangiovese with a little Colorino.

Poggio Valente – *cru* from Le Pupille in Scansano, from Sangiovese and Alicante.

Poggio Venti – pure Sangiovese from Massa Vecchia in Massa Marittima.

Le Pratole – pure Merlot from Rocca di Castagnoli.

Le Prime Donne – best Brunello di Montalcino from Donatella Cinelli's estate, il Casato.

Promis – third wine from Gaja's Bolgheri estate; 55 per cent Merlot, 35 per cent Syrah and 10 per cent Sangiovese.

Pulleraia – IGT Merlot made by Agricoltori del Chianti Geografico in Chianti Classico.

Querciolaia – *cru* of old Alicante from Mantelassi in Scansano.

Rainero – blend of Cabernet Sauvignon, Merlot and Sangiovese from the Castello di Meleto in Chianti Classico.

Rancia – Chianti Classico *riserva* from Felsina Berardenga, a pure Sangiovese and a *cru*.

Redigaffi – pure Merlot from Tua Rita in Suvereto.

Reflesso Antico – pure Montepulciano from Ambrosini in Suvereto.

I Renai – pure Merlot from San Gervasio near Pisa.

Il Rennero – pure Merlot from Gualdo del Re in Suvereto.

Rinascimento – blend of Malvasia Nera and Canaiolo, from Dievole in Chianti Classico.

Ripa – second wine of Sopra la Ripa in Sovana.

Rocca Guicciarda – Chianti Classico produced by Brolio.

La Rocorma – pure Merlot from San Giusto a Rentennano in Chianti Classico.

Romitoria di Santedame – 65 per cent Colorino and 35 per cent Merlot from Tenimenti Ruffino.

Rondinaia – pure Chardonnay from Terriccio near Montescudaio.

Rosso degli Appiani – Sangiovese with 30 per cent Montepulciano from Bonti in Piombino.

Rosso delle Miniere – blend of Sangiovese, Cabernet Sauvignon and Malvasia Nera from Sorbaiano in Montescudaio.

Rosso del Senatore – pure Sangiovese from Aiola in Chianti Classico.

Rovo – Tuscan blend with some Cabernet Sauvignon from Poggio Gagliardo in Montescudaio.

Sabazio – Rosso di Montepulciano from La Braccesca.

Saffredi – blend of Cabernet Sauvignon, Merlot and Alicante from Le Pupille in Scansano.

Sagrato – Chardonnay *cru* from Montauto in San Gimignano.

Salamartana – blend of Cabernet Sauvignon and Merlot aged in new oak, from Montellori near Pisa.

Salarco – *riserva* Vino Nobile di Montepulciano from Fassati.

Salco – top Vino Nobile di Montepulciano from Salchetto.

San Biagio – San Gimignano Rosso from Vagnoni; a blend of Sangiovese and Merlot.

San Gennaro – oak-aged Sangiovese *cru* from Fattoria di Fubbiano in the Colline Lucchesi.

Sangioveto – Badia a Coltibuono's best wine, a pure Sangiovese.

San Giusto – pure oak-aged Sangiovese from Bonti in Piombino.

Sanice – oaked Vernaccia di San Gimignano from Cesani.

San Lorenzo – pure Ciliegiolo from Sassotondo in Pitigliano.

San Marcellino – *riserva* from Rocca di Montegrossi in Chianti Classico.

Sanmarco – from Castello dei Rampolla, Cabernet Sauvignon with a drop of Sangiovese.

San Martino – Sangiovese *cru* from Cafaggio in Chianti Classico.

Sansovino – top wine from Contucci in Montepulciano.

Santa Catarina – 30 per cent each of Sangiovese, Cabernet Sauvignon and Syrah with 10 per cent Petit Verdot from Dei in Montepulciano.

Santa Cristina – Toscano Rosso from Antinori; Sangiovese with 10 per cent Merlot.

Sant'Amato – pure Sauvignon from Montellori near Pisa.

Sassaloro – pure Sangiovese from the Castello di Montepò in Scansano.

Sassicaia – Cabernet Sauvignon and Cabernet Franc blend from the eponymous estate in Bolgheri.

Il Sasso – IGT from Piaggia in Carmignano, but same blend as for the DOCG – 70 per cent Sangiovese, with 20 per cent Cabernet Sauvignon and 10 per cent Merlot.

Sassobianco – Trebbiano and Malvasia with a drop of Ansonica from Mantelassi in Scansano.

Sassotondo rosso – IGT from the eponymous estate in Pitigliano; a blend of Ciliegiolo, Sangiovese and Alicante.

Saxa Calida – Merlot and Cabernet Sauvignon blend from Il Paradiso in San Gimignano.

Schidione – Cabernet Sauvignon, Sangiovese Merlot blend from the Castello di Montepò in Scansano.

Scrio – pure Syrah from Le Macchiole in Bolgheri.

Selciaia – Rosso di Montepulciano from Fassati.

Selene – second wine of La Stellata in Pitigliano.

Selvascura – pure Merlot from Fattoria di Cusona in San Gimignano.

Le Sentinelle – Sangiovese with a little Alicante, from Mantelassi in Scansano.

Seraselva – Merlot Cabernet Sauvignon blend from Poggio al Sole in Chianti Classico.

Le Serre Nuove – second wine of Ornellaia in Bolgheri.

Siepi – *cru* from Fonterutoli in Chianti Classico, a Sangiovese and Merlot blend.

I Sistri – Chardonnay from Felsina Berardenga in Chianti Classico.

Il Sodaccio – *cru* from Montevertine, currently being replanted.

I Sodi del Paretaio – Chianti from Badia a Morrona near Pisa.

Sodole – *riserva* Vernaccia di San Gimignano from Fattoria di Cusona in San Gimignano.

Soianello – Sangiovese, with a touch of Malvasia Nera, Ciliegiolo and Canaiolo from Bruno Moos near Pisa.

Solaia – blend of Cabernet Sauvignon, with 20 per cent Sangiovese, produced by Antinori.

Solalto – dessert wine from Le Pupille in Scansano, a blend of Sauvignon, Traminer and Sémillon.

Solare – Sangiovese with 20 per cent Malvasia Nera, from Capannelle in Chianti Classico.

Solengo – Cabernet Sauvignon, Merlot, Syrah blend from Argiano in Montalcino.

Sono Montenidoli – oak-aged Rosso di Toscana from Montenidoli in San Gimignano.

Sotto il Vento – pure Sangiovese from Villa Vestri near Pisa.

Spante – pure Chardonnay from Terre del Sillabo in the Colline Lucchesi.

Le Stielle – IGT from Rocca di Castagnoli in Chianti Classico, a blend of Sangiovese and Cabernet Sauvignon.

Le Stoppie – pure Sangiovese from San Gervasio near Pisa.

Subetum – Sangiovese, Merlot, Syrah blend from Ambrosini in Suvereto.

La Suvera – oak-aged Chardonnay from Badia a Morrona near Pisa.

Tabarò – unoaked Sangiovese from Ambrosini in Suvereto.

Tassinaia – equal parts Cabernet Sauvignon, Merlot and Sangiovese from Terriccio near Montescudaio.

Templare – Bianco Toscano from Montenidoli in San Gimignano; a blend of Vernaccia, Trebbiano and Malvasia.

Terre di Chianti – Chianti *normale* from Corzano e Paterno in the Colli Fiorentini.

Terre Eterea – Sangiovese and Ciliegiolo from La Busattina in Sovana.

Terrine – IGT from Paneretta in Chianti Classico; a blend of Sangiovese and Canaiolo.

Terziere – pure Alicante or Grenache Noir from Massa Vecchia in Massa Marittima.

Tignanello – the first super-Tuscan, after Sassicaia; from Antinori, Sangiovese with 20 per cent Cabernet Sauvignon.

Tinscvil – blend of Sangiovese, with 25 per cent Cabernet Sauvignon and 5 per cent Merlot from Monsanto in Chianti Classico.

Tiziano – blend of Merlot and Lambrusco from Rietine in Chianti Classico.

Torre a Destra – *riserva* from Paneretta in Chianti Classico.

Torricella – Chardonnay from Brolio in Chianti Classico.

Torrione – Sangiovese with a drop of Merlot from Fattoria Petrolo in the Colli Aretini.

Trappolino – Chardonnay and Pinot Bianco blend from Badia a Coltibuono in Chianti Classico.

I Tre Borri – Chianti *riserva* from Corzano e Paterno in the Colli Fiorentini.

Trinoro, Tenuta di – from the eponymous estate in the Val d'Orcia. A blend of Cabernet Sauvignon and Franc, Merlot and Petit Verdot.

Valentina – pure Vermentino from Gualdo del Re in Suvereto.

Varramista – pure oak-aged Syrah from the eponymous estate near Pisa.

Vasario – pure Pinot Bianco from Fattoria di Buonamico in Montecarlo.

Venerosa – 50 per cent Sangiovese, 45 per cent Cabernet Sauvignon and 5 per cent Merlot from Tenuta di Ghizzano near Pisa.

Ventesimo – blend of Sangiovese with a little Cabernet and Merlot, from Monteverdi in Chianti Classico.

Ventunno – Chianti Colli Senesi from Panizzi in San Gimignano.

Vermiglio – Sangiovese, with 20 per cent Merlot and 10 per cent Cabernet Sauvignon from Costanti in Montalcino.

Vescovo II – second Syrah from Fattoria di Manzano near Cortona.

Vialetto – Capalbio *bianco* from la Parrina.

Vigna Alata – Sangiovese from Badia a Morrona near Pisa.

Vigna Bellavista – *cru* from Castello di Ama; a blend of Sangiovese and Malvasia Nera.

Vigna d'Alceo – Castello dei Rampolla's best vineyard, planted with Cabernet Sauvignon and some Petit Verdot.

Vigna degli Aiali – blend of Trebbiano, Vermentino and Ansonica from Mola on Elba.

Vigna dei Fiori – *cru* from Fattoria dei Barbi in Montalcino.

Vigna a Solatio – Vernaccia di San Gimignano from Falchini, made from overripe grapes.

Vigna del Sorbo – Sangiovese with a small proportion of Cabernet Sauvignon, made by Fontodi in Chianti Classico.

Vigna di Pallino – pure Sangiovese from Sette Ponti near Arezzo.

Vigna le Stipe – Procanico, Vermentino and Ansonica from Sapereta on Elba.

Vigna Regis – white wine of Vecchie Terre di Montefili in Chianti Classico, made from 80 per cent Chardonnay, 15 per cent Sauvignon and 5 per cent Traminer.

Vigna Thea – oak-aged Sangiovese and Cabernet Sauvignon from Sapereta on Elba.

Vigneto Antica Chiusina – Vino Nobile di Montepulciano *cru* from Fattoria del Cerro.

Vigneto Carpinaia – pure Sangiovese from Monteverdi in Chianti Classico.

Vigorello – pioneering super-Tuscan from San Felice in Chianti Classico; a blend of Sangiovese with some Cabernet Sauvignon.

Virente – blend of Syrah, Cabernet Sauvignon and Merlot from Fattoria di Wandanna in Montecarlo.

Vocato – Sangiovese with 20 per cent Cabernet Sauvignon from Villa Cilnia near Arezzo.

Le Volte – third wine of Ornellaia in Bolgheri; includes some Sangiovese with Cabernet and Merlot.

HELPFUL HINTS

Visiting wine estates

Some producers are more organized than others for visitors. Many of the bigger estates will have a shop with a tasting room, as will the various *cantine sociali*, such as Capalbio and Scansano, who depend on local custom for a large part of their revenue, while a few of the more tourist-orientated producers will even run cellar tours. Inevitably, there is a seasonality about these, with tasting rooms unlikely to be open during the winter months.

Friendly tasting rooms include:
- ❖ Aiola outside Vagliagli in Chianti Classico.
- ❖ Brolio; the castle is also open to visitors.
- ❖ Castello di Nipozzano in Rufina.

Cellar tours are available at San Felice in Chianti Classico, Banfi and Fattoria dei Barbi in Montalcino, and in the town of Montepulciano at both Contucci and the Cantina del Redi.

On Elba there are tasting rooms at La Chiusa and Sapereta, while Mola has a tasting stand on the main road near the winery.

As for visits to other producers, often it is a question of timing. Phone in advance and if they are not too busy, there may well be someone who can give you a tasting and show you round. At the risk of stating the obvious, it is inconsiderate to turn up unannounced, especially at meal-times, and not to buy even a single bottle, if you take up someone's whole afternoon. However, most Italians are naturally hospitable, and enjoy sharing their knowledge and enthusiasm with interested visitors. And if you are tasting more than a couple of wines, spitting is *de rigueur*. It is not a waste, for you will have enjoyed all the flavour of the wine. It is only the alcohol you are avoiding, and this is just as well, given that many estates are off the beaten track down winding roads.

Maps

The British are quite spoilt by the quality of the Ordnance Survey maps, a fact I had not appreciated until I came to use Italian walking maps.

However, the following, on a scale of 1:25000, and published by Edizioni Multigraphic in Florence, are helpful, but by no means cover the whole of the region.

- Chianti Classico – Val di Pesa – Val d'Elsa
- Isola d'Elba
- Val d'Orcia
- San Gimignano – Volterra
- Appennino Toscomagnolo, which includes Rufina
- Parco dell'Uccellina – Monte Argentario
- Alta Maremma Parco di Montioni

The province of Grosseto has introduced several waymarked walks; you will often see signs for these in the villages, but the reassuring red markers do have a disconcerting habit of disappearing. The only walk that is not generally open to the public is one to the original Sassicaia vineyard.

Agriturismi

The websites for the *agriturismi* where we stayed:

- Fontodi – www.fontodi.com
- Camigliano – www.camigliano.it
- Frascole – www.frascole.it
- Montenidoli – www.montenidoli.com
- Sassotondo – www.agriturismo.regione.tos.it
- Fubbiano – www.fattoriadifubbiano.it
- Montefabbrello – www.montefabbrello.it

Bibliography

Brunello to Zibibbo: the Wines of Tuscany, Central and Southern Italy, Nicholas Belfrage, Mitchell Beazley 2002.

Tuscany and Its Wines, Hugh Johnson, Mitchell Beazley 2000.

The Food and Wine Lover's Companion to Tuscany, Carla Capalbo, Chronicle Books 2002.

Walking and Eating in Tuscany and Umbria, James Lasdun and Pia Davis, Penguin Books 1997. Second edition in the pipeline.

Landscape of Tuscany, Elizabeth Mizon, Sunflower Books 2000.

Index